NEIGHBOR NETWORKS

Neighbor Networks

Competitive Advantage Local
and Personal

Ronald S. Burt

OXFORD

UNIVERSITY PRESS

OXFORD

UNIVERSITY PRESS

Great Clarendon Street, Oxford ox2 6dp

Oxford University Press is a department of the University of Oxford.
If furthers the University's objective of excellence in research, scholarship,
and education by publishing worldwide in

Oxford New York

Auckland Cape Town Dar es Salaam Hong Kong Karachi
Kuala Lumpur Madrid Melbourne Mexico City Nairobi
New Delhi Shanghai Taipei Toronto

With offices in

Argentina Austria Brazil Chile Czech Republic France Greece
Guatemala Hungary Italy Japan Poland Portugal Singapore
South Korea Switzerland Thailand Turkey Ukraine Vietnam

Oxford is a registered trade mark of Oxford University Press
in the UK and in certain other countries

Published in the United States
by Oxford University Press Inc., New York

British Library Cataloguing in Publication Data

Data available

Library of Congress Cataloging in Publication Data

Data available

Typeset by SPI Publisher Services, Pondicherry, India
Printed in Great Britain
on acid-free paper by
Clays Ltd, St Ives plc

ISBN 978–0–19–957069–0

1 3 5 7 9 10 8 6 4 2

Mama may have,
Papa may have,
But God bless the child that's got his own.

from "God Bless the Child"
Billie Holliday and Arthur Herzog Jr.
recorded by Billie Holliday in 1941
first sung by Billie Holliday in 1939

PROLOGUE

The moral I take away from this book is a bit of Confucian wisdom often ignored in social network analysis: "Worry not that no one knows you, seek to be worth knowing."[1] The old saying speaks to a tension we all feel at one time or another, a tension between hope and suspicion. The hope: people are rewarded for their ability and effort. The suspicion: rewards go to people with well-connected friends.

I present evidence on analysts, bankers, and kinds of managers showing that rewards in fact do go to people with well-connected colleagues. Look around your organization. The individuals doing well tend to be affiliated with well-connected colleagues.

The advantage obvious to the naked eye is spurious. It disappears when the individual's own characteristics are held constant. Well-connected people have their own interests. They do not have to affiliate with people who wish to affiliate but bring nothing to the affiliation. The research to be presented shows that affiliation with well-connected people adds stability but no advantage to a person's own connections. Advantage is concentrated in people who are themselves well-connected. Advantage is a phenomenon local and personal. In the words of Confucian disciples, "seek to be worth knowing." For readers more down home, there is the immortal Billie Holliday, "God bless the child that's got his own."

This book is a trail of argument and evidence that leads to the conclusion that individuals make a lot of their own network advantage. In the end, the social is affirmed, but with an emphasis on individual agency and the social psychology of networks. The network around you is not a device separate from you. You are woven into it. It is a trellis to friends and colleagues on which certain people develop and others decay. Certain network structures develop people more adept at certain kinds of tasks. The research to be presented gives new emphasis to Coleman's (1988) initial image of social capital as a forcing function for human capital.

I wrote this book for colleagues interested in a new angle on familiar data, and as a supplemental reading in graduate courses on social networks, stratification, or organizations. I presume that the reader is familiar with the imagery of network brokers, bridges, and relations embedded in closed networks.

---

[1] My phrasing is colloquial for a contemporary audience. Sources are given in the note at the end of the chapter.

The book began as a by-product of another project, *Brokerage and Closure* (Burt, 2005), in which key properties of what we know about the network structure of social capital were brought together in four stylized facts. Reviews of what we know highlight where we are ignorant, and on my long "need to figure this out" list following *Brokerage and Closure* was a question about spillover: Given the evidence of social capital in the immediate network around a person, how does competitive advantage spread between adjacent networks? I was looking for new kinds of evidence to corroborate the evidence reviewed in *Brokerage and Closure*.

The project I had in mind was a cameo—one of those projects intended to reinforce basic results elsewhere. For a while, I put it aside as a discursion that could be quickly executed, or could be given as an exercise to a graduate student to help flesh out a rookie vita. I anticipated producing a book chapter, or an article in a specialty journal; nothing that would break new ground, but something that would broaden and reinforce the foundation on which I built the review in *Brokerage and Closure*.

What I expected to be an innocuous implication turned out to be complicated and consequential. The empirical results on spillover from neighbor networks had implications for how we conceptualize, study, and apply network concepts of social capital.

The empirical results on network closure turned out much as I expected. The results are an incremental extension of previous research. There are interesting subtleties, such as spillover closure promoting brokerage, but the primary finding is that closure in the immediate network around a person is reinforced by closure in the broader network among friends of friends. The closure results are completely consistent with the broad review in *Brokerage and Closure*, anchored on Coleman's (1988, 1990) discussion of closure as social capital and Granovetter's (1985, 1992) discussion of embedding. At the same time, the results highlight the significance of a closure dimension rarely discussed in social-capital discussions of closure: social monopoly. As much as reputation and network stability are enhanced by dense connections within a closed network, stability is further enhanced by the network having a monopoly on its members indicated by their lack of contacts outside the network.

In contrast, the empirical results on network brokerage were a surprise. More, the results raised troubling questions about the mechanism by which brokerage has its effect. I expected to see advantage spill over between adjacent networks. Given the known advantage of friends in separate groups through whom you have access to diverse information, and given ready connections across the world through the internet and wireless communication, it is a short step to conclude that network-advantaged access to information would be enhanced if your friends themselves had networks of scattered contacts providing even broader access. Well-connected friends should provide some advantage over having ill-connected friends. How much advantage was an empirical question, but I expected some advantage. I was surprised to find no advantage at all. I wrote up my early results and submitted them in 2005 for publication (Burt, 2007), then began the deeper analysis reported in this book. The early results are corroborated and generalized here. The social psychology of networks moves to center stage and personal responsibility emerges as a key theme. The competitive advantage of brokerage does not come to people who passively wait for the network to deliver it. The advantage provided by network brokerage depends on personal engagement with conflicting opinion and practice.

What you have in this book is a line of work arriving at a branch in the road. Next steps could go this way or that. Forced to make a consequential choice, I use contrasting study populations and extensive data displays to be confident in taking the right path. I use generic procedures so that others can readily replicate the evidence. The diverse study populations provide grounds to talk about how the results should vary across the populations if alternative mechanisms were responsible for the spillover I observe. On the replication point, I include detailed appendices on the network data and their use to measure social structure.

The data collection and analyses reported here were supported by work with private clients. I am grateful for summer support provided by the University of Chicago Booth School of Business that allowed me to work on the book free of consulting obligations.

Argument and evidence here have been improved in response to colleague comment. Foremost among these is Edward C. Smith. I was fortunate to have Ned read the manuscript from beginning to end to help identify blocks of choppy text and ambiguous links in the argument. Ned worked with me as a Teaching Assistant for two years (and was voted one of the best by Chicago's Executive MBA students), so he came to the manuscript as an expert, knowing the material and having successfully communicated it. In addition, I am indebted to the patience and curiosity of colleague audiences at the 2007 Distinguished Scholar lecture for the Organization and Management Theory division of the Academy of Management, an Organization Behavior and Industrial Relations workshop at the University of California at Berkeley Haas School of Business, the 2007 "Management and Social Networks" conference at the Groupe ESC Clermont Graduate School of Management, an Organizations and Markets workshop at the University of Chicago Booth School of Business, the 2006 "Search and Diffusion in Networks" conference at Cornell University, a Sociology Department seminar at Duke University, the 2005 and 2008 Intra-Organizational Network Conferences at Emory University and the University of Kentucky, the "Age of Networks" speaker series at University of Illinois Center for Advanced Study, a Strategy workshop at INSEAD Fontainebleau, an Organization Behavior workshop at INSEAD Singapore, an Information Systems Group seminar at the New York University Stern School of Business, the 2008 Nobel Symposium "Foundations of Organization," the 2007 Distinguished Speaker lecture at Northwestern University's Institute on

Complex Systems, the Nuffield College Sociology Seminar Series at Oxford University, a research workshop at the University of Pennsylvania Wharton School and the 2006 "Networks in Context" conference at the University of Pennsylvania Department of Sociology, a Distinguished Scholar lecture at the University of Pittsburgh Katz School of Business, an Economics and Business seminar at Universitat Pompeu Fabra, the Economics/Sociology workshop at Princeton University, a research seminar at Queen's University School of Business, the Russell Sage Foundation Working Group on Formation and Decay of Economic Networks, the 2006 "Annenberg Workshop on Network Theory" at the University of Southern California, the 2006 annual Sunbelt Network Conference, a strategy workshop at the University of Toronto Rotman School, and the Network Roundtable at the University of Virginia McIntire School.

The book includes material adapted from earlier publications. Chapters 2, 3, and 4 each contain bits from "Secondhand brokerage: evidence on the importance of local structure for managers, bankers, and analysts," *Academy of Management Journal* 50 (2007): 119–148. Chapter 3 contains a section from "Structural holes and good ideas," *American Journal of Sociology* 110 (2004): 349–399. Chapter 5 draws on "Industry performance and indirect access to structural holes," Pp. 315–360 in *Advances in Strategic Management*, edited by Joel A. C. Baum and Timothy J. Rowley, Elsevier (2008). Chapter 6 draws on "Closure and stability: persistent reputation and enduring relations among bankers and analysts," Pp. 100–143 in *The Missing Links: Formation and Decay in Economic Networks*, edited by James Rauch, Russell Sage Foundation (2007). Chapter 7 contains material from "The gender of social capital," *Rationality and Society* 10 (1998): 5–46. Chapter 8 contains material from "Actor interests in a social topology: foundation for a structural theory of action," *Sociological Inquiry* 50 (1980): 107–132. Appendix G contains material from "Detecting role equivalence," *Social Networks* 12 (1990): 83–97, "Social contagion and social structure," by R. S. Burt and Gregory A. Janicik, Pp. 32–49 in *Networks in Marketing*, edited by Dawn Iacobucci, Newbury Park: Sage (1996), and from "The social capital of opinion leaders," *Annals of the American Academy of Political and Social Science* 566 (1999): 37–54.

Note: Sources

The bit of wisdom cited at the top of the chapter is from the second substantive sentence in Verse 4.14 of *The Lun Yü*, also known as *The Analects*, a collection of snippets from disciple discussions with or about Confucius. Wording varies across translators and revisions, but obedience is the consistent theme: good people do good work without meddling in the distribution of rewards. My phrasing in the text is colloquial for a contemporary audience. There is no single correct translation into English. Waley (1938:96) provides a widely circulated translation: "The Master said. He does not mind not being in office; all he minds about is whether he has qualities that entitle him to office. He does not mind failing to get recognition; he is too busy doing the things that entitle him to recognition." Brooks and Brooks (2001:16) translate from an earlier version more likely reflecting Confucius' original words: "The Master said. He does not worry that he has no position; he worries about whether he is qualified to hold one. He does not worry that no one recognizes his worth; he seeks to become worthy to be recognized." The Confucius Publishing Company website www.confucius.org/lunyu/ed0414.htm provides multi-lingual translation, the English of which is: "Confucius said. Do not be concerned when without official position, be concerned with where a stand is established. Do not be concerned when not appreciated, seek what can be appreciated."

CONTENTS

LIST OF FIGURES

LIST OF TABLES

ONE

Introduction

I F social networks can be an advantage (the well connected do well), and networks are jointly owned by the people in them (not equally, but jointly), there should be advantage to affiliation with well-connected people. Your neighbors should matter. On the first point, we know quite a bit about social networks creating competitive advantage for certain people while holding back others. We know that opinion and behavior move between people adjacent in social networks. Does advantage work the same way? Is there advantage to affiliation with the well connected?

The common-sense answer is yes: Well-connected neighbors can be a source of opportunity and resources. This bit of common sense is nicely illustrated by a pair of quotes Rowley and Baum (2004:122) offer from their interviews with investment bankers: "Information and access to it are king . . . being close to the source is the name of the game . . . I don't have time to know everyone, but I need to be close to those that have the best contacts." "The best players in the industry build reputations by getting the biggest clients and controlling information, and carefully passing it out to others. It makes you a hot commodity, like a hot concert ticket or restaurant—everybody wants some." Well-connected contacts also can be a helpful signal. They signal to observers that you have standing among the right people. When once asked to invest in a friend's new venture, Baron de Rothschild is said to have replied that he would not invest, but would walk arm-in-arm with his friend across the exchange floor. In short order, there would be investors to spare. People observing the pair would infer that Rothschild had thrown into the venture, which would ensure the venture's success. When affiliation has obvious benefit, it can be expensive. People who obtain exceptional prerogatives through affiliation often pay with selfless loyalty. Examples are Court Jews in Baroque Germany, Christian renegades in the Ottoman Empire, royal mistresses and eunuchs in the Orient more generally. Claims to beneficial affiliation can backfire in ways long familiar. Well before the Baron de Rothschild or Suleiman the Magnificent, Aesop spoke in ancient Greece of a pretentious monkey claiming social connections he did not have, drowned by an otherwise philanthropic dolphin. The advantage of affiliation, the cost of that advantage, and retribution for false claim to affiliation, are illustrative costs and benefits of neighbor networks. You are somehow made better off, or dragged down, by the networks around your neighbors.[1]

The performance effects of neighbor networks are substantively interesting in their own right, but uniquely important for research. Social processes difficult to discern within one's own network can be distinguished in the spillover from neighbor networks. The extent to which advantage spills over from neighbors is a criterion that can be used to determine the process by which social networks constitute social capital. This book is an exploration of that criterion. I begin by distinguishing your network from the networks around your neighbors, offer three reasons for wanting to know how advantage spills over from neighbor networks, then sketch a quick overview of the chapters to come.

People You Know versus the People They Know

Figure 1.1 is a sociogram of the network around a person, ego, whose performance is to be explained. Dots represent people. Lines represent relationships. A direct contact is someone with whom ego communicates directly. There are eight in Figure 1.1. The eight direct contacts define ego's immediate network. I use a possessive form, but of course, the network does not "belong" to ego. It is co-owned with the contacts. A more accurate label would be "the interface between ego and social structure," but the label is clumsy. The structure of relations among the contacts defines the immediate network around ego, which is typically what we mean when we talk about a person's network (also discussed as ego's personal network, or an ego network).

Social capital in the immediate network: Direct access to structural holes

Inherent in the structure of ego's network is a level of social capital, a competitive advantage that ego enjoys as a result of the network. The advantage is conceptualized using structure as a proxy for information. The proxy is based on two facts taken from a vigorous stream of research on communication and influence that began after World War II (e.g., Festinger, Schachter, and Back, 1950; Asch, 1951; Lazarsfeld and Katz, 1955; Schachter, 1959; Coleman, Katz, and Menzel, 1957—all work to be discussed in this book, all classics that still shape today how scholars think about communication and influence): (1) People cluster into groups as a result of interaction opportunities defined

---

[1] Sources for the stories in this paragraph are given in the note at the end of the chapter.

by the places where people meet; the neighborhoods in which they live, the organizations with which they affiliate, the projects in which they are involved. (2) Communication is more frequent and influential within than between groups such that people in the same group develop similar views of the history that led to today, similar views of proper opinion and behavior, similar views of how to move into the future. People tire of repeating arguments and stories explaining why they believe and behave the way they do. They make up short-hand phrases to reference whole paragraphs of text with which colleagues are familiar. Jargon flourishes. Not only jargon, but a whole system of phrasing, opinions, symbols and behaviors defining what it means to be a member of the group. Below the arguments and experiences labeled are many awaiting a label, more understood than said within the group. What was once explicit knowledge interpretable by anyone becomes tacit knowledge meaningful only to insiders. With continued time together, new combinations and nuances emerge to make the tacit knowledge more complex, making knowledge more difficult to move to other groups. Information in the group becomes "sticky" (von Hippel, 1994). Much of what we know is not readily understood beyond the colleagues around us. Inside the tribe, one only needs to say the punch line of a popular joke to elicit bonding recollection of the whole story. Explicit knowledge converted into local, tacit knowledge makes information sticky such that holes tear open in the flow of information between groups. These holes in the social structure of communication, or

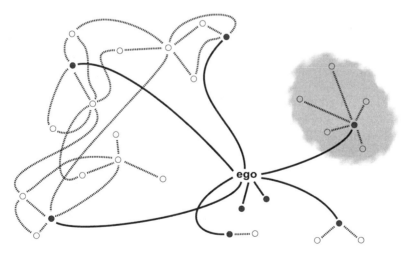

(Solid dots are direct contacts. Hollow dots are indirect contacts. Solid lines are connections within immediate network. Dashed lines are connections within neighbor networks. Shaded area identifies a neighbor's network.)

Figure 1.1 Immediate Network and Neighbor Networks

more simply "structural holes," are missing relations that inhibit information flow between people ("like an insulator in an electric circuit," Burt, 1992:18).

Structural holes distinguish two network sources of advantage: Brokerage and closure. These are forms of social capital in as much as they originate, evolve, and decay as a function of the surrounding network. Closure is about staying on your side of a structural hole. It is about the benefits of protection from variation in opinion and behavior, protection provided by focusing on connections with your own kind. Structural holes are boundary markers in the division of labor. By not having to attend to the interpretations of people beyond the boundary around my specialty, I can focus on deepening my knowledge of what I already know pretty well, becoming more efficient in doing what I already do. Without structural holes, we would be overwhelmed with the diversity of knowledge available. If structural holes were taken away, we would quickly re-create them to re-establish a sense of control over our lives. That desire to live within a world understood is a source of advantage for the hardy souls among us who rise above it. Brokerage is about the benefits of exposure to variation in opinion and behavior provided by building connections across structural holes. Network brokerage and closure both provide advantage, but by different mechanisms toward different performance goals. To use colloquial business terms, network brokerage drives top-line growth and closure drives bottom-line growth. People, process, product, and market enhancements provided by network brokerage grow the business. Labor, management, and speed efficiencies provided by closure cut costs so that business is more profitable.

In this book, I focus on network brokerage, measured in terms of opportunities to coordinate across structural holes. Where everyone you know knows everyone else, you have no access to structural holes. The more disconnected a manager's contacts, the more likely her network spans structural holes in the surrounding organization and market. In Figure 1.1, for example, ego's five contacts to the east have no connections with one another and their contacts have no connection with one another. The eastern part of the network is rich in structural holes. Because the contacts to the east have no connection with one another, they are more likely to operate with different ideas and practices, taking for granted different ways of looking at problems. People whose contacts are all in the same group know only their own group's opinion and practice. People who connect across structural holes (call those people network brokers, connectors, hubs, or entrepreneurs) are exposed to the diversity of opinion and behavior in the surrounding organization and market. Such people are presented with opportunities to coordinate people otherwise disconnected, and derive ideas or resources from exposure to contacts who differ in opinion or the way they behave. Connecting across more holes means broader exposure. Broader exposure provides a vision advantage in selecting early between alternative ways to go, synthesizing new ways to go, framing a proposal to be attractive to needed supporters, and detecting likely supporters/

opponents to implementing a proposed way to go. This is not to say that every connection across a structural hole is valuable. Coordination between some groups does not warrant the cost. Many novel combinations of existing opinion or practice are worthless. Network brokerage is not a guarantee. It is a probability: Connecting across structural holes increases the risk of productive accident—the risk of encountering a new opinion or practice not yet familiar to colleagues, the risk of envisioning a new synthesis of existing opinion or practice, the risk of finding a course of action through conflicting interests, the risk of discovering a new source for needed resources. Bridging structural holes creates a vision advantage in detecting and developing productive opportunities. The advantage is manifest in standard performance metrics. Network brokers enjoy more-positive evaluations than their peers, higher compensation, and faster promotions.

Questions about the returns to network brokerage lead me to network closure later in the book. Closure is measured by the extent to which everyone in a network is connected to everyone else, through a central person in the network, or through direct connections between people in the network. In Figure 1.1, ego and his three contacts to the west are densely connected, in part directly and in part through several friends of friends. Closed networks are detrimental with respect to the vision advantage of brokerage, but can be an advantage with respect to coordinating work. Reputation is the mechanism by which closure delivers its effect. As connections close the network around a manager, people are more informed about one another and benchmark opinion and behavior against one another. Reputations emerge to distinguish the peripheral from the best among us. I am using reputation to refer broadly to the vertical axis of social organization: Some people are prominent, respected members of a network. Other people are on the periphery, barely considered members of the network. To preserve reputation among colleagues well-informed about one another's behavior, people are careful to behave well (which lowers the risk of trust within the network) and people work to keep up with colleagues (which lowers cost within the network by increasing the quality and quantity of work and decreasing the need for a supervisor to monitor individual behavior). Closure's advantage is manifest as enhanced collaboration, productivity, and stability that speed a group down its learning curve.

Social capital from your neighbor's network: Indirect access to structural holes

The preceding cryptic remarks are fleshed out in the forthcoming chapters. I need the overview to frame the research question for this book: What about contacts beyond the immediate network?

Beyond the immediate network are numerous indirect contacts, friends of friends at various distances. In Figure 1.1, hollow dots represent the 21 people with whom ego has indirect contact through his eight direct contacts. Dashed lines represent connections with and among the indirect contacts. The network around each of ego's contacts is a "neighbor network." Ego's three direct contacts to the west in Figure 1.1, for example, are interconnected through friends of friends. To the east, each of ego's direct contacts leads to indirect contacts disconnected from the others. I shaded an area containing the network around one of ego's contacts. That contact should be doing well since her network is rich in structural holes (no connections between her six contacts). As managers vary in their direct access to structural holes within the immediate network, managers vary in their indirect access to structural holes among friends of friends.

I want to know the extent to which advantage spills over between adjacent networks such that neighbor networks are a factor to consider in social capital. Does any of the network-induced success of the shaded-area colleague in Figure 1.1 spill over to ego? Does ego benefit from the stability expected in the closed network among his western contacts? Moreover, if neighbor networks affect ego's performance, how does the neighbor-network effect compare to the effect of ego's own network? The effect of ego's network could be magnified or reversed by effects, even small effects, from a multitude of neighbors.

So What?

Given replicated results on the network structure of social capital, measuring the effects of neighbor networks might seem to be little more than an academic exercise, a consistency check on a well-established theme. There is some truth to the suspicion, but three issues press for taking a closer look at neighbor networks.

Business practice

First, many admired business practices are based on an assumption that neighbor networks do matter. Businesses have made increasing use of network ideas in their efforts to integrate operations. Employees are encouraged and expected to "network" through colleagues. Colleges, professional schools, and companies tout the value of access to their alumni network. "Mentoring" programs are based on well-connected senior people facilitating the recognition and development of promising junior people. "Onboarding" programs use well-connected insiders to facilitate the social integration of new hires (e.g., Cisco's famous "manager of the intangibles," a well-connected insider appointed to facilitate the social integration into Cisco of employees from a company just acquired by Cisco). These programs, and the many like them, assume that advantage spills over between neighbor networks. If advantage does not spill over, then these programs operate somewhere between irritating and irrelevant. For any such program that has proven valuable, the factor responsible for its value would have to be something other than neighbor networks.

Research design

In contrast to business practice, much of the research evidence on returns to network brokerage rests on an assumption that neighbor networks do not matter. The usual survey-network research design involves gathering data on relations with and among direct contacts to define the immediate network around a survey respondent—the solid lines and dots around ego in Figure 1.1 (for details, see Appendix A on measuring networks). Measures of structure in the immediate network, such as network size and density, are then added to traditional stratification models predicting the respondent's achievement and rewards. This can be a powerful research design when used with a stratified random sample of managers in a large heterogeneous population (e.g., Burt, 1992; Podolny and Baron, 1997; Hansen, Podolny, and Pfeffer, 2001; Mizruchi and Sterns, 2001; Seibert, Kraimer, and Liden, 2001). The same research design underlies DiMaggio and Louch's (1998) use of the General Social Survey, a national probability survey, to describe closure effects on preferences for buying and selling "within network" items such as a house or a car. Structure beyond the respondent's immediate network (the dashed lines and hollow dots in Figure 1.1) is ignored in these research designs, as in other studies based on the same survey-network research design. If neighbor networks are a factor in social capital, the above research is wrong in its assumption, the reported estimates of returns to network structure are inconsistent, and much of what has been taken as evidence is called into question.

Social capital process clues

Third, neighbor networks are interesting for the criterion that spillover provides to identify processes by which social networks constitute social capital. Empirical success in predicting performance with network models has far outstripped our understanding of the way information and behavior in networks are responsible for network effects. Information and behavior are almost never observed directly. Both are inferred from the structure of relations in which they occur. As discussed above, information is assumed to have a clustered distribution in which information is relatively homogeneous within groups and heterogeneous between groups. That clustered distribution is assumed to create a vision advantage for people who have connections across groups because they are exposed to a broader range of alternative opinion and behavior, so they are more likely to see alternative ways to go, synthesize new ways to go, and see a broader range of ways to support an initiative. Finally, it is assumed that people who see more opportunities are more likely to act on at least one of the opportunities, so the vision advantage creates an achievement advantage manifest in evaluations and compensation as performance metrics.

Thus, structure has been used as a proxy for process assumptions about information, opportunity, and behavior. Using network structure as a proxy for process has facilitated research because structure can be measured more reliably and at lower cost than would be true of measuring information or behavior directly, and research can focus on the more interesting task of explaining performance differences. Given success in predicting performance with network structure, the process responsible warrants closer inspection, and we now see papers reporting ethnographic description of network brokerage (Obstfeld, 2005), richer survey data on network content and brokerage (e.g., Rodan and Gallunic, 2004), authoritative archival data on network content and brokerage (Aral and Van Alstyne, 2007), and rigorous speculation with network simulations of brokerage processes (e.g., Centola and Macy, 2007; Buskens and van de Rijt, 2008; Reagans and Zuckerman, 2008). The elaborate research designs and novel research strategies are an exciting development, but more can be done than has been done with existing data. Familiar cross-sectional and panel data can be used to measure the extent to which advantage spills over from neighbor networks, and spillover can be used to make inferences about network processes otherwise indistinguishable in the immediate network around ego. That is the central point developed in the next chapter.

Overview of the Book

In the next chapter, I introduce network measures of direct versus indirect access to structural holes, then describe how spillover evidence can be a criterion for distinguishing three broad categories of processes potentially responsible for social capital: Global processes (indicated by increasing spillover from information flow expanding exponentially through friends of friends), local processes (indicated by decreasing spillover from information flow only meaningful between people who are socially close), and personal processes (indicated by a lack of spillover because information flow is irrelevant to advantage except as it leaves behind a by-product of learning to communicate across structural holes).

Chapters 3 and 4 introduce the most surprising results, the lack of advantage from affiliation with network brokers. Managers in five diverse study populations show a strong correlation between performance and affiliation with well-connected colleagues, but the correlation is spurious. The correlation disappears when ego's job and her own network are held constant. The evidence in Chapter 3 is from populations in which groups are separated by strong boundaries. People focus on others like themselves. Knowledge is unlikely to move easily across groups. Such "balkanized" populations are the places in which local processes are likely to be important. The first population is composed of employees active in the Asia-Pacific launch of a new software product. The employees are segregated by regional divisions. A second population is the supply-chain organization in a large electronics company segregated by geography and technology. In Chapter 4, I turn from balkanized populations to populations integrated through dense ties to a single, central elite. In populations so integrated, knowledge should move more easily through the short connections that span the population, so indirect access to structural holes among friends of friends is more likely to be valuable. The three study populations in Chapter 4 are a human resource organization, investment bankers in a financial organization, and senior analysts in the organization. My research results are consistent across the five very different populations in Chapters 3 and 4: Performance increases with direct access to structural holes and has no association with indirect access. Therefore, when describing the advantage provided by affiliation with network brokers, I choose at the end of Chapter 4 to use the diminutive label "secondhand" brokerage—rather than spillover, pre-owned, leveraged, or some other more positive adjective.

The negligible spillover between adjacent manager networks is consistent with personal processes and distinct from what would be expected from local or global processes. It is not enough to affiliate with known brokers. Such affiliation should be an advantage if brokerage creates advantage by providing quick, early access to distant, novel information. Consistently negligible re-turns to secondhand brokerage in diverse populations lead me to conclude that the advantage of network brokerage is not about quick, early access to distant, novel information so much as it is about what happens to a person who has to manage communication across a network full of structural holes. Either way, ego has a vision advantage in detecting and developing rewarding opportunities. The question is whether the vision advantage comes from better glasses or better eyes. A network that spans structural holes could provide a manager with better information access and control, which would be an advantage, or it could, by exercising one's ability to manage heteroge-neous information, make the managers better able than less "exercised" peers to see opportunities, which would amount to the same advantage. Brokerage exposes ego to diverse opinion and behavior in other groups. In the course of managing contradictory relationships, ego develops cognitive skills of analogy and synthesis, and emotional skills for reading, engaging, and motivating colleagues. One is perhaps less troubled by sharp differences in opinion or practice. One becomes, perhaps, more skilled in analogy and metaphor in order to communicate across differences. Whatever specific skills are involved (and I look into some in the final chapter), brokerage is not valuable for the information it provides so much as it is valuable as a forcing function for the cognitive and emotional skills required to manage communication between colleagues who do not agree in their opinion or behavior. It is the cognitive and emotional skills produced as a by-product of bridging structural holes that are the proximate source of competitive advantage. In a phrase, brokerage opportunities could be a forcing function for human capital (the theme in Coleman's, 1988, initial network discussion of social capital in the creation of human capital).

The conclusion is attractive on several counts: It is simple, surprisingly robust, puts a welcome emphasize on personal responsibility at the same time that it greatly simplifies the study of strategic behavior in networks, creates an incentive for social psychologists to join in the expanding work on network brokerage, and creates an incentive for the people working on the structure-performance association to seek out social psychology as a corollary competence.

On the other hand, the conclusion creates a problem. The fact that managers do not benefit from indirect access to structural holes raises a question about the traditional network-theory strength of consistency across levels of analysis. It is not the empirical fact of secondhand brokerage that is troubling so much as the fact's implication that returns to brokerage within the immediate network are a result of social psychological processes. The role of cognition and emotion in network brokerage makes sense when applied to people. It is not obvious how the metaphor of sentient individuals applies at the macro level. Organizations, and the industries and regions in which they operate, are assemblies of people who individually think and feel. To attribute thinking and feeling to macro units such as organizations, industries, or regions, requires an unattractively anthropomorphic metaphor. To continue the above "better glasses or better eyes" metaphor, the "better glasses" metaphor generalizes readily to the macro level of organizations and markets. The "better eyes" metaphor, with its emphasis on enhanced cognitive and emotional skills, does not. It would be useful to see macro-level evidence on performance and indirect access to structural holes.

That is my purpose in Chapter 5. I describe a network brokerage model at the industry level that is analogous to the model used to describe manager performance in Chapters 3 and 4. I use the model to describe performance and producer access to structural holes among suppliers and customers based on data in the 1987 and 1992 benchmark input–output tables of the American economy. The manager and industry evidence offer complementary strengths (similar returns to brokerage at the two levels of analysis, greater variety in the manager networks, less endogeneity in the industry networks). In contrast to the manager evidence showing no performance association with indirect access to structural holes, there is clear industry evidence of positive association. About 24 percent of the industry-structure effect on performance can be attributed to structure beyond the industry's own buying and selling, to networks around the industry's suppliers and customers.

At the same time, manager and industry evidence are similar in important ways. I conclude in Chapter 5 that the industry evidence is not qualitatively distinct from the manager evidence so much as it describes a more extreme business environment. I speculate on information and inhibition as factors making the industry environment more extreme (industry information codified into routines can move more quickly, further, with more accuracy, and industry buying and selling is less inhibited by social norms of proper behavior). One thing is clear: A wide range of business environments—from corporate bureaucracies up through the mature capital markets in which investment bankers and analysts work—show no performance advantage to brokerage beyond the immediate network of direct contacts. There is a detectable performance advantage at the extreme of industry market relations; but short of that extreme, advantage is limited to the immediate network of direct contacts.

Chapters 6 and 7 report on closure effects from neighbor networks. In Chapter 6, relations and reputations are analyzed over time among the investment bankers and analysts introduced in Chapter 4. As expected, relations are enhanced and reputations more stable when colleagues are connected so as to close the network around participants.

More, and in contrast to brokerage, closure's effect is strengthened by closure in neighbor networks. The evidence on spillover closure is consistent with local processes, processes in and just-beyond the immediate network around a person. The evidence is distinct from what would be expected if spillover closure resulted from population-spanning global processes, or was a by-product via personal processes. The evidence is reassuring more than surprising since spillover effects were expected from closure. The vision provided by brokerage enlightens ego. The reputation provided by closure aligns ego with neighbors. Enlightening ego is a less social outcome than aligning neighbors, so it is not surprising to see closure spillover between neighbor networks.

Closure spillover from neighbor networks emphasizes an aspect of closure that is rarely discussed. The trust and alignment associated with closure is a story that can be told in two ways: As a social integration story about strong connections within the closed network, or as a social monopoly story about the lack of strong connections beyond the closed network. The social integration story lends itself to positive rhetoric about community and strong relationships. The social monopoly story is more nakedly a story about control, access denied. Closure is often discussed, and closure strategies proposed, in terms of the positive, social integration story. The social integration story is valid, but the results in Chapter 6 show that social monopoly matters. Closure is about control. Whatever the closure within the immediate network around ego, each person in the network—each of ego's neighbors—is a potential backdoor through whom contradictory opinion and practice can enter to disrupt trust and alignment within the network. Having neighbors embedded in their own closed networks significantly reduces the risk.

Closure spillover in Chapter 6 sets the stage for the analysis in Chapter 7. Chapter 7 is about what would seem to be an obvious case of managers benefiting from affiliation with a network broker—which would contradict the secondhand brokerage conclusion in Chapter 4. Communication across groups can be difficult when the communicator is viewed with suspicion. In some organizations, certain kinds of people are deemed outsiders in the sense that they are denied the advantages of connecting across groups. Sometimes women are the outsiders. Sometimes age is the criterion with young men excluded as outsiders until they prove themselves. Sometimes the criterion is nationality, or religion. Whatever the criterion, network models provide a useful diagnostic identifying the people deemed outsiders in a specific organization: Outsiders are the people whose careers are slowed or reversed when they try to broker connections across structural holes. The corrective action is simple to do and has demonstrable benefit: Affiliate with an insider rich in structural holes who legitimates outsider access to insider opportunities for brokerage. In Chapter 7, I discuss such an insider as a strategic partner. Outsiders benefiting from affiliation with an inside broker look like an exception to the finding in Chapters 3 and 4 that managers do not benefit from affiliation with network brokers. Outsiders clearly do. In fact, this is one of those exceptions that proves the rule. Strategic partners do not create advantage by affecting ego. Partners create advantage by making ego more acceptable to colleagues. The spillover effect of strategic partners is an instance of strategic partners closing the network to facilitate trust. As evidence of closure inducing trust, the positive effect of strategic partners does not contradict the negligible returns to secondhand brokerage in Chapters 3 and 4. It corroborates the trust and alignment returns to closed networks documented in Chapter 6.

Driven by the evidence of local and personal processes, I speculate in the concluding chapter on the role individual people play in the process by which network structure constitutes social capital. This is the question of agency: How much do individuals matter relative to the social structure around them? I begin with a lament, as have many others, on the lack of attention to agency. Scholars typically assume agency away or hold it constant in order to focus on the network connection with performance. That performance connection is my focus in the first seven chapters here. However, networks also affect what people want to do, what they see as valuable. How much of the performance association with networks is due to differences in network advantage versus individual differences in seeing or seizing network advantage? Action that can seem worthwhile to one person can seem trivial, even status-eroding, to another person. Are networks the performance factor to manage, or would it be more effective to manage incentives to act on network advantage? Network advantage is worthless until someone acts on it.

In Chapter 8, I argue that networks create a pressure on ego to act by defining the frame of reference through which ego evaluates alternative actions. Ego is lured to action by the prospect of moving ahead and pushed to action by fear of falling behind. Preferences are bent in predictable ways by network context. Connection between felt and actual resources is taken from psychophysics. Concepts of structural and role equivalence in sociology provide context. Context dependence is neither new in general, nor in the particular discussed here. With respect to the generally familiar idea of context dependence, the proposed bent preference model is promising in its simplicity, precise description, and compatibility with economic, psychological, and sociological analysis. The model combines marginal evaluation from economics and psychophysics with the sociology of network structure, shifting context from psychophysics lab to social network, extending contagion from behavioral communication to symbolic role play, and defining motivation in terms of advantage relative to peers in a network. The proposed model would fall under the relative income hypothesis in economics, social comparison theory in psychology, and reference group theory and the concepts of relative advantage and deprivation in sociology. With respect to the particular model proposed, I draw on earlier work that is timely to revisit because diffusion research has clarified the network condition used in the model as a frame of reference for perception, accumulating evidence on the performance correlates of network structure has widened the audience interested in the motivation question, and the evidence in the first seven chapters brings individual differences in cognition and emotion to center stage in the social capital of network structure.

I derive from the model three broad hypotheses around which Chapter 8 is organized. First, the motivation that networks create is disproportionately about fear, specifically, fear of falling behind peers. In defining the frame of reference through which ego evaluates alternative actions, the network around ego creates pressure to act. Ego is lured to action by the prospect of moving ahead and pushed to action by fear of falling behind. The bent preferences model predicts that the push is stronger than the pull; the network pressure on ego to act is less about the lure of gain, than the fear of loss. The following *network fear hypothesis* is implied: The feelings of loss as peers overtake ego are more severe than the feelings of gain in overtaking peers, but the feelings of loss fade as peers continue to do well. This hypothesis is a bridge between the sociology of networks and the psychology of loss versus gain. The prediction is that feelings of loss versus gain are not a psychological primitive. Rather, the feelings are in some large part a function of the social context in which prospective action is evaluated.

Second, networks differ predictably in the intensity of fear they generate. The difference between felt loss and gain predicted by the first hypothesis is larger for people with more obvious peers. With peers defined by a network criterion of structural equivalence, more obvious structural equivalence makes falling behind peers more obvious, which ensures the pain, and so fear, of relative deprivation. Network brokers are relatively unique within their networks. There is often no one structurally equivalent to a broker. Brokers having no structurally equivalent peers are free from the competitive pressure of peers, so they are less subject to the pain of relative deprivation, and therefore more free to evaluate and espouse something new for its benefits. An *intrepid broker hypothesis* is implied as a contingency version of the network fear hypothesis: When evaluating a new idea or practice, network brokers are more motivated by the lure of gain, and less troubled by a fear of failure. I discuss this hypothesis with respect to interpersonal influence, opinion leaders, displayed emotion, and high-performance teams.

Where the second hypothesis describes correlates of the freedom provided to brokers by their lack of peers, the third describes corrective moves expected when brokers feel the need for a social frame of reference. Freedom from the competitive pressure of structural equivalence is an incentive to be a broker, but everyone at one time or another needs a social frame of reference to make sense of ambiguous events. The question "Who is like me?" sometimes needs to be answered, presupposing an answer to the identity question "Who am I?" For brokers, the lack of obvious peers means that a social frame of reference has to be found in more abstract images of social structure, implying the following *network identity hypothesis*: Brokers are less guided by structural equivalence in identifying peers (including claims that they have no peer), and are more likely to be guided by abstract images of social structure in which broker peers are more obvious. I discuss this hypothesis with respect to categorizing people, the social construction of market boundaries, and identity defined in terms of role rather than network.

What emerges from the book is a sense of the central role played by social psychology in the network advantage known as social capital. Technological advances have given us the ability to reach across previously unimagined distance, but value is still produced close to home. Despite technological advance, social capital remains a phenomenon local and personal.

A quick historical note is in order before I lay out my argument and evidence. About a half-century ago, the social psychology of organizational life took a leap forward with images of people satisficing under bounded rationality (March and Simon, 1958; Cyert and March, 1963), socially constructing the meaning of events around them (Weick, 1969), with social psychology offering refinements to basic questions about morale, motivation, productivity and efficiency, power and control, leadership and change (Katz and Kahn, 1966). The images of people shaping and reacting to their surrounding situation found fertile ground in organization and management research (Scott, 2004; Scott and Davis, 2007: chaps. 4, 5). Without detracting in any way from the substance of the 1960s leap forward, I suspect that there would not have been such a leap without the vigorous prior and coterminous wave of research on communication and influence in small groups (which was also the foundation on which network models of social capital developed, see pages 2–3 in this chapter). The 1950s were a golden age of research on small groups, and elements of that golden age inspired the 1960s social psychology of organizational life. I mention the leap forward leveraged on a wave of what we would now call network research because over the last decade, we have had another vigorous wave of research on social networks, research showing a substantial network association with individual, organization, and industry performance. Along the way, we gave individual people little attention as the agents through whom social networks come alive. Evidence from closer study is pushing us back to reconsider our previous lack of attention. The stage is set to re-engage social psychology. The basic questions so long ago sketched by Katz and Kahn (1966) are by our new analytical tools laid open once again. The result is an engaging vista of interesting, consequential, and tractable puzzles. I don't know what will come of social psychology playing a more central role in network studies of social capital, but it is another view, and if the research on network brokerage has shown anything, it is that more lines of attack improve the odds of productive advance.

Note: Sources

My source for the Rothschild anecdote is Kilduff and Krackhardt (1994), who cite Cialdini (1989) as their source. Cialdini does not give a source, and I could not find a source. The anecdote is perhaps no more than a succinct didactic illustration. Coser (1974) describes examples of people given exceptional prerogatives in return for selfless loyalty. Aesop's fable is "The Monkey and the Dolphin," the gist of which is: "When people go on a voyage they often take with them lap-dogs or monkeys as pets to while away the time. Thus it was that a man returning to Athens from the East had a pet Monkey on board with him. As they neared the coast a storm burst upon them, and the ship capsized. All on board were thrown into the water and had to save themselves by swimming, the Monkey among them. A Dolphin saw the Monkey, and, supposing him to be a man, took him on his back and began swimming towards the shore. When they got near the Piræus, which is the port of Athens, the Dolphin asked the Monkey if he was an Athenian. The Monkey replied that he was, and added that he came from a very distinguished family. 'Then, of course, you know the Piræus,' continued the Dolphin. The Monkey thought he was referring to some high official or other, and replied, 'Oh, yes, he's a very old friend of mine.' At that, detecting the Monkey's hypocrisy, the Dolphin was so disgusted that he dived below the surface, and the Monkey was quickly drowned." The graphic on the book cover is Gustave Doré's 1896 illustration for Jean de La Fontaine's seventeenth-century rhyming version of Aesop's fable.

Part I

ESTABLISHING SECONDHAND BROKERAGE

TWO

Process Clues in Network Spillover

Two sociograms set the stage for the analysis to be presented. In Figure 2.1A, you see the network of colleague relations around a New York investment banker in 1997. The network data come from the employer's annual evaluation process in which bonus-eligible employees are asked to indicate the colleagues with whom they have had substantial business in the year preceding, and evaluate what it was like to work with each colleague. Average evaluations are used to develop employees and monitor employee reputation with colleagues. Dots in Figure 2.1A are employees. Lines connect employees where one cited the other in the annual evaluation process as a colleague with whom substantial business was done last year.

To the right, in Figure 2.1B, you see the discussion network around a supply-chain manager in a large electronics company in 2001. The manager was asked in a network survey (Appendix A) to name colleagues with whom he most often discussed his work, then to describe relations among them. He named three discussion partners and said that two of them often spoke with one another.

These are simple pictures, but they describe actual networks reported by actual people, and they are the pictures captured by the network size and density measures so often used to predict opinion, behavior, and performance. Network size is the number of a person's contacts. Density is the average connection between contacts. Figure 2.1A shows a banker connected to eight colleagues (network size), most of whom do not cite one another as colleagues (network density is .14, four observed connections over 28 possible). Figure 2.1B shows a manager connected to three interconnected colleagues. Network size is three. Network density is .67 (two observed connections over three possible).

There is reason to expect the banker to be more successful than the manager. The network around the banker is rich in structural holes. As introduced in the previous chapter, a structural hole refers to missing relationships that inhibit information flow. Structural holes typically separate people in different divisions or offices, but they are also common between groups within the same division or office. In contrast to the manager's interconnected discussion partners in Figure

2.1B, the lack of connections between the banker's colleagues in Figure 2.1A implies that many of the banker's colleagues are separated by structural holes. The colleagues are connected through their mutual relations with the banker, but each is disconnected from most or all of the other colleagues. For simplicity of expression, I will refer to such contacts as disconnected to indicate that the person at the center of the network has disconnected contacts. People with disconnected contacts—that is to say people whose networks bridge structural holes—have a competitive advantage over peers confined to a single group of interconnected people. Information, opinion, and practice are more homogenous within than between groups, so the people whose networks span structure holes (call those people network brokers, connectors, hubs, or entrepreneurs) have a vision advantage in early exposure to diverse information and a political advantage as a hub in the information flow. As in previous studies, results in the next two chapters show that the banker and manager in Figure 2.1 worked in organizations where people connected to many, otherwise disconnected, colleagues were more successful than peers surrounded by a small, dense network of colleagues.

For the banker and manager in Figure 2.1, however, the theory seems wrong. In contrast to low expectations of the manager's closed network, the manager was successful. He received a top performance evaluation in the year the network data were gathered, and his compensation was above average for managers at his rank with his background (.59 residual z-score for salary plus bonus).[1] In contrast to high expectations of the banker's network reaching

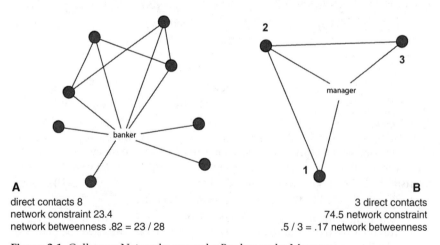

A
direct contacts 8
network constraint 23.4
network betweenness .82 = 23 / 28

                                    B
                    3 direct contacts
               74.5 network constraint
    .5 / 3 = .17 network betweenness

Figure 2.1 Colleague Networks around a Banker and a Manager

---

[1] Throughout the book, I am concerned with relative performance within populations rather than absolute performance so I measure performance as a z-score. Relative performance can be compared across populations and keeps confidential the compensation

disconnected colleagues, the banker was not particularly successful. His colleagues gave him evaluations slightly below what others in his job rank received (−.32 residual z-score) and he received about a million dollars in compensation, which was less than the average given to bankers at his rank with his background (−.49 residual z-score).

I do not want to blow the exceptions out of proportion. On average, there is a strong association between brokerage and compensation in the manager and banker populations. The manager and banker are each a single datum in their respective organizations. Individual variation from the average is to be expected. Some people with networks rich in structural holes do not do as well as others. The prediction is only that the people with networks rich in structural holes are at higher risk of success; bumping into ideas with which they can create value, seeing ways to develop their ideas, and so on.

Nevertheless, a broader view of the networks in Figure 2.1 makes less surprising the relative performances of the manager and banker. The sociograms in Figure 2.2 extend the manager and banker networks into the contacts around their colleagues. Here, as in the other complex sociograms to be presented, two people are close together to the extent that they are connected directly and indirectly through mutual colleagues.[2] The manager's three interconnected discussion partners were themselves brokers into disconnected parts of the company (Figure 2.2B). Through his three discussion partners, the manager was connected indirectly with 20 people, most of whom are disconnected

---

magnitudes within populations. To make it clear when performance is measured relative to an individual's peers in a population (versus the average for the whole population), I use the term "residual z-score" to refer to what is left of performance after holding constant job rank and other control variables. Residual z-scores are computed in three steps: Run a regression predicting performance from job rank and other control variables, compute the difference between a person's predicted versus actual performance, express the residual as a z-score. See footnote 3 below for reference to individual populations.

[2] Spatial representations of the networks in this book are heuristic multidimensional scalings in which proximity is proportional to path distance. People connected through intermediaries are further apart than people connected directly. The spatial representations are heuristic in that a network can have multiple representations depending on start values for the algorithm. The algorithm (variously named "spring-embedding" in NetDraw, or "energy" in Pajek, or "force-directed" in some texts) represents path distance by a spring connecting people. Given unit elasticity for the spring representing direct connection, elasticity increases with the number of intermediaries through whom people are connected, up to an infinitely elastic spring between people who cannot be connected through intermediaries. The algorithm finds a two-dimensional display that minimizes the stretch on the springs (using models from the physical sciences such as Hooke's law for the force of a stretched or compressed spring). Neither NetDraw (used for the spatial representations in this book, Borgatti, 2002) nor Pajek is provided with explanation of how network data are used to measure force. Spatial displays from either program have face validity when you see similar kinds of people in clusters (e.g., people in the same work group) and see in the center of the space people connected across an organization. I use the spatial representations only to provide an intuitive sense of complex network structures.

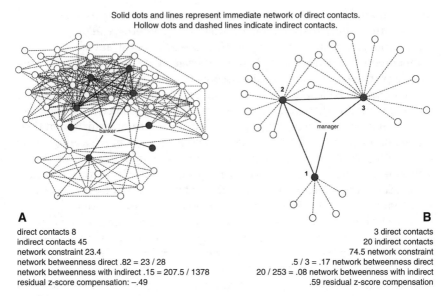

Solid dots and lines represent immediate network of direct contacts.
Hollow dots and dashed lines indicate indirect contacts.

A

direct contacts 8
indirect contacts 45
network constraint 23.4
network betweenness direct .82 = 23 / 28
network betweenness with indirect .15 = 207.5 / 1378
residual z-score compensation: –.49

B

3 direct contacts
20 indirect contacts
74.5 network constraint
.5 / 3 = .17 network betweenness direct
20 / 253 = .08 network betweenness with indirect
.59 residual z-score compensation

Figure 2.2 Direct and Indirect Contacts

from one another, many of whom are senior people in the company (job rank is not indicated in the sociograms). It turns out that the manager led a team that coordinated an aspect of work in the offices of the three senior people in different parts of the company. The manager must have been discussing his work with more than three people, but he only cited the three senior people as his key discussion partners. For his coordination efforts, the manager was well compensated and received a top performance evaluation.

The sociogram in Figure 2.2A reveals that the banker's contacts were less disconnected than they seem in Figure 2.1A. The banker was connected indirectly with 45 people beyond his eight direct contacts, but his contacts were clustered into two groups. The primary cluster, at the top of Figure 2.2A, is composed of other investment bankers. Most of the banker's direct contacts are in the banker cluster. These contacts are not often connected directly, but they are frequently connected indirectly through mutual ties to other bankers in the cluster. The banker's one contact disconnected from everyone in Figure 2.2A is in another banker cluster, but newly hired to a junior rank so no one in the banker's primary cluster cited her as a colleague (direct contact to the southeast of the banker). That leaves one contact to a senior person outside the banker's own cluster: The contact to the southwest of the banker is in the cluster at the bottom of Figure 2.2A, which is a group of people who specialized in a specific kind of financial instrument. Three of the instrument specialists are connected to bankers. The instrument specialist connected to the focal banker in Figure 2.1A is central among the specialists, directly connected with everyone in the specialist cluster. In contrast to the Figure 2.1A image of the banker spanning many structural holes, Figure 2.2A shows the banker bridging one hole, between bankers and the instrument specialists.

My purpose in this and the next two chapters is to understand the performance implications of the difference illustrated by the banker and manager. I want to know the extent to which predicting performance from a network of direct contacts (Figure 2.1) is strengthened when the prediction includes data on indirect contacts (Figure 2.2). The networks in Figure 2.1 define opportunities to move information between direct contacts. This is direct access to the structural holes between your contacts. The networks in Figure 2.2 define brokerage opportunities more distant, opportunities to move information between friends of friends. This is indirect access to the structural holes in networks around your contacts.

The lack of brokerage opportunities among the manager's direct contacts in Figure 2.1 is misleading. In Figure 2.2, the manager has indirect access to a rich diversity of structural holes. In other words, the manager is poor in direct access, rich in indirect access—and we know he was successful relative to his peers, so indirect access is a possible explanation.

The banker's opportunities for brokerage among his direct contacts in Figure 2.1 largely disappear when his network is expanded to include indirect contacts in Figure 2.2. Looking past his direct contacts, indirect access to structural holes is limited by dense connections among his indirect contacts. The banker was rich in direct access, poor in indirect access—and we know he was not particularly successful relative to his peers, which makes indirect access a possible explanation.

Direct Access to Structural Holes

A cluster of related network concepts emerged in the 1970s developing the general idea that there is advantage in having connections to multiple, otherwise disconnected, groups and individuals. At the center of the concept cluster are Granovetter (1973, 1983) on weak ties as bridges between groups, Freeman (1977, 1979) on network centrality as a function of being the connection between otherwise disconnected people, Cook and Emerson (1978; Cook *et al.*, 1983) on the advantage of having alternative exchange partners, Burt (1980, 1982) on the advantage of disconnected contacts, later discussed as access to structural holes (Burt, 1992, 2005), and Lin, Ensel, and Vaughn (1981) on the advantage of distant, prestigious contacts, later elaborated in terms of having contacts in statuses diverse and prominent (Lin, 2002). Empirical research has remained lively in predicting performance at the level of people, teams, organizations, and industries. Network measures are discussed in Appendix B relative to the summary index, network constraint, used in this book.

Direct network constraint

It is sufficient for the purposes here to say that network constraint is a concentration index (see equation B1 in Appendix B for formal definition). The index, which I will reference by the letter C, measures the extent to which a person's network time and energy is concentrated in a single group. The index varies with three network dimensions: Size, density, and hierarchy (see Figure B2 in Appendix B). Network constraint on a person is high if the person has few contacts (small network), and the contacts are connected to one another directly (dense network) or indirectly through a central, mutual contact (hierarchical network). I multiply proportional scores by 100 to discuss integer levels of constraint. A score of 100 indicates a person with no access to structural holes. Like a social straight jacket, a high-constraint network provides no opportunities to broker connections. Everyone knows everyone else. As a person connects with more and more different groups, the person is less constrained by any one group. Constraint scores approach zero for people with many disconnected contacts.

Figure 2.3 illustrates the network constraint index and my use of it to distinguish direct from indirect access to structural holes. There are six groups in Figure 2.3, each containing two roles: Persons 11 through 28 are "group members" in the sense that they are only connected to other people inside their own group (e.g., 11 is connected to 12, 13, and 5). The other role, "group leader," refers to people connected to someone outside their own group (persons 5 to 10). Persons 1 through 4 play a third role. They are "brokers" in the sense that they connect people across groups. The first column of the table in Figure 2.3 reports network constraint scores for the three roles. Constraint is lowest for the brokers who link across groups (33.3), higher for the group

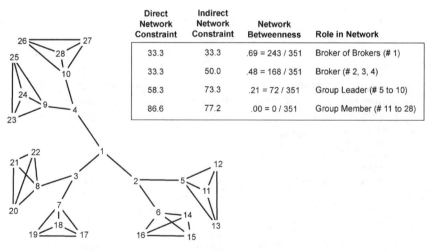

Direct Network Constraint	Indirect Network Constraint	Network Betweenness	Role in Network
33.3	33.3	.69 = 243 / 351	Broker of Brokers (# 1)
33.3	50.0	.48 = 168 / 351	Broker (# 2, 3, 4)
58.3	73.3	.21 = 72 / 351	Group Leader (# 5 to 10)
86.6	77.2	.00 = 0 / 351	Group Member (# 11 to 28)

Figure 2.3 Illustration of Direct and Indirect Network Constraint

leaders who have at least the brokerage opportunity of linking their group to an outside person (58.3), and highest for the group members who only know people within their own group (86.8). Note that the network constraint scores for banker and manager are the same in Figure 2.1 and Figure 2.2: 23.4 for the banker, 74.5 for the manager. Network constraint is defined for direct contacts, so expanding the networks in Figure 2.2 to include indirect contacts does not change the constraint scores.

Known returns to direct access

The broad prediction from theory and research is that brokers do better. People with direct access to structural holes (people in low-constraint networks, such as persons 1 to 4 in Figure 2.3) have an advantage—in detecting and developing productive opportunities—over people without access (in closed, high-constraint networks, such as group members 11 to 28). More constrained networks span fewer structural holes, so returns to brokerage are indicated by a negative association between performance and network constraint.

The association is illustrated in Figure 2.4 for the six populations of managers to be analyzed in this book (see Burt, 2005:56, for similar association across eight study populations). The horizontal axis of the graph distinguishes people by network constraint. High-constraint people to the right are surrounded by a network of interconnected colleagues (illustrated by the closed-network sociogram below the horizontal axis). At the other extreme, to the left in the graph, low-constraint people have numerous bridging connections to disconnected colleagues (also illustrated by a sociogram below the horizontal axis).

The vertical axis of the graph in Figure 2.4 distinguishes people by relative performance. Criterion variables differ between populations; sometimes compensation, sometimes evaluation, sometimes idea quality, sometimes promotion. The vertical axis is a z-score measure of residual performance, a measure of how well a person is doing relative to peers.[3] Senior investment bankers

---

[3] I am not being specific here because it would require an unproductive detour into the analyses of each study population which will be reported in the upcoming chapters. For persons interested in the details, my measure of residual performance in Figure 2.4 is the measure used to summarize brokerage results in Table 5.2. Listing the study populations in the order that they will be discussed in the book, I have 258 observations on the product-launch employees in Chapter 3, and 455 observations on the supply-chain managers. From Chapter 4, I have 283 observations on the HR employees, 469 annual observations on the investment bankers, and 354 annual observations on the analysts. From Chapter 7, I have 170 observations on senior male managers in the electronics firm. To simplify the graph in Figure 2.4, each dot is an average of performance and network scores within five-point intervals of network constraint in each study population (distinguished by ticks on the horizontal axis). Among the investment bankers, for example, the three-year average of network constraint scores between 20 and 25 is 22.10, and the corresponding average z-score residual performance for observations within the interval is −.44, which defines a dot at (22.10, −.44) in the graph.

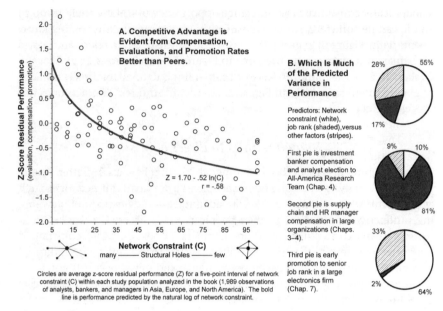

Figure 2.4 Social Capital of Brokerage

typically enjoy high compensation, but the issue here is the degree to which a specific banker's compensation is higher or lower than the average compensation received by peers. A residual performance score of zero indicates a person doing as well as his peers. A score of one indicates a person one standard deviation ahead of peers.

The regression line in the graph describes a performance advantage for people with direct access to structural holes. The higher the network constraint, the lower the performance relative to peers. The performance association with network constraint is statistically significant across the six study populations, and you will see in the forthcoming chapters that it is statistically significant within each study population.[4]

---

[4] There is a −6.54 routine t-test for the regression line through the 85 aggregate observations in Figure 2.4, which describe 1,989 observations on individual managers. The association so evident in Figure 2.4 does not occur in every population. As mentioned in the previous chapter, returns to brokerage are greater for people in more unique, less routine job assignments. Returns can be negligible among people in lower job ranks, whose work is less shaped by themselves than it is shaped by peer pressure and company processes. Returns can be negligible among people doing routine work, for whom the information diversity provided by brokerage is more disruptive than productive. However, the work in the study populations analyzed in this book involves nonroutine coordination tasks, which is work in which brokerage can be valuable. There is a strong performance association with network constraint in each population.

Statistical significance is no guarantee of magnitude. Effects small in magnitude can be sufficiently clear statistically to reject the null hypothesis. The pie charts in Figure 2.4 provide a sense of effect magnitude relative to other performance factors. Predicted performance variance is disaggregated into three sources: A portion attributed to network constraint (white), a portion attributed to job rank (shaded), and a portion attributed to other factors such as age, product, and geography (stripes).[5]

The network effect is large in populations where people have substantial control over their work, in other words, where work is less structured by formal job ranks than by informal relationships. Drawing from Chapter 4, the first pie chart in Figure 2.4 describes performance differences among investment bankers and analysts in a large financial organization. Direct access to brokerage opportunities accounts for the largest percentage of explained performance differences (55%). Senior job rank makes a difference (17%), leaving 28 percent attributed to other factors.

The network effect is large but indirect through job rank in populations structured by formal job ranks. The second pie chart describes compensation differences among supply-chain managers in a large electronics company (Chapter 3) and human resource managers in a commercial bank (Chapter 4). Brokerage measured by network constraint contributes a statistically significant, but substantively small, 10 percent of predictable compensation differences. Demographic and geographic factors make about the same contribution

---

[5] The pie charts are useful in communicating the relative magnitude of effects, but they are only presented as a heuristic. Using the middle pie chart as an illustration, here are the details on how I constructed the chart: Create a correlation matrix among four variables; performance, log network constraint, job rank, and a linear composite of other control variables predicting performance in a population. For the 455 supply-chain managers, performance is measured by annual compensation, log network constraint is measured with sociometric choice data, job rank is a variable distinguishing five levels of managers to vice president, and "other" is a linear combination of the eight control variables in Table 3.2 as they predict compensation (Heise, 1972, describes summary effects from a subset of predictors in a regression equation). Run the same operation on the 283 human-resource employees in Table 4.1 (except job ranks of individual contributors and managers are combined into a single dimension of job rank as it predicts compensation). Standardize the four variables within each population. Stack the standardized scores in a single data set containing 738 observations on the four variables with observations weighted so the two populations contribute equally to correlations (supply-chain managers weighted .62). Here are the correlations with compensation: $-.526$ for log network constraint, .829 for job rank, and .395 for other factors (cf. Appendix E for correlations within each population). Regressing compensation across the predictors yields a squared multiple correlation of .727 and the following standardized regression coefficients: $-.131$ for log network constraint, .714 for job rank, and .169 for other factors. The middle pie chart in Figure 2.4 shows that 9.5% of the explained variance in compensation is attributed to network constraint ($-.526$ times $-.131$ divided by .727), 81.4% is attributed to job rank (.829 times .714 divided by .727), and 9.2% is attributed to other factors. The other two pie charts in Figure 2.4 were constructed the same way.

(9%). What matters most is job rank. In a bureaucracy, compensation is a function of job rank. The key to high compensation is high job rank. Compensation differences between the supply-chain and HR managers are largely determined by job rank (81%). However, getting to a senior job rank is largely a function of network brokerage. The third pie chart in Figure 2.4 shows that brokerage contributes two-thirds of the explained variance in early promotion to senior job rank in a large electronics company (Burt, 1992). Thus, compensation continues to be closely associated with network constraint, but the association is indirect through job rank in a bureaucratic organization: Network brokers get promoted to senior rank earlier than peers, where they enjoy high compensation.

Structure as a proxy for process

At the same time that Figure 2.4 exhibits a robust and substantial association between performance and network constraint, it illustrates the practice discussed in Chapter 1 of using structure as a proxy for process. None of the studies combined in Figure 2.4 include data on network information or behavior. Returns to brokerage are indicated by the performance association with network constraint when other performance factors are held constant. The measure of network structure is a proxy for measures of network process under the assumptions in Chapter 1: Information has a clustered distribution in which it is relatively homogeneous within groups and heterogeneous between groups. The clustered distribution creates a vision advantage for people who have connections across groups because they are exposed to a broader range of alternative opinion and behavior, so they are more likely to see alternative ways to go, synthesize new ways to go, and see a broader range of ways to support an initiative. People who see more brokerage opportunities are more likely to act on one, so the vision advantage is manifest in superior evaluations and compensation as performance metrics. Access to structural holes is discussed as synonymous with access to diverse information and seeing brokerage opportunities, both of which are discussed as synonymous with brokerage behavior.

Discussing information, opportunity, and behavior as synonyms is not without justification. There is the precedent of the early diffusion research cited in Chapter 1 describing the clustered distribution of information. Recent work on network content and behavior provides richer description (e.g., Obstfeld, 2005; Rodan and Gallunic, 2004), but the breakthrough in studying the information assumptions directly emerged a few years ago in algorithms for encoding electronic messages so the content of individual information exchanges can be compared while preserving sender and recipient confidentiality. For example, Aral and Van Alstyne (2007) analyze email traffic in a small headhunter company (73 recruiters in 14 offices in 2001) along with traditional survey network data and company data on recruiter backgrounds and performance. Knowing the (encoded) content of email messages allows Aral and Van Alstyne to measure the information heterogeneity in which each recruiter is involved. They show that information heterogeneity is associated with bridging structural holes (people rich in information heterogeneity have many colleagues not closely connected with one another), and is associated with higher recruiter performance in terms of billable hours and bringing in contracts. Aral and Van Alstyne's analysis is a "proof of concept" prototype for authoritative network analyses of information flow in large heterogeneous populations.

Justification notwithstanding, the three terms—information, opportunity, and behavior—are not synonyms. Access to a structural hole can be an opportunity to broker connection across the hole, but neither is behavior, and opportunities to broker need not trigger acts of brokerage.[6] This is not the book in which distinctions will be ironed out between brokerage information, opportunity, and behavior. I can, however, use estimates of spillover from neighbor networks to narrow the range of processes by which the three terms likely come together to create the performance advantage associated with structural holes.

---

[6] I suspect that measuring brokerage by its opportunities rather than its occurrence exacerbates a problem predicting performance. In the absence of data on brokerage behavior, I have only my suspicion. The prediction problem is heteroscedasticty: Performance variance is uneven across levels of network constraint. Performance is typically low in the absence of brokerage opportunities because there are no returns to brokerage where there is no brokerage, which means low performance variance at high levels of network constraint. At the other extreme, where brokerage opportunities are numerous, performance varies widely because managers differ in the extent to which they act on opportunities, which means high performance variance at low levels of network constraint. Here are four reasons to expect high performance variance where brokerage opportunities are abundant: (1) Some people with opportunities show no performance benefit because they do not act upon their opportunities (for various reasons from incompetence to sloth). (2) Some people with opportunities are rewarded for talking a good game about what could be done without ever taking action (e.g., Burt, 2005:240–244). (3) Sometimes there is no value to moving information between disconnected people (e.g., explain to your grandmother the latest technology in your line of work). (4) Benefit does not increase deterministically with opportunity. The performance benefit of brokerage can result from a few bridge relations. For example, a sociologist might do more creative work because of working through an idea with a colleague from economics. That does not mean that the sociologist would be three times more creative if she also worked through the idea with a colleague from psychology, another from anthropology, and still another from history. Rather, the odds of her having a creative insight increases with the number of diverse colleagues with whom the sociologist discusses her idea. The four points can be true of brokerage measured in terms of behavior, but under the assumption that people invest less in brokerage work that earns no rewards, the points will be more true of brokerage measured in terms of opportunities.

Indirect Access to Structural Holes

Neighbor networks lie just beyond the immediate network around a manager. Quickly repeating the explanation in Chapter 1, direct contacts are the people with whom a manager has personal contact and indirect contacts are friends of friends reached through direct contacts as intermediaries. As managers vary in direct access to structural holes within their immediate network, managers vary in indirect access to structural holes among friends of friends.

Indirect network constraint

With network constraint measuring direct access to structural holes, my corresponding measure of indirect access is the average constraint on a person's direct contacts (equation B3 in Appendix B). Constraint on a manager's contact is indirectly a constraint on the manager. I will reference indirect network constraint by the letters IC. A manager with low indirect constraint has colleagues with networks rich in brokerage opportunities, which are the structural holes to which the manager has indirect access.[7]

In Figure 2.1, the manager's three discussion partners are senior people who have disconnected contacts. Network constraint is low on the discussion partners (scores of 16.4, 15.1, and 25.0), the average of which indicates low indirect network constraint on the manager (indirect constraint score is 18.8). The fact that the manager's discussion partners have some flexibility with their contacts means that the manager has some added flexibility working with the three discussion partners.

The second column of the table in Figure 2.3 shows indirect constraint scores for the illustrative network. Person 1 is connected to persons 2, 3, and 4, all of whom have constraint scores of 33.3, so the indirect constraint on person 1 is reported in the table as 33.3. Persons 2, 3, and 4 are each connected to person 1 and two people who are embedded in a group, so the indirect constraint on them is higher: 50.0. Group leaders are each connected to a broker and three group members, so indirect constraint on them is higher still (73.3). Finally, group members face the highest indirect network constraint (77.2) because their friends of friends are primarily other members of the group.

---

[7] I tried more sophisticated aggregations, but the alternative measures are strongly correlated with the simple arithmetic average (see discussion following equation B3 in Appendix B). In addition to alternative measures of indirect access, there is variation in the distance over which access is indirect. Indirect contacts could be friends of friends as in Figure 2.3, or more distant contacts such as friends of friends of friends, and so on. I began with a broad distinction between direct and indirect contacts, assuming that brokerage among indirect contacts would be some amount less valuable than brokerage among direct contacts. I discovered so little value to brokerage among friends of friends that I had no incentive to make finer distinctions among indirect contacts. In this book, therefore, I focus on direct contacts versus their friends as indirect contacts.

The third column of the table in Figure 2.3 is included to illustrate how direct and indirect constraint are associated with Freeman's (1977) between-ness index. This index too is explained with illustration in Appendix B. Betweenness measures a person's monopoly access to structural holes any-where in the network. There is no distinction between direct versus indirect access to the structural holes. Person 1, the broker of brokers, has the highest score. She brokers connections between 243 pairs of other people in the network, which is 69 percent of all 351 pairs possible. Persons 2, 3, and 4 broker fewer connections (168 of 351, or .48 betweenness). The group leaders broker connections with their team members (72 of 351 connections, or .21 betweenness). Team members are connected only to people already con-nected, so the team members broker no connections between direct or indirect contacts.

Research design: Network spillover versus network contagion

My research design is simple: I propose to add indirect network constraint (measuring a manager's indirect access to structural holes in the networks around his contacts) to the usual regression model, illustrated in Figure 2.4, in which manager performance is predicted from direct network constraint (measuring manager access to structural holes in his own network) and con-trols for manager differences on other performance factors, such as job rank, seniority, and so on:

$$P = b_1 \ln(C) + b_2 \ln(IC) + BX + R,$$

where P is a measure of manager performance, R is a residual score of unpre-dicted performance, C is network constraint on the manager from direct contacts (first column of the table in Figure 2.3), and IC is the indirect network constraint on the manager from connections among indirect contacts (second column in the table). The natural logarithm of constraint is used as a predictor because performance changes more across low levels of network constraint than it does across high levels (illustrated by the nonlinear regression line in Figure 2.4).

The X term in the model is a matrix containing a regression intercept and various control variables appropriate for the performance measure being pre-dicted. Job rank is especially important to hold constant to ensure that returns to bureaucratic authority do not get confounded with returns to brokerage. Brokerage opportunities increase, on average, with rank. Senior people have separate groups reporting to them, which gives them direct access to the structural holes between their subordinates and indirect access to the struc-tural holes among the subordinates of their subordinates. In this light, the illustrative network in Figure 2.3 resembles a traditional corporate hierarchy with six teams reporting to three middle managers and the middle managers reporting to a senior executive.

Coefficients b_1 and b_2 in the above model describe performance associations with direct versus indirect access to structural holes. I expect b_2 to be contingent on b_1. I do not expect advantage from indirect access to structural holes if there is no advantage from direct access (b_2 should be zero if b_1 is zero). However, where direct access is an advantage ($b_1 < 0$, as illustrated in Figure 2.4), I expect evidence of returns to indirect access ($b_2 < 0$) under the intuition with which I began the book: If social networks provide an advantage, and networks are jointly owned by the people in them, then there should be advantage to affiliation with well-connected people.[8]

Not a contagion effect

The proposed analysis resembles a network analysis of social contagion, but it is different in an important way. The regression model illustrated in Figure 2.4 expresses manager i's performance as a function of network constraint, holding job rank and other performance factors constant: $P_i = f(C_i, X_i)$. The function predicts performance for each other manager j in the same population: $P_j = f(C_j, X_j)$. If advantage spills over between adjacent networks in the population, and j is a close colleague for manager i, then P_i and P_j are not independent. Network advantage affecting j's performance affects i's performance. The contingency can be modeled as an aggregate contingency between outcomes (P_i is a function of P_j), or as contingency between ego's outcome and a specific condition in alter's network (P_i is a function of C_j). Network contagion models do the former. I propose to do the latter, discussing it as a network spillover effect to distinguish it from the former, which is the contagion effect familiar in sociology.

If this were a contagion analysis, I would predict—with controls for individual differences in experience and kind of work—manager i's performance from the performance of her contacts ($\Sigma_j \, \delta_{ij} \, P_j$ where δ_{ij} measures the extent to which person j is a close colleague for manager i; see equation G1 in Appendix G). The model is general in that it includes all factors responsible for performance similarity between manager and contacts. Specific factors are not distinguished. Their aggregate effect is the correlation between manager performance and contact performance (also discussed as a spatial, or network, autocorrelation, e.g., Ord, 1975; Doreian, 1981; Dow, Burton and White, 1982). The correlation describes the extent to which performance is homogeneous within the immediate network around a manager; able managers

---

[8] In keeping with the results to be presented, I focus on positive returns to neighbor networks. In the conclusion to Chapter 4, I discuss the negative returns that would be expected if brokers made their gains by exploiting their neighbors. I find no evidence of negative spillover from affiliation with brokers in the diverse manager populations, but there are conditions in which such effects could be expected.

discussing work with other able managers, unable managers finding solace in one another's company.

Network models of social contagion became familiar in sociology with studies of interpersonal influence (e.g., Lazarsfeld, Berelson, and Gaudet, 1944; Festinger, Schachter, and Back, 1950; Katz and Lazarsfeld, 1955; Rogers, 1962; Coleman, Katz, and Menzel, 1957), and more recently with studies of corporate behavior influenced by the other organizations with which a corporation is connected (e.g., Davis, 1991; Greve, 1995; Davis and Greve, 1997). For example, Coleman, Katz, and Menzel (1957) show that a physician is likely to begin prescribing a new antibiotic at about the same time it begins to be prescribed by other doctors in the town with whom the physician discusses cases. Davis (1991) reports contagion in the spread of the "poison pill" strategy through the late 1980s. The strategy involved issuing a dividend to shareholders that would allow them to purchase shares at steep discount if ever a takeover attempt occurred without board approval. Davis shows that firms tended to adopt the strategy at about the same time as the companies with which a firm was interlocked through its board of directors.

I am proposing a research design more limited than contagion. I do not wish to estimate the aggregate performance correlation between colleagues. I wish to estimate the extent to which a manager's performance is affected by a specific condition in the colleague's network, namely, access to structural holes. I propose to predict manager performance from the network constraint on the manager's contacts ($IC = \Sigma_j \; \delta_{ij} \; C_j$, where δ_{ij} weighs colleague j's relevance to manager i; see equation B3 in Appendix B), holding constant background variables (X) and the level of constraint in the manager's own network (C). If performance contagion between colleagues in a population is the result of conditions other than access to structural holes, it would be possible for me to find no evidence of spillover from neighbor access to structural holes at the same time that there is substantial evidence of performance contagion.[9]

---

[9] I am drawing a distinction between contagion and spillover effects but they can be mixed in the same model. Rao, Greve, and Davis (2001) offer an example. The spillover effects are weaker than the broader contagion effects, but both kinds of effects are in the model. The study population is firms listed on the NASDAQ exchange from 1987 to 1994. The criterion variables are how many analysts begin to cover a firm during a year, how many discontinue coverage, and how many make discernibly optimistic earnings forecasts for the firm. The three network predictors are (1) the number of analysts that began covering the firm last year, (2) the number who discontinued coverage last year, and (3) both network variables weighted by the status of the research department in which each analyst was employed (with status measured as the summed election recognition the department received in last year's election of analysts to the *Institutional Investor*'s All-America Research Team, the criterion variable for analyst performance in Chapter 4). Under the assumption that analysts are colleagues in the same network, the count of analysts initiating/discontinuing coverage last year is a network contagion measure of peer behavior. Peers initiating/discontinuing coverage last year should trigger imitation this year. There is also a spillover measure: as Stuart, Hoang, and

Back to spillover

The network spillover design is less familiar than contagion in sociology, but it is not without precedent. Stuart, Hoang, and Hybels (1999) use a network spillover model to estimate performance attributable to contact status. They study start-up organizations in biotechnology as the start-ups move toward their initial public offering (IPO). There is always an element of uncertainty in the value of a start-up, but the uncertainly is less when the start-up is affiliated with established, high-status companies. As an organization's status is a signal of quality to customers and suppliers (Podolny, 1993, 2005), the status of a start-up's alliance partners is a signal of low risk to investors.[10] Alliance-partner status spills over to the start-up. Stuart, Hoang, and Hybels (1999) measure

---

Hybels (1999) measure the status of partners in a company's alliance network, Rao, Greve, and Davis (2001) measure the status of analysts covering the focal firm. Whatever the number of analysts who initiated/discontinued coverage last year, the pressure to imitate this year should be higher if the initiation/discontinuation came from analysts in high-status departments. The authors report strong evidence of contagion on the decision to begin covering a firm, with analysts affected by contagion more likely to forecast overly optimistic earnings for the firm, become disappointed, and discontinue coverage early. There is no evidence of contagion in the decision to discontinue coverage, and no evidence of a spillover effect, on coverage initiation or discontinuation, from the behavior of analysts in high-status banks and brokerage houses. As the authors summarize (page 521, cf. Greve, 1995): "Potential adopters rely on the actions of others to infer the value of a course of action because they are uncertain of its value. Once they have adopted and can make direct evaluations, they do not use external cues to make choices about abandonment."

[10] In fact, every study that reports a status effect using the eigenvector measure of status made popular by Podolny (1993) is reporting a spillover effect because direct and indirect contacts are combined in the eigenvector measure. The eigenvector measure defines status as a weighted sum of relationships: $S_i = \Sigma_j z_{ji} S_j$, where z_{ji} measures the strength of relation from j to i and S_j is the status of the source of the relationship. You gain status (S_i) by receiving attention from high-status people ($z_{ji} S_j$). When relation measures are made row stochastic ($\Sigma_j z_{ij} = 1.0$), the matrix of relations has an eigenvalue of one, and status scores are entries in the left-hand eigenvector of the matrix. Bonacich (1972) provides a clear, succinct statement of the model, which he later generalizes to positive and negative centrality (Bonacich, 1987). Hubbell (1965) begins the analogy to input–output models of the economy (see Doreian, 1986, for an improved measure) and Coleman (1966, 1972) provides a theoretical discussion in which the eigenvector, measuring resources or power, is defined by a network of overlapping interests and control. Note the combination of direct and indirect contacts: Direct contacts are the people with whom you are connected. Indirect contacts are the people whose connections to your contacts make your contacts high or low status ($\Sigma_j z_{ji} S_j$ defining status corresponds to $\Sigma_j \delta_{ij} C_j$ defining indirect network constraint in equation B3, Appendix B). This point is not a criticism, just a note that direct is mixed with indirect in the eigenvector measure. The confounding can interfere with tests for spillover, which is avoided by Stuart, Hoang, and Hybels (1999) when they measure status as a count of direct contacts. I follow their lead in using employee choice status to measure status in Chapter 6 when I estimate status spillover effects among investment bankers and analysts (see footnote 18 in Chapter 6).

status with the number of alliances in which an alliance partner is involved, and the frequency with which the partner's patents are cited by other patents. Status scores are aggregated across the alliance partners of a start-up to show that start-ups in alliances with high-status partners move more quickly to IPO, subject to controls for company value, and sell at a higher premium when they reach IPO. Another signal of low risk is the status of an investment bank endorsing an IPO. IPO stock is priced below market price as an incentive for investors to take the risk of purchasing the stock. The higher the risk, the steeper the discount. Investment banks maintain high status by endorsing low-risk investments, so endorsement by a high-status bank is a signal of low risk. Carter and Manaster (1990) measure IPO discount by the increase between initial offer price and selling price two weeks later. They show that start-ups endorsed by high-status banks are less subject to IPO discounts. Which start-ups are endorsed by high-status banks? Gulati (2007:chap. 9) continues the Stuart, Hoang, and Hybels analysis to show that biotechnology start-ups are more likely to be endorsed by a high-status bank when the start-up senior staff have, or have had, affiliations with established high-status firms in biotechnology, or downstream, with high-status pharmaceutical and health care companies.

Jensen (2003) takes advantage of a change in policy to test for status spillover between market segments. The 1989 Federal Reserve Board decision to allow commercial banks to underwrite corporate bonds was followed by commercial banks entering what had been a protected market for investment banks. In the subsequent years, how often were commercial banks selected to be the lead bank for a corporate bond issue? Did management's choice of a commercial bank as lead vary with (a) the bank's status in commercial banking, or (b) having a commercial loan with the bank before selecting it to be lead on the corporate bond issue? Jensen measures status as an eigenvector—which in this case means that bank status increased with the extent to which the bank participated in multi-bank loan syndicates (commercial bank status) or led underwriting syndicates composed of high-status banks (investment bank status)—and reports positive spillover. Previous commercial business with a bank, or the bank's status in commercial banking, both increase the odds that it will be selected to be lead bank on a corporate bond issue. Corroborating the idea that status was used by management as a signal of bank quality, the effect of commercial bank status decreases as the bank spends more time in the investment banking market. In short, company status in commercial banking provided a discernible, but temporary, advantage in obtaining business when the company sought to lead bond syndicates in investment banking.

As affiliation with attractive neighbors can be an advantage, affiliation with tainted neighbors can be a disadvantage. Begin with what it means to be tainted: Suspicion of fraud damages a firm's reputation, damage evident from decrease in a firm's stock price, and evident more broadly in lost opportunities for business and difficulty in obtaining new funds (Karpoff and Lott,

1993). Kang (2008) looks at the negative effect of affiliation with tainted neighbors. He identifies 143 firms in the Lexis-Nexis database over a period of four years that were publicly announced targets of U.S. Securities and Exchange Commission (SEC) investigations for accounting irregularities. Thirty of the 143 firms are selected conditional on suffering an abnormal drop in stock price when their investigation was announced (following Karpoff and Lott, 1993). Whatever the reality of the alleged irregularities, the 30 were "tainted" in the sense that investors reacted negatively to the announced investigation. Kang assembles a snowball sample of 244 neighbor firms by tracing directors of the 30 tainted firms into other firms where they were also directors. The 244 neighbor firms were untainted in the sense of not being announced targets of SEC investigation. Nevertheless, the evidence of negative spillover is that the 244 untainted neighbors suffer a statistically significant drop in stock value within a couple of days of the announced investigation of the tainted firm with which they are affiliated (Kang, 2008:149).[11]

Another research design is to study negative by-products from positive spillover. Silverman and Baum (2002) offer evidence from Canadian biotechnology.

---

[11] Two caveats warrant mention. The first concerns timing and spillover-effect magnitude. Kang studies SEC activity from 1998 through 2002, which was a period prone to spillover, bringing to mind the public hysteria of witch hunts discussed in Chapter 7. Consider the below graph of data from SEC annual reports. Over time, increasing SEC budget facilitates an increasing number of new investigations, which results in an increasing number of enforcement actions. Budget, investigations, and actions are all strongly correlated with time (respectively, .93, .86, and .93). Summary change over time obscures a dramatic shift at the turn of the century. The Public Company Accounting Reform and

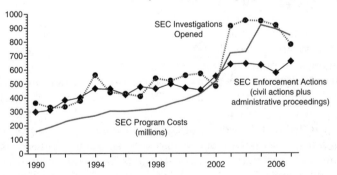

Investor Protection Act (Sarbanes Oxley) went into law in 2002 in response to major corporate and accounting scandals (e.g., Enron bankruptcy in 2001). The SEC program budget increased by 21% from 2001 to 2002, and increased by a record 39% from 2002 to 2003 (versus less than 10% annual increases during the preceding decade). New investigations opened by the SEC increased by a record 90% from 479 in 2002 to 910 in 2003 (versus 4% annual increases during the preceding decade). Things start to calm after 2005, with the SEC program budget decreasing by 8% from 2005 to 2007, and new investigations decreasing by 18%. The turn of the century is a period when investors

If a strong alliance network is an asset, and one company's gain comes at the expense of its rivals, then a company's strong alliance network should have a negative effect on the company's rivals. Silverman and Baum report the expected effect: Firms are more likely to exit the industry if they face rivals with strong alliance networks. Jensen (2008) corroborates his (2003) evidence of spillover for commercial banks entering the corporate bond market. With incumbent investment banks hurt by strong competitors entering the market, investment banks can be expected to make entry difficult for strong commercial banks by excluding them from bond syndicates. Sure enough, Jensen (2008) reports that investment banks, when they are the lead bank on a bond issue, seek out other investment banks advantaged by bridging structural holes and avoid commercial banks comparably advantaged by bridging structural holes.

Spillover has been long familiar in economics as a kind of externality, often discussed with Marshall's (1920) image of industrial districts as concentrations of specialized labor, related production activity, and knowledge spillover.[12]

---

were especially sensitive to news of fraud. I suspect that spillover would be less pronounced when investors were more calm. A second caveat concerns sample selection. To know that a firm's stock price was eroded by affiliation with tainted neighbors, you need to know what the price would have been without the affiliation. All of Kang's untainted firms are affiliated with tainted firms, so his baseline for judging whether a firm's stock value declined is limited to projecting a stock price from historical company and industry data, which involves considerable guesswork. Ideally, the study would have begun with a sample of tainted firms, and a matched sample of untainted firms, then traced interlocking directors into matched samples of neighboring untainted firms. The spillover effect, ceteris paribus, could be estimated from differences between firms interlocked with the tainted versus firms interlocked with the untainted. So, the strength and clarity of negative spillover remains to be seen in replication work. Meanwhile, Kang's (2008) evidence of negative spillover is consistent with the prior evidence of positive spillover.

[12] Marshall's image of spillover within industrial districts is nicely phrased in the eighth edition of his *Principles of Economics* (Marshall, 1920: Book 4, chap. 10, section 3): "When an industry has thus chosen a locality for itself, it is likely to stay there long: so great are the advantages which people following the same skilled trade get from near neighbourhood to one another. The mysteries of the trade become no mysteries; but are as it were in the air, and children learn many of them unconsciously. Good work is rightly appreciated, inventions and improvements in machinery, in processes and the general organization of the business have their merits promptly discussed: if one man starts a new idea, it is taken up by others and combined with suggestions of their own; and thus it becomes the source of further new ideas. And presently subsidiary trades grow up in the neighbourhood, supplying it with implements and materials, organizing its traffic, and in many ways conducing to the economy of its material."

Marshall's "in the air" criterion can be seen in contemporary efforts to adapt the spillover research design to study contagion. For example, Grinblatt, Keloharju, and Ikäheimo (2008) report "social influence" effects estimated from a spillover design. By combining tax records with detailed car purchase data, Grinblatt *et al.* know when a person purchased a car and they know when each of the person's 500 geographically most-proximate neighbors purchased cars. Grinblatt *et al.* predict a person's car purchase today from the number of 10 closest neighbors (inner-ring neighbors) who bought cars during

Spillover occurs when actions taken by my neighbors for their own benefit have consequences for me. The investment my neighbor makes in keeping his landscape and property attractive for his own gratification increases the price for which I can sell my house. If many of my neighbors own computers, my own transition to first computer ownership is easier than if I am the first in my neighborhood to own one (Goolsebee and Klenow, 2002). Similarly, R&D investments by other companies in my line of business can be a factor in the returns to my own R&D investments. For example, Jaffe (1986) shows that a company's R&D productivity increases with R&D investments by what he terms "technology neighbors" (see Griliches, 1992 for an overview of R&D spillover effects). Technology neighbors are defined as follows: Aggregate patents into 49 broad categories to characterize a firm's technology position as a profile of the firm's patents in each of the 49 categories over two time intervals. To measure the extent to which firms compete in the same technology space, compute a normalized cross-product, δ_{ij}, between the patent profiles for firms i and j (an imagery similar to market niches defined by structural

---

alternative time intervals before today (yesterday, within the last two days, a week, a month, etc.), and the number of 40 next-closest neighbors (outer-ring neighbors) who bought cars during the same period. Inner-ring neighbors live an average of 26 meters away. Outer-ring neighbors live an average of 93 meters away. Since inner- and outer-ring neighbors both live close to ego, holding constant purchases by the outer-ring neighbors is an ingenious control for unobserved location factors that could account for similar behavior by ego and the inner-ring neighbors. The analysis offers rich detail on when "social influence" is strongest (during the first few days after neighbors purchase cars), from whom "social influence" is strongest (the closest two or three neighbors), and on whom "social influence" is strongest (people in lower income brackets). What the analysis does not reveal is social influence or how it happens. Influence is left an undefined force responsible for simultaneous car purchases by neighbors. Something is "in the air"—to use Marshall's phrase—such that people who live close together influence one another, breathing the same air as it were. This is the point at which the sociology and social psychology reviewed in Appendix G can be valuable in distinguishing mechanisms by which influence occurs. For example, Goolsbee and Klenow (2002) argue that their estimated spillover effects result from access to information. People are more likely to make the transition to owning their first computer when they live in an area containing a large proportion of people who own computers because the prevalent existing owners provide a ready source of information and infrastructure on computers. If access to information is the mechanism responsible for the observed spillover, then spillover should be stronger where access is better. To illustrate, Goolsbee and Klenow (2002: 328, 337) show that their strong spillover effects at the city level (t-tests of 5 to 9) are stronger between family and friends between whom communication is more likely (t-tests of 20 to 40). Grinblatt et al. (2008:735), in contrast, offer the startling claim that "little empirical research exists on how social connections influence consumption." For quick reference into the sixty years of empirical research missed by such a claim, see Appendix G. Putting aside the rhetoric (and speculative interpretation after the analysis), there is a relative deprivation mechanism implicit in Grinblatt et al.'s analysis, and their empirical findings offer exceptional illustration cited in the theoretical argument in Chapter 8.

equivalence in network analysis, e.g., Burt, 1992:208–215). What Jaffe terms the "spillover pool" for firm i of R&D investments by firm i's technology neighbors is the average of each firm j's R&D spending weighted by the δ_{ij}. When patents granted to a company are predicted by company production factors and the spillover pool from the company's technology neighbors, successful patenting is associated with larger spillover pools (Jaffe, 1986:994).

Possible Returns to Indirect Access

Turning now to the spillover expected from neighbor access to structural holes, there is a wide range of possibilities, depending on the process by which social networks constitute social capital. Perhaps most obviously, the advantage derived from access to brokerage opportunities in neighbor networks can be expected to vary with the difficulty of communication through friends of friends. Consider the following situation: You are talking with a handful of people at a social gathering drawn from diverse groups. Conversation around you turns to a recent event for which you offer a quick sentence of explanation followed by an illustrative example. A discussion partner looks puzzled, puts you a clarifying question, and conversation is renewed. Occasionally, a colleague interjects clarification; you assumed familiarity with a concept that the colleague believes is not familiar to your discussion partner. The less often the colleague has to interject, the less often you find yourself making analogies to translate terms, the more clearly we can say that knowledge moves easily between your group and your discussion-partner's group. When communication is difficult, it could be due to differences between the groups (certain groups have more in common than other groups), the specific knowledge being communicated (certain knowledge is more tacit and indexical), or the individuals trying to communicate (some people are so buried in their specialty they always require a more-broadly experienced colleague to enable their communication outside the specialty). Whatever the specifics, a distinction can be drawn between situations in which knowledge moves easily, or with difficulty, between groups.

Global processes imply increasing spillover

The broad distinction between easy and difficult is foundation for distinguishing social capital created from global versus local information processes. Information moves through networks, exchanged one person to another, to create the advantage known as social capital. By global processes I refer to social capital created by communication in which information retains its meaning as it moves quickly and easily through chains of indirect connections across a network. Capital markets are the quintessential example. Early information on the exchange value of yen can be an advantage in decisions about dollar investments. There must always be an element of local interpretation, but capital markets are mature in the sense that news about investments and company developments in distant locations routinely flashes around the globe to affect plans and share price in London, New York, Tokyo. Under global processes, an invisible hand can seem to guide interpersonal exchanges such that it makes sense to focus on a balance of forces that defines the population at equilibrium as is characteristic of a neoclassical view on markets.

General implication for social capital

Suppose for a moment that global processes are responsible for social capital in a specific population. Then the benefit, the social capital, provided by a network would increase as the network provided access to more relations. The more easily that meaningful information can move quickly between distant places, the more benefit there would be to the diverse information that indirect contacts can provide. Small starts can leverage into big finishes (engagingly illustrated in Gladwell, 2000). Some relations must be more beneficial than others, and friction can lower the benefit of access to relationships between distant contacts. With information able to move over wide distances, value lies not in knowing specific groups in detail so much as knowing how groups differ—which means substantial returns to brokerage among friends of friends because of the diversity of groups they can reach beyond the immediate network. Performance scores would be highest for brokers like person 1 in Figure 2.3. Through her connections to persons 2, 3, and 4, person 1 is exposed to the greatest diversity of opinion and behavior via her indirect connections to all six groups (person 1 has the highest betweenness score in the network).

In fact, benefit could increase exponentially with network size. Whatever the number of people you count as friends, they have other friends. The combination of your friends plus their friends is a number equal or larger than the number of your friends alone. If you have five friends and they each have five friends (you plus four unique others), your five contacts put you in contact with 20 friends of friends, for a total of 25 contacts. Go out further to friends of your friends' friends. If the friends of friends each add four unique contacts, the total expands to 105 contacts. The number increases quickly. And this is just the connections to you. More generally, there are $N(N-1)/2$ pairs of people in a network of N people. Each pair adds a relationship. You have access to 10 relationships among your five direct contacts, another 215 relationships involving friends of friends, and another 5,160 involving your friends of friends of friends.

Here is a concrete example: The next chapter includes a network analysis of 331 people active in the regional launch of a software product. Of 54,615 possible connections (pairs) among the 331 employees, 1,034 are observed.

A direct connection between two people is observed when one person in the survey named the other as a colleague with whom he or she often discussed the product launch. Indirect connections can be derived from the direct. There are 3,934 instances in which two people did not talk directly, but cited a mutual colleague as discussion partner. In network terms, the 3,934 indirect connections through a mutual colleague correspond to a path distance of two. Path distance is the shortest chain of relations required to connect two people; one for a pair of people who speak directly with one another (friends), two for people who do not speak directly but do speak with mutual colleagues (friends of friends), and so on. Number of people encountered at increasing path distance is a metric on how a network provides access to relations. In the product-launch, the ratio of 3,934 two-step path distances to 1,034 direct connections is 3.80. In other words, there were 3.8 new connections at path distance two for every one direct connection. Continuing, there were 10.20 additional new connections at path distance three for every direct connection, 16.69 new connections at path distance four, and so on.[13]

This imagery of exponentially increasing benefit is often applied to computer networks. Processes in computer networks are typically presumed to be global. Once information is encoded in a packet, it can be shipped to distant locations where a receiving machine decodes the packet. The information transmitted equals the information received. The exponential imagery applied to computer networks is often discussed as "Metcalfe's Law," according to which the value of a network increases with the square of the number of nodes in the network (there are N^2-N ordered pairs of nodes in a network of N nodes).[14] As Spence (2002:453) referenced the imagery in his lecture on the occasion of receiving the Nobel Prize in economics for his work on the dynamics of information flow in markets: "Metcalfe's law states that the value of a network to the entities attached to it is proportional to the square of the number of connected entities. In economic terms this probably means that the value and hence the speed of connecting accelerates as the number increase. This is sometimes referred to as the network effect."

---

[13] It can be helpful to have the raw numbers to be able to work through the ratios. The numbers of new connections reached within the product-launch network at path distances 1, 2, 3, and 4 respectively are 1,034, 3,934, 10,550, and 17,261. The corresponding ratios plotted in Figure 2.5 are 1.00, 3.80, 10.20, and 16.69.

[14] Metcalfe's Law is not an empirical regularity. It is an engineer's intuition discussed as a law in a business magazine article (e.g., see Briscoe, Odlyzko, and Tilly, 2006). The functional form of the association between network benefit and nodes was not the essence of the intuition. Robert Metcalfe, inventor of Ethernet networks, had the productive intuition that the value of an Ethernet network increases exponentially (with the number of communication possibilities it provides) while the cost of the network increases linearly (with the number of nodes in the network), so at some number of nodes the exponential benefit curve exceeds the linear cost curve, before which the network is inefficient and after which the cost/benefit ratio for additional nodes is increasingly attractive.

If global processes are responsible for social networks constituting social capital in a population, in sum, then ego's social capital would be increasingly a function of the networks to which ego has access through her neighbors. The advantage of brokerage would be improved by having many connections to people who have many connections (and closure would be strengthened by distant people knowing of your deeds). A person rich in social capital would be "known far and wide."

Global processes within a specific population

Social networks are less exponential than the imagery in Metcalfe's Law. Your friends count as their friends many of the same people that you count as friends, so access to new relationships does not expand as quickly as is possible in theory. How quickly access expands depends on network size and density. In small networks of people who know one another well, many of your friends are my friends.

The empirical association between access and path distance is illustrated in Figure 2.5 using three of the study populations to be analyzed in the next chapters. Path distance is on the horizontal axis. Number of new connections

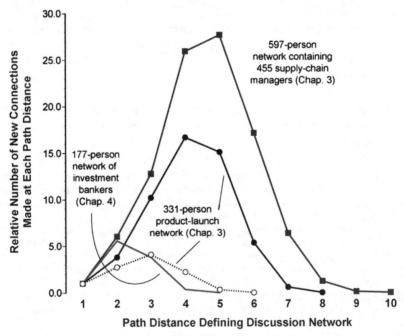

Figure 2.5 Network Connections at Increasing Path Distance

relative to direct connections is on the vertical axis. Note the exponentially increasing number of relations initially reached at longer path distances. In the product-launch, one direct connection on average generates 3.8 two-step connections, 10.2 three-step connections, and 16.69 four-step connections.[15] Second, the increase varies with population size. Bigger populations provide access to more relations. There were 331 people in the product-launch organization. The higher line through squares in Figure 2.5 describes connections among 455 supply-chain managers introduced in the next chapter. The lower solid line in Figure 2.5 describes connections among 177 investment bankers introduced in Chapter 4. Third, the increase reverses well before path distances reach the boundary of the population. As new connections are made in a bounded population, fewer remain to be made. At some inflection point, new connections are less frequent at longer path distances, until all possible connections that can be made have been made. The inflection point for the supply-chain managers is five. The solid line through squares shows fewer new connections at path distances longer than five steps. In the product-launch organization, the inflection point is four. Among the investment bankers, who were connected through mutual colleagues at the center of their organization, the inflection point is two.

Implication for spillover from neighbor networks

The pattern illustrated in Figure 2.5 has implications for the magnitude of spillover effects. You can maintain a limited number of relationships yourself. Access to people with access would be the key to reaching large numbers of relationships. People will not have these connections equally. Some connect with well-connected neighbors. Others connect with dead-ends. Whatever differences exist between people in their immediate network will be amplified as some people expand their network through neighbors while others circulate within a closed network of interconnected neighbors. Figure 2.5 plots the average number of new connections reached at successive path distances. If I compute the standard deviation of new connections it mirrors the plots in Figure 2.5 (.93 correlation). Where there is a high average number of new connections there are wide differences between people in their connections. People locked in closed networks become more clearly distinct from people who have extensive connections.

Therefore, if global processes are responsible for social networks constituting social capital, then ego's social capital should be more a function of the networks to which ego has access through neighbors than it is a function of the immediate network. Whatever the performance effect for the immediate network, I would expect a stronger effect from neighbor networks (test statistic

---

[15] The counts of relations defining these ratios were given in footnote 13.

and correlation for b_2 larger than for b_1), and still stronger effect from networks around more distant neighbors in larger, less-connected populations, as illustrated by the higher lines in Figure 2.5.

Local processes imply decreasing spillover

There is exhilaration in the promise of global processes. Images come to mind of strangers connected across vast distance. Geographic boundaries fade hazy in the "death of distance" (Cairncross, 1997). This imagery makes intuitive sense applied to computer networks. Server nodes receive packets of data. They send packets of data. Message meaning is irrelevant to transmission, and even message integrity is best left to initial sender and ultimate receiver (the "end-to-end" principle proposed by Saltzer, Reed, and Clark, 1984).

But there is social meaning to information even in computer networks (Brown and Duguid, 2000), and social capital in particular is a function of substantive meaning in human communication, with all its nuance, imperfection, and likely misunderstanding between groups.

Local processes are at work in a population when people are balkanized into groups such that information does not retain its meaning across groups. Knowledge across groups emerges in fits and starts as entrepreneurs limited to local knowledge experiment with alternative combinations. The contrast between global and local processes can be sketched in terms of tacit knowledge moving between groups, but von Hippel's (1994) concept of "sticky" information provides apt description and has the virtue of doing less violence to Polanyi's (1958) concept of tacit knowledge as a Kuhnian-paradigm feature of the perceiver rather than the information perceived. Information is sticky to the extent that it would be difficult to move (von Hippel, 1994:430): "We define the stickiness of a given unit of information in a given instance as the incremental expenditure required to transfer that unit of information to a specified locus in a form usable by a given information seeker. When this cost is low, information stickiness is low; when it is high, stickiness is high." Von Hippel (1994:430–431) offers four reasons why information can be sticky: It can be tacit so it is difficult, if not impossible, to transmit in recorded form. It can be voluminous such that absorbing the information would be expensive. It can require complementary knowledge to process the information. It can interact with characteristics of sender, receiver, or channel to resist transmission. Although "sticky" is an adjective modifying "information," it is not a characteristic of information so much as it is a characteristic of moving information. Information can resist communication through certain relationships at the same time that it flows readily through others. "The knowledge necessary for the development of the personal computer, for example, was developed at the Xerox research center in Silicon Valley but would not travel into the rest of the corporation—it simply stuck. Yet the same knowledge leaked out of the company, providing a highly lucrative resource for Apple, Adobe,

3Com, other Silicon Valley firms, and eventually Microsoft" (Brown and Duguid, 2002:430; see Brown and Duguid, 2000, for elaboration). People in groups can be so immersed in their own way of thinking they easily overlook the value to them of a development outside the group. Even if insiders become aware of the outside development, they can fail to recognize its value to them. This image of knowledge within groups inhibiting communication between groups is foundational to brokerage and closure as social capital. The more sticky the knowledge, the less likely it will move from one group to another without a broker to facilitate the transmission.

I use local in a broad way and in a narrow way. The two are deeply linked, but distinct. I use local broadly to refer to a social cluster around ego, an affiliation within which a variety of understandings are taken for granted, and beyond which those understandings are problematic. This is the image of social cluster central in the communication and influence research discussed in the Introduction as foundational for concepts of social capital. More specifically, I use local to refer to ego's close, personal relationships. With respect to closed networks, the two meanings overlap entirely. Close relationships are concentrated within the social cluster around ego. With respect to brokerage, however, the two meanings are less redundant. Brokers by definition have relationships that bridge across social clusters. The broker's close contacts can be in other groups, other organizations, other cities, other places around the world. I nevertheless refer to direct connections as local in that ego's personal presence brings a human texture and flavor to whatever the connection. Appropriate qualifications to this broad and narrow use of local will be apparent from context, but most often the two uses overlap rather than contradict one another.

The distinction I have in mind between global and local processes is analogous to the distinction between neoclassical and "Austrian" market processes. Even a mature capital market reveals local processes when the market is studied in terms of regulations affecting capital flow between specific regions, or accounting rules or local conventions differing between regions. Investors know they can benefit from insider information on the organizations coming together in a deal. And relative to a mature capital market, most markets (and most certainly resource "markets" in organizations) are less fluid, more sticky, more shaped by the politics of who supports an idea and who rises in opposition. Population equilibrium has less felt reality than the path-dependent processes by which local prices emerge and diffuse in a continuous disequilibrium—which is a characteristic of the Austrian perspective on markets. This view holds that commercial activities (Rosen, 1997:140–141; cf. Ferrier and Smith, 1999:373–374): "...evolve as the amalgamation and interactions of trials and errors among economic agents. Entrepreneurial ventures and experiments, arbitrage activities, and survival of the fittest play crucial roles in this process.... This approach begins with the premise that there is an enormous amount of ignorance in the system. No one knows or can ever know what is being maximized overall. Decentralization is fundamental because specialization is extreme." Where the neoclassical perspective focuses on the balance that defines market equilibrium, the Austrian focuses on process by which markets move toward equilibrium. If a market seems to clear as if it contained a central pricing mechanism, it would be because there are sufficient intermediaries to carry local prices across otherwise segregated locations (Hayek, 1945:524–526; cf. Baker, 1984).

The global–local distinction also can be found in recent simulations of processes by which information moves across network bridges. For example, Centola and Macy (2007) simulate the spread of ideas, distinguishing "simple" ideas that ego would be likely to adopt once aware of the idea from "complex" ones that ego would be hesitant to adopt without corroborating adoptions by neighbors. Dense clusters of connections provide the "wide bridge" that Centola and Macy conclude is required for the spread of "complex" contagions. In complement to Centola and Macy's focus on ego's reluctance to adopt an idea before neighbors, Reagans and Zuckerman (2008) focus on ego's attraction to ideas expressed by neighbors. Their concept of "homophilic" value puts a premium on information obtained from socially proximate sources. Information obtained from neighbors is more relevant to ego and more readily understandable since ego and neighbor are more likely than distant contacts to share concerns, unspoken assumptions, and vocabularies. Where there is no premium on information obtained from neighbors, Reagans and Zuckerman describe information as having "uniform" value. The images of "simple" information that can travel with impact across distant relations, and information that retains "uniform" value as it travels across long distances, are global processes responsible for network structure constituting social capital. The images of "complex" information delayed pending neighbor adoptions, and a premium for "homophilic" information expressed by neighbors, are local processes responsible for network structure constituting social capital.

General implication for social capital

Local information misunderstood and miscommunicated through indirect connections can be expected to erode returns to brokerage among friends of friends. The more closed the networks around a group, the more likely that people in the group use tacit knowledge in the form of mutually understood, unwritten language and routines to coordinate with one another. The more they have worked together, the more complex and subtle their coordination can become. In all, their knowledge becomes difficult to move, sticky to its local context. As knowledge becomes sticky within groups, a premium emerges for people who can coordinate it across the groups. The more sticky the information to be moved between groups, the more likely there will be misunderstandings in moving the information, so the more valuable it will be to anticipate and manage the misunderstandings by knowing the two groups through personal contacts in the groups. In other words, the more sticky the information to be moved between groups, the higher the premium to direct rather than indirect brokerage. Performance scores in Figure 2.3 would be highest for the three brokers who have direct contacts in the groups, that is, persons 2, 3, and 4. Their direct connections into separate groups give them an advantage in translating opinion and behavior between the groups.

Imagine an economist and a psychologist trying to explain to economists the value of research on a psychological mechanism. Whatever the psychologist's advantage from knowing the mechanism, the economist has an advantage in knowing the economic vernacular so she is more likely to know an attractive way to frame and communicate the mechanism to the target audience (e.g., consider the development of behavioral economics as an area).

So it is in organizations more generally. A manager familiar with the tacit knowledge in a group has an advantage over outsiders in knowing a way to frame and communicate a new idea to make it attractive to the group. For illustration, consider Fleming and Waguespack's (2007) analysis of appointments to leadership positions in the Internet Engineering Task Force (IETF), the "de facto standards-developing organization for the Internet." A consistent finding in the analysis is that the odds of getting appointed are higher for programmers who co-author with colleagues from different working groups (which is the usual brokerage–performance association just illustrated in Figure 2.4, and the center–periphery network structure typical of "invisible colleges" in which leading academics at the center connect people in otherwise disconnected groups at the periphery, Crane, 1969). Beyond what is usual, Fleming and Waguespack show the importance of personal contact to brokerage. Personal contact in the organization does not directly affect a programmer's chances of getting appointed to a leadership position. Many programmers continue to be active at the periphery. It is the combination with brokerage that matters. The odds of getting appointed to a leadership position are significantly higher for programmers who exercise their brokerage network with extensive face-to-face contact.[16]

---

[16] My use of Fleming and Waguespack in this paragraph does not make the same emphases as the authors so I want to tie my point to the specific results they report. My reference in the text to "consistent finding" refers to the consistently statistically significant association between network constraint and appointment to a leadership position (Fleming and Waguespack, 2007:174, "social brokerage" in the table is negative one times network constraint) and the consistently significant increase in the association for programmers who make more effort to meet with other programmers in the organization (termed "presence," and measured by a function of attending many IETF conferences at great distance from home, Fleming and Waguespack, 2007:172–173). "Presence" has no direct association with appointment to a leadership position, but a consistent interaction effect with network constraint in which low-constraint programmers with high presence are especially likely to get appointed to a leadership position (Fleming and Waguespack, 2007:174). On a more general note, the analysis is relevant to

So it is in markets and industries more generally. Burt (2003:657) describes local Cornish men having a competitive advantage over well-financed London investors in detecting and developing lucrative 19th century mining opportunities: "... the Cornish had access to immediate, first-hand information that could be verified from several different quarters, while London speculators received only partial, second-hand reports that had to be taken on dubious trust. Similarly, Cornish networks were tight and efficient, exploiting strong filial, religious, and cultural links that extended across the country and to emigrant communities in all of the world's major minor districts. By comparison the City's networks, although themselves multifarious, were looser, based mainly on commonality of economic interest rather than deeper societal connections."

Local processes within a specific population

Local processes imply that the spillover benefit of a network reaching new people through longer path distances is less impressive than implied by global processes. Groups are smaller and more densely connected than the broader networks in which they occur. Most friends of friends are inside the group. Many of their friends are inside the group. Beyond that, indirect contacts are often in other groups.

For example, the product-launch network used as an example in Figure 2.5 is shown in the next chapter to contain seven groups. The groups correspond to regional and administrative divisions. One group is the China operation. Another is the India operation. A third is the Australia operation, and so on across seven groups.[17] The dashed line in Figure 2.5 shows for the product-launch network how connections within groups are fewer and peak sooner than connections across the whole network. The solid line through solid

---

promotion to senior job rank in an organization, but it is as much, perhaps more, an illustration of brokerage in political mobilization. The leadership positions are largely self-created. The process has three steps: (1) Ego interested in creating a new working group on a topic circulates a BOF (Birds of a Feather) message soliciting participation from others in the organization. (2) If many people sign up in response to the BOF message, ego gets physical space at the next (tri-annual) IETF conference to have a session on the BOF topic. (3) If the BOF session is well attended, a working group is created and a chair is appointed, where the chair is "generally, but not always, the BOF organizer" (Fleming and Waguespack, 2007:167). Thus, "new working groups emerge mainly from grassroots interest in a topical area and are typically preceded by a Birds of a Feather (BOF) meeting convened during a conference" (Fleming and Waguespack, 2007:167).

[17] The text contains sufficient information to understand the point being made here, but if you are curious about the distinctions between groups, Figure 3.2 in the next chapter contains a sociogram of the product-launch discussion network, and a density table of average relations within and between the seven groups.

circles in Figure 2.5 describes the number of new product-launch connections *within and across* groups. The dashed line describes new connections *within* groups. The dashed line increases much less than the corresponding solid line, and peaks at path distance three instead of the four steps at which the solid line for the product-launch network peaks.

Another way to illustrate the point is to show the percent of new connections that are within group at increasing path distance. Corresponding to the dashed line through circles in Figure 2.5, the dashed line through circles in Figure 2.6 describes the percentage of new connections in the product-launch network that are within group at each path distance. In other words, the dashed line through circles in Figure 2.6 equals the ratio of the dashed line in Figure 2.5 over the corresponding solid line in Figure 2.5. Of the 1,034 direct connections between people in the product-launch network, 903 were between people in the same group (87%). Of the 3,934 additional connections made by two-step path distances, 2,481 were between people in the same group (63%), and so on.[18]

The point illustrated is that most direct, and a majority of two-step, contacts reach colleagues in the group surrounding ego. At path distance three, however, indirect contacts are likely to be in other groups (35% in ego's group on the dashed line through circles in Figure 2.6, leaving 65% in other groups), and most contacts at path distance four are in other groups (12% in ego's group leaves 88% in other groups). The other dashed lines in Figure 2.6 show a similar majority of friends of friends within ego's group for the supply-chain managers and the bankers, and more distant indirect contacts similarly concentrated outside the group around ego.[19] The low dashed line for the bankers shows that they have the most direct contact across groups—the banker network is well-integrated across regional boundaries—but the banker line shows the same relatively high within-group percentages for direct and two-step connections, followed by steep decline across higher path distances.

Research can be found consistent with the implication of limited benefit from connections longer than path distance two. For example, Friedkin (1983) describes a limited "horizon of observability" in organizations. The probability that two directly connected professors know something about one another's current work drops to 28 percent as likely if their connection is only indirect

---

[18] Continuing footnote 13, it can be helpful to have the raw numbers to be able to work through the ratios yourself. The numbers of new connections reached within one's own group in the product-launch network at path distances 1, 2, 3, and 4 respectively are 903, 2,481, 3,704, and 2,011. The percentage of new connections within group given the total number of new connections at each path distance (from footnote 13: 903/1034) is 87% for direct connections, 63% for two-step paths, 35% for three-step paths, 12% for four-step paths, and so on.

[19] Within-group relations are in one of nine groups distinguished among the supply-chain managers (Figure 3.7 density table), and in one of four banker groups (Figure 4.4 density table).

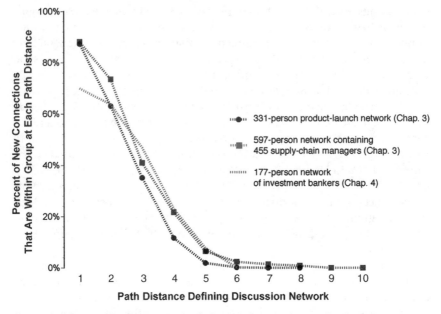

Figure 2.6 Percent In-Group Network Connections at Increasing Path Distance

through a mutual colleague, then to a near-zero 3 percent as likely if their connection is less direct. Killworth and Bernard (1978) found in their "reverse small world" experiments that people searched for an unfamiliar target person in a distant location by jumping to someone they knew in the target's region from whom a local search can begin. Studying neighbor effects on car purchases, Grinblatt, Keloharju, and Ikäheimo (2008:744) show that my two closest neighbors exercise much stronger social influence on my own decision to purchase than the third closest or less-close neighbors. More generally, Stuart and Podolny (1996) infer "local search" from the tendency for organizations to file patents drawing on technology similar to the technology on which they drew for previous patents (despite the fact that such "crowding" is likely to produce a "dead end" patent, Podolny and Stuart, 1995), Sorenson and Stuart (2001) describe the concentration of venture capital investments in companies that are within a few-mile radius around the investor, and Owen-Smith and Powell (2004) describe how successful patenting in biotechnology is predicted by brokerage within the local network more than brokerage in the extra-local network. Analyzing team networks and performance in a large electronic company, Hansen (1999, 2002) reports that teams with direct connections across business units are faster at completing tasks that require non-routine information from other business units. Teams with the same kind of network are slower on tasks that only require routine information, presumably because team members are slowed by the (now superfluous) costs of maintaining connections across business units. Against a backdrop of patent co-author networks in Boston and the Silicon Valley (two inventors are connected if they have co-authored a patent within a five-year window), Fleming *et al.* (forthcoming) tell a story about segregated groups in Silicon Valley becoming connected via people who had insider connections with one another from their time as post-docs at IBM's Almaden Valley Labs. As Sorenson and Stuart (2001:1584) conclude: "Whenever personal and professional networks play a central role in economic activity, we will likely observe spatial patterns in the unfolding of that activity."

Implication for spillover from neighbor networks

If local processes are responsible for social networks constituting social capital in a population, then information will likely be misunderstood through indirect connections beyond the local group, so ego's social capital is a function of direct access beyond the group and thorough access within the group. A person rich in social capital would be "the leading person in the area." The contradiction to global processes is that coefficient b_2 for neighbor networks should not be substantially stronger than coefficient b_1 for ego's immediate network. Direct contact facilitates moving sticky knowledge, so direct access to the brokerage opportunities of structural holes should be more rewarding on average than indirect access.[20] How much more rewarding depends on the social structure of the specific population. There would be no benefit from indirect access to relations in other groups when local processes generate social capital, so network measures based on connections far removed from ego would be based on connections that do not provide productive information, which obscures differentiation on the local connections responsible for social capital. The result would be weaker evidence of spillover effects on performance. If the decline in spillover effect follows the rate at which new connections occur beyond ego's group, then I would expect spillover effects to decline in proportion to the graphs displayed in Figure 2.6. There would be social capital benefit from the immediate network of ego's direct contacts, and to an extent the networks around direct contacts (because most of those friends of friends are within ego's group). Benefit would decrease sharply for neighbors

---

[20] The greater reward can be obscured in current data-collection methods because the distinction between direct and indirect contacts can vary with research design. The fewer relations recorded as direct contacts, the more likely that some direct contacts will be coded as indirect contacts. Brokerage among such "indirect" contacts would in fact be brokerage among direct contacts erroneously coded as indirect contacts. Assuming that closer contacts are more likely to be recorded as direct contacts in any research design, however, average returns to brokerage among direct contacts should be higher than average returns to brokerage among indirect contacts. Methodological confusion between direct and indirect contacts should become quickly irrelevant with increasing path distance.

further removed because a decreasing proportion of indirect connections would reach local contacts not already reached.

Personal processes imply no spillover

A third broad possibility is that the performance association with network structure is not about the social so much as it is about the person, ego, at the center of the network. In a trivial sense, this is always true: Networks do not act. Networks can facilitate action by making success likely for certain people. They can inhibit action by making success unlikely for certain people. Ultimately, it is individuals who act, successfully or unsuccessfully. While the source of action is obvious, the process responsible for successful action is not. Social capital created by local or global processes is an advantage in the flow of information. People who broker the flow of information between groups are more familiar with the diversity of opinion and practice elsewhere, which gives them an advantage in detecting and developing rewarding opportunities. Advantage need not be a direct result of information flow. It could be a by-product. People develop cognitive and emotional skills to manage information as it flows through their network. The cognitive and emotional skills associated with kinds of networks could be the proximate cause of enhanced performance.

In a phrase, network structure would be a forcing function for human capital (the theme in Coleman's, 1988, initial description of social capital). Brokerage exposes ego to diverse opinion and practice in other groups. In the course of managing contradictory relationships, ego develops cognitive skills of analogy and synthesis, and emotional skills for reading, engaging, and motivating colleagues. The growth and innovation associated with brokerage would not result from a vision advantage provided by access to conflicting information but instead from a vision advantage provided by cognitive and emotional skills enhanced as a by-product of ego managing the contradiction and conflict inherent in translating information across structural holes.[21] Either way, ego has an advantage in detecting and developing rewarding opportunities. The question is whether the vision advantage comes from better glasses or better eyes. A network that spans structural holes could provide ego better

---

[21] Personal processes are not limited to brokerage. Closure protects ego from the diversity of opinion and practice in other groups, which frees ego to specialize within a group of trusted colleagues on a narrow range of alternatives. The result is a person who thinks deep rather than wide, a person adept at ironing out inconsistency. The trust of insiders, suspicion of outsiders, alignment and speed associated with network closure need not be determined by reputation within the information boundary provided by a closed network. They could be determined instead from cognitive or emotional skills enhanced by freedom from the contradiction and conflict inherent in translating information across structural holes.

information access and control, or it could, by exercising ego's ability to manage heterogeneous information, make ego better able to see.

With the social working through the personal, it seems appropriate to describe the better-eyes process as an instance of personal processes being responsible for the advantage discussed as social capital. The social is still present. In fact, the social is emphatically present since it is shaping the person. However, the benefits of social capital created by personal processes do not result from network structure directly, but rather from the kind of person ego becomes by dint of the networks in which she operates. A person rich in social capital would be known as "wise."

Particularly good evidence of such personal processes is available from Kohn and Schooler's research with colleagues at the National Institute of Mental Health on a panel study with a national probability sample of employed American men in the 1960s and 1970s (Kohn, 1969; Kohn and Schooler, 1983). They link work to personality through what they term the "substantive complexity" of a man's work and his "intellectual flexibility." Substantive complexity is measured by coding detailed descriptions of a job for the extent to which it "requires thought and independent judgment" (Kohn and Schooler, 1978:30–36). Intellectual flexibility is measured with a variety of techniques capturing a man's thoughtfulness together with his ability to see and describe alternative solutions (Kohn, 1971: 464n; Kohn and Schooler, 1978:36–39). Men have a level of intellectual flexibility that continues through time as human capital, but that level can be raised or lowered by their work. Kohn and Schooler (1978: 24, 44) summarize: "the effect of substantive complexity of work on intellectual flexibility is real and remarkably strong—on the order of one-fourth as great as the effect of men's earlier levels of intellectual flexibility on their present intellectual flexibility." This research was conducted before network measures were readily available, but I suspect that people with access to structural holes would report higher substantive complexity in their work. The lower a man's network constraint score, the more his work involves juggling opinion and practice across separate groups—the more complex his work. The higher a man's network constraint score, the less he is exposed to alternative opinion and practice, the more likely he works in the two-layer offices that Kohn (1971) earlier linked with low intellectual flexibility (two-layer refers to an office of employees under a single boss, or under a single layer of managers). In short, I interpret the research by Kohn and his colleagues to be evidence of network brokerage enhancing individual cognitive and emotional skills.

The implication for spillover is that there should not be any. If ego's social capital advantage comes from cognitive and emotional skills developed as a by-product of managing her immediate network, then the zero-order association between performance and neighbor networks should disappear when ego's immediate network is held constant because her skills are based on the relationships she herself manages, not the relations her neighbors manage.

Whatever the performance association with brokerage in ego's immediate network (coefficient b_1), there should be no association with the networks around her neighbors (coefficient b_2 should be zero, allowing for the possibility of direct connections miscoded as indirect, see footnote 20).

Spillover diagnostic

Global, local, and personal processes are indistinguishable in the immediate network around ego. Any or all of the processes could be responsible for performance enhanced by the immediate network around ego. Ego's cognitive and emotional skills are certainly present, so personal processes are candidate explanations. Local and global connections reach ego through the immediate network, so local and global processes cannot be ruled out.

Since I have no power of resolution between processes within the immediate network, I use it as a frame of reference for comparing spillover effects, which do offer process clues. Whatever the strength of the performance association with the immediate network around ego, is the association with neighbor networks higher, about the same, or negligible?

Lines in Figure 2.7 show performance associations with network structure for each of the three processes at each path distance relative to the association with the immediate network around ego. The lines in Figure 2.7 are hypothetical, but based on the connection distributions displayed in Figures 2.5 and 2.6 for study populations to be analyzed in the next chapters. The three lines in Figure 2.7 begin by definition at unit strength within the immediate network, then diverge immediately, indicating the process clue that spillover can provide. The bold line, following the shape of the curves in Figure 2.5, describes the increasing spillover effects expected if global processes are responsible for social capital. The solid thin line, following the shape of the curves in Figure 2.6, describes the decreasing spillover expected if local processes are responsible for social capital. The dashed line describes the lack of spillover expected if personal processes are responsible for the social capital effects in a population. All three lines converge on zero at some point as distant network structure becomes irrelevant to ego's social capital. Empirical data offer the most powerful distinctions between processes where the three lines are furthest apart. The lines are most distinct in Figure 2.7 for neighbors at path distances three or four. However, I can make distinctions almost as powerful, with less measurement complication, by going just one step beyond ego's immediate network to the networks around ego's direct contacts, the neighbor networks. That is what I do in this book.

Reverse the inference. Instead of describing the spillover effects expected if a certain process is responsible for social capital, ask what process is implied by the spillover observed in a population. Following the bold line in Figure 2.7, the more advantage I see spill over from neighbor networks in a population—in other words, the more performance-relevant the structure of neighbor

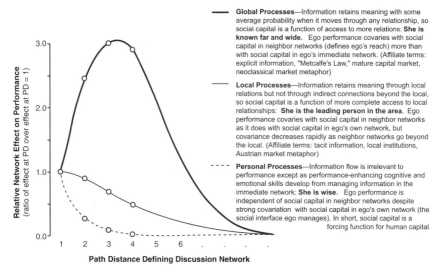

Figure 2.7 Neighbor Network Clues to Processes by which Social Networks Could Constitute Social Capital

networks—then the more likely that global processes are at work in the population, and so the more appropriate a neoclassical market metaphor would be for explaining performance differences in the population.

Following the thin solid line, if returns to neighbor networks are about the same or less than the returns to the immediate network around ego, then advantage is probably based on local processes in the population, so the more appropriate it would be to explain performance differences using an Austrian market metaphor, with its emphasis on tacit, sticky knowledge about local norms and practice. Note that one need not conduct a network analysis to distinguish groups before deciding whether advantage is limited to relations within groups. It is sufficient to study the returns to neighbor networks.

Following the dashed line, a lack of spillover from neighbor networks implies that social capital in the population is not based on information flow so much as it is based on cognitive and emotional skills developed as a by-product of managing flow. Performance differences in such a population are to be explained by kinds of people created by the networks in which they operate. Note the simple generality of the spillover test for personal processes. A traditional research design testing for personal processes would add measures of cognitive or emotional skill to a network study of performance, then describe how the skill measures work with network measures to predict performance. For example, Mehra, Kilduff, and Brass (2001) describe how the psychology of self-monitoring works with network brokerage to enhance performance. They show that both brokerage and self-monitoring are associated with performance, leading them to conclude that ego's personality has an independent, additive effect on performance, holding constant the immediate network around ego. Mehra, Kilduff, and Brass selected self-monitoring to study. They could have selected the intellectual flexibility indices used by Kohn and colleagues to analyze the link between personality and work (Kohn and Schooler, 1983), a locus of control index to study whether people in closed networks are more likely to believe that events are determined by forces beyond the control of individuals (Rotter, 1966), or a self-efficacy index to study whether people in brokerage networks are more likely to believe that they personally can make a difference (Bandura, 1997). Beyond these three options is a thicket of alternative personality and skill measures, with new measures proposed annually by academics and consultants eager to distinguish themselves from past work. Results with any one measure leave open the possibility of very different results with other measures. In comparison, the spillover test for personal processes is simple and general: if personal processes are responsible for social networks constituting social capital, there should be no spillover advantage from neighbor networks.[22]

Summary

To diagnose the information process by which social networks constitute social capital in a population, I propose to study spillover from neighbor networks. Distinct processes—here discussed as global, local, and personal—could be responsible for the known performance association with bridging structural holes (illustrated in Figure 2.4). The three processes cannot be distinguished empirically within the immediate network, but they can be distinguished, to an extent, in the advantage that spills over from well-connected neighbors.

---

[22] Inferring process from spillover is not quite so neat as implied in the text. The text is adequate to the specific empirical results to be presented in this book but not to the general case. I do not cover the general case because I have seen the data and can limit the space of all possible outcomes to the few that actually occur. Still, there is value in sketching the more general space for applications in other domains. If I see evidence of increasing spillover in a population, it is likely that global processes are at work, but it is possible that local and personal processes are also at work under the cover of global processes. If I see decreasing spillover, it is likely that local processes are at work, but it is possible that personal processes are also at work under the cover of local processes. If I see no evidence of spillover, it is unlikely that global or local processes are at work in the population. I am left with personal processes by elimination. In other words, the process clue provided by spillover involves triage down a hierarchy of alternative processes more than it identifies a specific process. Global processes are ruled out by two levels of spillover. Local processes are ruled out by one. Personal processes are never ruled out. This issue is discussed again after the evidence is in (see discussion following Figure 4.7). I appreciate Matthew Bothner calling my attention to this issue.

The research design is simple. Add indirect network constraint (measuring a manager's indirect access to structural holes in the networks around his contacts) to a regression model predicting manager performance from direct network constraint (measuring the manager's access to structural holes in his own network):

$$P = b_1 \ln(C) + b_2 \ln(IC) + BX + R,$$

where P is a measure of manager performance, R is a residual score of unpredicted performance, C is network constraint on the manager from direct contacts (first column of the table in Figure 2.3), and IC is the indirect network constraint on the manager from connections among indirect contacts (measured as the average direct network constraint on each of a manager's contacts, see second column of the table in Figure 2.3). The X term is a matrix containing a regression intercept and various control variables for the performance measured predicted in a specific study population.

The advantage provided by direct versus indirect access to structural holes is described by coefficients b_1 and b_2 respectively. The two effects combine to provide a diagnostic on the process by which networks constitute social capital in a population.

High returns to indirect access indicate global processes. Global processes are at work in a population if information retains its meaning as it moves quickly and easily through chains of indirect connections. Under such processes, an invisible hand can seem to guide interpersonal exchanges such that it makes sense to focus on a balance of forces that defines the population at equilibrium—as is characteristic of a neoclassical view on markets. With information able to move over wide distances, value lies not in knowing specific groups in detail so much as knowing how groups differ—which means substantial returns to brokerage among friends of friends because of the diversity of groups they can reach beyond the immediate network. If global processes are responsible for social capital in a population, then ego's social capital would be increasingly a function of the networks to which ego has access through her neighbors. Following the bold line in Figure 2.7, the more advantage I see spill over from neighbor networks in a population, the more likely that global processes are at work in the population.

Modest returns to indirect access indicate local processes. Local processes are at work in a population when people are balkanized into groups such that information becomes sticky in the sense that it is difficult to move between groups. Information can be tacit so it is difficult, if not impossible, to transmit in recorded form. It can be voluminous such that absorbing the information would be expensive. It can require complementary knowledge to process the information. It can interact with characteristics of sender, receiver, or channel to resist transmission. The more closed the networks around groups, the more likely that people in the groups work with tacit knowledge in the form of mutually understood, unwritten language and routines to coordinate with one another. The more they have worked together, the more complex and subtle their coordination can become. In all, their knowledge becomes difficult to move, sticky to its local context. As knowledge becomes sticky within groups, a premium emerges for people who can coordinate it across the groups. The more sticky the information to be moved between groups, the more likely there will be misunderstandings in moving the information, so the more valuable it will be to anticipate and manage the misunderstandings by knowing the two groups through personal contacts in the groups. In other words, the more sticky the information to be moved between groups, the higher the premium to direct rather than indirect connections, and discussion networks show indirect connections longer than friends of friends increasingly cross group boundaries. Following the thin solid line in Figure 2.7, if the spillover from neighbor networks is about the same or less than the returns to the immediate network around ego, then advantage is probably based on local processes in the population, so the more appropriate it would be to explain performance differences using an Austrian market metaphor, with its emphasis on tacit, sticky knowledge about local norms and practice.

Negligible returns indicate personal processes. Social capital created by local or global processes is an advantage in the flow of information. People who broker the flow of information between groups are more familiar with the diversity of opinion and practice elsewhere, which gives them an advantage in detecting and developing rewarding opportunities. Advantage need not be a direct result of information flow. It could be a by-product of flow. People working in certain network structures develop cognitive and emotional skills to manage information as it flows through their network. Those cognitive and emotional skills could be the proximate cause of enhanced performance. With the social working through the personal, it seems appropriate to describe this possibility as an instance of "personal" processes being responsible for the advantage discussed as social capital. The implication for spillover is that there should not be any. If ego's social capital advantage comes from cognitive or emotional skills developed as a by-product of managing ego's immediate network, then zero-order association between performance and neighbor networks should disappear when ego's immediate network is held constant because ego's skills are based on the relationships she herself manages, not the relations her neighbors manage. Following the dashed line in Figure 2.7, a lack of spillover from neighbor networks implies that social capital in the population is not based on information flow so much as it is based on cognitive and emotional skills developed as a by-product of managing flow. Performance differences in such a population are to be explained by kinds of people created by the networks in which they operate. With Figure 2.7 as frame of reference, it is time to present evidence.

THREE

Balkanized Networks

G ROUP boundaries indicate the likely extent to which a population operates on local, tacit knowledge, making knowledge sticky to its current
location. The stronger the boundaries between groups, the more likely groups
evolved separate from one another to develop group-specific understandings
that can be difficult to communicate across groups. This chapter is about
brokerage in two such populations. The populations are not unusual. They
can be found in most organizations. They are "balkanized" in the sense that
each population is an assembly of cohesive groups with sparse relations between groups and dense relations to a strong center. Clear network boundaries
between groups mean that operations in both populations probably involve
local, tacit knowledge so analysis is likely to reveal evidence of local rather
than global processes. I expect some evidence of spillover from neighbor
networks (thin solid line in Figure 2.7), but not the exponential benefit
expected with global processes (bold line in Figure 2.7).

Product Launch Network

I begin with a study population of employees active in the Asia-Pacific launch
of a new product from a large software company. People leading the launch
faced the usual market uncertainties of customer enthusiasm for the new
product, appropriate margins, protecting intellectual property, limiting legal
liability, and so on. Beyond the usual uncertainties, the product launch is
interesting for the diversity it involved. The launch involved a wide range of
employees—individual contributors, managers, and executives—coordinated
across strong organizational and cultural boundaries.

   Coordination challenges are quickly apparent from the sociogram in Figure
3.1 of the formal organization. The dots represent people and a line connects
two people if one reported to the other. The job-function and supervision data
needed to create the sociogram come from company personnel records and a
network survey, described in a moment, in which respondents were asked to
name "the person to whom you report." The 300 people active in the regional
product launch are indicated by shaded dots. Shapes distinguish four kinds of

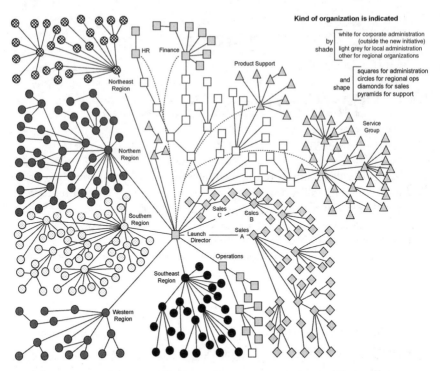

Figure 3.1 Sociogram of Product Launch Formal Organization

activities: Administration, sales, product service and support, and the local regional organizations. In addition to the study population, the network contains 31 senior administrative people outside the study population indicated by white dots in Figure 3.1, and bringing the total number of people in the network to 331. The senior outsiders were added to the network as needed to complete the chain of command between people in the study population, or if they were cited in the survey as discussion partners.

The leadership team for the product launch contained 14 people plus a senior executive, the "launch director," at the head of the team. The launch director is identified at the center of the sociogram in Figure 3.1. Connected directly to him are five heads of sales and operations organizations and five heads of regional organizations. Finance and human resources (HR) were represented on the team by people separated from the team leader by long chains of command that run through company headquarters (follow the dotted lines to the top of the sociogram). This is not unusual. Finance and HR processes are often held in tight control by corporate headquarters. A more unique challenge was the long chains of command through which the launch director was connected with company service and product support (follow the dotted lines to the east and northeast of the sociogram). The product launch was a new set of activities imposed on the existing organization. Established groups were asked to add the product launch to already busy schedules. Getting already-busy groups focused on the product launch was its own challenge.[1]

There is the further challenge of coordinating across cultures. The five regional organizations range from Australia, to India, to Japan. The regions are diverse in history and belief. Some spent time as colonies. Some have prominent periods of imperialist activity. Majority religion is in some areas Christian, in some Buddhist, in some Hindu, in some Muslim. With clear structural holes between groups, local operations can be expected to involve tacit knowledge, knowledge taken for granted by local people and easily misunderstood by visitors. Decoding that knowledge to effectively coordinate across groups will require direct, personal contact between the groups. Tension is to be expected between the interests of local and corporate leaders, the former best positioned to know customer preferences, the latter responsible for preserving company processes and presenting a coherent company face to the world.[2]

---

[1] As illustration of the challenge, HR staff for the product launch had difficulty obtaining company data on employees who reported to supervisors not in the study population (viz., the finance, HR, product support, and service people in Figure 3.1). As the HR staff explained: "We don't have visibility." They had to make a formal request to cross organization boundaries. Access was a special favor not always granted. An initial data request was granted, but subsequent data on supervision relations were taken from organization charts on the company website and the generous patience of the HR staff for the product launch.

[2] For the purposes of this analysis, the product-launch population is interesting for its strong boundaries between groups. More generally, the product launch can be studied to answer questions about brokerage in Asia. For example, popular belief distinguishes Asia for an emphasis on the collective over the individual, and success contingent on connections aligned with the formal chain of command (e.g., Morris, Podolny, and Ariel, 2000: Competition is undesirable within work groups, p. 71; friends are a more likely source of advice and exchange is more likely with friends, p. 75; acknowledged friends are more likely to occupy higher statuses, p. 77; and dense networks are more likely to increase felt obligation to help a peer, p. 82). An Asian emphasis on the collective raises questions about network brokerage. Brokerage involves individuals distinguishing themselves from peers and building bridges across chains of command. As such, brokerage could clash with local social norms such that returns to brokerage are non-existent or even negative. Hitler (2009) explores such issues in the product-launch network and reports statistically significant returns to brokerage under a variety of controls for more and less "Asian" segments of the network. In contrast, Xiao and Tsui (2007) report negative returns to brokerage in four Chinese technology organizations (16, 12, four, and three thousand employees), but it is difficult to interpret the results because the respondents are young (29 years, versus 39 in the product-launch network) and in low job-ranks where work is defined by superiors and company processes so brokerage is not typically an advantage in detecting and developing opportunities (9% of the Xiao-Tsui respondents were junior managers and 6% were middle or senior managers, versus 38%

A network survey was conducted to determine where coordination was strong and where it might need to be facilitated or encouraged. At the center of the study population are 87 employees targeted for study by the launch director. The social network connecting the 87 people involved chains of command through people elsewhere in the company and discussion relations with colleagues adjacent to the target population. In the interest of replication, details on the survey are provided in Appendix A. Respondents were representative of the study population. The final network contains 300 employees active in the product launch and 31 senior outsiders (the white dots in Figure 3.1). The average employee has 6.2 contacts; a boss plus five colleagues with whom the employee had his or her most "frequent and substantive work contact." The average varies from a single contact for people at the periphery of the network, to 28 for the most-connected person who responded to the survey, 27 for the most-connected person in the study population who did not respond to the survey, and eight for the most-connected of the 31 senior people not invited to the survey.

Brokerage opportunities between regions

The product launch was rich in brokerage opportunities. Structural holes were deep between the regions, and there were extensive holes within each region.

Figure 3.2 is a sociogram of the discussion relations. Six network clusters are linked through an administrative hub at the center. The clusters are distinguished by discussion more likely within than between clusters (high diagonal cells in the table at the bottom of Figure 3.2). The administrative hub is indicated by a shaded area at the center of the sociogram. The nine people in the hub include the launch director (square), the head of a sales group and a lieutenant from the group (diamond), the head of another sales group and a lieutenant from that group (diamond), and four people from the operations group (squares). The table at the bottom of Figure 3.2 shows that each cluster has more discussion with the administrative hub than with any other cluster— despite the fact that there are only nine people in the hub.

Structural holes between the regions are apparent from the sociogram, but numerically striking in the table. The Northeast and the Southern regions have few discussion relations beyond the region. The Northern region is also self-contained. There is in the Northern regional organization a small group of

---

and 43% respectively in the product-launch network). It would have been useful to see the Xiao-Tsui returns to brokerage broken down by firm and job rank to see how much returns varied between the four companies and how returns increased or decreased with job rank. Returns increase with rank as work involves more coordination across groups (Burt, 2005:156–162). In the product-launch network, compensation regressed on the log of network constraint produces a negligible −.59 t-test among employees below managerial rank, a −4.25 t-test for junior-rank managers, and a −6.13 t-test for managers in middle and senior ranks (coefficients of $40.15, −$654.51, and −$1,640.84 American dollars change in compensation with a one-unit increase in network constraint in a linear model; see Burt, 1992:133, 138; 2004:371, for similar results in other technology firms).

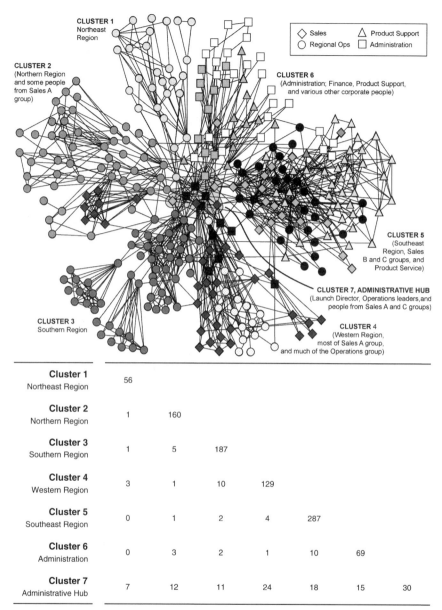

Cluster 1 Northeast Region	56						
Cluster 2 Northern Region	1	160					
Cluster 3 Southern Region	1	5	187				
Cluster 4 Western Region	3	1	10	129			
Cluster 5 Southeast Region	0	1	2	4	287		
Cluster 6 Administration	0	3	2	1	10	69	
Cluster 7 Administrative Hub	7	12	11	24	18	15	30

Note: Cells are counts of discussion relations within and between the clusters in the sociogram. For example, there are three between people in Cluster 1 and the people in Cluster 4. There are 56 between people within Cluster 1.

Figure 3.2 Sociogram of Discussion Relations within the Product Launch

people from one of the sales groups (cluster of diamonds among the dots, Figure 3.2), but the sales people primarily discuss work with colleagues in the region. Product-launch administration is integrated into the Western region in that the Western cluster (Cluster 4 in Figure 3.2) contains employees in the regional organization (dots) plus a substantial number of people from one of the sales organizations (diamonds) plus more than half of the people from the product-launch operations group (squares). The administration is most integrated into the Southeast region. The Southeast cluster (Cluster 5 in Figure 3.2) contains employees in the regional organization (dots) plus one of the sales organization (diamonds) plus all of the service organization (pyramids). The sales and service groups embedded in the Southeast cluster are connected to little outside the region. A sixth cluster, at the top of the sociogram in Figure 3.2, is composed of administrative people who largely talk to one another. Product support for the launch is embedded in the administrative cluster. The sociogram shows little direct contact between the six clusters. Another way to describe the segregation between clusters is to compare the counts of relations in the Figure 3.2 table to counts expected if relations occurred independent of cluster boundaries.[3] Relations within the six clusters occur with a frequency more than seven times the number expected under independence (758% average). Relations between the six clusters occur at a small fraction of the frequency expected under independence (6% average across the 15 cells for relations between the six clusters).

In short, there is uneven integration of sales, service, and support across the regions, which leaves a difficult coordination task for a few people in the administrative hub since so much of communication between the regions is indirect through the administrative hub. Opportunities for brokerage between the regions are substantial and numerous.

Brokerage opportunities within regions

Brokerage is not limited to connections between regions. Opportunities exist within each region. For example, the three sub-clusters within the Southern organization are obvious. A main cluster is linked to the product-launch administrative hub. There are also two country clusters in which discussion is almost entirely with colleagues in the same country. Some of the opportunities within regions are less obvious. For example, Cluster 5 to the southeast in Figure 3.2 is a dense blob of discussion among sales, service, and regional

---

[3] The frequency of relations expected under independence is computed in the usual way as row marginal times column marginal divided by table total, so ratios of observed to expected are not exact. Exact expectations would require correction for relations cited by the same respondent. For the purposes here, the reported ratios of observed to expected frequencies are a heuristic provided to put a familiar metric on the tendency for people to talk primarily with colleagues in their own cluster.

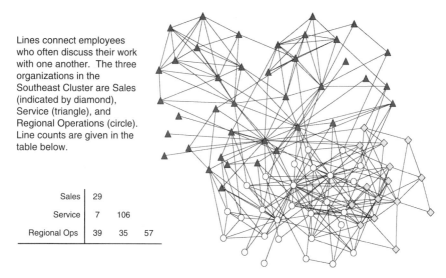

Lines connect employees who often discuss their work with one another. The three organizations in the Southeast Cluster are Sales (indicated by diamond), Service (triangle), and Regional Operations (circle). Line counts are given in the table below.

Sales	29		
Service	7	106	
Regional Ops	39	35	57

Figure 3.3 Detail of Discussion within the Southeast Cluster

operations. However, closer inspection of the cluster shows that discussion is concentrated within the three functions, with discussion especially infrequent between the sales and service employees (Figure 3.3).

There are extensive opportunities for brokerage within regions largely because discussion is so closely tied to the chain of command. Figure 3.2 shows discussion concentrated within the regional clusters, but that does not mean everyone is equally likely to talk to anyone else in the region. Employees most often discuss work with colleagues close to them in the chain of command. For example, 32 percent of all discussion relations are between boss and subordinate, and another 28 percent are between people separated by one intermediary in the formal organization. The probability of discussion drops to 15 percent between people separated by two intermediaries, and quickly disappears thereafter. Discussion is neither random nor ubiquitous within regions; it is concentrated between people who are close together in the chain of command, which leaves open extensive opportunities for brokerage between local offices within each region.

Employee returns to brokerage

Informal discussion relations cut across reporting relations in the product launch. Path distance is the shortest chain of relationships required to connect two people. Average path distance through the formal organization in Figure 3.1 is six. Informal discussion is quicker by two intermediaries (dropping from an average path distance of 6.17 reporting relations in Figure 3.1, to 4.13 discussion relations in Figure 3.2).

The empirical question is whether people are rewarded for cutting across the formal organization. It turns out that they are. Employees whose discussion relations reach across structural holes enjoy higher compensation than their peers and more positive performance evaluations. Figure 3.4 shows how compensation varies with brokerage. The vertical axis is relative annual compensation (salary plus bonus). The data, taken from company personnel records, are converted by the company to a common currency and expressed here as z-scores adjusted for regional differences. A score of 0.0 indicates an employee whose compensation was average for his or her region. A score of 1.0 indicates compensation one standard deviation higher than the regional average.[4]

Network constraint varies on the horizontal axis, distinguishing employees by their opportunities for network brokerage. As illustrated by network icons below the graph, employees to the left have networks that reach across structural holes. They have many opportunities for brokerage. Employees to the right are embedded in closed networks, which is to say that the people with whom they discuss work are well known to one another. Employees to the right have few opportunities for brokerage.

Returns to direct brokerage are described by the solid, downward-sloping line in Figure 3.4 (−7.62 t-test). The form of the association is generic. I have elsewhere discussed such graphs as a stylized fact in social capital (Burt, 2005:56) and the association in Figure 3.4 looks just like the aggregate association discussed in the previous chapter (Figure 2.4). People whose networks span structural holes enjoy significantly higher compensation than peers whose networks do not span structural holes. Returns to brokerage are also

---

[4] From the company personnel records, I have compensation data on 258 of the 300 employees in the study population. The 42 missing data are people not visible to the HR staff attached to the product launch, as discussed earlier in the text. I searched for correlates of the missing data to see what kinds of people are more likely to be missing. I estimated a logistic equation predicting whether compensation data are missing for an employee from the available characteristics in Table 3.1 (e.g., age and seniority are not available where compensation is not available) plus dummy variables distinguishing the clusters in Figure 3.2 (Table A1 in Appendix A contains tests for selection bias). The four factors associated with the missing data are job rank, network, administration, and being targeted for this study. Compensation to senior-rank employees within closed networks is more likely to be missing. Compensation is more often missing on the administrative people in Cluster 6 in Figure 3.2. Last, the HR staff made a concerted effort to obtain compensation data on the 87 people initially targeted for the study, so compensation is especially likely (but not entirely) available on the target population. I conclude that the results in Table 3.1 are characteristic of people more involved in the product launch. As a final check on the stability of the results, I re-estimated the compensation prediction in Table 3.1 using the data on two subpopulations in which I have more complete survey and company data. There are statistically significant associations with network constraint if I limit estimation to the 87 people in the target population (−2.47 t-test) or the 168 survey respondents (−2.63 t-test). Corresponding associations with indirect network constraint are negligible (−.55 and .60 t-tests, respectively).

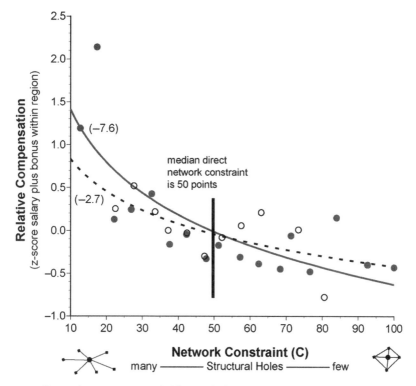

Constraint scores are pooled for 5-point intervals on horizontal axis. Solid symbols and line indicate performance at levels of direct constraint. Hollow symbols and dashed line indicate performance at levels of indirect constraint. Test statistics are given in parentheses.

Figure 3.4 Employee Compensation and Network Constraint

statistically significant if I limit the estimation to individual contributors (−2.27 t-test) or managers (−4.40 t-test).

The dashed line in Figure 3.4 shows a weaker, but statistically significant, performance association with indirect network constraint (−2.65 t-test). These are returns to employees who discuss their work with well-connected colleagues. To the left in the graph are employees who discuss their work with colleagues whose networks span structural holes. To the right in the graph are employees connected with colleagues embedded in closed networks.

The performance association with neighbor networks is not as clear as it seems in the Figure 3.4 graph. I excluded "entourage" employees from the graph, that is to say, people embedded in a closed network around someone well-connected beyond the closed network. An example would be a deputy or executive assistant, whose position in the community depends on affiliation with a strong leader. As people who do not themselves have wide connections, but affiliate with people who have wide connections, these people are part of the entourage around their prominent affiliate. Figure 3.5 shows that entourage employees are not paid to be brokers. The graph displays relative compensation across levels of indirect network constraint. The entourage employees are in the shaded corner to the bottom left of the graph. They are among the least-well compensated people in the product launch. Few entourage employees made it into the study population, but they are such outliers that I add a control for them in the model.[5]

---

[5] The control is irrelevant after I hold constant the immediate network, but the zero-order association between compensation and indirect network constraint is obscured without a control for the eight entourage employees ($-.04$ t-test). I identified entourage employee as follows: Multiply an employee's direct network constraint times one minus the employee's indirect network constraint. For constraint bounded by zero and one, the product varies from zero to one measuring the extent to which the employee has limited direct access to structural holes (high direct network constraint) and extensive indirect access to structural holes (low indirect network constraint). Second, order the employees from the person with the highest score to the person with the lowest score. The eight outliers shaded in the lower-left corner of Figure 3.5 are the eight people at the top of the rank order. Scores drop after the eight top-ranked people, and continue to decrease slowly across the rank order. I created a dummy variable distinguishing the eight people as "entourage" employees. I removed the eight people from the data to get the results reported in Figure 3.4. The zero-order association with indirect network constraint is stronger with the entourage employees removed, however, there is no effect on the multiple regression results in Table 3.1. Age and job rank, in particular, act as controls for entourage employees because they tended to be older people (2.03 logit z-score) in junior ranks (-2.40 logit z-score with job rank). If I add to the compensation prediction in Table 3.1 the dummy variable distinguishing entourage employees, I find that they do not receive significantly lower compensation than other employees with the same job rank, age, etc. ($-.80$ t-test). If I add the variable to the ordinal prediction of evaluations in Table 3.1, entourage employees do not receive significantly more or less positive evaluations (-1.52 logit z-score). Looking ahead to the supply-chain managers, what I here term entourage employees do not obscure zero-order associations between performance and brokerage (Figure 3.8), and the measure used here to identify entourage employees adds no statistically significant prediction to the equations in Table 3.2.

Moran (2005:1140) reports a similar issue at the other extreme of network constraint. In a population of 120 product and sales managers for a large drug company, Moran finds that half of the managers had network constraint scores over 80. A third had completely closed networks (C = 100). The performance association with brokerage is clear across the managers right up to the completely closed networks (Moran, 2005:1143). The people in completely closed networks did not perform as badly as would be expected. Instead of performing least well, the complete-closure managers were about average in their performances. There were no isolates in the population, so it would be interesting to see what manager characteristics distinguish the many people in the complete-closure networks. A constraint score of 100 with multiple contacts is more than high closure; it is complete segregation. Perhaps certain products were developed in completely closed networks (as sometimes occurs in the defense industry), or certain sales managers had embedded long-term client relations in completely closed networks (as sometimes occurs in business services), or the completely closed networks are concentrated in small, isolated offices. Whatever the explanation for the completely closed networks, it would be good to identify the explanation so that it could be held constant with a company-specific control rather than complicating the association between performance and brokerage.

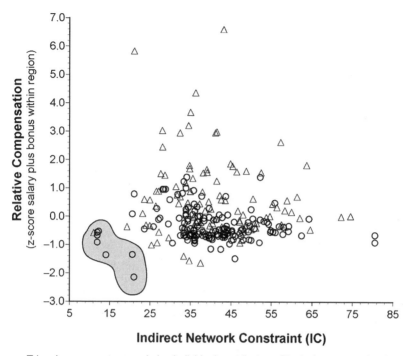

Triangles are managers, circles individual contributors. Shaded area contains the entourage employees (see footnote 5). Test statistic for association is −0.60 across all employees, −2.65 excluding the entourage employees.

Figure 3.5 Detail on Employee Compensation and Indirect Network Constraint

With controls for alternative explanations, the first column in Table 3.1 shows compensation returns to brokerage. Means, standard deviations, and correlations are given in Table E1 in Appendix E. Employee characteristics were obtained from company personnel records just after the network survey was completed, so there is no time order between network and performance. Job rank is measured by two variables: Four job ranks of individual contributors, and four job ranks of managers. Job rank is measured separately for the two kinds of employees because data plots of compensation by job rank show that the managerial ranks were more a separate track than a continuation of individual-contributor ranks. Average compensation for the most junior managerial rank is lower than average compensation for the highest-rank individual contributor, and compensation increases more quickly with increasing managerial job rank. The latter point is illustrated by the coefficients for job rank in Table 3.1. There is a .27 z-score increase in relative compensation associated with moving one level up in the individual-contributor ranks. The compensation increase associated with moving up one managerial rank is twice as large (.62). Apart from job rank, function matters. Compensation is substantially higher for the employees in

Table 3.1 Predicting Performance within the Product Launch

	Annual Compensation	Annual Performance Evaluation	
		Interval	Ordinal
Intercept	−1.49	4.49	−9.23
			−6.16
Direct Network Constraint	−.27 (.10)*	−.56 (.20)*	−1.11 (.42)*
Indirect Network Constraint	.14 (.14)	−.37 (.26)	−.61 (.52)
Job Rank (Ind. Contributors)	.27 (.05)**	.03 (.09)	.03 (.18)
Job Rank (Managers)	.62 (.06)**	.05 (.13)	.21 (.25)
Age	.02 (.01)*	−.03 (.01)*	−.06 (.03)*
Female	−.09 (.10)	−.11 (.17)	−.10 (.35)
Sales Function	.76 (.09)**	−.17 (.16)	−.41 (.33)
Years with Company	−.03 (.01)*	.01 (.02)	.02 (.04)
Regional HQ	.57 (.15)**	.14 (.26)	.47 (.52)
Targeted by Study	−.07 (.12)	.03 (.24)	−.11 (.49)

Note: The first two models predict annual compensation and annual performance evaluation measured as z-scores (.67 and .10 squared multiple correlations, 258 and 182 observations; zero-order correlations in Appendix E, Table E1). The third column is an ordinal logit model predicting the three categories of annual evaluation (the two intercepts are the cut points between the three categories, 20.23 chi-square with 10 d.f., P = .03). Network constraint is the log of constraint. The job-rank variables distinguish four levels of individual contributors and four levels of managers. "Targeted by Study" distinguishes employees who were the initial targets of the network study. Standard errors are given in parentheses (* p < .05, ** p ≤ .001).

sales (8.75 t-test). Compensation is higher for people in the regional headquarters (3.90 t-test). Nevertheless, the people deemed central to the launch so as to be targeted by the network survey turn out to be a representative sample of the study population in that they are neither more or less compensated than anyone else in the population (−.60 t-test).

The company compensation system is blind to gender, but age matters in the sense that older employees enjoy higher compensation (.02 coefficient). The advantage of age is undone by a corresponding loss of compensation for each year spent with the company (−.03 coefficient). Business is expanding rapidly and the new product involves many new employees. The average person in the study population is 38 years old, but that average middle-age person has only been with the company for 5.4 years and in their current job for 1.7 years. Almost half have been in their current job for less than a year (42%). The age premium here is for experienced employees recruited from other companies.

The key result is the strong compensation returns to brokerage despite controls for employee characteristics. There are returns to structural holes in the immediate network, but no returns to having discussion partners rich in structural holes. The company rewards employees who connect across the structural holes defined by discussion within and between regions (Figure 3.2),

but only if the employees themselves connect. There is no statistically significant evidence of benefits to employees who merely affiliate with colleagues
who connect across the structural holes.

The other models in Table 3.1 corroborate the key result. Company performance evaluations recognize people who connect across the structural holes
within and between regions, but again only if they themselves connect. The
criterion variable is the summary judgment from each employee's most recent
annual performance evaluation: Outstanding, average, or poor (synonyms for
the words actually used). Evaluations are not a useful criterion variable here (as
they often are elsewhere) because so many initiative employees are new to
their job. Recall that 42 percent have been in their current job for less than a
year. It is too early to evaluate a large proportion of the employees so they are
"missing" on the evaluation variable. I have compensation data on 258 employees, annual performance evaluations on only 182. Given evidence of
compensation returns to brokerage already established, however, finding the
same returns for evaluations is useful corroboration of the more complete
compensation evidence. The second model in Table 3.1 predicts a z-score
measure of evaluation. For comparison with the compensation results, I computed from integer values and the distribution of managers a z-score for each
level of evaluation (2.12 for outstanding, .51 for average, and -1.11 for poor).
The third model in Table 3.1 is a logit regression predicting ordinal differences
between the three levels of evaluation.

The interval and ordinal predictions support the same conclusions: Almost
every kind of employee is at equal risk of receiving a positive evaluation, or for
that matter, a negative evaluation. Performance evaluations are not associated
with job rank, being in sales, gender, years with the company, location, or being
targeted for the study as a central employee.[6] The one exception is age. Older
employees are less likely to be judged "outstanding" (though they are no more
likely to be judged "poor").[7] Other than age, employee network is the factor
associated with evaluations. Employees who connect across structural holes
receive more-positive job evaluations (-2.78 t-test for interval prediction,

---

[6] This sentence refers to the statistically negligible associations between evaluations and
the employee characteristics in Table 3.1. With respect to geographic location, evaluations
are no higher for employees at the regional headquarters than they are elsewhere. More,
I get negligible results when I try to predict evaluations from dummy variables distinguishing the five regional clusters in Figure 3.2. The five dummy variables have no association
with z-score evaluations (.64 F-statistics with 5 and 176 d.f., P = .67) and no association
with the ordinal distinction between the three levels of evaluation (3.12 chi-square statistic, 5 d.f., P = .68). Holding constant the employee characteristics in Table 3.1, in other
words, employees in each region are equally at risk of positive evaluations.

[7] If I replace the three-category criterion variable in the Table 3.1 ordinal logit regression
with a dummy variable distinguishing employees who received a "poor" evaluation, I find
no association with employee age (1.65 logit z-score). If I replace the three-category
criterion variable with a dummy variable distinguishing employees who received an
"outstanding" evaluation, I find the negative association with age (-2.43 logi z-score).

−2.64 logit z-score for ordinal prediction). There is no evidence of positive evaluations going to employees who merely affiliate with well-connected colleagues (−1.42 t-test for interval prediction, −1.17 z-score for ordinal).

Supply-Chain Organization

My second study population is supply-chain managers in a large American electronics company. The clusters are less segregated from one another than in the product launch, so tacit knowledge could be less important to coordination within clusters, so coordination could be more feasible across clusters through indirect access to structural holes. In the product-launch network, structural holes were reinforced by employee differences in culture, history, language, as well as the more familiar differences in function, geography, and chain of command. The supply-chain managers were less diverse: They had worked in the United States for most of their lives, they all held managerial rank, and it was relatively easy for them to discuss work with distant colleagues in that they were supply-chain managers in the same company.

Segmented by geography and product

Still, the managers were segregated in their own way. With respect to history, the managers had worked for a long time in legacy organizations acquired by the parent company and retained substantial freedom to purchase supplies where they wished. The average manager was 50 years old, had been with his or her organization for 18 years, and had known his or her discussion partners for 8 years. Many had been in the industry for their entire career. With respect to geography and product, consider the sociogram in Figure 3.6. This is the formal organization. Supply-chain managers are represented by dots and a line connects two managers when one reported to the other (taken from company personnel records). In the center of the sociogram are managers located in the company headquarters (white squares). Headquarters is surrounded by supply-chain organizations within the company business units. I have located business units roughly as they are distributed geographically. A senior executive runs the large Eastern division, which contains three sub-divisions. Eastern-division managers are represented by diamond-shaped dots in Figure 3.6. Circles indicate managers in two separate divisions to the Southeast and South. Pyramid-shaped dots represent managers in the largest division. I have distinguished three sub-divisions reporting to the senior executive in charge of the largest division, but concentrations of reporting relations make clear that there are distinct groups within the three sub-divisions. The business units operate in distant locations within the United States, producing distinct kinds of electronic output. In each product line within the legacy

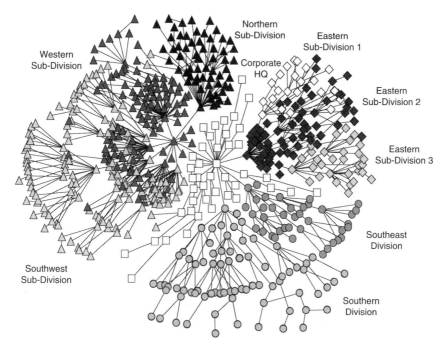

Figure 3.6 Sociogram of Supply-Chain Formal Organization

organizations, managers knew the products for which they ordered supplies and vendors from whom they had ordered supplies. They had little incentive to know the supply chain in other product lines. The supply-chain managers are substantially less diverse than the product-launch employees, but they are diverse in their own way.

I have network data on the population as it was going through a leadership change triggered by exogenous events. The incoming leadership thought that a network analysis would be a quick way to become familiar with the current informal organization. Knowing the current organization would be useful for thinking about and communicating future strategy.

The supply-chain network was mapped by the same procedure just described for the product-launch network, so I can be brief here. The online network survey contained two name generators. Managers were asked to describe their best idea for improving supply-chain operations, then asked if they had discussed the idea with anyone. If yes, they were asked to name the person. Next, they were asked, "More generally, who are the people with whom you most often discuss supply-chain issues?" The 455 survey respondents are representative in the sense that there are no significant differences between respondents and non-respondents in geographic region, business unit, job rank, age, race, gender, or education (Burt, 2004:360–365). Respondent reports on relations between their cited contacts are used to fill in the network around non-responding managers. A logit model predicting sociometric citations from reports on relations, shows that the managers make a deep distinction between relations perceived as "often" versus the less-strong relations perceived as "sometimes" or "rarely" (Burt, 2004: 361n; cf. Table A2 in Appendix A). I connect two managers when they are perceived by a colleague to meet "often," or, of course, when one cites the other directly as a discussion partner. The sociogram in Figure 3.6 contains 597 supply-chain managers, which is the 455 managers who responded to the survey plus managers required to complete the chain of command to each respondent plus discussion partners named by two or more respondents (all such "snowball" contacts were also in the supply-chain). Network indices are computed on the entire system of 597 people, but for this analysis, I focus on the networks around each of the 455 survey respondents because I have complete data on the respondents (see Burt, 2004, for broader analysis). The manager networks vary in size from one to 25 discussion partners, around a median of seven.

Figure 3.7 is a sociogram of discussion relations across the managers. The sociogram shows the managers segregated by geography and product, but it also shows more discussion across groups than occurred in the product-launch network. In particular, discussion across the Eastern sub-divisions has the grey and white diamonds mingled together in the sociogram, and many of the grey diamonds are mingled with circles indicating managers in the Southeast Division. On the other side of the sociogram, discussion between managers in the Western and Southwest sub-divisions blurs the organizational boundary between them. Dark and grey pyramids are mingled together in the sociogram. The managers at headquarters are particularly connected into the Eastern, Western, and Southern divisions.

On average, informal discussion provides a significant short-cut across the formal organization. Average path distance through the formal organization in Figure 3.6 is six links (specifically, 5.93 links). That average drops through discussion relations to two and a half links in Figure 3.7 (specifically, 2.45 links).

Improved connectivity notwithstanding, discussion is concentrated inside the business units. The dark and grey pyramids in the Western and Southwest sub-divisions stand apart from the cluster of black pyramids indicating managers in the Northern sub-division. The grey circles indicating managers in the Southern division stand apart from the rest of the organization. The table of discussion relations in Figure 3.7 offers quantitative evidence of discussion concentrated within the business units. Averaging across the nine diagonal cells of the table in Figure 3.7, the observed frequency of discussion relations between managers in the same business unit are nine times the number expected if relations were independent of business unit (882%). Frequencies between divisions are, on average, a fraction of the number expected if relations were independent of business unit (25%; higher than the 6% in Figure 3.2

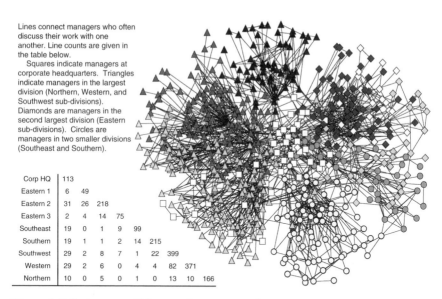

Lines connect managers who often discuss their work with one another. Line counts are given in the table below.

Squares indicate managers at corporate headquarters. Triangles indicate managers in the largest division (Northern, Western, and Southwest sub-divisions). Diamonds are managers in the second largest division (Eastern sub-divisions). Circles are managers in two smaller divisions (Southeast and Southern).

Corp HQ	113							
Eastern 1	6	49						
Eastern 2	31	26	218					
Eastern 3	2	4	14	75				
Southeast	19	0	1	9	99			
Southern	19	1	1	2	14	215		
Southwest	29	2	8	7	1	22	399	
Western	29	2	6	0	4	4	82	371
Northern	10	0	5	0	1	0	13	10	166

Figure 3.7 Sociogram of Manager Discussion Relations

for the product-launch network, but still much lower than the 882% between managers in the same business unit).[8]

Manager returns to brokerage

Figure 3.8 displays three measures of manager performance, all associated with both direct and indirect access to structural holes. There is no time order between network and performance. Data on manager networks and the quality of a manager's idea for improving operations were gathered in the same survey. I am predicting performance evaluations and salary figures defined about six months after the network survey was conducted, but salary is strongly correlated between adjacent years (.98 correlation between salary in the predicted year and salary the year before) and performance evaluations, though more subject to change than salary, are also strongly correlated between adjacent years (.82 correlation).

Relative compensation is dollars of salary measured as a z-score on the vertical axis of Figure 3.8A. In round numbers, salaries varied across the managers from $50,000 to $200,000. A score of zero on the z-score salary variable in Figure 3.8A indicates a manager paid an average salary. Variables

---

[8] As explained in footnote 3, the ratios of observed to expected frequencies are a heuristic provided here to put a familiar metric on the tendency for managers to talk primarily with colleagues in their own business unit.

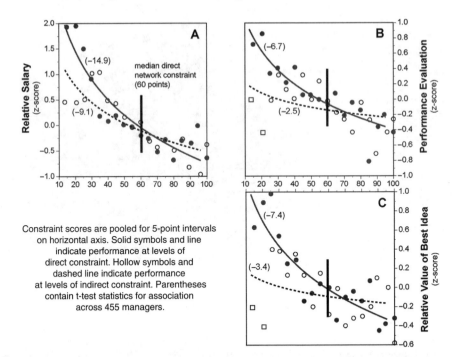

Constraint scores are pooled for 5-point intervals on horizontal axis. Solid symbols and line indicate performance at levels of direct constraint. Hollow symbols and dashed line indicate performance at levels of indirect constraint. Parentheses contain t-test statistics for association across 455 managers.

Figure 3.8 Looking at Colleagues Shows that Affiliation with Brokers is an Advantage

predicting salary are listed in Table 3.2, with means, standard deviations, and correlations in Table E2 in Appendix E. Salary and the manager-background variables are taken from company personnel records. "Job Rank" is a five-category distinction between vice presidents, senior directors, directors, senior managers, and managers. "Age" is measured in years. The two education variables refer to college graduation or completing a post-graduate program. "Minority" is a dummy variable distinguishing women, African-Americans, Asians, and Hispanics. "Hightech Organization" and "Lowtech Organization" are dummy variables respectively distinguishing divisions in which supply-chain managers had to have some technical expertise or no technical expertise. "Regional HQ" distinguishes managers who worked in the headquarters of the largest division in the company. "Corporate HQ" distinguishes managers who worked in corporate headquarters (squares in Figure 3.7). Returns to direct brokerage are shown in Figure 3.8A by the solid line describing a strong association between salaries and direct network constraint (−14.92 t-test for the regression line in the graph). Returns to brokerage opportunities in neighbor networks are shown by the dashed line, which describes a strong salary association with indirect network constraint (−9.12 t-test).

Relative performance evaluation is the criterion in Figure 3.8B. Managers were assigned in their annual performance evaluation to one of three categor-

Table 3.2 Predicting Manager Performance

	Annual Salary	Annual Performance Evaluation		Value of Best Idea
		Interval	Ordinal	
Intercept	−.59	1.58	−5.08	2.01
			−2.64	
Direct Network				
Constraint	−.17 (.05)**	−.33 (.11)*	−.71 (.25)*	−.50 (.12)**
Indirect Network				
Constraint	−.08 (.05)	.09 (.12)	.22 (.25)	−.11 (.12)
Job Rank	.55 (.02)**	.19 (.05)**	.37 (.10)**	.08 (.08)
Age	.01 (.00)**	−.02 (.01)**	−.04 (.01)*	.00 (.01)
College Degree	.02 (.05)	.14 (.11)	.09 (.24)	.16 (.12)
Graduate Degree	.01 (.05)	−.06 (.11)	.12 (.24)	.05 (.11)
Minority	−.05 (.04)	.23 (.10)*	.46 (.21)*	.09 (.10)
High-Tech Businesses	.09 (.05)*	−.05 (.10)	−.16 (.22)	.08 (.11)
Low-Tech Business	−.22 (.08)*	−.21 (.17)	−.46 (.37)	.29 (.18)
Regional HQ	.20 (.06)*	.19 (.14)	.36 (.30)	−.05 (.14)
Corporate HQ	.30 (.06)**	−.11 (.13)	−.10 (.28)	.04 (.13)

Note: For 455 supply-chain managers, columns one, two, and four respectively predict z-score annual salary, annual performance evaluation, and the value of a manager's best idea for improving the supply-chain organization (.85, .19, and .14 squared multiple correlations; zero-order correlations in Appendix E, Table E2). The third column is an ordinal logit model predicting three categories of annual evaluation (the two intercepts are cut points between the categories, 74.8 chi-square with 11 d.f., P < .001). Network constraint is the log of constraint. Standard errors are given in parentheses (* p < .05, ** p ≤ .001).

ies: Outstanding, average, or poor (synonyms for the words actually used). For comparison with the salary metric, I computed from integer values and the distribution of managers a z-score for each level of evaluation (1.88 for outstanding, .06 for average, and −1.58 for poor). The solid line in Figure 3.8B shows that managers with disconnected contacts were likely to receive an outstanding evaluation and managers with inter-connected contacts were likely to receive a poor evaluation. There is a strong performance association with direct network constraint (−6.72 t-test for the bold regression line in Figure 3.8B). The dashed line shows a detectable, but weaker, performance association with indirect network constraint (−2.45 t-test).

Idea quality is the criterion in Figure 3.8C. The idea data are useful to show how the performance association with network brokerage is similar for performance measured by compensation, evaluations, or idea quality. The idea data are a more direct measure of the vision advantage that network brokerage is argued to provide. Detailed analysis of the manager ideas is available elsewhere (Burt, 2004). Each of the supply-chain managers was asked to describe his or her best idea for improving operations ("From your perspective, what is the one thing that you would change to improve [the company's] supply-chain management?"). Ideas were evaluated by the heads of the two largest divisions in the company. They were asked "How much value could be generated if the idea were well executed?" The answer scale ranged from one ("low value or can't say") to five ("value could be high"). Evaluations by the two judges are averaged then converted to z-scores to define the relative value of a manager's idea on the vertical axis in Figure 3.8C. The solid line shows the tendency for less-valuable ideas to come from more-constrained managers (-7.41 t-test).[9] The dashed line shows that less-valuable ideas come from managers whose contacts are subject to high constraint (-3.16 t-test).

The results in Table 3.2 show what happens when the network variables are combined with job rank and the other background variables to predict performance: Performance is closely associated with brokerage opportunities in your own network (row of results for direct network constraint). There is no performance association with brokerage opportunities in your neighbors' networks (indirect network constraint).

Job rank is the key control variable. Managers in more senior job ranks had more direct and indirect access to structural holes in that their direct contacts were people in separate groups who managed across groups of lower-rank people ($-.58$ and $-.41$ correlations for job rank with direct network constraint and indirect constraint). Holding job rank constant eliminates the indirect-network-constraint association with compensation (-9.12 t-test in Figure 3.8A drops to -1.24), performance evaluation (-2.45 in Figure 3.8B drops to 0.59), and idea value (-3.16 in Figure 3.8C drops to -0.95). None of the background variables in Table 3.2 are associated with idea quality, but there are strong zero-order associations between idea quality and a manager's rank and education. The associations disappear when network structure is held constant (Burt, 2005:380). Idea quality is less associated with manager position and background than it is associated with the way the manager connects with colleagues.

---

[9] Fleming, Mingo, and Chen (2007) report a similar result with better data by comparing patents. Patents are classified by the U.S. Patent Office into one or more of a hundred thousand categories. Some patents are novel in the sense that they are assigned to categories not combined in previous patents. Fleming *et al.* measure creativity by the frequency with which the inventor's patents combine previously uncombined patent categories. They measure network closure by the extent to which the inventor co-authors patents with people who co-author with one another on other patents that do not involve the inventor. Analogous to the display in Figure 3.8C, creativity is significantly lower for inventors embedded in closed networks. The more densely connected an inventor's collaborators, the less often the inventor files patents that involve new combinations of patent categories.

Summary

I estimated returns to brokerage in two study populations that can be described as "balkanized" in that work discussion revealed multiple cohesive groups with sparse relations between groups and dense relations to a strong center. Balkanization is common in large organizations, whether the organization is global such as the one analyzed here for one of its product launches, or domestic such as the one analyzed here for its supply-chain organization. In both study populations, performance is closely associated with brokerage, but only within the immediate network around a manager. Indirect access to brokerage opportunities in networks around the manager's discussion partners has no independent association with performance.

The product launch employees and supply-chain managers are a useful place to begin because they are so typical of contemporary organizations—and I expected to find evidence of advantage spilling over from neighbor networks. Having not found the expected evidence, I turn to study populations in which well-connected neighbors are more likely to be valuable.

FOUR

More Connected Networks

THIS chapter is about performance and network brokerage when people can easily exchange information. The people described in the previous chapter were segregated into separate clusters by culture, geography, or product. In comparison, the people in this chapter face negligible barriers to communication. The three study populations are all in financial services. All three have a center–periphery structure in the sense that sociograms of colleague relations do not show clustering so much as they show a dense center of interaction that fades in all directions toward a social periphery. There are abundant structural holes in the study populations, but the holes are not reinforced by the segregation displayed in Chapter 3. Less segregation between social clusters means lower barriers to making sense of opinion and practice received from distant colleagues. In other words, indirect access to structural holes is more likely to be valuable in these populations than it was in the Chapter 3, balkanized, populations.

A Human Resources Organization

The sociogram in Figure 4.1 describes reporting relations within the human resources (HR) organization of a large commercial bank. Anticipating acquisitions, bank leaders were interested in understanding how HR processes were integrated across current operations. Human resources can be a difficult line of work in that you are expected to be both policeman and den mother. HR employees have to ensure obedience to company processes at the same time that they facilitate recruitment, talent development, and interpersonal relations. Violations of company HR policy can expose the company to costly intrusions from the outside in the form of lawsuits and regulatory interventions. Accordingly, corporate headquarters usually maintains tight control on HR processes. As essential as HR processes can be, they are usually more valuable in the long run than they are in the short run so they are often viewed as a gratuitous burden on the daily business activities of employees outside HR. Employees have to be monitored for compliance. Resentment is to be expected. In response, it is also to be expected that people in HR develop their own tribal identity as a group in, but distinct from, the surrounding organization. Their shared tribal identity can facilitate the enforcement component of HR work at the same time that it increases the probability of policies insensitive to business needs. A network analysis was commissioned to see where HR coordination in the bank was strong, where it might need some assistance, and where it might do well to back off.

The sociogram in Figure 4.1 shows strong coordination across the formal organization. The dots are the 283 full-time HR employees in the bank's top three job ranks of individual contributors and subsequent four manager ranks. A line indicates where company records said that one person reported to the other as their primary supervisor, or, for a few people with matrix responsibilities, their secondary supervisor. The sociogram is densely connected at the center, with the density fading toward a social periphery in all directions. This is very different from the segregated regional and administrative clusters in the product-launch organization (Figure 3.1), or the segregated product and business clusters in the supply-chain organization (Figure 3.6). There is some clustering in the network. The squares in the center of the sociogram are HR employees at company headquarters. Employees at headquarters are interspersed to the west of Figure 4.2 with "back office" employees (dark grey dots). All HR employees are part of the bank's back office in a certain sense, but back

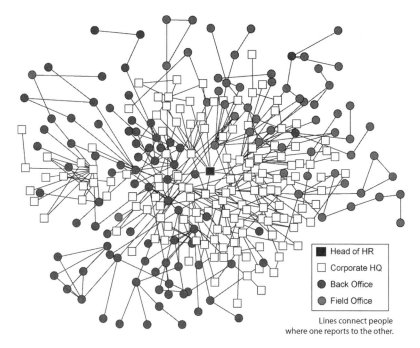

Figure 4.1 Sociogram of HR Formal Organization

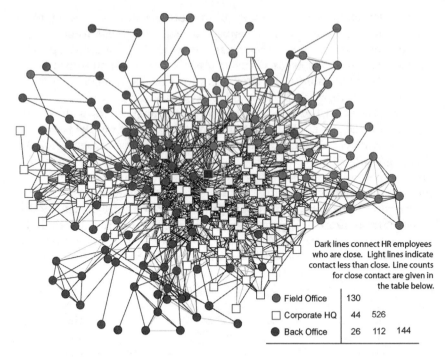

Dark lines connect HR employees who are close. Light lines indicate contact less than close. Line counts for close contact are given in the table below.

● Field Office	130		
□ Corporate HQ	44	526	
● Back Office	26	112	144

Figure 4.2 Sociogram of Discussion Relations within HR

office here specifically means HR employees who worked in an office separate from, and less expensive than, company headquarters. Headquarters employees are interspersed to the east in Figure 4.2 with "field office" employees (grey dots). These are HR employees who worked in the bank's local offices, which varied greatly in size.

The center–periphery structure is more obvious in the Figure 4.2 sociogram of discussion relations. The table below the sociogram shows that discussion is more likely within than between the three groups of HR employees, but there is extensive discussion across groups such that they are less like segregated clusters than they are shadings on the center–periphery structure of HR. The 219 survey respondents were representative of all 283 HR employees in the sense that respondents are scattered across the network and there are no significant differences between respondents and non-respondents in compensation, performance evaluation, job rank, age, seniority, race, gender, or office location. The survey included a dozen name generators eliciting discussion partners for important matters, informal socializing, essential work support, company policy, competition, and new job opportunities (see Figure A3 in Appendix A). All of the 283 HR employees were cited as discussion partners by one or more of the 219 survey respondents. Also, 159 bank employees outside HR were cited by two or more of the survey respondents so I added the

159 outsiders to the network analysis (for a final network of 542 people). I used respondent reports on relations between cited contacts to complete the network around non-respondents as in Chapter 3. A loglinear model of perceived and cited relations shows that the HR employees made substantive distinctions between close, especially close, and less-close relations, so the distinctions are preserved with continuous measures of relation strength in the network analysis (see Table A3 and Figure A5). Within the final network of 542 people in and beyond HR, the 283 HR employees vary from one to 39 contacts around a median of eight contacts.

HR Returns to Brokerage

Figure 4.3 shows compensation returns to brokerage for the HR employees. The vertical axis is annual compensation measured as a z-score. Compensation is salary plus bonus. Salary varied across the 283 HR employees from twenty thousand dollars to a few hundred thousand. Bonuses, concentrated in the manager ranks, varied from zero dollars to a couple-hundred thousand. Bonuses could increase or decrease more freely between years, so I checked my results predicting bonuses separate from salary. I get the same results.

There is no time order between network and performance. The network data were gathered a few months before compensation figures were announced, but compensation this year is strongly correlated with compensation last year (.96 correlation, .89 partial correlation holding constant job rank and age). Solid dots and the solid regression line in Figure 4.3 show the compensation association with direct network constraint (−8.20 t-test). Hollow dots and the dashed line show statistically significant association with indirect network constraint (−4.49 t-test).

Three factors predict an HR employee's compensation: Time, rank, and network. Non-network variables are taken from company personnel records. Means, standard deviations, and correlations among the predictors in Table 4.1 are given in Table E3 in Appendix E. At the time of the network survey, the average HR employee was in his or her mid thirties, and had spent the last seven years with the company. White males comprised less than half of the population (40.2%). Several dummy-variable controls expected to affect compensation in Table 4.1 turned out to be negligible: Getting a positive or average evaluation on the most recent performance evaluation (versus a poor evaluation), being a woman or racial minority (versus white male), working with business leaders in corporate headquarters or a field office (versus the back office).

Time matters in the sense that compensation increases significantly with the years a person had been with the company. This can be interpreted in terms of acquired skills, familiarity with the company, loyalties accumulated in a rise through the job ranks, or other factors. Alternative interpretations are narrowed because factors such as office location, performance evaluations, and job rank are

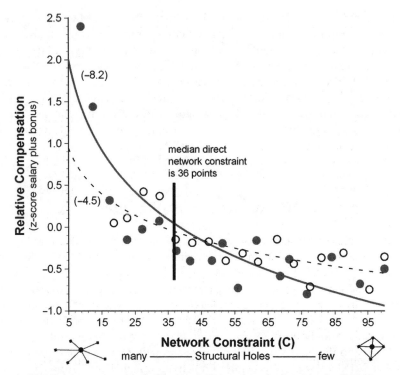

Constraint scores are pooled for 5-point intervals on horizontal axis. On the vertical axis, compensation is measured as a z-score to describe relative compensation. Solid symbols and line indicate compensation at levels of direct constraint. Hollow symbols and dashed line indicate compensation at levels of indirect constraint. Parentheses contain t-test statistics across the 283 HR employees in the bank.

Figure 4.3 HR Compensation and Network Constraint

held constant. The association with time is a duration effect. Just staying with the company was rewarded with higher compensation in this HR organization.

Promotion to senior rank was the most effective route to high compensation in HR. I say "most effective" because the coefficient is large (half a standard deviation in compensation for every job rank acquired) and the test statistic is far and away the largest in Table 4.1. The job-rank effect is concentrated in the managerial ranks. Compensation increases only slightly across individual-contributor ranks (1.43 t-test). It increases sharply up the manager ranks (13.34 t-test). You can get a sense of the shift from the distribution of the solid dots in Figure 4.3. Note how compensation increases only slightly with network constraint above the median level of network constraint (indicated by a vertical bar in the graph). The t-test for association between compensation and log network constraint is a negligible −.27 for the 139 employees with constraint

Table 4.1 Predicting HR Compensation

	Total Annual Compensation	Bonus Only
Intercept	−.06	.43
Direct Network Constraint	−.30 (.07)**	−.42 (.09)**
Indirect Network Constraint	−.03 (.13)	.03 (.16)
Job Rank (Ind. Contributors)	.06 (.04)	.08 (.05)
Job Rank (Managers)	.53 (.04)**	.39 (.05)**
Job Evaluation Was Positive	.11 (.12)	.02 (.15)
Job Evaluation Was Average	−.02 (.11)	−.03 (.13)
Years with Firm	.02 (.01)*	.03 (.01)**
Minority	.00 (.10)	−.04 (.12)
Corporate Headquarters	.08 (.09)	.05 (.11)
Field Office	.24 (.12)	.15 (.15)

Note: Regression coefficients are presented (283 observations). Compensation next year is predicted from row variables this year. Network constraint is the log of constraint. Annual compensation includes salary and bonus. Compensation is measured as a z-score to indicate relative annual compensation. The job-rank variable distinguishes three levels of individual contributors and four levels of managers. Squared multiple correlations for the two equations are .65 and .46 (zero-order correlations are given in Appendix E, Table E3). Standard errors are given in parentheses (* $p < .05$; ** $p \leq .001$).

scores higher than the median 36 points. Below the median in Figure 4.3, compensation increases sharply as network constraint decreases (t-test is −6.23 for the 142 employees with constraint scores less than 36 points).

The third factor that matters is the employee's contact network. Holding constant the other employee differences in Table 4.1, employees connected to otherwise disconnected colleagues were more likely to enjoy compensation higher than their peers (−4.35 t-test for total compensation, −4.92 for bonus in particular). These were the employees who most contributed to holding together the HR organization in Figure 4.2. Job rank explains the compensation ostensibly associated with well-connected neighbors. The strong −4.49 t-test for association between compensation and indirect network constraint in Figure 4.3 drops to a negligible 1.46 when the two job-rank variables are held constant in Table 4.1. The other controls in Table 4.1 only reduce the negligible association to near-zero (−.21 t-test in Table 4.1). In sum, the dashed-line performance association with neighbor networks in Figure 4.3 is spurious.

Two Divisions in Financial Services

Having failed to find evidence of a performance association with neighbor networks in three typical organization settings, I go to an extreme case in which indirect connections are more likely to be valuable—mature capital markets. Motivated people, ready communication through strong connections, and reliable capital transfers across the globe mean that information can move quickly and accurately between distant people in this world. There must always be an element of local interpretation, but news about investments and company developments in distant locations routinely flashes around the globe to affect plans and share prices in London, New York, and Tokyo. The more easily that meaningful information moves quickly between distant places, the more benefit there should be to the diverse information available through well-connected colleagues. If neighbor networks are an information asset anywhere, they should be an asset in a mature capital market.

I have network and performance data on senior people in two divisions of a large American financial organization during the late 1990s, just before the dot-com bubble. The people in one division craft investments and offer advice on investments. I will call them bankers. People in the second division produce predictions about the market value of investments. I will discuss the second group of people as analysts.[1]

The bankers and analysts play distinct, related, roles that evolved significantly in the twenty years preceding the data to be described. Beginning in the 1970s, market pressure on commissions for buying and selling stocks led to analyst work becoming increasingly tied to investment banking. Especially through the 1990s, analysts became a prominent and powerful factor in investment business. The trend intensified a conflict of interest for analysts between making accurate forecasts versus supporting employer-sponsored investments. The conflict of interest drew public attention when the dot.com bubble burst in 2000 and it became apparent that analyst opinions expressed in emails with colleagues sometimes contradicted their opinions expressed in published reports. The point significant for this analysis is that as analysts rose above their traditional back-room staff role to become contenders in the bonus pool, they were included in peer evaluations like bankers and other people with leadership responsibilities in financial organizations. Their inclusion provides the network data for this analysis.

Annual network data

As in other organizations moving to more adaptive, less bureaucratic structures during the 1990s, work in financial organizations required flexible cooperation

---

[1] Nothing is revealed here that would be awkward for the organization, but to honor management's wish for anonymity, I am deliberately vague on job ranks in the study population, and vague on the number of people in lower ranks with whom study-population people had relations. The people I discuss as bankers and analysts could be described with other job labels. I use "banker" and "analyst" because the labels are short and not inappropriate.

between employees. It was difficult, if not impossible, to monitor cooperation through traditional chains of command when cooperation crossed chains of command. Organizations began to use multi-source evaluation processes, processes in which employees were evaluated by their immediate supervisor as well as colleagues above, below, and around them. Rare in the 1970s, multi-source evaluation swept through corporate America during the 1980s and 1990s to help managers adapt to the ambiguity of flatter organizations in which bureaucratic chains of command were replaced with networks of negotiated influence. Estimates at the end of the century had as many as 90 percent of the *Fortune* 1000 using some form of multi-source evaluation (Atwater and Waldman, 1998). Such evaluations create data on the social network in an organization, each evaluation indicating a relationship between the employees sending and receiving an evaluation. In the organization from which this chapter's study population is drawn, bonus-eligible people were instructed in an annual evaluation process to identify colleagues with whom they had worked closely during the preceding year, then asked to describe their experience with the colleague as poor, adequate, good, or outstanding (my synonyms for the words actually used). The average evaluation of an employee was then a factor in promotion and bonus decisions.

I have four years of evaluations with which to measure annual networks around the analysts and bankers. As network data, each evaluation is a claim that the person making the evaluation had substantial contact with the person evaluated—they probably communicated, coordinated, and were otherwise "in touch" during the year. I do not know what they did, or what roles they played to one another (other than broad divisional role of banker, analyst, sales, administration, etc.), or how much they gained from the interaction. The evaluation data measure an employee's opinion about which people were colleagues during the year, and what it was like to work with each.

Not knowing what people were doing with one another raises a question about how much discretion people had in the relations. At one extreme, people could have been assigned to work with certain colleagues, whereupon network decay is determined exogenously; you work with whomever you are assigned to work. At the other extreme, people could have been free to select the colleagues with whom they worked.

The truth is some mixture of exogenous assignment and endogenous choice, with the mix different for different individuals. Nevertheless, an attractive feature of this study population is that the network data on average are probably closer to the endogenous alternative. I cannot prove this, but I have two reasons for believing it. First, there is the nature of the work. These are upper-level bankers and analysts. The analysts received average annual incomes of several hundred thousand dollars and the bankers averaged well over a million dollars a year. They were not paid that level of compensation to take orders. They were expected to find ways to create value. In fact, the company invests substantial resources in annual peer evaluations precisely because it is otherwise difficult to keep track of collaborations. The bankers and analysts so often cut across vertical chains of command that a supervisor cannot know how her direct reports are working with other employees. The only way to monitor collaborations is to survey the upper-level employees, asking each to name the people with whom they had substantial work contact during the year. Second, evaluations determined by exogenous assignment should be symmetric and correlated within dyads. People assigned to the same project would evaluate each other and project factors they have in common would create correlation between their evaluations (more positive evaluations, perhaps, in more successful projects). Instead, the evaluations are asymmetric and contradictory. Less than half of evaluations are reciprocated (38%), and when reciprocated, they are inconsistent; one person saying the relationship was good while the other says it was ok (.27 correlation between reciprocated evaluations scored 1 to 4). In short, I believe that the bankers and analysts had wide latitude in naming colleagues with whom they had substantial work contact.

Regional segregation

Figure 4.4 contains annual sociograms of relations among the senior bankers. Adding middle-rank bankers to the sociograms makes the regional clusters denser but shows the same structure displayed in Figure 4.4. Each dot is a senior banker. A line connects bankers where either cited the other as a colleague in that year's evaluation process.

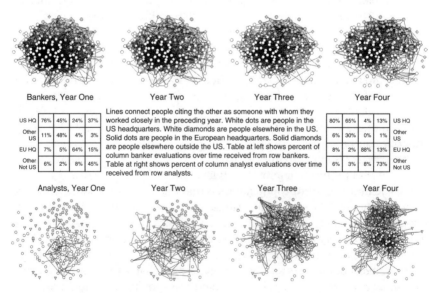

				Lines connect people citing the other as someone with whom they worked closely in the preceding year. White dots are people in the US headquarters. White diamonds are people elsewhere in the US. Solid dots are people in the European headquarters. Solid diamonds are people elsewhere outside the US. Table at left shows percent of column banker evaluations over time received from row bankers. Table at right shows percent of column analyst evaluations over time received from row analysts.					
US HQ	76%	45%	24%	37%		80%	65%	4%	13%	US HQ
Other US	11%	48%	4%	3%		6%	30%	0%	1%	Other US
EU HQ	7%	5%	64%	15%		8%	2%	88%	13%	EU HQ
Other Not US	6%	2%	8%	45%		6%	3%	8%	73%	Other Not US

Figure 4.4 Banker and Analyst Sociograms

There are about 150 senior bankers each year, but with turnover from exit, hires, and promotions, there are 177 senior bankers across the four years. I identified contacts cited by each banker and contacts who cited the banker, then looked at each contact's evaluations to see how the contacts were connected with one another. The network around a banker contained a median of 20 senior contacts in and beyond the banking division. The location of each banker in Figure 4.4 was determined in a sociogram of all relations among all 177 people, then held constant across the annual sociograms so that network change is not obscured by individuals shifting position.

There is little change to see. The bankers are connected each year through a single center indicated by dense conjunctions of lines at the center of each sociogram (though individual bankers shift position within the network from one year to the next, and there is extensive change in relations between individual bankers described in Chapter 6). Such structures are often described as "center–periphery" structures in that they are characterized by dense relations at the center fading in all directions toward the periphery. The "center" for the bankers is US headquarters. There is a headquarters office in the United States and another in Europe (EU HQ in Figure 4.4). In addition, there are bankers scattered across the globe in offices of one to a dozen bankers per office. Note the white dots at the center of the sociograms in Figure 4.4 with dense ties out to other bankers. Those central white dots are people at the US headquarters. In fact, each banker sociogram in Figure 4.4 is so densely connected it looks like a cloud of gnats more than the globally dispersed network it is.

The density table to the left in Figure 4.4 corroborates the sociograms. A cell in the table is the percent of evaluations of column bankers that come from row bankers. The table includes middle and senior bankers. Diagonal cells in the table are the largest, showing that evaluations often come from colleagues in the same regional category. The primary feature of the table is the central role played by the US headquarters, with some segregation between operations in the US and operations outside the US (recall that these data describe operations before September, 2001). Reading across the first row of the table, US headquarters provide 75 percent of the banker evaluations for other bankers in the US headquarters, 45 percent for non-headquarters bankers in the US, and 37 percent for non-headquarters bankers outside the US. Bankers in the European headquarters are most independent of the US headquarters, but even they draw 24 percent of their banker evaluations from the US headquarters.

The analyst structure is similar to the bankers, but less-well documented and more segmented by geography. Annual sociograms of colleague relations between senior analysts are displayed at the bottom of Figure 4.4. Again, I constructed an over-time sociogram among the 197 people who ever held senior rank as an analyst during the four years, then held each analyst's position constant in year-specific sociograms. The analyst sociograms in Figure 4.4 show relations expanding across the years, from a few US relations in the first year to two dense clusters of relations in the fourth year. The apparent change is about documentation more than structure. In the first year, analysts were only included in the evaluation process when they were cited to be included by other employees. In the second year, US analysts were more systematically included. In the third and fourth years, analysts in general were included. The telling fact is that four out of five analysts in Figure 4.4 were hired before the first of the four years displayed (153 of 197, or 78%). In other words, most of the isolated dots in the analyst sociograms are employees whose network connections had not yet been recorded. Network structure is not changing across the analyst sociograms so much as it is becoming better documented. Thus, these data are not suitable for studying the formation of relations so much as they are suited to studying stability and decay after a relationship has been included in the evaluation process, and the third and four years provide the most complete data for cross-sectional analysis. As was done for the bankers, I identified for each year contacts cited by each analyst and contacts who cited the analyst, then looked at each contact's evaluations to see how contacts were connected with one another. In years three and four, analysts had a median annual network of ten colleagues.

Relative to the bankers, analysts in the US are more segregated from analysts outside the US. The table to the right in Figure 4.4 highlights regional segregation. Column entries are the percent of column analyst evaluations received from row analysts. The table includes middle and senior analysts. Non-headquarters analysts in the US are strongly connected to headquarters analysts, but analysts outside the US are much less connected than the bankers. Only 4 percent of evaluations of analysts at the European headquarters come from analysts in the US (versus 24 percent for bankers in the European headquarters). The percentage is 13 percent for other analysts outside the US (versus 37% for non-headquarters bankers outside the US). The analysts form a connected network in the sense that every analyst is connected through analyst intermediaries to every other analyst—and there are numerous intermediaries in the US headquarters. Nevertheless, relative to the bankers, geographic segregation is more obvious among the analysts because colleagues in the US do not play the integrative role they play for the bankers.

In sum, the bankers and analysts formed in a network of connected colleagues scattered across the globe. Specifically, the network is a center–periphery structure anchored in the US headquarters. "Center–periphery" is more descriptive of the bankers than the analysts, but both of the fourth-year sociograms in Figure 4.4 are center–periphery structures relative to the regional clusters in the product-launch network (Figure 3.2) or the product-region clusters in the supply-chain organization (Figure 3.7). Both of the discussion networks in Chapter 3 have a center, but they fan out into separate clusters, like spokes on a wheel. Given strong connections across the network and clear rules for currency exchange across the globe, information should move easily across the network, which would make more valuable the broad diversity of information provided by indirect connections. The most efficient way to stay in touch with developments across the network would to be to work with colleagues broadly connected across the network. I expect indirect connections to be valuable for the bankers and analysts, reflecting the advantage of proximity to the vortex of the "deal stream."

Banker Returns to Brokerage

Compensation is an obvious performance metric distinguishing bankers. There are other criteria, such as integrity or teamwork, but compensation is a primary dimension (see Eccles and Crane, 1988: chap. 8, on deliberations over banker compensation). I have compensation data on the bankers from the organization's personnel records. Total annual compensation—which includes salary, bonus, and the cash value of other compensation—varied from several hundred thousand dollars to several million. To obscure exact dollar amounts and remove year-to-year fluctuation, I standardize compensation for each year. A score of zero on the z-score compensation variable indicates a banker who received an average level of compensation for that year. A score of 1.0 indicates a banker with compensation one standard deviation higher than average, and so on. For each year, I know the banker's compensation and background from company personnel records, and have data on the banker's network constructed from citations with and beyond senior colleagues in the banking division. I predict compensation next year from variables measured this year. With people entering and leaving the organization, there are a total of 469 banker observations.[2]

Model A in Table 4.2 shows returns to brokerage opportunities in a banker's own network (means, standard deviations, and correlations are given in Table

---

[2] Network and control data in year one are used to predict compensation for the 156 senior bankers in year two. Network and control data in year two are used to predict compensation for the 159 senior bankers in year three. Network and control data in year three are used to predict compensation for the 154 senior bankers in year four. I want the statistical power of repeated observations over time, but compensation is strongly correlated between adjacent years, so standard errors have to be increased to take into account the fact that repeated observations of the same person are not independent observations. Salary does not change much between years, but salary is a small portion of total compensation (14% on average). In theory, total compensation could vary between years. However, gossip ensures stable reputations, which in turn ensure high correlation between compensation in adjacent years (see Burt, 2005:chap. 4, for detailed evidence of reputation stability increasing with network closure): Total compensation is correlated .93 between the second and third years, .94 between the third and fourth years. Even if I hold constant the predictors in Table 4.2 (job rank, tenure, minority, US headquarters, and average peer evaluation), the partial correlations between compensation in adjacent years are .88 for the second and third years, .91 for the third and fourth years. Standard errors in Table 4.2 are increased as a function of correlation in compensation across years ("cluster" option in STATA).

Table 4.2   Predicting Banker Compensation

	Total Annual Compensation			Bonus Only
	A	B	C	D
Intercept	−1.63	−1.92	−1.41	−1.41
Direct Network Constraint	−.38 (.09)**	—	−.32 (.09)**	−.34 (.09)**
Indirect Network Constraint	—	−.39 (.11)**	−.18 (.12)	−.16 (.12)
Senior Job Rank	.73 (.08)**	.79 (.09)**	.73 (.08)**	.68 (.08)**
Peer Evaluation	.51 (.09)**	.58 (.10)**	.51 (.09)**	.53 (.09)**
Years with Firm	.02 (.01)	.03 (.01)*	.02 (.01)	.02 (.01)
Minority	−.05 (.19)	−.14 (.19)	−.07 (.19)	−.06 (.19)
US Headquarters	.28 (.11)*	.23 (.11)*	.27 (.11)*	.28 (.11)*

Note: Regression coefficients are presented for annual data pooled across three years (469 observations). Compensation next year is predicted from row variables this year. Network constraint is the log of constraint. Annual compensation includes salary and bonus. Compensation is measured as a z-score within each year to indicate relative annual compensation. Squared multiple correlations for the equations are .31, .28, .31, and .31 (zero-order correlations in Appendix E, Table E4). Standard errors, given in parentheses, are adjusted for autocorrelation within individuals across years (* $p < .05$; ** $p \leq .001$).

E4 in Appendix E). Compensation increases as network constraint decreases (−4.51 t-test). In other words, higher compensation went to bankers whose contacts in separate groups gave them opportunities to broker connections between groups. With respect to background variables, compensation is higher for bankers currently in the senior rank, who work in the US headquarters, and especially those who receive more positive evaluations from other employees. "Peer Evaluation" is the average evaluation of the banker in the annual peer evaluations. Some bankers in senior rank by the third year were not in senior rank two years earlier. "Senior Job Rank" is a dummy variable distinguishing bankers in the senior rank from those who will reach but have not yet reached the senior rank. "Years with Firm" is the years that the banker has been with the firm. "Minority" is a dummy variable distinguishing females, African-Americans, Asians, and Hispanics. "US Headquarters" is a dummy variable distinguishing bankers working that year in the US headquarters office.

Model B shows returns to neighbor networks. Compensation increases as indirect network constraint decreases (−3.70 t-test). I do not provide for the bankers a graph showing performance increasing with brokerage opportunities in neighbor networks—as I did for the product-launch employees (Figure 3.4), the supply-chain managers (Figure 3.8), and the HR employees (Figure 4.3)—because the association here survives controls for background differences in the bankers. An observant person entering the senior ranks of bankers would see that higher compensation went to bankers whose contacts' contacts were in a position to broker connections between groups.

Nevertheless, the returns to neighbor networks are spurious. When direct and indirect network constraint are included in the same equation as alternative predictors, the performance association with direct constraint remains strong while the association with indirect constraint is reduced to negligible (Model C). The same results occur if the prediction is limited to bonus pay, which, unlike salary, is free to increase or decrease from one year to the next (Model D). In predicting total compensation or bonus, brokerage opportunities within a banker's own network is the key control variable.[3] Bankers with many, disconnected contacts tended to have contacts who themselves had many, disconnected contacts (.47 correlation between direct and indirect network constraint in Table E4 in Appendix E). The compensation advantage attributed in Model B of Table 4.2 to bankers with disconnected indirect contacts, is in fact due to the banker having his or her own disconnected direct contacts.[4]

Analyst Returns to Brokerage

Given the banker results, I was keen to see results on the analysts. Information arbitrage is the essence of analyst work—speeding a bit of information found here

---

[3] There is a difference in compensation to more-senior bankers in this study population (all test statistics for job rank are statistically significant in Table 4.2), but controlling for job rank does not eliminate the compensation correlation with indirect network constraint— as it did in the product-launch, the supply-chain, and the HR organizations. The bankers operate in a loose formal organization, each banker very much the author of his or her job, so one could infer from the negligible job-rank control that position in the formal organization (job rank) matters less for banker compensation than position in the informal organization. However, it is also true that this is a senior population in which job-rank differences are minor relative to the distinction between the senior population and colleagues at lower ranks. What I have done with this study population is sample to get good data on variation in returns to their position in the informal organization so I can compare the performance correlations with direct versus indirect network constraint. Extending the population to less senior ranks would likely reveal more compensation differences by job rank. But estimating returns to job rank is not my concern here. My concern is to hold constant job-rank differences, however minor, so I can compare returns to direct versus indirect access to structural holes.

[4] The network data distinguish positive from negative relations. I do not discuss the distinction in the text because positive and negative relations have the same association with performance in this study population. For each banker, each year, I computed two average levels of indirect network constraint: Average constraint on the colleagues with whom the banker had a negative relationship (banker or colleague evaluated the relationship as adequate or poor), and average constraint on the colleagues with whom the banker had a positive relationship (banker or colleague evaluated the relationship as good or outstanding). If I re-estimate Model B in Table 4.2 with indirect constraint through positive relations, I get a -3.84 t-test for indirect constraint. I get a similarly strong -3.36 for indirect constraint through negative relations. Model C in Table 4.2 re-estimated with indirect constraint through positive relations yields a -1.10 t-test for indirect constraint and a similarly negligible -1.16 for indirect constraint through negative relations.

to a customer over there. A priori, I expected the analysts to benefit more than bankers from the access to diverse information that indirect connections through neighbors can provide. I have relatively rich data on the network pattern of an analyst's work with colleagues in the third and fourth years of the four-year panel in Figure 4.4. I use the third-year control variables and network data to predict analyst performance in the fourth year. I use the fourth-year control variables and network data to predict analyst performance in the fifth year. Combining the two years, I have 351 observations. If I use annual compensation as the performance indicator, there is a strong performance correlation with the network around the analyst, and the networks around his contacts. Compensation is lower for analysts in closed networks, whether the constraint of a closed network is direct (-3.83 t-test, $P < .001$) or indirect (-3.69 t-test, $P < .001$).

Industry recognition as a performance metric[5]

There is a more sophisticated indicator of analyst performance. The substantial impact of analyst opinion on corporate finance was an incentive to rate analysts for the quality of their opinions (see Hayward and Boeker, 1998; Zuckerman, 1999; Phillips and Zuckerman, 2001; Fang and Yasuda, 2005, for complementary illustration and research review). With the growing celebrity of analysts in the 1990s, rating services multiplied.

The "All-America Research Team" is a premium service closely watched and discussed by analysts, investors, and the institutions in which both are embedded. The October issue of the trade magazine, *Institutional Investor*, names a first, second, third, and runner-up analyst in each of several industries. The election is based on votes from a few thousand institutional investors in several hundred financial organizations. Polling for the 1999 ratings was explained as follows (*Institutional Investor*, October 1999:105–106): "To select the members of this year's All-America Research Team, *Institutional Investor* sent questionnaires covering 90 industry groups and investment specialties to the directors of research and chief investment officers of major money

---

[5] I am going to show the same results for the industry recognition indicator of performance that I reported for the earlier populations: Strong performance association with direct network constraint and negligible association with indirect network constraint. I also get that pattern of results if I use analyst compensation as a performance indicator, except compensation is higher for senior job rank as reported in Table 5.1 for the bankers rather than the negligible association to be reported with industry recognition in Table 5.2 (-2.51 t-test for analyst compensation with direct network constraint, -1.62 for indirect network constraint, and a 3.58 t-test for senior job rank). I use industry recognition of analysts as a performance indicator for two reasons: It is reliable and less subject to individual differences between senior managers making internal performance evaluations and compensation decisions. Second, finding the same results with the external industry performance indicator that I found with internal performance indicators broadens the evidence base from which I draw conclusions about the lack of spillover from neighbor networks.

management institutions. Included were those managers on our rankings of the largest institutions in the U.S., as well as other key U.S., European and Asian institutions. . . . The opinions of more than 2,300 individuals—representing approximately 90 percent of the 100 largest U.S. equity managers, as well as more than 300 other key money management firms—were tapped." Analysts are rated for their stock selection, earnings forecasts, written reports, and service. The highest-rated analyst in an industry is named to the first team, the next highest to the second team, and so on. Recognition in the All-America Research Team is a coveted award associated with professional status and financial reward (Eccles and Crane, 1988:153–154; Hayward and Boeker, 1998). In fact, the award is coveted to such an extent that the election process is deliberately kept vague. Here is an excerpt from the 2005 *Institutional Investor* website: "To mitigate the likelihood of extraordinary, vote-generating activities on the part of firms or analysts during the fieldwork, it is the policy of *Institutional Investor* not to reveal the details relating to certain aspects of the survey execution process."

Election to the All-America Research Team is an indicator of analyst success, and to the extent that analyst success depends on rich and varied perspectives on the companies analyzed, I expect successful analysts to be connected to separate groups as diverse sources of information. In other words, I expect successful analysts to have social networks rich in structural holes. The empirical question is whether recognition of an analyst's performance from outside the organization employing the analyst can be predicted from the analyst's network inside the organization. The information access indicated by an analyst's network is certainly believed to be a factor. Baldwin and Rice (1997) describe personal and institutional factors correlated with rankings in the All-American Research Team. The data are more exploratory than authoritative (telephone interviews with 100 analysts, from a stratified sample of 266 contacted), but a prominent theme to the data is that personal sources of information dominate archival sources: Analysts elected to high rank on the All-America Research Team tend to work in a large company with staff colleagues, speak directly with company executives, and tend not to use library archives.

My criterion performance variable is recognition of an analyst in this year's election. Level of recognition is set to the highest level that the analyst achieved in the election: 0 for not recognized, 1 for runner-up, 2 for third team, 3 for second team, 4 for first team. I give analysts with non-zero scores in more than one industry the score for the highest recognition they achieved in any industry. I get the same associations with the network variables if I predict an analyst's aggregate recognition across industries. Analysts in my data who were recognized across industries tended to be extremely good in at least one industry. Half of the ones with non-zero scores in multiple industries were elected to the first team in at least one industry. I also include a measure of election recognition as a z-score (0 to 4 raw score minus the mean for the year across analysts in the study population, quantity divided by the standard deviation for the year). This is not a claim that election to the first versus second team is the same difference in recognition as election to the third team versus runner-up. I include predictions of z-score recognition together with logit models predicting ordinal levels of recognition to show that either provides the same results, so I can use the z-score measure in a summary graph across populations later in the book.

Who gets elected?

Table 4.3 contains the predictions. To preserve confidentiality, intercepts are not reported for the logit models. Means, standard deviations, and correlations are given in Table E5 in Appendix E.[6]

Table 4.3 Predicting Analyst Election to the *Institutional Investor* All-America Research Team

	A	B	C	D
Intercept	—	—	−.67	—
Direct Network Constraint	−2.11 (.46)**	−1.50 (.45)**	−.30 (.07)**	−1.42 (.45)**
Indirect Network Constraint	−3.04 (.84)**	−1.66 (1.03)	−.18 (.11)	.17 (.71)
Senior Job Rank	—	−.36 (.94)	−.06 (.21)	−.90 (1.04)
Peer Evaluation	—	2.49 (.94)*	.45 (.18)*	2.55 (.98)*
Years with Firm	—	−.02 (.03)	−.01 (.01)	.01 (.03)
Minority	—	.33 (.52)	.14 (.19)	.25 (.58)
US Headquarters	—	.01 (.57)	−.07 (.34)	.48 (.68)
Office in the US	—	2.31 (1.26)	.44 (.33)	2.99 (1.25)
Forecast Accuracy	—	1.60 (.61)*	.32 (.13)*	−.15 (.63)
Published Forecasts	—	—	—	2.96 (.77)**

Note: Regression coefficients are presented for annual data pooled across two years (351 observations). Election this year is predicted from the two forecast variables for this year (bottom two rows) and the other row variables for last year. Network constraint is the log of constraint. Models A, B, and D are ordinal logit regressions predicting an analyst's highest rating for the year (4 for first team, 3 for second, 2 for third, 1 for runner-up, 0 for not being named; chi-square statistics of 27.99, 40.52, and 46.28 with 2, 9, and 10 d.f.). Model C is a least-squares regression predicting the numerical value of the five rating categories expressed as a z-score for the year (.23 squared multiple correlation; zero-order correlations in Appendix E, Table E5). Standard errors, given in parentheses, are adjusted for autocorrelation within individuals across years (* $p < .05$; ** $p \le .001$).

---

[6] I use network structure one year to predict election recognition next year, but I do not make too much of the time order because election recognition is so stable over time: 84% of analysts in my data who were elected in the fourth year were re-elected in the fifth year, and there is a .91 correlation between z-score recognition in the two years (the dependent variable in Model C in Table 4.3). Standard errors in Table 4.3 are adjusted for autocorrelation in election recognition between years ("cluster" option in STATA).

Model A shows that the analysts recognized in the election this year were well-connected last year and affiliated with well-connected colleagues. Election recognition decreases with direct network constraint (−4.56 test statistic, P < .001). In other words, analysts who were network brokers this year are more likely to be elected to the All-America Research Team next year. The analyst's own network is not the key control variable as it was for the bankers. Recognition decreases significantly with indirect network constraint (−3.61 test statistic, P < .001). Holding constant an analyst's own network, analysts who worked with network-broker colleagues this year are more likely to be recognized in the election next year.

Models B, C, and D add controls for analyst location, background, and work quality. There is no longer a performance association with indirect network constraint. Models B and D predict ordinal levels of recognition. Model C predicts z-score levels of recognition. In all three models, election recognition is associated with an analyst's own network, but has no association with the networks around the analyst's contacts.

There are two kinds of controls: Six variables holding constant differences in analyst backgrounds, and two variables controlling for differences in analyst accuracy. The background variables are defined as they were in Table 4.2 for the bankers, and are similarly taken from company personnel files. The one additional background variable is "Office in the US," which equals one for analysts working in the US at the time the network was measured, zero for analysts outside the US. I added the US control variable to test for effects from a US focus in the election or the segregation between US and non-US analysts evident in the Figure 4.4 sociogram. When both network constraint variables are in the prediction, the US control variable has no association with election outcomes, from which I infer that being in the US is not as consequential for election recognition as brokering the flow of market information, which happens to be anchored in the US for this study population. Of the six background variables in Table 4.3, "Peer Evaluations" is the only one associated with election recognition across the models: Positive reputation inside the company is a robust correlate of positive reputation in the broader market outside the company.[7]

Work quality is the other significant control variable, here measured by the accuracy of an analyst's forecasts. I follow Phillips and Zuckerman (2001) in

---

[7] I suspect that job rank would be associated with election recognition if the population were expanded to lower ranks. However, estimating job-rank effects on election recognition is not the goal here. To better distinguish components in the election association with network structure, I focus on senior people, the people most at risk of recognition across institutional investors, and so most at risk of election to the All-America Research Team. "Senior Job Rank" in Table 4.3 distinguishes analysts in senior rank for both years from those promoted into senior rank during the first year. It is included in the table to control for the minimal job-rank differences between the analysts.

measuring analyst accuracy relative to competitors. "Forecast Accuracy" in Table 4.3 is the extent to which an analyst's earnings forecasts have been more accurate this year than forecasts by other analysts covering the same companies (see Appendix C). Accuracy is an aspect of analyst work often discussed, and previous research with broader samples of analysts shows that analysts who publish more accurate forecasts are more likely to get elected to the All-America Research Team (Stickel, 1992, for 1981–85; Fang and Yasuda, 2005, for 1983–2002). In keeping with past research, Models B and C show that analysts who made more accurate forecasts this year are more recognized in this year's election (respective test statistics of 2.62 and 2.37).

Accuracy alone is not the entire story. It is accuracy in published forecasts. Many people with an "analyst" job title in their organization do not publish forecasts. Specifically, I could not find forecasts in the I/B/E/S data for 74 of the 197 analysts in my data. All 197 analysts are senior people in a large financial organization, so they are not peripheral people. In fact, three of the 74 unpublished analysts were elected to the All-America Research Team during the two years under study. One explanation for the unpublished analysts is that analysts can choose not to have their name listed with their forecasts in the I/B/E/S data. Another explanation is that the "analyst" job category includes people, a great many judging from this study population, who do not make earnings forecasts about individual companies. For example, the three unpublished analysts elected to the All-America Research Team each managed a team of analysts.

Whatever the reason for the unpublished analysts, they create a problem for holding accuracy constant. The problem does not arise when a study population is defined by available archival data, because analysts who do not publish forecasts do not appear in the data (e.g., Stickel, 1992; Phillips and Zuckerman, 2001; Fang and Yasuda, 2005).

For Models B and C in Table 4.3, I solved the problem in an ad hoc way by giving unpublished analysts a z-score accuracy of zero—average—in as much as I had "found no forecasts more or less accurate than forecasts from other analysts."

I tried alternative solutions to the problem, all of which result in the same conclusion, so I present the simplest of the alternatives as Model D in Table 4.3. Model D is an ordinal logit model identical to Model B except that Model D contains in the bottom row a dummy variable, "Published Forecasts," that distinguishes analysts for whom I found forecasts in the I/B/E/S data.

Three things happen when I control for unpublished analysts. First, the negligible association between election recognition and neighbor networks drops still lower to near zero (0.24 test statistic for indirect network constraint in Model D versus -1.62 in Model B).

Second, unpublished analysts were unlikely to be recognized in the election. Publishing forecasts in the I/B/E/S data is strongly associated with election recognition (3.85 test statistic). I get the same result if I add "Published Forecasts" to Model C predicting z-score election recognition (4.62 t-test, not reported in Table 4.3). I computed a more sophisticated measure that increased with the visibility of the companies an analyst covered, but covering more visible companies added nothing to the prediction by the dummy variable "Published Forecasts" (see the last paragraph in Appendix C).

Third, accuracy is no longer directly associated with election recognition. I also obtain this result if I predict z-score election recognition, or estimate Models B and C using only observations on the analysts for whom I found forecasts in the I/B/E/S data (reducing the 351 observations in Table 4.3 to 211 observations). Publishing accurate forecasts was less important for election recognition than the publishing itself. Reporting on a broader selection of analysts, Phillips and Zuckerman (2001:410–411) also report a near-zero correlation between forecast accuracy and election recognition.

In sum, an analyst's chances of being elected to the All-America Research Team increased with publishing forecasts (so as to appear in the I/B/E/S data) and having good relationships with disconnected colleagues (positive peer evaluations and brokerage opportunities within the analyst's own network). Election recognition was not enhanced by affiliation with well-connected colleagues (indirect network constraint). Having one's own personal contacts in separate groups mattered for the analysts, as it did in the other study populations.

Conclusions

I have presented returns to network brokerage in five study populations that span a range of work environments. The performance association with brokerage has been consistent from one population to the next. I draw three conclusions from the analysis so far.

Consistent returns to brokerage

First, the results on all five populations agree with previous studies in showing returns to brokerage opportunities within a person's immediate network. People in the software product launch enjoyed higher compensation (Figure 3.4). Supply-chain managers in the large electronics company enjoyed higher compensation, more positive job evaluations, and were at higher risk of producing good ideas (Figure 3.8). HR employees in the large commercial bank enjoyed higher compensation (Figure 4.3). Investment bankers in the large financial organization enjoyed higher compensation (Table 4.2, Models A and B) and analysts in the organization were more likely to receive industry recognition for excellence (Table 4.3, Model A).

The two graphs at the top of Figure 4.5 summarize the evidence of returns to brokerage in the five study populations analyzed in this and the preceding chapter. The graphs show a performance association with network brokerage before and after other factors are held constant.

The zero-order association with network constraint is displayed in the graph to the top-left. Performance is measured relative to the average person in the same study population (z-score for an employee averaged across the one or more performance variables discussed in this and the previous chapter). I measured performance with annual evaluations and compensation, so the negative association in the graph shows that network brokers are more often praised, and better compensated, than their peers.

The graph to the top-right of Figure 4.5 shows that the association with network brokerage survives controls for other performance factors. The criterion variable in the graph is residual performance, residual in the sense that it cannot be explained by job rank, neighbor networks, or the other control variables used in each study population. For example, employee compensation in the Asia-Pacific product launch was predicted by the equation in Table 3.1, deleting "Direct Network Constraint" from the prediction. The standardized residual from that prediction is the vertical axis in the graph to the top-right in Figure 4.5. Residuals were similarly constructed in the other populations. Where I have multiple performance variables, I averaged residuals across the variables.[8] The graph is a more severe version of the graph in Figure 2.4 used to introduce the evidence of returns to network brokerage. The graph is more severe in that the controls in Figure 2.4 for year and job rank here include indirect network constraint and the other control variables in this and the previous chapter.[9]

These companies had no policy encouraging network brokerage. No company leaders had seen the networks around their employees until the studies reported here were carried out. Yet rewards went disproportionately to the employees who were network brokers. The reason is simple. When compa-

---

[8] For example, Table 3.2 contains brokerage effects on compensation, annual evaluations, and idea quality. I predicted the criterion variables in the first, second, and fourth models in Table 3.2, excluding direct network constraint, then computed standardized residuals for each model, and averaged a manager's three residual scores to define the manager's residual z-score performance score in Figure 4.5. In the product-launch network, I predicted employee compensation and evaluation separately, then computed standardized residuals for each model, and averaged an employee's two residual scores. Mean performance score remains at zero, but to re-establish unit variance, I multiplied the average residuals in these study populations by a scalar.

[9] Another difference, a minor one, is that Figure 2.4 includes seven data points from the study population to be analyzed in Chapter 7 (Figure 2.4 contains 85 data points versus 78 in the graphs at the top of Figure 4.5). The Chapter 7 population was studied with a probability sample that only provided network data on the immediate network around a respondent. The graphs at the bottom of Figure 4.5 require network data on the broader network among a respondent's friends of friends.

nies reward good work, they are rewarding employees who connect across structural holes because those are the employees more likely to do good work, because those are the employees with a competitive advantage in detecting and developing opportunities to be productive, as discussed in Chapters 1 and 2.

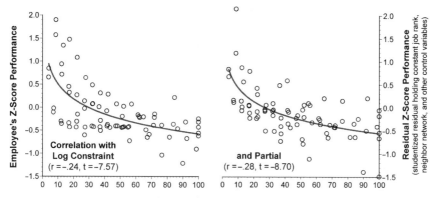

Lack of Structural Holes
in Employee's Immediate Network of Direct Contacts
(network constraint averaged within five-point intervals)

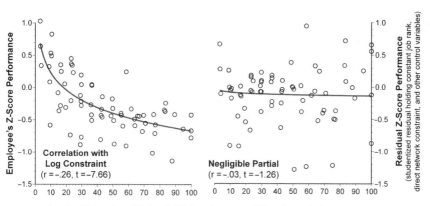

Lack of Structural Holes in Networks around Employee's Contacts
(average network constraint on contacts, averaged within five-point intervals)

Within each of five populations (analysts, investment bankers, HR employees, product-launch employees, and supply-chain managers), a dot indicates a population average on performance and network constraint within five-point intervals of network constraint. Correlations and routine test statistics are computed across 1,819 observations, with correction for repeated annual observations of the analysts and bankers.

Figure 4.5 Returns to Structural Holes in Immediate and Neighbor Networks

Negligible returns to secondhand brokerage

Second, there is no advantage to affiliating with colleagues rich in access to structural holes. The two graphs at the bottom of Figure 4.5 summarize the evidence. The two graphs were constructed for indirect network constraint just as the graphs at the top of Figure 4.5 were constructed for direct network constraint.[10]

In each population, I have found a strong correlation between performance and indirect network constraint. The criterion variable in the graph to the lower-left in Figure 4.5 is observed relative performance. The negative association in the graph is what people see when they look around the office. The people celebrated and well paid tend to be connected to network broker colleagues. It is not surprising that people sometimes think that advantage comes from affiliation with well-connected colleagues.

Also in each population, I have found that the obvious correlation is spurious. Personal characteristics that make someone an attractive contact at work—her senior job rank, her own network bridging structural holes, the visibility and quality of her work—account for the ostensible benefit of having well-connected friends. The performance association with indirect network constraint disappears in each of the populations when I control for ego's own assets. The criterion variable in the graph to the lower-right in Figure 4.5 is residual performance holding constant job rank, direct network constraint, and the other control variables used in this and the preceding chapter. There is no residual performance association with indirect network constraint when other performance factors are held constant. What makes someone an attractive contact can be different in different populations. Senior job rank makes people attractive in the more structured organizations. For the bankers, it is having your own valuable network. For the analysts, it is accurate published forecasts. Whatever the characteristic valued in a population, holding it constant eliminates the performance association with indirect network constraint

---

[10] The two graphs to the left in Figure 4.5 are based on the same criterion variable, z-score performance, but the range of scores for direct network constraint is wider than the range for indirect network constraint (−1.5 to 2.0 in the top graph, −1.5 to 1.0 in the bottom graph). The plotted data are averages within five-point intervals of network constraint, and indirect network constraint is an average score across contacts. Averaging across contacts pulls observations toward the center of the distribution so average scores within intervals of indirect network constraint pool extremely successful and unsuccessful managers with average managers. This compresses differences as discussed in Appendix B (see Table B1). For example, 17.4% of observations are contained in the central three five-point categories of direct network constraint, versus 58% for the central three categories of indirect network constraint. The standard deviation of mean performance scores in the direct network constraint graph to the upper-left in Figure 4.5 is .539, versus .451 for in the indirect network constraint graph to the lower-left. Display differences notwithstanding, the key point is that the two graphs show performance similarly correlated with direct and indirect network constraint.

at the same time that the association with direct network constraint remains strong.

I am led to the conclusion that ego's own network matters significantly for his performance, while the network around his individual colleagues matters not at all. With respect to the three processes distinguished in Figure 2.7 as potentially responsible for network advantage, the results in this and the previous chapter strongly favor personal processes. From this point forward in the book I will use the diminutive label "secondhand" brokerage—rather than spillover, leveraged, or some other more positive adjective—when describing brokerage in neighbor networks. Where direct brokerage refers to information moved across disconnected people in the immediate network, secondhand brokerage refers to information moved across disconnected friends of friends in the networks around one's colleagues. The benefit from direct brokerage is substantial. The benefit from secondhand brokerage is negligible.

The boss in particular

Certain colleagues can be singled out for closer attention. For example, the boss is in a unique position to affect returns to brokerage. The boss can get in the way of a subordinate participating in a rewarding opportunity, cauterize support for a subordinate's idea, give better assignments to preferred subordinates. More generally, a boss has opportunities to share with subordinates as a function of the boss's network access to structural holes. Returns to secondhand brokerage are negligible when measured for colleagues on average, but would the conclusion be different if the boss were considered apart from other colleagues? It turns out no. Figure 4.6 presents evidence to illustrate the conclusion.

People are compared across the horizontal axes in Figure 4.6 for the extent to which their boss reaches a large number of disconnected contacts. Specifically, the horizontal axis is the network-constraint score for ego's boss. For example, suppose that person 5 reports to person 2 in the Figure 2.3 organization. Person 2 has a network constraint score of 33.3, so person 5 would appear at 33.3 on the horizontal axes in Figure 4.6. People to the left in each graph have a boss rich in access to structural holes (low constraint). People to the right in each graph have a boss embedded in a closed network (high constraint). I have no data on formal reporting relations among the bankers and analysts. However, I am more likely to find evidence of subordinates benefiting from a well-connected boss in populations more structured by reporting relations, such as the three populations in Figure 4.6: The product launch, the supply chain, and the human resource organizations.

The graph to the left in Figure 4.6 suggests that subordinates do benefit from the social capital of their boss. Performance here is the same as in the graph to

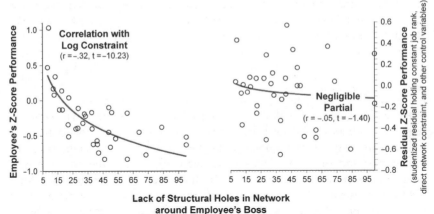

**Lack of Structural Holes in Network
around Employee's Boss**
(network constraint on boss, averaged within five-point intervals)

Each dot is a population average on the Y axis and X axis for a five-point interval on the X axis
(HR employees, product-launch employees, and supply-chain managers). Correlations and
test statistics are estimated across individual observations.

Figure 4.6 Advantage from a Well-Connected Boss

the left in Figure 4.5. For the product launch employees and HR, the graph
shows that people with a less-constrained boss enjoy higher compensation
(−5.79 t-test for the product launch, cf. Figure 3.4; −6.17 for HR, cf. Figure 4.3).
For the supply-chain managers, performance is the average of three z-score
indicators: Higher compensation, more positive job evaluations, and higher-
value ideas. All three are associated with having a less-constrained boss (−6.70
t-test for summary measure in Figure 4.6, −6.85 for compensation alone,
−3.40 for evaluations, −3.30 for idea value, cf. Figure 3.8).

The graph to the right in Figure 4.6 shows that the performance association
disappears when job rank and other background variables are held constant.
More specifically, I get a negligible −1.00 t-test for the product-launch employees if I replace "Indirect Network Constraint" in Table 3.1 with the log of
constraint in the boss's network. The association with residual compensation
is similarly negligible in the HR organization when I replace "Indirect Network
Constraint" in Table 4.1 with the log of boss constraint (−0.12 t-test). Test
statistics are negligible in Table 3.2 for log boss constraint predicting supply-
chain manager compensation, job evaluation, or idea value (respective t-tests
of 0.44, −.55, and −1.34).

In sum, there is no benefit to having a boss whose network spans structural
holes. Such bosses tend to occupy high job ranks so their subordinates occupy
high job ranks, and job rank is associated with having connections across structural holes. The association could reflect the increasing diversity of connections
required by jobs higher in the corporate hierarchy, or it could be that bosses rich

in access to structural holes develop, or attract, subordinates with networks that span structural holes. Either way, Figure 4.6 shows that advantage to a subordinate depends on having one's own connections across structural holes.[11]

Best-connected colleague

If not the boss, the key could be one well-connected colleague. The colleague could be the boss, but it does not have to be. One well-connected colleague could be sufficient to reveal or support a great opportunity.[12] The two graphs in Figure 4.7 correspond to the two graphs in Figure 4.6 except the contact whose network constraint is measured on the horizontal axis in Figure 4.7 is not the boss; it is the colleague who reaches the largest number of disconnected contacts. The colleague with the broadest reach is ego's "best-connected" colleague, identified by searching across ego's direct contacts for the person with the lowest network constraint score. For example, person 2 in Figure 2.3 has three colleagues. The three colleagues have constraint scores 58.3 (for persons 5 and 6) and 33.3 (for person 1), so person 2's best-connected colleague is person 1, and person 2 would appear at 33.3 on the horizontal axes in Figure 4.7. The bankers and analysts are included here since I can identify their "best-connected" colleague.

The pattern of data in Figure 4.7 looks very similar to the pattern in Figure 4.6 and the pattern in Figure 4.5. Data are more compressed in Figure 4.7 since these are best-connected colleagues, but the data patterns are otherwise very

---

[11] These results assume that each employee has full access to his or her boss' network. In fact, what the boss has in terms of opportunities is distributed to the boss' subordinates. If the boss has a favorite subordinate, that subordinate will get a disproportionate share of whatever the boss has to distribute. There might be no boss-constraint effect because favorite subordinates (who benefit from the boss' network) are balanced by other subordinates (who do not benefit from the boss' network). Span of control is another consideration. Where a boss has fewer subordinates, each can expect a larger share of whatever the boss has to offer. For the moment, these considerations, and others like them, are an interesting aside. The main result here is that a strong association between performance and boss constraint (left-graph in Figure 4.6) disappears when job rank, ego's own network, and other controls are held constant (right-graph in Figure 4.6).

[12] The imagery here is analogous to networks providing social support: When you are depressed or going through an emotionally difficult time, a large network of contacts can be too diffuse to provide support, or even be a burden to maintain, while having just one very close confidant can be a great assistance. Reporting on a panel survey of people in a metropolitan area, Lin, Ye, and Ensel (1999) predict the level of a respondent's depression from respondent participation in community organizations, frequency of contact with kind of people, and having a spouse or partner confidant. Participation in the community had no effect on depression, contact frequency slightly alleviated depression, and having a confidant strongly alleviated depression. In an earlier panel study, Lin, Dumin, and Woelfel (1986) found that the number of a respondent's contacts increased depression while having a confidant strongly decreased depression.

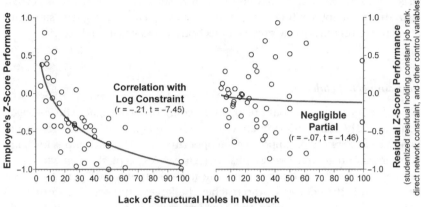

Lack of Structural Holes In Network
around Employee's Least-Constrained Colleague
(network constraint on least-constraint direct contact, averaged within five-point intervals)

Each dot is a population average on the Y axis and X axis for a five-point interval on the X axis
(analysts, bankers, HR employees, product-launch employees, and supply-chain managers).
Correlations and test statistics are estimated across individual observations with
correction for repeated annual observations of the analysts and bankers.

Figure 4.7 Advantage from Best-Connected Colleague

similar. To the left, there is a strong performance association with the brokerage available through a person's average colleague (Figure 4.5), boss (Figure
4.6), or best-connected colleague (Figure 4.7). To the right, the performance
association disappears when job rank, the immediate network, and other
controls are held constant. The graph in Figure 4.7 shows no pattern of
association between residual performance and constraint on a person's best-
connected colleague. The negligible aggregate association displayed occurs in
each study population: I get a negligible 0.30 t-test for the product-launch
employees when I replace "Indirect Network Constraint" in Table 3.1 with
constraint on an employee's best-connected colleague. The association with
compensation is similarly negligible in the HR organization when I replace
"Indirect Network Constraint" in Table 4.1 with best-connected-colleague
constraint (0.81 t-test). Test statistics are negligible in Table 3.2 for best-connected-colleague constraint predicting supply-chain manager compensation,
job evaluation, or idea value (t-tests of 0.15, −.76, and −1.49 respectively).
The same result occurs among the investment bankers and analysts (respective
t-tests of −1.64 and −.72 in Tables 4.2 and 4.3).

Negative spillover

Negligible returns to secondhand brokerage exclude positive and negative
returns, so this segment might seem redundant to the preceding text. However, this is a convenient place to address the sometimes-voiced concern that

brokers make their gains by exploiting their neighbors. Up to this point, I have discussed possible benefit available from neighbor networks. There is a frame of reference within which brokers are dangerous neighbors.

The suspicion that brokers advance by exploiting their neighbors can be made more specific in analogy to Karen Cook's work with various colleagues on performance in laboratory exchange networks. The lab networks are similar to the Figure 2.3 sociogram in containing brokers at increasing removes from the center, person 1 more central than persons 2, 3, 4, and so on (Cook and Emerson, 1978:726; Cook *et al.*, 1983:280). The lab networks are different from Figure 2.3 in that people at the periphery of the lab networks (persons 11 to 28 in Figure 2.3) have weak rather than strong relations with one another. Performance in the lab networks is measured by "profit points" accumulated from negotiated exchanges with partners defined by network links (e.g., person 1 in Figure 2.3 would be allowed to exchange with person 2; see Cook *et al.*, 1983:290–293, for the network design and basic results). The results show that brokers earn high scores by exploiting neighbors who depend on them. Brokers take a disproportionate share—71 percent to be exact—of "profit points" from exchanges with dependent neighbors.[13]

To illustrate, imagine that the strong relations between group members in Figure 2.3 were made weak, as in the lab networks. Advantage would be concentrated in the group leaders (e.g., person 5) because their exchange alternatives would include group members (e.g., persons 11, 12, 13) whose best exchange options would be with their group leader while the group leader had other equally good options. Over time, group leaders would emerge as the most successful people because they can exploit the dependence of subordinates in their group. Group members would do poorly because they have no attractive alternative to exchange with their group leader. Brokers more central than the group leaders would do poorly because they have no exclusive relations through which they can abuse a neighbor.[14]

Strong connections within the groups make a difference. Group members in Figure 2.3 can turn to one another for exchange and support. Group leaders do not have exclusive exchange relations with the people in their group.

---

[13] This number is from results reported by Cook *et al.* (1983:293). Of the 24 profit points possible in an exchange, brokers with an incentive to maximize profit take an average of 17.19 with more-central neighbors, and 16.91 with more-peripheral neighbors (see next footnote). Average the two results and divided by the 24 points possible to get the 71% reported in the text. Like Cook *et al.* (1983:293) I use results from the final period of the experiment, "since the emergence of power use is expected to occur over time."

[14] Group-member dependence is exploited sooner than other-broker dependence. Across three blocks of exchange in the high-incentive experiment, each block containing nine transactions, here are the average profit points taken by team leaders from exchanges with group members (Cook *et al.*, 1983:293, these are the position E exchanges with position F in the lab network):

$$15.52 \ (2.38) \qquad 16.66 \ (2.10) \qquad 16.91 \ (2.46)$$

But this assumes people have fungible resources, such as the "profit points" in the laboratory experiment, that can be exchanged equally well between any two people linked in the network.

Suppose instead that success comes from bringing together different kinds of information. Then group members are again at a disadvantage because their only option to exchanging with the group leader is to exchange with other members of the group, and people in the same group have the same information. In addition, most of each group leader's exchange partners are within their group. Each group leader has a single connection to information beyond the group: Their relationship with the middle brokers, persons 2, 3, or 4. The middle brokers are best positioned to move information across groups because their contact with different groups provides access to different kinds of information at the same time that their proximity to groups increases the odds of them understanding each group sufficient to successfully translate information from one group into the interests of another. Moreover, middle brokers are the only source to the groups for information about the center (person 1), and the middle brokers are gatekeepers for center access to information on the groups. Over time, the middle brokers would emerge as the strongest people, followed by the center, followed at some distance by the group leaders, then the group members. The less easily information moves between groups, the greater the potential advantage to exclusive-access brokers just outside the groups.

The imagery here is a zero-sum game in which people drift toward preferred exchange partners with whom they can transact more advantageous exchanges. People with less choice in exchange partners are abused by brokers, who have more choice. These results make intuitive sense and can fuel a suspicion that the documented advantages enjoyed by network brokers come at a cost to their neighbors (Brass, 2009; Fernandez-Mateo, 2007; Bidwell and Fernandez-Mateo, 2007; cf., Foster's, 1965, 1972, description of peasants understanding the world as a place of "limited good" such that people who move ahead must have done so at the cost to the rest of us so it is wise to be suspicious of people who do well).

---

where standard deviations are given in parentheses. Here are the points taken by team leaders from exchanges with their contact more central in the network (Cook *et al.*, 1983:293, these are the position E exchanges with position D in the lab network):

$$12.90 \ (3.71) \qquad 13.72 \ (4.40) \qquad 17.19 \ (5.25)$$

There is more variability in the points taken from the more-central broker, exchanges begin with close to a 50/50 split of profit points (across the first nine exchanges, team leader takes an average 12.90 of the 24 points available, leaving an average of 11.10 points for the more-central broker), then shift to match the exploitation of group members in the final exchanges. Group members are more obvious objects of exploitation, judging from the fact that they are exploited in the first exchanges as much as they are in the final exchanges.

Negative spillover can certainly exist. I expect that a person who has exclusive access to another person for a long time can become accustomed to asymmetry in the relationship such that extracting a disproportionate share of resources is not seen as exploitation so much as it is just the natural order of things, the accepted market price for the transaction. This is the evidence from Cook's lab exchange networks in which brokers learn over time to exploit the people dependent upon them (e.g., Cook *et al.*, 1983:293–294). It is the evidence from Bidwell and Fernandez-Mateo's (2007) detailed analysis showing that contingency workers receive a decreasing share of their earnings the longer they stay with the same placement firm. This kind of negative spillover is not exclusive to brokerage, but it could occur with prolonged dependence on a broker. The more general point is that prolonged dependence on a stronger person can foster feelings of *droit de seigneur* in the stronger person and learned helplessness in the weaker person (Peterson, Maier, and Seligman, 1993), whatever the criterion for deeming the other person stronger.

To say negative spillover can exist is not to say it is the norm. Without implying that network brokers are pleasant company, or never abusive, I can say that the image of brokers succeeding by abusing neighbors does not fit the five populations analyzed here. Associations between performance and broker neighbors are positive in each population (graphs to the left in Figures 4.5, 4.6, and 4.7). The positive associations go to zero when controls are introduced, but there is no evidence in any population of a negative effect from affiliation with network brokers.

The lack of negative spillover here could be attributed to the impropriety of zero-sum behavior between colleagues. Zero-sum behavior can seem reasonable in industry buying and selling, and will be discussed in the next chapter. A price that benefits the seller comes at a cost to the buyer. Between colleagues, however, the same behavior is rude, and potentially harmful over time. If negative spillover is limited to zero-sum behavior, and zero-sum behavior is avoided between colleagues, then I would be surprised to see evidence of negative spillover in colleague discussion networks.

Whatever the explanation, the consistent lack of negative spillover in diverse populations leads me to the conclusion that such spillover is not a typical feature of organizations. I am left to repeat the conclusion that there is neither positive nor negative performance effect to affiliation with a broker, whether the broker is the boss, a manager's average contact, or the manager's best-connected colleague.

Probably true in organizations generally

My third conclusion concerns the scope of my second: Secondhand brokerage is unlikely to be valuable in any organization.

It is common practice—in some part a result of efforts to make efficient use of scarce space in prestigious journals—to report and cite empirical findings on an organization as if the findings were true of all organizations. Reports sometimes move higher on the research-quality dimension by including a comment about the study organization being strategically suited to research on the findings, but the fact remains that inference is being drawn from a cluster of observations related by dint of being in the same organization, not a probability sample of independent observations in a heterogeneous population.

By common practice, any of the five study populations introduced in this or the previous chapter could have been used to draw my conclusion about second-hand brokerage. None of the study populations show returns to secondhand brokerage, and it would certainly be more efficient to present results on a single population.

Results are not identical across populations, so my job as author would include selecting the population to present that provides the most compelling evidence. The HR organization provides strong results in the sense that it provides the largest test statistic for returns to brokerage. The supply-chain managers provide robust results given replication with three performance indicators. The analysts provide interestingly subtle results since there is evidence of returns to second-hand brokerage right up until I control for publishing reports.

However, result differences between the populations pale in comparison to the consistency across populations. A feature of this and the previous chapter is the consistent lack of returns to secondhand brokerage in populations showing substantial returns to direct brokerage.

Result consistency is only a feature if the five study populations differ such that consistency would not be expected a priori. Consistent results in identical populations indicate reliability, not replication. There is face validity to claiming that the populations are different. Managing supplies for a large electronics company is a kind of work profoundly different from the work of investment bankers or analysts in a global financial organization.

Beyond face validity, the five populations were selected for their differences in network connectivity, which is relevant here because brokerage opportunities in neighbor networks are more likely valuable in better-connected groups. If people are segregated into separate groups, complex tacit knowledge within groups is more likely, making clear communication across groups difficult without direct brokerage. Research that does not find evidence of returns to neighbor networks in populations segregated into separate groups is open to criticism that the research site was biased in favor of the null hypothesis. In contrast, where people in separate groups are connected by short indirect connections, the people are more likely to communicate often such that they are able to more clearly com-municate opinion and practice from their respective business activities—so they are more likely to benefit from the broad reach of brokerage opportunities in neighbor networks. Research that does not find returns to neighbor networks in populations where people can communicate clearly through indirect connec-tions raises a serious question about the value of secondhand brokerage.

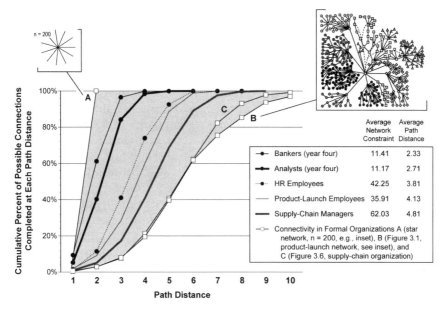

Figure 4.8 Connectivity in the Five Study Populations

Figure 4.8 shows how the study populations used here differ in connectivity. The graph shows the distribution of path distances and provides a frame of reference for comparing populations. The horizontal axis measures path distance, the shortest chain of relations needed to connect two people. With respect to the formal organization of the product-launch displayed in Figure 3.1, the 330 reporting relations are path distances of one step. The people to whom your boss reports are two steps away from you in the formal organization, and so on. The vertical axis in Figure 4.8 is possible connections completed at each level of path distance. For example, the 330 reporting relations in Figure 3.1 are 0.6 percent of the 54,615 possible connections between pairs of 331 people (N[N–1]/2 possible connections in a network of N people). The table in Figure 4.8 reports the mean level of network constraint and mean path distance in each population (patterned after Watts and Strogetz's, 1998:441, use of mean density and mean path distance to indicate small-world properties in a population). Higher average constraint indicates people more surrounded by interconnected discussion partners. Higher path distance indicates that communication across the population required more intermediaries.

The shaded area in the graph is where I expect most organizations to exist. The left side of the area is bounded by a thin solid line (labeled "A") that describes strong connectivity. Consider what the highest level of connectivity in a formal organization would look like. Everyone can reach everyone else in an organization through symmetric reporting relations, so the most connected organization would be a "star" structure in which everyone reported to the same boss. Each employee would be one step from the boss and two steps from everyone else. A Figure 4.8 cumulative plot of connectivity in such a network would have two levels: A small percentage for direct connections (specifically in a population of N people, [N–1] connections between boss and employee divided by N*[N–1]/2 connections possible), then 100 percent for two-step indirect connections between employees through the boss. In a star structure of 200 people, for example, one percent of the 19,900 possible connections would be realized in one step, then 100 percent realized in two steps. That organization is the left-most side of the shaded area in Figure 4.8.

The right side of the shaded area describes weak connectivity. The line labeled "B" describes connectivity in the Figure 3.1 formal organization of the product-launch network. This is a baseline in that the organization contained long path distances because employees were segregated in regional clusters. The 330 direct reporting relations are 0.6 percent of the network. Adding the 1,206 two-step indirect connections brings connectivity to 2.8 percent. Adding the 2,813 three-step indirect connections brings connectivity up to 8.0 percent, and so on, out to path distances of ten steps with which 97.0 percent of the network is connected. As mentioned in Chapter 3, the longest path distance was a 14-step connection between a finance person at corporate and one of the field employees. The line in Figure 4.8 labeled "C" describes connectivity in the Figure 3.6 formal organization of the supply-chain managers. This is a baseline in that the supply-chain managers were the largest of the five study populations analyzed and there were numerous maximum-length path distances between the managers because they were segregated by geography and product into legacy organizations (there were 10 path distances of 14 steps among the supply-chain managers).

The other lines in Figure 4.8 describe connectivity in the informal organization of the five study populations. The point illustrated is that the study populations span the space of the area shaded in the graph. The thin solid line without dots in Figure 4.8 describes the product-launch network. People are connected by shorter path distances in the informal organization than they were in the formal organization (line B in Figure 4.8), showing that discussion cuts across formal chains of command to improve connectivity: 1.9 percent of connections were direct, 7.2 percent of possible connections were complete with two-step indirect connections, and so on. Path distances of eight or fewer discussion relations were sufficient to connect everyone in the product launch. The bold solid line without dots is to the right of the product-launch line, showing that the supply-chain managers were less connected than the employees in the product launch—path distances were slightly longer on average (4.81 steps versus 4.13) and the managers were much more likely to discuss work within a densely connected cluster of colleagues (62.03 mean network constraint versus 35.91). The dashed line in the middle of the shaded area shows that the HR organization was much more connected than the supply-chain organization and more connected than the product launch (though the tendency was similar to discuss work with interconnected colleagues). Further to the left, the analysts and bankers were more connected than the HR employees. There was low clustering around the bankers and analysts (respective means of 11.14 and 11.17 for network constraint) and short path distances to colleagues (respective averages of 2.71 and 2.33). The bankers were the most connected of all: 61 percent of the bankers are friends of friends and 97 percent can reach one another in path distances of three steps or less. The thin line describing path distances among the bankers is close to the maximum-connectivity line bordering the left side of the shaded area. The bold solid line describing connectivity among the supply-chain managers is close to the weak-connectivity line bordering the right side of the shaded area. In other words, the five study populations span the shaded area in the graph.

That leaves uncovered the area to the right of the shaded area in Figure 4.8. Organizations to the right are more segregated into separate groups than the segregation visible between regional and administrative groups in the product launch (Figure 3.1). Such organizations surely can be found, but there is a more certain way to expand to the right in Figure 4.8: Study employees deeper in the organization. Imagine an organization composed of two divisions only connected by a relationship between the two top people in each division. In a study population composed of the leadership team in each division, the longest path distance will be three: One step to your boss, another step to the boss of the other division, and one step to his subordinates. Expand the population to include people two levels down in each division and the longest path distance in the population would be seven steps. Expand two more levels and the longest path distance would be 11 steps. The example is extreme in that there are typically multiple connections between the organization silos in a company. The point illustrated by the simple example still holds: With people focused on the immediate environment around them, connections between organization silos are more likely between people at the top of the silos, so path distances will be longer in study populations that include people in lower job ranks. Longer path distances move the grey area in Figure 4.8 further to the right. However, employees at lower job ranks in the organizations studied in this book, or employees in other organizations to the right in Figure 4.8, do not upset my conclusion about secondhand brokerage. People in organizations to the right in Figure 4.8 are more segregated into separate groups than the people studied in this book. More segregation increases the likelihood of complex, tacit knowledge within groups, which makes communication between groups more difficult without direct brokerage, which decreases the odds of returns to secondhand brokerage.

In short, the study populations analyzed in this and the preceding chapter span the space of organizations such that my conclusion about secondhand brokerage has broad application. Pending authoritative evidence to the contrary, I do not expect to see returns to secondhand brokerage in any organization.

The evidence presented so far strongly supports an inference that social capital advantage results from the personal processes described in Chapter 2 (the dashed line in Figure 2.7). The evidence severely weakens an inference that advantage results from the global processes described in Chapter 2 (the bold line in Figure 2.7). There is consistent evidence of negligible returns to neighbor networks for the managers (implying personal processes) and no evidence of increasing returns to neighbor networks (which would have implied global processes). As I mentioned in Chapter 1, technological advances have given us the ability to reach across previously unimagined distance, but value, on average, is still produced close to home. Social capital seems to be a phenomenon personal and local.

Part II

TESTING THE PERIMETER

FIVE

Industry Networks

A central tenet in network theory, perhaps the central tenet, is that causal spark is released by the pattern in which relations intersect. Something about the pattern of relations intersecting in a network node encourages, facilitates, or inhibits. Specific models focus on the spark released by a specific pattern. Whatever the causal spark, it is expected from the relational pattern regardless of where the pattern occurs; in a person, a team, an organization, a geographic region.

For example, the network status model that Podolny (1993) uses to explain why certain investment banks are able to obtain capital at more attractive rates is the same eigenvector model used by Kadushin (1995) to describe the status of individuals in the French financial elite.

The network brokerage model that Freeman (1977) uses to explain why certain people are more satisfied in a laboratory task is the same model used by Owen-Smith and Powell (2004) to explain why certain companies are more likely to file successful patent applications. The network brokerage model that Burt (1992: chap. 3) uses to explain why profit margins are high in certain markets is the same model used in the subsequent chapter of the same book to explain why certain managers are promoted more quickly to senior job rank in a large organization.

The simple embedding model used to describe mutual contacts increasing the persistence of relationships and reputations (e.g., Feld, 1997; Krackhardt, 1998; Burt, 2005:chap. 4) is the same model that Gulati and Gargiulo (1999) use to describe the higher odds of repeated alliances between firms with mutual alliance partners, that Ingram and Roberts (2000) use to describe mutual friendships enhancing the survival of hotels, that Rowley *et al.* (2005) use to describe mutual contacts lowering the probability of exit from investment-bank cliques.

Consistent network theory across levels of analysis is attractive because the consistency is a bridge for analogies between otherwise disparate research results, which is all the more powerful because disparate research results are likely to have complementary strengths if the results can be compared in a meaningful way. As illustrated by the examples cited in the previous paragraphs, network explanations for performance differences between people can be used to draw inferences about performance differences between macro units of analysis such as organizations or industries or regions—just as network explanations for macro performance differences can be used to draw inferences about performance differences between people. The integrative and cross-fertilizing potential of network theory consistent across levels of analysis has contributed in some part to the widespread use of network models in studies of competitive advantage.

Now the problem: My conclusion in the preceding chapter that managers do not benefit from indirect access to structural holes raises a question about consistency across levels of analysis. It is not the empirical fact that is troubling so much as the fact's implication that returns to network brokerage are a result of social psychological processes in the broker rather than a result of the broker having early access to distant information. The role of cognition and emotion in network brokerage makes sense for sentient individuals. It is not obvious how the image of sentient individuals applies at the macro level. Organizations, and the industries and regions in which they operate, are assemblies of people who individually think and feel. To attribute thinking and feeling to macro units such as organizations, industries, or regions, requires an unattractively anthropomorphic metaphor. To continue the "better glasses or better eyes" metaphor in the discussion of network brokerage as a forcing function for human capital, the "better glasses" explanation generalizes readily to the macro level of organizations and markets. The "better eyes" story, with its emphasis on enhanced cognitive and emotional skills, does not. News media and students often talk about organizations as though they were sentient beings, for example, when emotions result in one company paying too much for another. Those emotions were not the company's. Any emotion involved resided in the managers responsible for the acquisition.

It would be useful to see macro-level evidence on performance and indirect access to structural holes to know how the secondhand brokerage results for people play out across the broader organization and market networks in which people are embedded. Is the lack of returns to secondhand brokerage a generic feature of network structure, or something specific to the way that individual people are advantaged by their surrounding network? In this chapter, I regress industry profits across network measures of producer access to structural holes among their suppliers and customers. Holding constant differences in producer rivalry within industries, profits increase significantly with the structural holes among suppliers and customers. The industry returns to direct brokerage resemble the returns documented in the previous two chapters for people. As previous work has shown, there is a micro-macro consistency for network models of brokerage applied to people, organizations, and industries.

I then add to the prediction indirect producer access to structural holes in the networks around their suppliers and customers. Indirect access is an advantage. Industry profits increase significantly with the extent to which producers do business with suppliers and customers who are themselves advantaged by their own network of suppliers and customers. With respect to the three mechanisms illustrated in Figure 2.7, there is no evidence of the global processes that would generate increasing advantage from business with advantaged suppliers and customers. There is clearly no empirical support for the personal processes supported in the previous two chapters. I am left with local processes as the mechanism responsible for returns to brokerage in industry networks. This is a boundary condition for the secondhand brokerage reported in the previous two chapters, a boundary condition I discuss as a function of the way information moves between industries versus people.

Fair warning: Data are treated differently here than in the preceding chapters. In the previous chapters, measurement detail was often pushed to the appendices. I outsourced data collection to Appendix A, and network measures to Appendix B. More data detail is retained in this chapter. The change reflects the data. Measuring interpersonal networks involves several decisions that vary from scholar to scholar: Population boundaries are defined in different ways, different kinds of relations are recorded, different scales are used to record relations, and so on. I use the appendices to make my decisions explicit so that the results reported here can be replicated and assessed, but I saw no need to drag readers through the details of idiosyncratic measurement decisions. In contrast, industry networks are measured with census data from input–output and concentration tables. The data are the same for every scholar, so results should be point-estimate comparable across scholars, and measurement is a key element in any research hypothesis. Relative to the previous chapters, therefore, I speak with a little more precision about the data in this chapter.

Direct Access to Structural Holes

As manager networks rich in structural holes provide an advantage in detecting and developing opportunities by exposing managers to diverse business opinion and practice, advantage comes twice at the macro level to producer organizations with hole-rich networks of suppliers and customers. (1) Within supplier and customer industries, structural holes mean more likely variation in business practice so there is something for producers to learn from the industry (groups separated by structural holes are more likely to evolve on separate paths), and competing organizations within the industry mean that producers can play them against one another to negotiate attractive prices. (2) Between supplier and customer industries, structural holes mean that large firms are unlikely to have integrated operations across the industries, so the producer advantages of within-industry holes occur between industries: More likely exposure to variation in business practice, and more likely independent competitors that can be played against one another. Using gross profit margins to measure performance, producer margins on average should increase with the structural holes in their immediate network of suppliers and customers. This was the initial intuition for returns to network brokerage at the macro level here stated in a multiplicative form as a baseline model for the chapter:

$$A = \alpha \, (k-O)^\beta \, C^\gamma,$$

where A is producer "structural autonomy," an advantage provided by an industry's network position in the economy, α is an intercept term, O is a measure of producer coordination within an industry, k is a constant just above the upper limit of O so $(k-O)$ measures the lack of coordination between industry producers, β measures the corrosive effect of disorganized producers, C is a network constraint measure of producer dependence on well-organized suppliers and customers, and γ measures the corrosive effect of organized suppliers or customers (Burt, 1980, 1983, 1992:chap. 3; Burt *et al.*, 2002).

Network constraint C at the industry level is defined by the same weights that define network constraint at the level of individual people (c_{ij} in equation B2 in Appendix B), but there is now a question of contacts organized within customer and supplier industries to exploit producer dependence on them. Producer dependence on another industry is not a problem if establishments in the other industry can be played against one another. Dependence is a problem when there are few alternatives within a key supplier or customer industry. Network constraint on industry i is a weighted sum of dependence on supplier-customer industries j in which business in industry j is concentrated in a few dominant companies:

$$C_i = \Sigma_j \, c_{ij} O_j, \, i \neq j,$$

where O_j is the coordination of businesses in market j, measured as it is measured for the producer market. The $c_{ij}O_j$ term is a network measure of the condition that Pfeffer and Salancik (1978:51) so productively explored as resource dependence: "Dependence can then be defined as the product of the importance of a given input or output to the organization and the extent to which it is controlled by a relative few organizations." The network constraint index C is the sum of such dependencies, measuring the extent to which producers are dependent on coordinated suppliers or customers. With respect to Porter's (1980:4) five-forces metaphor—grounded in the economics of industrial organization (e.g., Caves, 1992) and a close relative in time and content to Pfeffer and Salancik's resource dependence metaphor—β measures the negative effect on industry profits from producer "rivalry" within the industry and γ measures negative effects from "supplier power" and "buyer power."

In sum, structural autonomy is a baseline industry model in which estimates of β and γ should be negative (Burt, 1992:85): "where the distribution of structural holes in a product network gives producers a negotiating advantage, producers can be expected to negotiate prices in their favor, visible as higher profit margins. The specific hypothesis is that profit margins increase with absent structural holes between producers, O, and decrease with the lack of holes between suppliers and customers, C." Estimates of β and γ have been significantly negative in the American economy since the 1960s and in other economies where estimates are available (Burt *et al.*, 2002). The estimates express empirically the old idea that monopolists do well exploiting disorganized partners. The optimum industry network for profits combines coordination inside the industry with brokerage outside the industry (high O combined with low C; see Burt, 2005:139–146 for a performance surface plot of industry data; cf. Shipilov, 2006:599; Baum, van Liere, and Rowley, 2008: Figure 3a, for similar graphs describing company data within an industry).

Network data on industry dependencies

Much of the data needed to estimate industry network effects can be obtained at high quality in the U. S. Department of Commerce benchmark input–output tables. Each table is a network of dollar flows between sectors of economic activity: Cell (i,j) is dollars of goods purchased by organizations in sector j from organizations in sector i. In theory, organizations assigned to the same input–output sector, or industry, draw supplies in similar proportions from the same supplier industries and sell product in similar proportions to the same customer industries. Thus, an input–output table is a summary network, like a density table, describing patterns of buying and selling between structurally equivalent organizations (Burt, 1988; Burt and Carleton, 1989), and an input–output industry composed of structurally equivalent organizations corresponds to a market in that the industry contains organizations competing for the same supplier and customer business (Burt, 1992:208–215). Regional markets, government regulations, business practice, and data limitations must create data deviations from theory, but the industry concept remains in theory a concept of industry organizations using similar processes, to produce similar goods, available to customers according to customer input requirements. Treating the input–output dollar flows as cells in a network density table, the contact-specific weight c_{ij} in equation (B2), in Appendix B, can be computed with p_{ij} defined as the proportion of industry i buying and selling across industries that is conducted with establishments in industry j: $p_{ij} = (z_{ij} + z_{ji}) / (\Sigma_k z_{ik} + \Sigma_k z_{ki} - z_{ii})$, where z_{ij} is dollars of sales from industry i to j in the input–output table, and k ranges across all production categories in the table (i.e., everything excluding government and final demand).[1]

---

[1] After suppliers and customers in an industry's immediate network are identified, proportions are normalized within the immediate network to compute network constraint. Proportions p_{ij} in the text are normalized to sum to one across all production industries in the economy. As reported in Table D2 in Appendix D, I get stronger network constraint effects if I compute constraint from p_{ij} normalized within the immediate network around an industry: $p_{ij} = p_{ij} / \Sigma_k p_{ik}$, $i \neq j$, where the sum is across all industries k in the immediate network excluding industry i itself. This assumes that the connections most relevant to the focal industry are the connections within its immediate network, not connections across the economy. Normalizing within the immediate network is what is done with manager networks when relations beyond the immediate network are unknown (as is often the case in survey network data), so I am comfortable using the same operationalization with industry networks to obtain stronger network effects.

Defined by these proportions, contact-specific weight c_{ij} varies from 0 to 1 with the extent to which producer buying and selling is directly (p_{ij}) or indirectly ($\Sigma_q\, p_{iq}p_{qj}$) with establishments in market j. The dependence asymmetry matters between two industries as supplier and customer (Casciaro and Piskorski, 2006), but I can make my point in this chapter with aggregate producer dependence on another industry as supplier or customer.

In this chapter, I estimate effects for detailed manufacturing industries in 1987 and 1992. I use the most detailed input–output categories to preserve the highest level of structural equivalence available between producers treated as competitors in the same industry. I focus on the years 1987 and 1992 for consistent, reliable sector definitions. The US Department of Commerce expanded distinctions between service sectors in the 1987 benchmark input–output table, then shifted from Standard Industrial Classification (SIC) business categories to the North American Industrial Classification System (NAICS) for 1997 and later benchmark input–output tables (Lawson *et al.*, 2002). Sector definitions in the 1987 and 1992 panels are similarly expanded from earlier benchmark tables, but still based on SIC categories familiar to the operations people at the Department of Commerce before they changed over to the substantially different NAICS categories. Dollar flows between industries can be downloaded from the US Department of Commerce, Bureau of Economic Analysis website (www.bea.gov/industry/io_benchmark.htm). Excluding government and final demand, the 1987 benchmark input–output table distinguishes 469 production sectors, of which 362 are manufacturing (Lawson and Teske, 1994). Respective numbers for the 1992 table are 485 and 361 (Lawson, 1997). There is almost no difference between manufacturing industries in the two tables. The one difference is that chewing gum and a portion of candy manufacturing are separate sectors in 1987, but combined in 1992 (sectors 142001 and 142003 in 1987 are combined as sector 142005 in 1992). For consistency across the tables, I combined the two 1987 candy categories to correspond to their combined category in the 1992 table. Thus, I have 361 manufacturing industries in 1987 and 1992.

Each industry is subject to some level of network constraint in its buying and selling with suppliers and customers in the other 402 industries. Producer dependence is combined with the data on organization within other industries to compute measures of direct and indirect network constraint. To compute the network constraint scores for an industry, I need a measure of coordination within each of the 402 potential supplier or customer industries.

Industry concentration

I follow standard practice in using market shares to measure the extent to which producers are coordinated within an industry. The four-firm concentration ratio for an industry varies from 0 to 100 as the percent of industry output that comes from the four firms producing the largest volumes of industry output. Higher concentration is presumed to indicate more coordination, less rivalry, so producers can price for higher profit margins. The four-firm concentration ratio of 91 percent in the 1987 "Tire and Cord Fabric" industry indicates that almost all industry output came from establishments operated by one of the four leading firms in the industry. In contrast, concentration in the 1987 "Sheet Metal Work" industry indicates that only 10 percent of industry output came from the four leading firms, so there must be numerous other competitors within the industry.

Concentration ratios for manufacturing industries in 1987 and 1992 are available from the US Census Bureau website for four-digit Standard Industrial Classification (SIC) categories (www.census.gov/epcd/www/concentration. html). The input–output tables are published with a list of SIC categories that map into each input–output category. Of the 361 manufacturing industries on which I have input–output data, 320 correspond to a unique four-digit SIC category. The other 41 correspond to multiple four-digit SIC categories. For example, the input–output "Sugar" industry (141900) is composed of three four-digit SIC categories (2061 "Cane Sugar," 2062 "Cane Sugar Refining," and 2063 "Beet Sugar"). For the 41 manufacturing industries that correspond to multiple four-digit SIC categories, concentration is averaged across component SIC categories, weighting by the volume of business in each component category: $\Sigma_k CR_k*(S_k /[\Sigma_k S_k])$, where CR_k is the four-firm concentration ratio in component SIC category k, and S_k is dollars of sales by establishments in SIC category k.

Buying and selling with 42 aggregate industries beyond manufacturing is included in the network measures. The industries are taken from a network analysis of boundaries between detailed input–output categories of agriculture, mining, construction, distribution, and services. The 42 non-manufacturing industries are described in Appendix D and listed with concentration scores for 1987 and 1992. There are no authoritative concentration scores in these industries. Input–output tables provide dollar-flow data beyond manufacturing, but there are no measures of producer organization comparable to the concentration data on manufacturing. Concentration in non-manufacturing can be estimated using data on the relative size of companies (e.g., Burt, 1992:89–91), but the practice is disconcerting because companies often operate in multiple industries and competition in non-manufacturing industries is often more local and regulated than competition in manufacturing industries (e.g., Burt *et al.*, 2002). For example, Ingram and Roberts (2000) analyze the relative performance of international hotels in Sydney, Australia within the Australian Hotel Association, New South Wales Division. The central finding is that high-performing hotels are operated by managers who have friendships with managers in competing hotels. The nuanced analysis is rich with text and quotes enthusiastic about the advantages of cooperation between producers. Here is a gem from a trade magazine that would lead to government intervention in many manufacturing industries (Ingram and Roberts, 2000:392): "You must get together with your fellow-managers in each city, once a week if necessary, and talk rates. Stick to the idea that you can't control occupancy, but you can control rates. . . . Fight the situation by cooperating with your competitors in an effort to maintain your rates." Ingram and Roberts (2000:396) nicely summarize the reason for having a measure of producer cooperation in the baseline network model (variable O in the baseline model): ". . . the greatest benefit for Sydney hoteliers comes not from maximizing structural holes in the intra-industry friendship network, but from minimizing the structural holes faced by customers." A national concentration ratio for the industry cannot capture competition this local and personal. Neither is it realistic to accurately capture local competition to aggregate it across locations into a national industry ratio. In Appendix D, I report tests with alternative approximations to concentration in non-manufacturing. Approximations based on company size provide the clearest results. So, effect estimates in this chapter are based on network constraint computed from size-based approximations to concentration in non-manufacturing.

I now have a measure of concentration (O) in each of the 403 manufacturing and non-manufacturing industries in 1987 and 1992. I can compute network constraint C in the baseline model and can compute the measures of indirect network constraint to be presented in a moment.

I focus on predicting performance in certain industries because the concentration scores are not equally valid across industries. The scores in which I have the most confidence are those for the 320 manufacturing industries that correspond to a unique four-firm SIC category. These are the industries in which producer concentration is defined by the same industry boundaries that define producers buying and selling with suppliers and customers. Concentration scores in the 42 non-manufacturing industries are crude size-based approximations. Scores in the other 41 manufacturing industries are an average of scores within segments of the industry so it is impossible to know the extent to which the four leading producers within industry segments account for total industry output. I compute network constraint scores for all 361 manufacturing industries and test for selection bias from my focus on the 320 that correspond to unique four-digit SIC categories. I obtain similar results for the 320 and the 361 industries. Effect estimates based on all 361 manufacturing industries differ slightly in metric, and are statistically stronger since they are based on 82 additional observations across the two panels, however, I focus where I have the most authoritative industry-structure data: The 320 industries for which transaction data and concentration data are defined by the same industry boundaries.

Baseline effects on industry performance

The input–output data contain a measure of industry performance. Price–cost margins (PCM) are a performance measure of net income to sales introduced by Collins and Preston (1969) and widely used in market structure research: PCM as originally computed from *Census of Manufactures* data equals net income (dollars of value added minus labor costs) divided by sales. Computed from input–output data, PCM equals net income (dollars of "other value added" plus indirect business taxes) divided by volume of business. The input–output data could be argued to provide a better measure of performance because more production and distribution costs such as advertising and entertainment are removed from value added, but the final result is that the two data sources provide price–cost margins similarly associated with industry structure (Burt, 1988:372–378).

The average price–cost margin is .162 across manufacturing industries in 1987 and 1992, showing a price–cost profit of 16.2¢ on the average dollar of sales. As a concrete example, the 1987 input–output table shows $1,047.3 million in business by establishments in the "Tire Cord and Fabric" industry. Of that sum, $742.8 million were production and distribution costs, leaving $304.5 million in value added, of which $134.8 million was labor cost (input–output category 880000), $3.5 million went to indirect business taxes (category 890000), and $166.2 million was other value added not attributed to specific costs (category 900000). Removing labor costs from the value added, dividing by volume of business, and multiplying by 100 yields a price–cost margin of 16.2¢, the average across all manufacturing. The margin seems modest given the high 91 percent four-firm concentration in the industry, however, it is well known that industry margins have only a weak correlation with industry concentration (Schmalensee, 1989:973–976; Weiss, 1989).

Figure 5.1 shows that relative industry performance in 1987 continued by and large into 1992, but margins were slightly higher on average in 1987, and a few industries operated at a loss in one or the other year. No industry operated at a loss in both years. Beginning with the four negative price–cost margins in 1987 (to the left in Figure 5.1), the most extreme is in "Miscellaneous Ordnance and Accessories." The Department of Commerce distinguished six input–output categories in the armaments industry. Five of the six were about as profitable in 1992 as they were in 1987 (missiles, tanks, small arms, small-arms ammunition, and ammunition other than small-arms). The residual category, "Miscellaneous Ordnance and Accessories," was a small industry of about a billion and a half dollars producing assorted tactical weapons such as artillery, flame throwers, rocket launchers, etc. ($1.6 billion in 1987, $1.3 billion in 1992). The industry was highly concentrated and Honeywell was the leading producer (77% four-firm concentration ratio in 1987, 83% in 1992). Miscalculations following the collapse of the Iron Curtain resulted in large losses for Honeywell's operations in the industry. In 1990, the operations were spun off as Alliant Techsystems, and put on a more solid footing. In 1987, however, the large Honeywell losses summed into the industry operating at an extreme loss indicated in Figure 5.1. Switching to the five negative price–cost margins in 1992, "Primary Nonferrous Metals" ran the largest loss. The former

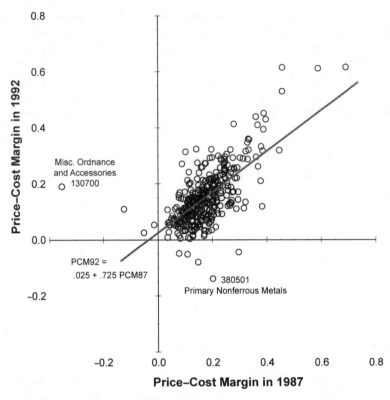

Figure 5.1 Industry Price–Cost Margins in the Two Benchmark Years

Iron Curtain was again an issue. When the Soviet Union collapsed, Russian smelters who had served the Soviet military dumped their low-priced aluminum on the world market, triggering a severe drop in the market price for aluminum from American producers.

Given that the nine negative price–cost margins are year specific (each is positive in the other panel), and would have disproportionate influence on estimated effects because they are at the extreme edge of the data distributions, I put the nine aside as intrusive outliers. This turns out not to affect conclusions about the statistical significance of effects, but it does make effects stand out more clearly since the nine temporary outliers do not have to be fit into the aggregate performance associations with industry structure.[2] As quick illustration, here are estimates for the baseline model fit across all 722

---

[2] I tested alternative treatments. I estimated effects with the nine outliers included as routine data, with the nine PCM scores truncated to a value of zero, with a dummy variable distinguishing the outliers, and with the nine outliers put aside to be explained on a case by case basis. I get the same results with the different treatments except industry-structure effects are slightly more clear with the nine outliers excluded or

observations of the 361 manufacturing industries, including adjustment for the slightly higher margins in 1987:[3]

$$PCM = 41.37 - 4.07 \ln(100 - O) - 3.99 \ln(C) + 2.45 \, D87,$$
$$(1.48) \qquad\qquad (.81) \qquad\quad (.41)$$

where standard errors are given in parentheses (adjusted for autocorrelation across repeated observations with the "cluster" option in STATA). There is a statistically significant -2.75 t-test for the negative effect of producer rivalry, and a -4.92 t-test for the negative effect of supplier-customer network constraint. Here are estimates for all 640 observations of the 320 industries that correspond to unique four-digit SIC categories:

$$PCM = 42.31 - 4.14 \ln(100 - O) - 4.18 \ln(C) + 2.51 \, D87,$$
$$(1.52) \qquad\qquad (.87) \qquad\quad (.41)$$

which define t-tests of -2.70 and -4.81 respectively for producer rivalry and network constraint. And here are estimates for the baseline model fit across the further subset of 632 observations in which price–cost margins were non–negative:

$$PCM = 48.41 - 5.42 \ln(100 - O) - 4.39 \ln(C) + 2.38 \, D87,$$
$$(1.41) \qquad\qquad (.80) \qquad\quad (.41)$$

which define t-tests of -3.83 and -5.47 respectively for producer rivalry and network constraint.

Three points are illustrated: First, the two industry-structure effects are, as expected, negative and statistically significant. Second, estimates do not differ much between the equation estimated across all 361 manufacturing industries and the one estimated across the 320 manufacturing industries that correspond to unique four-digit SIC categories. Third, effects are more clear—stronger magnitudes and smaller standard errors—in the equation for which I put aside the nine negative price–cost margins as temporary outliers.

Micro–macro connection

The two graphs in Figure 5.2 illustrate micro–macro consistency for performance as a function of direct access to structural holes. The graph at the top in Figure 5.2

---

distinguished by a dummy variable since the model does not have to fit them into the aggregate performance associations with industry structure. I put the nine outliers aside rather than add an "outlier" dummy variable to the network model to preserve the simplicity of the network model and because the dummy variable would be a temporary complication peculiar to the years observed here.

[3] Throughout this chapter, I use the structural autonomy score defined by industry structure (A in the baseline model) to predict exponential industry performance (e^{PCM}), rather than raw performance (PCM), where PCM is the industry price–cost margin. The exponential of performance yielded clearer results in Burt *et al.* (2002), and I find the same for the more narrowly defined industries analyzed here. Thus, natural logs of industry-structure variables predict price–cost margins in the text.

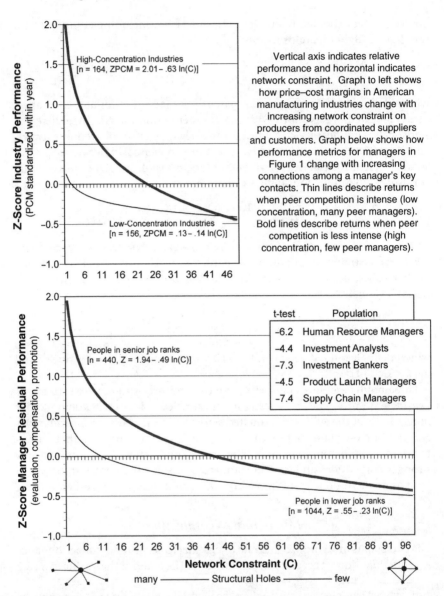

Vertical axis indicates relative performance and horizontal indicates network constraint. Graph to left shows how price–cost margins in American manufacturing industries change with increasing network constraint on producers from coordinated suppliers and customers. Graph below shows how performance metrics for managers in Figure 1 change with increasing connections among a manager's key contacts. Thin lines describe returns when peer competition is intense (low concentration, many peer managers). Bold lines describe returns when peer competition is less intense (high concentration, few peer managers).

t-test	Population
–6.2	Human Resource Managers
–4.4	Investment Analysts
–7.3	Investment Bankers
–4.5	Product Launch Managers
–7.4	Supply Chain Managers

Figure 5.2 Micro–Macro Connection for Direct Access to Structural Holes

describes the industry performance-structure association. I standardized price–cost margins within years to have a measure of relative industry performance comparable to the z-score performance metrics on managers in Figure 2.4. The z-score performance measure, ZPCM, is a function of the two industry-structure variables, O and C, in the baseline model:

$$\text{ZPCM} = 3.41 - .56 \ln(100 - O) - .46 \ln(C),$$
$$\phantom{\text{ZPCM} = 3.41 -} (.15) (.08)$$

where estimation is across the 632 non-negative margins in the 320 manufacturing industries that correspond to unique four-digit SIC categories, standard errors are given in parentheses, and the two network effects are clearly negative. Lines in the graph at the top in Figure 5.2 show how z-score price–cost margins vary with decreasing brokerage opportunities among suppliers and customers. The bold line shows the negative effect of coordinated suppliers or customers on industries in which producer rivalry is low (concentration is in the top quartile of manufacturing). The thin line shows the negative effect where producer rivalry is high (concentration is in the bottom quartile).

The graph illustrates two characteristics of the macro performance–structure association: First, the bold and thin lines both decrease, showing how producer margins are eroded by increasing dependence on supplier and customer industries in which rivalry is low. Second, producers in concentrated industries lose more. Dependence on coordinated suppliers and customers can erase the advantage of producer coordination. The bold line lies well above the thin line in the graph, showing the higher margins enjoyed by producers in concentrated industries. Where suppliers and customers are completely disorganized (far left in the graph), the difference between the bold and thin lines is almost two standard deviations (.13 z-score price-cost margin for the thin line, 2.01 for the bold line). The gap corresponds to 18¢ extra profit on a dollar of sales.[4] As producers become more dependent on supplier and customer industries in which rivalry is low (far right in the graph), the bold line decreases more quickly than the corresponding thin line, narrowing the gap between the lines (−.42 for the thin line at the far right in the graph, versus −.45 for the bold line, a difference that corresponds to a mere .3¢ profit advantage to industries in which concentration is high).

Similarity between the graphs in Figure 5.2 illustrate network-effect consistency across levels of analysis. The network model of brokerage applied to markets is a bit more complicated than the model applied to managers, but it is the same model. The difference is that applications to managers usually assume that each manager is equally able to act in his or her own interest. Consider the implications of making that assumption about producers in

---

[4] The statement is based on regressing observed price–cost margins across z-score margins, holding constant the slightly higher margins in 1987, which shows a 9.6¢ average increase in price–cost margin for a unit increase in z-score margin.

markets. If it could be assumed that producers were equally coordinated within each market, then O would be a constant, so industry network constraint C would reduce to the same sum of contact-specific weights used to define network constraint on individuals (equation B1 in Appendix B), producer concentration O would be absorbed into the intercept, so the baseline model would reduce to aC^γ (where a is the intercept α, plus an adjustment for constant O). The baseline reduced to aC^γ is precisely the model used to predict manager performance from log constraint as illustrated in Figure 2.4.

In fact, managers are not equally able to act in their own interest. When the assumption of equal ability to act is relaxed, returns to manager brokerage resemble the returns to market producer brokerage. Ceteris paribus, managers doing a job in which they have many peers are less able to act in their own interest. Numerous peers increase competitive pressure on each manager. Jobs in which there are many peers are more subject to company processes. Individuals are less the author of their own jobs, more a reflection of company prescriptions. Returns to brokerage decrease as the number of peers increases (Burt, 2005:156–162). In the graph at the bottom of Figure 5.2, I use job rank as a crude surrogate for number of peers and re-estimate the prediction in Figure 2.4 for managers in senior job ranks separate from managers in lower job ranks. The bold line in the graph at the bottom of Figure 5.2 describes for senior managers the rate at which performance erodes with decreasing access to structural holes. The thin line describes the same for managers in lower ranks. Both graphs in Figure 5.2 show higher returns to brokerage when people are free from competition—competition from other producers in their industry, or competition from other managers doing similar work.[5]

The two points made about the industry graph at the top in Figure 5.2 can be made equally well about the manager graph at the bottom in Figure 5.2. In both graphs, the regression lines decrease showing the corrosive effect on performance of increasing network constraint. The bold line is higher than the thin line, showing the advantage of being a producer in a concentrated

---

[5] Shipilov (2006) describes a related performance association at the level of organizations, that is, at a level midway between the industry and person results in Figure 5.2. Shipilov measures investment bank performance by the market share of a bank's deals, and brokerage by the extent to which the bank does deals with partners who otherwise do not do deals with one another. Association between market share and brokerage increases systematically with bank specialization, which Shipilov measures by the extent to which a bank's deals are concentrated in a single business sector. Analogy to the results in Figure 5.2 is as good as the analogy between bank specialization and the two measures in Figure 5.2 of freedom from rivals. Reinforcing the analogy, Shipilov's (2006:599) three-dimensional graph of bank performance across combinations of partner-network constraint with bank specialization resembles a graph of industry performance across combinations of extra-industry network constraint with producer concentration (Burt, 2005:139–146).

industry or a manager in a senior rank. Second, the advantaged lose more. The bold line decreases more quickly in both graphs as suppliers, customers, or colleagues, become more coordinated with one another.

The micro and macro effects are also complements in their differences. For one thing, there is a difference in network variability. Managers are more varied in network constraint. Once a manager finds a secure niche in a large organization, he or she can work it to personal advantage. Unproductive managers are not removed from organizations with the same ruthlessness by which competition removes unproductive organizations from markets. The two graphs in Figure 5.2 are drawn to scale. They are the same height, but the manager graph is wider. The industry graph is less wide because surviving industries rarely exist at the upper extremes of network constraint. Only two percent of industry observations used to estimate industry effects for Figure 5.2 lie above 40 points of network constraint on the horizontal axis. Only one percent of the observations lie above 50 points. The managers exist in more varied circumstances. A third of the manager observations used to estimate network effects for Figure 5.2 lie above 40 points of network constraint. A fifth of the observations lie above 50 points, and many managers are embedded in completely closed networks, networks that pose 100 points of constraint.

The industry data have their own strength: They provide a stronger foundation for claims that network structure affects performance. The stronger foundation is due to network data that are more authoritative, and network relations that are more exogenous to performance. With respect to more authoritative, the benchmark input–output tables defining industry networks are based on a census of business establishments. Anyone who studies industry networks defined by the tables begins with the same dollar-flow relations. Results are directly comparable across research projects. Manager network data, in contrast, are always open to questions about how networks have been sampled and measured, and whether the measured relations are real or a reflection of passing interests. With respect to more exogenous, the dollar-flow relations are not discretionary. They are defined by production technology, which makes them more exogenous to performance than is usually the case in network analysis. Car producers, for example, can purchase steel from one or another company, but they must purchase steel somewhere. Producers are dependent on another industry to the extent that existing production technology has them transacting a large portion of their business with the other industry. In contrast, relations in manager networks are typically cited and maintained at the discretion of individuals. Who I select as my "friend" is my choice, as is naming "frequent" or "valued" contacts. Where I have discretion in selecting friends, I can select for reasons other than friendship, which creates an endogeneity problem: A relationship can appear, or be obscured, because the person naming contacts is reacting to performance. Whatever the performance advantage provided by access to structural holes, for example, there must be some effect in the opposite direction. People seek out successful colleagues. Successful people will attract relations from colleagues from other groups such that a network measured after a manager has achieved success is likely to span structural holes. Input–output relations are more exogenous to performance. The relations are defined by production technology. Performance results from how producers execute the technology. This is not to say that industry performance and production technology do not have mutual effects over time. Both evolve and are subject to exogenous shocks (e.g., McGahan *et al.*, 2004). However, relative to the networks around managers, industry networks are more exogenous to performance.

In short, what managers do not provide in authoritative network data as a research site, they provide in variety. What industries lack in variety, they provide in authoritative data. Industries and managers are together a more powerful platform for network studies of competitive advantage than either would be alone.

Indirect Access to Structural Holes

That is, unless something disrupts the ability to draw research inferences between manager and industry networks, which is the central issue for this chapter: Advantage does not spill over between adjacent manager networks. Is the same true of industry networks?

Expected advantage: Maybe, yes, and no

A priori, the performance association with indirect access could be negligible, positive, or negative. Argument can be made for each of the three possibilities. Indirect access to structural holes in manager networks corresponds to industry networks: Organizations with which producers buy and sell define the producer industry's direct suppliers and customers. Organizations with which those suppliers and customers do business are the industry's indirect suppliers and customers. The effect on producers of structural holes among indirect suppliers and customers follows from the effect of holes among direct suppliers and customers.

A priori, my prediction would have been a negligible association in industry networks because the association in manager networks is so obviously negligible. Given the similar micro and macro performance associations with direct access to structural holes (Figure 5.2), and given no performance association with indirect access for managers (Figure 4.5), my default prediction would have been to assume similar micro and macro associations with indirect access, and so predict a negligible industry performance association with indirect access. The storyline would be that supplier and customers advantage is irrelevant to producer advantage. All that matters is whether producers are in a position to benefit from supplier or customer diversity and disunion.

A person unaware of the manager results could be expected to predict a correlation between producer margins and supplier-customer advantage—for much the same reason that correlation with manager performance was expected before the results in Figure 4.5 were known: Given the known advantage of direct access to structural holes, and the fact that networks are jointly owned (producers have nothing without customers and customers have nothing without suppliers), an advantage enjoyed by suppliers and customers must affect producer margins.

The performance effect could be positive. We know that direct access to structural holes is an advantage. Producers with direct access to structural holes among suppliers and customers are more exposed to variation in business practice and have more opportunities to play competing organizations against one another. Extend the immediate network one step to predict the performance association with having suppliers and customers advantaged by direct access to structural holes. Advantaged industries are more likely to have budget to experiment with new business practice so producers with advantaged industries as suppliers and customers are more likely to see new business practice and alternative ways to implement the practice. Advantaged industries in this view would be hubs in the spread of new business practice (e.g., Davis, 1991; Van de Ven *et al.*, 1999:173–178) and the abandoning of old practice (e.g., Oliver, 1992; Greve, 1995). There is a precedent for this possibility in Baum *et al.*'s (2008) analysis of U.K. investment banks predicting the value of a bank's bond deals from bridges in the bank's network and bridges in the networks around partners in the bank's bond deals (where network ties are defined by bank participation in the same syndicates). They report positive associations with the number of a bank's own bridges and the number of bridges that its partners have. Beyond information and access, the more-likely slack resources available to advantaged suppliers and customers (illustrated in the graph at the top of Figure 5.2), can make them more lucrative customers and suppliers. The summary story would be that advantaged suppliers and customers offer lucrative business opportunities and an enhanced portal into new business practices, so advantaged suppliers and customers have a positive association with producer performance.

The performance effect could equally well be negative. The performance advantage of direct access to structural holes is anchored on the assumption that producers gain advantage from supplier and customer disadvantage. The corollary is that producers lose advantage when dealing with advantaged suppliers and customers. Laboratory experiments with exchange networks clearly show that people with multiple exchange opportunities exploit their partners who have few opportunities (Cook and Emerson, 1978; Cook *et al.*, 1983). Outside the lab, Fernandez-Mateo (2007) reports disadvantage to contingency workers from continued affiliation with one placement firm that brokers access to jobs. Specifically, Bidwell and Fernandez-Mateo (2007) show that contingency workers receive a decreasing share of their earnings the longer they stay with the same placement firm. With respect to industry networks, the story would be that advantaged suppliers and customers extract a disproportionate share of profit from their business, so advantaged suppliers and customers have a negative association with producer performance.

Tire cord industry

To illustrate the alternative expectations, consider the Figure 5.3 sociogram of direct and indirect contacts for the tire cord industry in 1987 ("Tire Cord and Fabrics," SIC code 2296, input–output industry 170700). Lines in Figure 5.3 indicate volumes of business. Dots indicate industries. The tire cord industry is the square "dot" in the sociogram. This industry is a useful example because of its simplicity. The industry has one primary supplier and one primary customer. The bulk of tire cord supplies are purchased from the manmade fibers industry ("Manmade Organic Fibers," input–output category 280400). The bulk of tire cord output is sold to tire manufacturers ("Tires and Inner Tubes," input–output category 320100). Tire cord purchases from manmade fibers and sales to tire manufacturers are indicated by the two solid lines in Figure 5.3. The two relations together account for 86.7 percent of tire cord buying and selling with other production industries (33.9% with manmade fibers and 52.8% with tire manufacturers). I simplified Figure 5.3 by presenting only relations that constitute more than five percent of an industry's buying and selling (all p_{ij} greater than .05). I am using a broader 2 percent criterion to define suppliers and customers in the analysis, but a 5 percent criterion is better for the purposes of Figure 5.3. The lack of a solid line in Figure 5.3 between tire manufacturers and manmade fibers means that each does less than 5 percent of its business with the other. There is little more to report on the immediate network around tire cord producers. After the 33.9 percent of business with manmade fibers, the next largest volume of tire cord business is 3.1 percent with advertising, followed by 1.7 percent with the local electric utility, followed by still smaller percentages spread across 44 other industries with many relations constituting less than .01 percent of tire cord business. In short, the tire cord industry is little more than a way station in the flow of product from manmade fibers to tire manufacturers.

Seeing the immediate network helps explain why tire cord profits are low despite the high level of industry concentration. The tire cord price-cost margin of 16.2¢ equals the average margin across all manufacturing industries, but it should be higher given the lack of competitors in the industry (concentration ratio of 91% is well above the 40% average in manufacturing, 2.45 z-score). The sociogram in Figure 5.3 shows that concentration within the industry is counterbalanced by severe network constraint from suppliers and customers. Tire cord manufacturers are dependent on one primary supplier

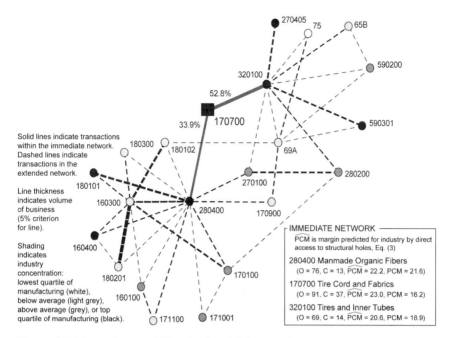

Solid lines indicate transactions within the immediate network. Dashed lines indicate transactions in the extended network.

Line thickness indicates volume of business (5% criterion for line).

Shading indicates industry concentration: lowest quartile of manufacturing (white), below average (light grey), above average (grey), or top quartile of manufacturing (black).

IMMEDIATE NETWORK
$\widehat{\text{PCM}}$ is margin predicted for industry by direct access to structural holes, Eq. (3)

280400 Manmade Organic Fibers
(O = 76, C = 13, $\widehat{\text{PCM}}$ = 22.2, PCM = 21.6)

170700 Tire Cord and Fabrics
(O = 91, C = 37, $\widehat{\text{PCM}}$ = 23.0, PCM = 16.2)

320100 Tires and Inner Tubes
(O = 69, C = 14, $\widehat{\text{PCM}}$ = 20.6, PCM = 18.9)

Figure 5.3 Network around Tire Cord and Fabrics Industry in 1987

and one primary customer. The industries on which they are dependent are highly concentrated. Concentration is shading coded in Figure 5.3 as high (black), above average (grey), below average (light grey), and low (white) distinguished by the median and interquartile range of 1987 scores. The text box shows that concentration is high in the direct supplier and customer industries: 76 percent in manmade fibers and 69 percent in tires and inner tubes. Dependence on concentrated supplier-customer industries defines a high level of direct network constraint on the industry (C equals 37 for tire cord and fabrics, well above the average of 15 for manufacturing, 2.36 z-score). Under strong pressure from suppliers and customers, tire cord profits should be lower than would be otherwise expected from high concentration in the industry—as they are.

But tire cord profits are even lower than predicted by industry concentration and direct network constraint together. The text box in Figure 5.3 shows a 23.0¢ price–cost margin predicted by the baseline model for the tire cord industry in 1987, which is well above the observed margin of 16.2¢ (z-score difference is .72).[6]

---

[6] The expected price–cost margin is predicted using estimates for the baseline model presented below as Model A in Table 5.1.

Explanation can be found in the industry's network of indirect suppliers and customers. Dashed lines in Figure 5.3 indicate buying and selling beyond the immediate network around tire cord producers. Network constraint computed within the immediate network around an industry—the solid lines in Figure 5.3—measures the extent to which industry producers have direct access to structural holes from which they could benefit. Network constraint computed within the broader network of suppliers and customers to the industry's direct suppliers and customers—the dashed lines in Figure 5.3—measures the extent to which industry producers have indirect access through their suppliers and customers to structural holes in the network structure around their suppliers and customers. In predicting tire cord profits from the baseline model, I held constant supplier and customer concentration as a component in direct industry network constraint (C). However, the supplier and customer industries for tire cord producers have a further advantage: They are subject to low network constraint from their own networks of suppliers and customers. Figure 5.3 shows that suppliers in the "manmade organic fibers" industry do business with many supplier and customer industries, few of which are especially concentrated—so tire cord suppliers face much less direct network constraint than tire cord producers (C for manmade fibers is 13 versus 37 for the tire cord industry, a 2.52 z-score difference). The lower direct network constraint on suppliers means that they enjoy a higher profit margin (PCM is 21.6¢ in manmade fibers versus 16.2¢ in tire cord), which could affect tire cord producers. Tire manufactures, the primary customer industry for tire cord producers, are similar subject to lower network constraint (C equals 13).

In this case of tire cord producers, having advantaged suppliers and customers seems to have a negative effect on producer margins. Advantaged suppliers and customers enjoy profits at a level expected from direct access to structural holes (PCM hat is about the same as PCM in the text box) while producer profits are well below expected.[7]

---

[7] The performance link with industry structure is all the more impressive because buying and selling as constrained as it is in the tire cord industry is rarely left exposed to the vicissitudes of market price. Such buying and selling is typically embedded in a corporate hierarchy to manage the risk (e.g., Pfeffer and Salancik, 1978; Burt, 1983). The typical pattern is borne out here. For example, one of the leading firms in the tire cord industry is Firestone Fibers and Textiles. Firestone is owned by BFS Diversified Products, which also runs establishments in Firestone's primary supplier industry, manmade fibers. BFS Diversified Products is owned by the Japanese tire company, Bridgestone, the American operations of which are a major tire supplier for automobiles produced in the United States. In other words, Bridgestone has embedded its American tire production in a corporate hierarchy. Bridgestone tire production can draw on Firestone tire cord, which can draw on BFS fiber output. Nevertheless, market advantage emerges in the transfer prices negotiated between business units. Tire cord production is anchored on three industries: itself, a supplier industry, and a customer industry. All three are highly concentrated. However, the supplier and customer industries are less subject to network constraint from their own suppliers and customers, which is manifest in them enjoying their expected level of profits while tire cord producers report margins well below expected.

Returns to indirect access

In contrast to the tire cord example, spillover is positive for manufacturing on average: Producers derive advantage from business with advantaged suppliers and customers. Results with alternative measures are presented in Table 5.1.[8] Suppliers and customers in Table 5.1 are the industries with which producers transact two or more percent of their business.[9]

As a point of reference, Model A in Table 5.1 provides estimates for the baseline model. The estimates show the negative performance effect of rivalry within the industry (reversed industry concentration in the first row of the table) and the negative effect of dependence on supplier-customer industries in which there is little rivalry (network constraint C in second row of the table).[10]

---

[8] I put aside the manufacturing industries that correspond to multiple SIC categories because their input–output industry boundary is not the boundary for which the concentration data are defined. As a check on that decision, I re-estimated the five effect estimates in Table 5.1 for measures of indirect network constraint with the deleted industries included in the estimation, increasing the number of observations from 632 to 713. Here are the coefficients in Table 5.1 and their corresponding t-tests (in parentheses): −5.09 (−3.84), −3.32 (−3.48), 1.48 (2.14), −.74 (−2.04), and −3.92 (2.03). When estimated across all manufacturing with non-negative price–cost margins, the results are similar, but with stronger test statistics because of additional observations: −5.33 (−4.41), −3.49 (−4.09), 1.38 (2.43), −.76 (−2.33), and −4.22 (−2.52).

[9] The 2% criterion is based on tests of higher and lower criteria reported in Table D2 in Appendix D. The 2% criterion keeps the immediate network to a minimum size without losing predictive power in the baseline model, and leaves more of the economy available as potential indirect suppliers and customers. I estimated the models adding as a predictor the percentage of industry business that was over the 2% criterion (74% on average, see Table D1). There is no zero-order association with performance (1.37 t-test) and no partial associations in the five models in Table 5.1 (respective t-tests of .81, −.63, −.42, −.95, and .66).

[10] Performance effects of access to structural holes can be expected to vary across industries. For example, by analogy with the higher returns for more senior managers—whose work is more ambiguous and unique to individual managers—returns might be higher in industries that are growing, perhaps higher returns in industries more dependent on new technology. I am only concerned here with the relative effects of direct and indirect access to structural holes, but I tested the network effects with some additional control variables. The effects in Table 5.1 are robust to the additional controls. For example, when I add to Model C in Table 5.1 a control for industry scale (measured by the log dollars of industry business), I get a negligible performance association with scale (1.57 t-test) and estimates (t-tests) for the three network effects that closely resemble the estimates reported in Table 5.1: −5.80 (−4.26), −2.94 (−3.60), and −5.13 (−3.86). When I control for industry value added as a measure of gross industry profit, I find higher margins in industries with higher gross profits (4.27 t-test) but similar estimates of network effects: −5.93 (−4.60), −2.50 (−3.03), −5.24 (−4.03). When I control for labor costs (measured by industry labor cost divided by total industry costs), I find lower margins in labor-intensive industries (−2.17 t-test), but similar network-effect estimates: −5.11 (−3.96), −3.04 (−3.69), −4.59 (−3.66). I find the same network-effect robustness with controls for the percent of industry business within the industry, the percent of industry business excluded by the 2% criterion for inter-industry relations to be included in the network measures, the extent to which industry business grew from 1987 to 1992 (measured by the difference between industry business in 1987 and 1992, divided by industry business in 1987), and the percent of industry business that is sales to government (state and local or federal).

Table 5.1 Price–Cost Margins and Industry Network Structure

	A	B	C	D	E	F
Rivalry within Industry (100 − industry four-firm concentration ratio)	−5.42** (1.41)	−5.71** (1.37)	−5.77** (1.37)	−5.95** (1.40)	−5.94** (1.37)	−5.41** (1.38)
Direct Network Constraint from Suppliers-Customers (C in Eq. 4)	−4.39** (.80)		−3.11** (.82)	−3.28** (.80)	−2.63* (.80)	−3.11* (1.02)
Indirect Network Constraint from Their Suppliers-Customers						
Unweighted Average Constraint on Industry Suppliers-Customers		−6.81** (1.30)	−5.09** (1.32)			
Weighted Average Constraint on Industry Suppliers-Customers				−3.32** (.95)		
Percent Industry Business with Low-Constraint Suppliers-Customers					1.48* (.69)	
Percent Industry Business with High-Constraint Suppliers-Customers					−.74* (.37)	
Total Constraint across Indirect Supplier-Customers						−3.92* (1.93)
Industry in 1987	2.38** (.41)	2.06** (.40)	2.16** (.41)	2.26** (.41)	2.20** (.41)	2.28** (.41)
Intercept	48.41	53.98	58.14	54.96	41.86	49.19
R^2	.15	.16	.19	.18	.19	.16
Percent Industry-Structure Effect from:						
Rivalry within Industry	56%	40%	48%	53%	49%	52%
Direct Network Constraint from Suppliers-Customers	44%	—	25%	29%	21%	29%
Indirect Network Constraint from their Suppliers-Customers	—	60%	27%	18%	30%	19%

Note: These are ordinary least-square regression equations predicting non-negative price–cost margins in manufacturing industries corresponding to unique four-digit SIC categories in 1987 and 1992 (N = 632). Criterion to be a supplier-customer is 2% of industry business. All predictors are measured as log scores except the dummy variable for 1987. Means, standard deviations, and correlations are given in Appendix E, Table E6. Standard errors (in parentheses) are corrected for autocorrelation across repeated observations of same industry using 'cluster' option in STATA. * P < .05 ** P < .001.

Zero-order correlation

As a further point of reference, Model B in Table 1 is the same as Model A, but with indirect network constraint replacing direct constraint. Recall the correlation between manager performance and indirect access to structural holes (graph to the left in Figure 4.5). Similarly, Model B shows a strong positive association between industry margins and indirect access to structural holes. The measure of indirect network constraint is average direct network constraint on supplier and customer industries, which is the exact analogue to the measure of indirect network constraint used for managers in the preceding chapters (equation B3 in Appendix B):

$$IC_i = \Sigma_j \; \delta_{ij} C_j, \; i \neq j,$$

where N is the number of other industries with which producers do more than the criterion volume of business. For example, 5 percent is the criterion for the tire cord network in Figure 5.3. Tire cord producers have one primary supplier and one primary customer, so N equals 2 and the δ_{ij} equal $1/2$. Indirect constraint on tire cord producers would equal direct network constraint on suppliers in the "Manmade Organic Fibers" industry ($C = 13$) averaged with direct network constraint on customers in the "Tires and Inner Tubes" industry ($C = 14$), which sums to 13.5 points of indirect network constraint on tire cord producers. Model B in Table 5.1 shows that producer margins increase with decreasing direct constraint on suppliers and customers (-5.21 t-test).

Returns to average indirect network constraint

Models C and D test direct and indirect network constraint as simultaneous effects on producer margins. The measure of indirect constraint in Model C is the average across suppliers and customer industries used in Model B. No consideration is given to the relative volume of producer business with different industries. Any supplier or customer industry over the criterion volume of business is equally a source of indirect network constraint on producers. This is a crude measure, but it is sufficient to show that producer margins increase with indirect access to structural holes in the networks of suppliers and customers, above and beyond the effect of direct access within their immediate network. The -5.09 coefficient for indirect network constraint in Model C generates a strong -3.84 t-test (cf. Baum *et al.*, 2008:Table 2, for association between investment bank performance and the average number of bridging ties in the networks around the bank's syndicate partners).

Model D differs from C in weighting for volume of business. The δ_{ij} weight aggregating customer/supplier networks equals $p_{ij}/\Sigma_k \; p_{ik}$ in Model D so suppliers and customers are weighted by their proportional business with producers. In Figure 5.3, for example, indirect network constraint on tire cord producers would be defined more by the network constraint on tire manufacturers than the constraint on manmade fibers because tire cord producers do more business with tire manufacturers. Specifically, the weight for tire manufacturers would be .61, which is 52.8 / (52.8 + 33.9), and the weight for manmade fibers would be the complement, .39. The two together define 14 points of weighted indirect network constraint on tire cord producers: $13.61 = .61(14) + .39(13)$. Weighting in Model D offers no improvement over the count of indirect suppliers and customers in Model C. The −3.32 coefficient in Model D for indirect network constraint generates a −3.48 t-test, about the same as the corresponding t-test in Model C.

Returns to high versus low indirect network constraint

In Model E, I disaggregate indirect network constraint into positive and negative elements to see whether either extreme makes disproportionate contribution to the spillover. Models C and D show that indirect network constraint erodes producer performance, but the effect is some mix of negative effect from indirect network constraint and positive effect from the lack of indirect network constraint. I suspected that the negative effect might be less negotiable in industry buying and selling, and so more likely to spill over between adjacent networks.

Measuring positive spillover potential in Model E, "Percent Industry Business with Low-Constraint Suppliers-Customers" is the percent of industry business transacted with suppliers or customers that are advantaged by their own networks of suppliers and customers, which could be an indirect advantage to producers. The measure is p_{ij} for producer industry i, summed across supplier-customer industries j, where industry j is under "low" network constraint from its own suppliers and customers, and "low" refers to the bottom quartile of network constraint scores (C less than 7.72 points). In Figure 5.3, tire cord producers score zero on this measure. The 13 points of network constraint on manmade fibers is above the 7.72 criterion for a low-constraint industry, and the 14 points of network constraint on tire manufactures is above the criterion.

Measuring negative potential, "Percent Industry Business with High-Constraint Suppliers-Customers" is the percent of industry business transacted with suppliers and customers weakened by severe network constraint from their own suppliers or customers. The measure is p_{ij} for producer industry i summed across supplier-customer industries j where industry j is under "high" network constraint from its own suppliers and customers, and "high" refers to the top quartile of network constraint scores (C greater than 17.43 points). In Figure 5.3, tire cord producers score zero on this measure. Network constraint on supplier and customer industries falls below the 17.43 criterion for a high-constraint industry.

The results for Model E show that producer performance is affected by both the positive and negative effects of indirect network constraint (t-tests of 2.14 for the positive and −2.04 for the negative).

Returns to constraint from the whole network of indirect suppliers and customers

Model F in Table 5.1 measures indirect network constraint for the whole extended network that does business with producer suppliers and customers. The measures of indirect network constraint in Models B, C, D, and E average network constraint in the networks around each supplier-customer industry. Business relations between networks are ignored. The measure of indirect network constraint in Model F defines constraint within and across the networks around an industry's suppliers and customers.

The measure is created as follows: Define the immediate network around a focal industry by identifying every other industry where focal-industry producers do more than 2 percent of their business. Second, define in the same way the immediate network around each industry supplier and customer in the immediate network. The M industries identified in the second step, but not the first, are indirect suppliers or customers for the focal industry. In Figure 5.3, for example, M equals 19. There are 19 indirect supplier-customer industries for tire cord producers. For the lower 2 percent criterion used in Table 5.1, the number of indirect supplier-customer industries increases to 26. Third, assemble from the input–output table buying and selling among the M industries to define the extended network of indirect suppliers and customers. By definition, the focal industry has no direct buying or selling (above the criterion) with its M indirect supplier-customer industries. I operationalized indirect relations with the strongest two-step connection through a direct supplier or customer.[11] Fourth, and finally, compute industry network constraint C from the network of buying and selling among indirect supplier-customer industries, and concentration data on producer rivalry within the industries.

Network constraint across indirect supplier-customer industries has a statistically significant effect on industry performance (2.03 t-test), but the effect is less clear than the corresponding effects for the more narrowly defined indirect constraint measures in Models B, C, D, and E. The implication is that what matters most for indirect network constraint is the immediate network around each supplier and customer industry, not the whole network of business

---

[11] The relation p_{ij} from focal-industry i to indirect supplier-customer industry j is set equal to the square-root of the maximum $p_{ik}p_{kj}$ across industries k in the immediate network around industry i, where p_{ik} is the proportion of industry i business conducted with industry k and p_{kj} is the proportion of industry k business conducted with industry j (where industry j is not in the immediate network around focal industry i).

relations within and between the immediate networks. That interpretation is made certain by adding to Model F the measure of average within-supplier-customer-network constraint (third row of Table 5.1), and seeing that the performance association with "total constraint" becomes negligible (-2.94 coefficient, 1.96 standard error, -1.50 t-test, $P \sim .13$) while the association with average within-supplier-customer-network remains strong (-4.83 coefficient, 1.36 standard error, -3.55 t-test, $P < .001$).

Conclusion

My goal in this chapter has been to connect the manager evidence in Chapters 3 and 4 with analogous evidence at the macro level of industries. A central tenet in network theory is that causal spark is released by the pattern in which relations intersect. Whatever the causal spark inherent in a specific pattern, spark is expected from the pattern wherever the pattern occurs; in a person, a team, an organization, a geographic region. We know that the performance association with direct access to structural holes is similar for individuals and industries (illustrated in Figure 5.2), which creates complementarities between manager and industry evidence on network brokerage (discussed here: Consistency across levels of analysis, greater variety in manager networks, less endogeneity in the industry networks). As with other lines of argument in network theory, generalizing across levels of analysis has been an attractive and productive feature of structural hole theory. The attractive and productive feature is put at risk by the conclusion at the end of Chapter 4—that the advantage of network brokerage does not result from early access to diverse information within the network so much as it results from enhanced cognitive and emotional skills that are a by-product of being in the network. Cognitive and emotional skills are more obviously qualities of people than qualities of organizations or industries. So my goal in this chapter has been to recalibrate the network theory's micro–macro consistency using evidence on industry networks analogous to the evidence in Chapters 3 and 4 on manager networks.

Using census data on industry performance and networks defined at the level of four-digit manufacturing industries, I analyzed price–cost margins in terms of three industry-structure effects: Rivalry within the industry, direct network constraint from industry suppliers and customers, and indirect network constraint spilling over from the networks around suppliers and customers. In contrast to the manager evidence in Chapters 3 and 4 showing no performance spillover effect from neighbor networks, there is clear evidence in this chapter of positive spillover from neighbor industry networks. The bottom rows in Table 5.1 show that about 24 percent of the industry-structure effect on price–cost margins can be attributed to structure beyond the industry's own buying and selling, to networks around the industry's suppliers and customers.[12]

Micro–macro consistency

The industry results could be cited as evidence that returns to network brokerage are inconsistent across micro and macro levels of analysis. However, much is consistent across the levels. Consider Table 5.2. Performance is reported for six study populations—the five manager populations in Figures 2.4 and 4.5, plus the industry population in Table 5.1. Alternative industry measures of indirect network constraint are used in Table 5.1. For Table 5.2, I use the measure in Model C, which is the industry measure most similar to the manager measure used in the previous two chapters. Observations in the six populations are divided into four network categories distinguished across the rows in Table 5.2 by direct and indirect network constraint, high versus low.

The manager and industry results are similar for extreme networks. The extremes are at the top and bottom panels in Table 5.2. At the top of the table are the networks around brokers who connect brokers. These are managers and industries with many disconnected contacts who themselves have many disconnected contacts. These networks provide both direct and indirect access to structural holes. Performance scores at the top of Table 5.2 are the highest in the table. Performance is a z-score residual holding constant job rank and year for the managers, concentration and year for the industries. At the bottom of the table are the closed networks providing neither direct nor indirect access to structural holes. These are managers and industries with densely interconnected contacts embedded in their own networks of densely interconnected contacts. Performance scores at the bottom of Table 5.2 are the lowest in the table.

The key results are in the middle of the table, describing networks that provide direct or indirect access to structural holes—but not both. In the second panel of Table 5.2, managers and industries are similarly advantaged by "only direct access" to structural holes. These are producers relatively free from the constraint of dependence on concentrated supplier or customer industries, but beyond those suppliers and customers are concentrated industries that pose severe indirect network constraint. The −.04 average residual price–cost margin reported for industries in the second panel of Table 5.2 is lower than the .34 residual margin enjoyed by producers free from direct and indirect network constraint, but significantly higher than the −.30 residual margin observed in industries oppressed by high direct and indirect network constraint (2.17 t-test). Test statistics in the second panel are sufficient to reject

---

[12] The 24% figure in this sentence is the average across the four percentages for indirect network constraint in Table 5.1. The specific averages across Models C through F are 50.5% for rivalry within the industry, 26.0% for direct network constraint, and 23.5% for indirect network constraint.

Table 5.2   Manager and Industry Returns to Direct and Indirect Access to Structural Holes

Network Category[a]	Network Constraint[b] Direct, Indirect	Study Population (N)	Residual Z-Score Performance[c]	Test Statistic[d]
Direct & Indirect Access				
	Low, Low	Product Launch (68)	.35	3.78**
		Supply Chain (134)	.44	6.33**
		HR (46)	.54	3.79**
		Bankers (134)	.46	5.09**
		Analysts (122)	.39	3.76**
		Industries (200)	.34	4.69**
Only Direct Access				
	Low, High	Product Launch (78)	.07	2.27*
		Supply Chain (97)	.10	3.18*
		HR (49)	.26	2.43*
		Bankers (88)	.26	4.44**
		Analysts (55)	.01	2.53*
		Industries (115)	−.04	2.17*
Only Indirect Access				
	High, Low	Product Launch (55)	−.20	.62
		Supply Chain (95)	−.29	.12
		HR (55)	−.09	.66
		Bankers (102)	−.28	1.37
		Analysts (123)	−.21	1.38
		Industries (129)	−.05	2.22*
Closed Network (no access)				
	High, High	Product Launch (57)	−.32	−2.45*
		Supply Chain (129)	−.31	−3.68**
		HR (133)	−.21	−2.10*
		Bankers (145)	−.39	−6.25**
		Analysts (54)	−.40	−3.35*
		Industries (188)	−.30	−3.26**

Note: (a) Focal manager or industry is dot in the center. Dashed lines are relations beyond immediate network.

(b) Constraint is dichotomized at its median in each population, except in the HR organization, where it is split to distinguish lowest 33% of scores.

(c) This is performance holding constant year and job rank for individuals, year and concentration for industries.

(d) These are test statistics for effects when z-score residual performance is regressed across the rows in each study population (analyst, banker, and industry results are adjusted for autocorrelation using "cluster" option in STATA). "Closed Network" is reference category.
* P < .05 ** P < .001.

the null hypothesis—a magnitude of two or three—but are for managers and industries similarly weaker than the test statistics for the broker-of-brokers networks in the top panel of the table.

The specific inconsistency

The manager and industry results disagree in the third panel of Table 5.2. These are networks that provide "only indirect access" to structural holes. Average manager performance in the third panel is no better than the low performance observed in closed networks (t-tests of .12 to 1.38). In contrast, price–cost margins for industries in the third panel of Table 5.2 are significantly higher than the margins in closed-network industries (2.22 t-test). The panel-three industries contain producers dependent on concentrated supplier-customer industries that are themselves relatively free from constraint. The network in Figure 5.3 is illustrative. Tire cord producers face severe direct network constraint. They are dependent on a concentrated supplier industry and a concentrated customer industry. Both the supplier industry and the customer industry do business in a wide variety of their own supplier-customer industries (dotted lines in Figure 5.3), which would put tire cord producers in the third panel of Table 4. However, the indirect supplier and customer industries are sufficiently concentrated to put tire cord producers in the "closed network" panel at the bottom of Table 5.2 (indirect network constraint score of 13.32 is higher than the median score of 8.53). In other words, industries in the third panel of Table 5.2 are less constrained than the example in Figure 5.3 in the sense that their indirect supplier-customer industries are more numerous, more disconnected, or more riddled with internal rivalry. That relative freedom from indirect network constraint is an advantage manifest in higher margins despite severe direct network constraint. In fact, margins in the third panel are about as high as the margins observed in the industries just above them with more attractive network structures (mean residual price–cost margins of −.04 and −.05 for industries in the second and third panels of Table 5.2, versus −.30 for "closed networks" at the bottom of the table).[13]

---

[13] The network cross-classification in Table 5.2 almost always elicits a workshop question about interaction effects. Do direct and indirect network constraint affect one another's effect on performance? They do not. To determine this, I multiplied log direct network constraint times log indirect constraint, and entered the interaction term to the performance prediction in each study population. The interaction term is a negligible addition: .45 t-test for compensation in the product launch (Table 3.1), .36 for supply-chain manager salary (Table 3.2), 1.71 for HR compensation (Table 4.1), .40 for investment banker compensation (Model C in Table 4.2), −.12 for analyst election to the All-America Research Team (Model D in Table 4.3), and .26 for industry price–cost margins (Model C in Table 5.1). The concentration of effect in panel three of Table 5.2 is a heuristic. It is true that the disagreement between manager and industry results is most apparent in panel three of Table 5.2, but the industry performance association with

Less inconsistent than more extreme

I conclude from the balance of similarity and difference that the industry evidence is not qualitatively distinct from the manager evidence so much as it describes a more extreme business environment. The disagreement between manager and industry results in the third panel of Table 5.2 is not a qualitative jump from managers to industries so much as it is a matter of degree. Returns to secondhand brokerage are not equally negligible in the third panel: Industries are over the line for statistical significance, but not by much (2.22 t-test; P < .05). The bankers and analysts are under the line for statistical significance (respective t-tests of 1.37 and 1.38, P ∼ .17). There is no association in the product-launch, supply-chain, and HR organizations (t-tests of .62, .12, and .66 respectively, P > .50).

Speculation

The order of results in the third panel of Table 5.2 can be used to make inferences about the way that industry networks are more extreme than the manager networks. What do analysts and bankers have in common with industries that distinguishes analysts and bankers from managers in the three, more bureaucratic, populations? I cannot answer this question in an authoritative way, but here is a working conclusion: Of the many dimensions that would put industries at one extreme of a continuum with bankers and analysts further along the continuum, and bureaucratic organizations at the other extreme, two dimensions stand out to me as candidates for productive network research in future: information and inhibition.

Information

The information dimension I have in mind is the familiar contrast between Austrian and neoclassical markets discussed in Chapter 2. At the Austrian end of the contrast lie networks in which information is tacit and complex so it is sticky, moving between groups slowly and inaccurately, if at all. At this end are the product-launch and supply-chain networks, balkanized by geography, technology, and legacy culture. Indirect connections beyond the immediate network have limited value, or, judging from Table 5.2, no value at all. At the neoclassical end of the continuum lie networks in which information travels great distance rapidly and accurately. Here are the mature capital markets in

---

indirect access to structural holes exists in the other three panels as well. If I delete the 139 industry observations in panel three of Table 5.2 from the estimation of Model C in Table 5.1, there is still a −3.36 t-test for the performance association with indirect network constraint. Binary distinctions in Table 5.2 are a useful heuristic. They do not fully capture the continuous-variable results in Table 5.1.

which I initially thought the investment bankers and analysts worked. There must always be an element of local interpretation, but capital markets are mature in the sense that news about investments and company developments in distant locations routinely flashes around the globe to affect plans and share price in London, New York, and Tokyo. The more easily that meaningful information moves quickly between distant places, the more advantage there is to the diverse information provided by indirect access to structural holes. I expected such advantage to be apparent among the investment bankers and analysts, but it was not. The advantage is only visible at the extreme of industry buying and selling, where information can be codified into routines and apparently moved with impact through indirect relations.

I focus on access to information, but I have no data on information flow. An alternative interpretation of the industry returns to secondhand brokerage is that advantaged suppliers and customers are inefficient in harvesting the benefits of their advantage so some of the benefit that would go to them spills over to producers. Why should producers be any more efficient than suppliers or customers in harvesting network advantage? It seems more likely that advantaged industries are centers for experimentation and innovation as discussed earlier in the chapter, and that organizations doing business with advantaged industries are at higher risk of learning about productive business practices. When those business practices are encoded in organization routines, they can be moved across industry boundaries.

If the transfer of business practice is a factor in the observed industry returns to secondhand brokerage, then returns should be higher in certain industries. Routines move between divisions in a company more easily than they move across companies in separate industries. Company headquarters can mandate the transfer. Senior managers keenly watch one another for new opinion or practice that gives advantage to peers. If routines move more easily within than between companies, then returns to secondhand brokerage should be higher in companies vertically integrated into their supplier and customer industries. I do not have the data to test the inference, but suppose companies in more concentrated industries are more likely to vertically integrate into supplier and customer industries (see footnote 7). Then returns to secondhand brokerage should be higher for producers in more concentrated industries. Here are estimated effects for indirect network constraint predicting price–cost margins in Model C of Table 5.1 for low, average, and high concentration industries:

−1.82	(−1.03)	Low Concentration (n = 156)
−3.71	(−2.11)	Average Concentration (n = 312)
−10.00	(−3.71)	High Concentration (n = 164)

The first column contains the coefficient corresponding to −5.09 in Model C in Table 5.1. The second column contains the t-test for the coefficient. The third column distinguishes industries in the bottom quartile of concentration, from those at an inter-quartile level of concentration, versus those in the highest quartile of concentration (this partition distinguished low from high concentration industries in Figure 5.2). There are no returns to secondhand brokerage for low-concentration industries, detectable returns for average-concentration industries, and high returns to the high-concentration industries. These results are only suggestive, but they are results I would expect to see if the industry returns to secondhand brokerage were in part due to organization linkages across industries facilitating the transfer of productive organization routines across industries.

Inhibition

At the other extreme of information flow, the social norms of proper behavior that inhibit information flow between people are less likely to affect flow between industries. The more personal and local the business, the more likely that people feel obligation to support friends and return favors. Of the six populations in Table 5.2, the HR, product launch, and supply chain show absolutely no returns to secondhand brokerage. In confidential talk with these people, I would expect to hear stories about actions justified by personal loyalty and favors that people owe one another. In contrast, no one "owes" his or her industry. No one counts their industry among their friends. You can drive a business into bankruptcy, but it would be poor form to hammer a friend insensible. There must always be some element of inhibition to corporate behavior. If you think corporations are wild based on what you know about their behavior, imagine what was ruled out as improper. The analysts and bankers in Table 5.2 show a negligible but nonzero advantage from indirect access to structural holes, so I put them somewhere between the extremes, distinct from the impersonal market behavior of industry buying and selling, but not quite the personal work environments of the HR, product-launch, or supply-chain organizations. Protection from competitive market forces can be discussed in terms of human decency or corrupt bureaucracy. Either way, it is a question for future research. One thing is clear: A wide range of business environments—from corporate bureaucracies up through the mature capital markets in which investment bankers and analysts work—show no performance advantage to brokerage beyond the immediate network of direct contacts. There is a detectable performance advantage at the extreme of industry market relations; but short of that extreme, advantage is limited to the immediate network of direct contacts.

What about organizations?

I have focused on the contrast between industries and people because that is where I have good evidence. Evidence at the intermediate level of organizations would be useful. Does indirect access to structural holes in interorganizational networks provide the advantage reported in this chapter for industry networks, or does it provide the negligible advantage reported in the earlier chapters?

The question is difficult to answer from previous research. Direct and indirect access are often combined, either in eigenvector measures of centrality/status (see footnote 18 to Chapter 6), or in betweenness measures of centrality/brokerage (see pages 297–299 in Appendix B). There are studies of spillover legitimating a firm, as in Stuart, Hoang, and Hybels' (1999) study of new ventures obtaining advantage from alliances with established companies. But, as explained in Chapter 7 with respect to outsiders gaining legitimacy from insider endorsements, such evidence is not evidence of returns to secondhand brokerage; it is evidence of spillover closure, which is readily apparent in the same networks that show no returns to secondhand brokerage (the subject of the next chapter).

Owen-Smith and Powell (2004) come close to testing for spillover across organization networks when they predict successful patenting by Boston biotech companies. They predict patenting from a company's Boston network versus its network beyond Boston. There are limits to inferring spillover from the data. Network correlations with patenting are near-zero (Owen-Smith and Powell, 2004:18) and the direct versus indirect distinction is not based on networks but geography (inside versus outside Boston). However, the results correspond to the lack of returns to secondhand brokerage reported in the previous two chapters: Patenting increases with membership in the Boston main component and does not increase with membership in the main component beyond Boston (Owen-Smith and Powell, 2004:Table 2).

Two recent studies contain results closer to the spillover analysis reported here: Baum *et al.* (2008) predict U.K. investment bank performance (log average value of bonds associated with the bank) from direct access to structural holes in the bank's immediate network of bond partners, and indirect access to structural holes in the networks around the bank's partners. Frankort (2008) predicts the number of a firm's successful IT patent applications from direct access to structural holes in the firm's network of alliance partners (holes are indicated by alliances with partners not allied with one another), and indirect access to holes in the alliance networks around the partners. Indirect access is measured in both studies by the average across partner networks, as it is measured in this and the preceding chapters. The two studies focus on interaction effects from combinations of network variables, effects beyond the scope of this discussion, but here are the reported zero-order performance correlations with direct and indirect network constraint:

Performance	1.00	−.74	.31
Direct Network Constraint	−.38	1.00	−.39
Indirect Network Constraint	−.06	.17	1.00

The upper-diagonal cells contain correlations from Baum *et al.* (2008: Table 1), the lower-diagonal cells contain correlations from Frankort (2008: Table 1), and network constraint is raw scores (rather than the natural log of scores used here).

There is a performance correlation with direct network constraint in both populations. The performance correlation with indirect network constraint is reversed for the investment banks, and direct constraint is negatively correlated with indirect, which together imply that many banks central in the network were connected directly to peripheral banks (C low and IC high for central banks, C high and IC low for peripheral banks), so path distances between the banks in this population might be too short to use the averaging measure of indirect network constraint (see page 302 in Appendix B).

Computing partial regression coefficients from the above correlation matrix shows a strong performance association with direct network constraint and no association with indirect network constraint. The respective regression coefficients are −.73 versus .02 for the investment banks, and −.38 versus .01 for the IT firms. In other words, returns to brokerage for these organizations look like the returns for analysts, bankers, and managers in Chapters 3 and 4.

Spillover between organization networks can be expected to vary between industries. If the above speculation about information and inhibition is correct, then spillover should be more obvious between organizations in industries within which information can be packaged into routines so it can be transferred more easily between organizations, and in industries within which business carries no personal obligation to support friends or return favors. In other words, spillover and corporate culture should be covariates. As economic performance is enhanced by a strong corporate culture in industries within which competition is severe (Burt *et al.*, 2002), spillover is more likely between organizations in industries within which competition is severe. To continue the above imagery of information flow inhibited by personal obligation to support friends, no one thinks of their industry as a friend, or feels obligation to support their industry, but people often develop such attachments to strong-culture organizations.

SIX

Closure and Stability

IN contrast to brokerage, closure does spill over into adjacent networks. The stability benefits of closing the network around collaborative relationships are enhanced when the broader networks around the collaborators are also closed. This chapter is about that spillover.

As the network around a set of people closes, it creates a competitive advantage very different from the advantage of brokerage. Where brokerage is about vision and growth from expanded horizons, closure is about control and productivity associated with people aligned on a shared goal. The gist of the closure argument—found in economics (e.g., Tullock, 1985; Greif, 1989), political science (e.g., Putnam, 1993, 2000), and sociology (e.g., Coleman, 1988, 1990; Granovetter, 1985, 1992)—is that closed networks create a reputation cost for inappropriate behavior which facilitates trust between people in the network. A network is closed to the extent that the people in it have strong relations with one another or can reach one another indirectly through strong relations to mutual contacts. As connections close the network, people are more informed about one another and calibrate with respect to one another. Reputations emerge to distinguish the peripheral from the best among us. People wary of news reaching colleagues that might erode their reputation in the network are careful to display appropriate opinion and behavior. With a reputation cost for inappropriate opinions and behavior, trust is less risky within the network, people are self-aligning to shared goals, transactions occur that would be difficult outside the closed network, and production efficiencies result from donated labor and the speed with which tasks can be completed (see Burt, 2005:93–166, for review and diverse examples).

Questions about network formation and decay are central to the social capital of network closure because stability is essential to the mechanism. For reputation to have its salutary effects, there has to be a credible threat that a person's reputation will persist to affect future relationships. From a woman's work in one project group, word gets around defining her reputation, which precedes her into her next project group. If negative reputation quickly dissolves, reputation loses its coercive power because yesterday's poor behavior is too soon forgotten. "Too soon" is relative. It could be a day, a month, a year. Relative stability is the key. Reputation has to persist longer than the productive relations it facilitates and the hurtful relations it protects against.

Stability cannot be taken for granted. Network closure varies from low to high, so closure-induced stability must vary. How does stability covary with closure? Current answers to the question are little more than speculation from cross-sectional evidence or assumptions convenient for formal models. Yet the question is central to any theoretical model that invokes a reputation mechanism and the question has broad substantive relevance.

Consider Munshi and Rosenzweig's (2005; 2007) work on community networks in India. They explain that people connected in the same village or by sub-caste (*jati*) across villages have traditionally had a social obligation to support one another (2005:428): "The fundamental marriage rule in Hindu society is that no individual can marry outside the *jati*. Marriage ties thus link all the members of the *jati*, either directly or indirectly, improving information flows and ensuring that members of the network do not renege on their obligations." For example (2005:428), "an individual making a job referral for another member of his *jati* will have a good idea of his ability, solving the basic information problem facing firms in labor markets with high rates of labor turnover. At the same time, the individual making the job referral can expect to receive similar support from his *jati* when he is unemployed in the future, giving rise to a decentralized reciprocal arrangement that only a long established and closed-knit community can provide." Munshi and Rosenzweig describe a decline in social obligation due to trends eroding attachment to community networks, a point to which I will return later in the chapter.

Readers familiar with Coleman's (1988) social capital argument will immediately recognize closure's reputation mechanism in Munshi and Rosenzweig's setting. Where Coleman discusses social obligation within rotating credit associations, Munshi and Rosenzweig discuss social obligation within *jati* and caste. All are concerned with reputation within a closed network, within the association, within the village, within the *jati*. Social obligation is enforced through a threat of losing face, eroded reputation, if one does not meet one's obligation of helping people who have a legitimate right to one's help. Which raises questions about variably strong reputation costs in variably closed networks: How closed must a network be to make reputation cost credible? How weak can closure in the *jati* beyond the local community become before *jati*-based reputation dissolves, whereupon felt obligation to the *jati* disappears?

To answer such questions, I study colleague networks around the bankers and analysts analyzed in Chapter 4. I measure reputation as the organization does, by the average evaluation a person receives from colleagues in the annual evaluation process. Reputation consistent in adjacent years I discuss as reputation stability. The tendency for colleague relations to disappear from one year to the next I discuss as decay. The empirical question is why certain reputations remain stable and certain relationships are prone to decay.

Consistent with received wisdom, closure is associated with stability: Where relations are more deeply embedded in a closed network, reputation is more stable and relationships are less subject to decay. Beyond the fact of association, three conclusions from the analysis describe the way in which stability covaries with closure:

First, reputation stability increases quickly with closure. I find that reputation has no stability from one year to the next in networks of colleagues who have little contact with one another. However—and this is an intriguing parallel to the social conformity induced by four peers in Asch's (1951) classic laboratory experiment—do the same work when you have four mutual contacts with colleagues, and reputation this year is a good predictor of reputation next year (see Figure G1 in Appendix G for a summary of Asch's experiment). With respect to the people studied here, Coleman (1988:S107) had it exactly right when he said: "Reputation cannot arise in an open structure."

Second, closure's stability effect is concentrated in new relationships. Closure is associated with more positive relations and relations are more robust to decay when embedded in closed networks. However, by the third year of a relationship, closure is less important than the strength of the relationship that has built up between the two people. In other words, closure keeps people in new relations longer than they would stay otherwise, thus protecting new relations from decay.

Third, closure's stability effect operates at a distance from the stabilized network element. Closure among indirect contacts (friends of friends) makes a statistically significant contribution to stability, emphasizing the importance of social monopoly to closure's stabilizing effect. My summary conclusion is that closure creates an endogenous force for the status quo that secures and expands the boundary around a network, protecting new relations until they are self-sustaining, and doing so even for people only indirectly connected at the periphery of the network.

Social Chaos in Financial Services

For this analysis, I return to the bankers and analysts introduced in Chapter 4. Viewed from outside, the banker and analyst networks have a center–periphery structure every year. There is little change to see (Figure 4.4). Inside the network, individual relations show dramatic rates of change.

The point is illustrated in Table 6.1. Cells are the percent of row evaluations this year that become the column evaluation next year. When relationships continue from this year to next year, they are likely to receive the same evaluation both years. The diagonal cells in Table 6.1 are the largest in each row for continuing relations (e.g., 21.3% of relations judged "outstanding" this year are again rated "outstanding" next year), and percentages are smaller in cells more removed from the diagonal (e.g., 1.3% of "poor" relations this year become "outstanding" relations next year).

However, most relations decay before next year. Seven of ten colleagues cited are new each year (72.9% at the bottom of Table 6.1). Banker relations are slightly more prone to decay than analyst relations, but decay is the typical outcome for relations in both groups: 73 percent for bankers, 71 percent for analysts. Strong relations are less subject to decay, but decay is the most likely outcome for strong and weak: Of relations judged "outstanding" this year, 69 percent are not cited next year. Of "poor" relationships this year, 80 percent are not cited next year. Life in the financial organization involves some long-term colleague relationships, but most relations fade as employees move to new projects: Of 16,505 relations to the bankers and analysts in the first of the four years, 4,418 are cited again in the second year, 1,233 continue to the third year, and 567 make it to the fourth year. And these are the relationships substantial enough to be cited in the peer evaluations. Less substantial relations must pass by like faces in a train going the other direction.

With relationships changing so dramatically, it is not surprising to see that evaluations are more about the people pair than either individual. Only 12 percent of variance in the evaluations can be attributed to agreement on the person evaluated. In fact, the best predictor of the number of positive evaluations a person receives is the number of negative evaluations received. Having a weak indicator of collaboration with colleagues is better than no indicator at all, but it is good to remember that only 12 percent of the variance in employee evaluations is consensus across colleagues. Another 23 percent of evaluation variance can be attributed to rater differences. Some colleagues give positive evaluations on average. Others use a more negative frame of reference. The remaining variance in evaluations, 65 percent, is unique to the two people connected by an evaluation. A person judged outstanding by one colleague is often incompatible with another colleague.[1]

Table 6.1 Turnover in Colleague Relations (row relations this year that receive column evaluation next year; based on 46,231 relations)

Colleague Relation This Year	Colleague Relation Next Year					
	Poor	Adequate	Good	Outstanding	Not Cited (decayed)	Total (%)
Poor	9.2	6.4	3.2	1.3	79.9	100
Adequate	3.1	10.5	8.9	1.7	75.8	100
Good	0.7	4.9	14.4	6.6	73.4	100
Outstanding	0.3	1.3	8.1	21.3	69.0	100
Total	1.5	4.9	10.6	10.1	72.9	100

---

[1] The percentages in this paragraph were computed from a regression equation predicting the evaluations from colleague i to employee j, e_{ij}, from the average evaluation

So much change from year to year makes this a productive study population for understanding the link between closure and stability. First, it increases the probability of seeing closure effects on stability even though I only have four years of data. Second, the high rate of change makes my time ordering consequential. Let "causal interval" refer to the time interval over which routine change occurs in a structure. If two observation periods are closer together than the "causal interval," structure will not appear to change. The two observation periods are ordered in time, but their similarity is less about stability than measurement reliability. High turnover in relations between annual observations means that I am in a stronger position to draw causal inference from correlations between networks in adjacent years.[2]

Direct and Indirect Embedding

I compute annual closure measures from the evaluation data. Consider the banker network in Figure 2.2 of Chapter 2. Six of the shaded dots are colleagues who evaluated the banker. The six colleagues are disconnected from each other. Thus, if limited to the immediate network around the banker, one could argue that there would be no reputation cost to the banker for poor behavior. The banker could drop a disgruntled colleague from the network without worrying about his reputation being tarnished by the erstwhile colleague talking to the other five. However, the six colleagues are embedded in a broader network through which they are connected indirectly so the banker could not easily escape the consequences of poor behavior toward any one of the colleagues. Beyond the six colleagues who evaluated the banker are 47 employees who evaluated one or more of the six who evaluated the banker. The 47 employees are indirect contacts to the banker. Following Granovetter's (1985, 1992) discussion of relations in context, there are three ways to think

---

made by the colleague (row mean) and the average evaluation of the employee (column mean). The 23% of evaluation variation due to rater differences is the variance predicted by the row mean. The 12% due to agreement on the employee is the variance predicted by the column mean. The remaining 65% is the residual variance unique to colleague i paired with employee j. The same percentages result if evaluations are standardized within years, and they only differ slightly if evaluations of analysts are predicted separately from the evaluations of bankers (63.0% residual variance for analysts versus 66.1% for the bankers). The tendency for relations to be more about the pair of people than either person individually is consistent with the substantial turnover in relationships in this study population, but it could be a more general phenomenon. Kenny and Albright (1987:399) report a similar pattern in networks of college students.

[2] High relationship turnover makes the study population analytically attractive for a third reason, but it is not productive to mention until I have introduced, in the next section, Granovetter's distinction between relational and structural embedding (see footnote 11).

about the broader network: Relational embedding, structural embedding, and what I will discuss as indirect structural embedding.

Relational embedding

Relational embedding refers to the relation accumulated between two people. It would be indicated in Figure 2.2 by the strength of the banker's relationship with each of his colleagues. Blau (1968:454) summarizes the process as follows: "Social exchange relations evolve in a slow process, starting with minor transactions in which little trust is required because little risk is involved and in which both partners can prove their trustworthiness, enabling them to expand their relation and engage in major transactions. Thus, the process of social exchange leads to the trust required for it in a self-governing fashion." In proposing the term "relational" embeddedness, Granovetter (1992:42) offers the following (cf. Granovetter, 1985:490): "That trustworthy behavior may be a regularized part of a personal relationship reflects one of the typically direct effects of relational embeddedness and explains the widespread preference of all economic actors to deal with those they have dealt with before. Our information about such partners is cheap, richly detailed, and probably accurate." The information advantage is illustrated in Uzzi's fieldwork on relational embedding in apparel (Uzzi, 1996), banking (Uzzi, 1999; Uzzi and Gillespie, 2002), and law (Uzzi and Lancaster, 2004). Similarly, Wong and Ellis (2002) describe how Hong Kong companies entering China decide more quickly between alternative venture partners when their information comes from family or close friends rather than casual friends or acquaintances.

Structural embedding

Now consider implications of the social network around the relationship. Every relationship is embedded in a network of people telling stories; not stories in the sense of deception, just stories in the sense of personal accounts about people; in other words, gossip. Gossip is the sharing of news, the catching up, through which we build and maintain relations (Dunbar, 1996; Gambetta, 1994). Reputations are defined by people monitoring and discussing individual behavior, and by defining reputations, mutual friends and colleagues constitute an adaptive control on behavior. The stronger and more numerous the connections between two people through mutual contacts, the more closed the network around the two people, and the greater their vicarious experience of one another. Alternative, redundant communication channels let numerous tellings of a story get around quickly, ensuring reliable, early warning. The omnipresent hydra-eyes of a closed network make it difficult for misbehavior to escape detection. The more closed the network, the more penetrating the detection and so the lower the risk of trust. This is the argument with which I began the chapter.

Coleman's (1988, 1990) closure argument is the most prominent with re-spect to social capital (in some part due to Putnam's, 1993, widely cited application of Coleman's argument to regional government in Italy), but it is not alone in predicting that closure facilitates trust (for review, see Burt, 2005: chap. 3). Anthropologists have long reported on gossip and trust in small communities. Merry (1984) offers review and ethnographic illustration that foreshadows Coleman's argument (Coleman, 1990:283–285). There is a clos-ure argument familiar in economics in which mutual acquaintances make behavior more public, creating an incentive for good behavior to maintain reputation, which decreases the risk associated with trust, and so increases the probability of trust (e.g., Tullock 1985; Greif, 1989). The other prom-inent closure argument in sociology is Granovetter's (1985, 1992) discussion of embeddedness (see Krippner and Alvarez, 2007, for broader review). "Structural" embeddedness refers to the relationship between people who share mutual friends (Granovetter, 1992:44): "My mortification at cheating a friend of long standing may be substantial even when undiscovered. It may increase when the friend becomes aware of it. But it may become even more unbearable when our mutual friends uncover the deceit and tell one another."

Indirect structural embedding

It is easy to imagine how closure and reputation work in the small, face-to-face groups measured by direct structural embedding. Not doing your share is quickly apparent, and immediately embarrassing.

But how effective is closure in creating reputation in the larger groups in which it is assumed—such as the Indian *jati* with which I began the chapter, or Grief's Maghribi traders, or Putnam's Italian regions, or contemporary profes-sional groups, or business groups more generally? In these larger groups, most connections are only indirect through colleague intermediaries.

With respect to the Indian example, Munshi and Rosenzweig (2005) de-scribe a decline in social insurance (what Coleman and Putnam would term community social capital) attributed to two events eroding attachment to community networks. One event was a farming innovation that created an economic advantage for one group over others, which made the advantaged group disproportionately wealthy and likely to be asked for favors, which in turn encouraged the advantaged group to marry outside the *jati*. Marriage ties outside the *jati* eroded felt obligation to the *jati*, thus explaining the decreased interpersonal economic assistance previously provided within the *jati*. The second event was the liberalization of the Indian economy in the 1990s, which led to higher incomes in commercial and corporate jobs, thus encour-aging parents to move their children to English-language schools (in prefer-ence to indigenous-language schools) so the children could better compete for the desired jobs. More able children were more likely to matriculate in the

English language schools, thus removing the more able participants in job referrals previously provided within the local network. Munshi and Rosenzweig's two disruptive events both eroded obligation to a group by creating attachments outside the group.

On the other side of the world, Frank Ellis is an instructive case. Ellis was one of the largest landowners in Ellickson's (1991) study of disputes resolved informally in closed networks. Ellis was a rancher and real estate broker in his late fifties when he bought his large tract of land in Shasta County. Ellis had risen to prosperity outside Shasta County. His primary affiliations were elsewhere. Ellis stands out in Ellickson's analysis for his immunity to the reputation mechanism by which Shasta County landowners resolved disputes. The area (Ellickson, 1991:57): "... remains distinctly rural in atmosphere. People tend to know one another, and they value their reputations in the community. Some ranching families have lived in the area for several generations and include members who plan to stay indefinitely. Members of these families seem particularly intent on maintaining their reputations as good neighbors." Residents (p. 57) "seem quite conscious of the role of gossip in their system of social control. One longtime resident, who had also lived for many years in a suburb of a major California urban area, observed that people in the Oak Run area 'gossip all the time,' much more than in the urban area. Another reported intentionally using gossip to sanction a traditionalist who had been 'impolite' when coming to pick up some stray mountain cattle; he reported that application of this self-help device produced an apology, an outcome itself presumably circulated through the gossip system." Returning to Frank Ellis (p. 58):

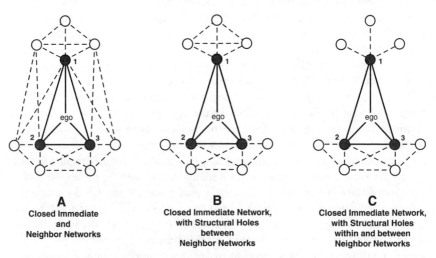

A
Closed Immediate
and
Neighbor Networks

B
Closed Immediate Network,
with Structural Holes
between
Neighbor Networks

C
Closed Immediate Network,
with Structural Holes
within and between
Neighbor Networks

Solid dots and lines represent immediate network of direct contacts.
Hollow dots and dashed lines indicate indirect contacts.

Figure 6.1 Variations on a Closed Network

"The ranchette residents who were particularly bothered by Ellis' cattle could see that he was utterly indifferent to his reputation among them. They thought, however, that as a major rancher, Ellis would worry about his reputation among the large cattle operations in the county. They therefore reported Ellis' activities to the Board of Directors of the Shasta County Cattlemen's Association. This move proved unrewarding, for Ellis was also surprisingly indifferent to his reputation among the cattlemen."

Frank Ellis illustrates a component to closure that is poorly captured by dense relations within the immediate network around ego. Closure is about control. It means closed to alternatives. It means social monopoly. The immediate network around ego, however much closed, is embedded in a broader network that can augment or erode trust and alignment within the immediate network.

Consider the three sociograms in Figure 6.1. The immediate network around ego is closed at the center of all three sociograms. Each of ego's contacts is connected to her other contacts. What differs across the sociograms is the network of ego's indirect contacts. In Figure 6.1A, the indirect contacts are connected. Closure in the surrounding network reinforces closure in the immediate network. In Figures 6.1B and 6.1C, in contrast, structural holes in the surrounding network could undermine closure in the immediate network. Person 1 in Figure 6.1B is part of a group separate from the group containing persons 2 and 3. Reputation lost in ego's network need not damage person 1's reputation in the outside group, which weakens pressure on person 1 to preserve reputation within ego's network, which increases the risk to ego of trusting person 1 and decreases person 1's incentive to avoid discussing opinion or practice contrary to what is currently accepted in ego's network. Like Frank Ellis among the cattlemen, person 1 is a backdoor for disruptive information entering ego's closed network. In Figure 6.1C, person 1 has multiple affiliations outside ego's network. Although a participant in ego's closed network, person 1 is exposed to a variety of alternative opinions and practices outside the network. Here again, alternative affiliations weaken the pressure on person 1 to maintain reputation within ego's network.

More generally, it is not unusual to see successful closed networks embedded in broader institutions. Within the closed network of the Jewish Maghribi traders described by Grief (1989:863), for example, traders appealed to the broader Jewish community to impose sanctions on errant members (cf. Woolcock, 1999:29–34, on closed networks of borrowers in a microfinance program embedded within a formal church hierarchy or pre-existing "affinity group;" Ingram and Roberts, 2000, on closed networks of hotel managers embedded in the local chapter of the national hotel trade association; Burt, 2003, on 19th Cornish mining networks embedded in Freemason Lodges). Each neighbor, illustrated by neighbor Frank Ellis among the cattlemen, is a potential backdoor through whom disruptive opinion can enter to disturb trust and alignment within the immediate network. Closure across neighbor networks shuts the backdoors. As Coleman (1988:S107–S108) summarizes: "Reputation cannot arise in an open structure, and collective sanctions that would ensure trustworthiness cannot be applied."

I will refer to closure through indirect contacts as indirect structural embedding. Closure in the immediate network around ego is "direct structural embedding" in the sense that contacts are directly connected so as to monitor one another. Consistent with Coleman's and Granovetter's discussions, perhaps implicit in both, is a broader domain of closure in which contacts are connected through people further removed in the network. In keeping with Granovetter's (1992) discussion, I use the term "indirect structural embedding." There are degrees. Continuing to more remote indirect connections eventually leads from network analysis to institutional analysis, but I limit myself in this book to the distinction between direct and indirect structural embedding.

Network metrics

To estimate the relative contributions of direct and indirect connections to closure, I compute the network measures illustrated in Figure 6.2. Let a 2-step connection refer to a connection between two people through a mutual contact. For example, the "1" under "D" for Jim in the first row of the table in Figure 6.2 refers to person 4 in the sociogram. Person 4 is the only contact linked directly to Jim and person 1. The "3" underneath the "1" in the table refers to three mutual contacts between Jim and person 2. The mutual contacts are persons 4, 6, and 7. Two-step connections measure direct structural embedding.

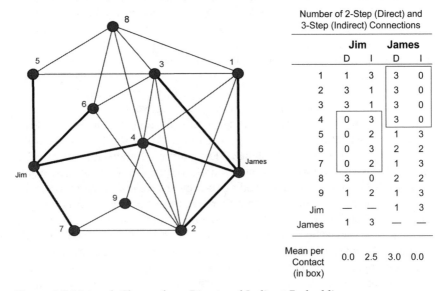

| | Number of 2-Step (Direct) and 3-Step (Indirect) Connections | | | |
| | **Jim** | | **James** | |
	D	I	D	I
1	1	3	3	0
2	3	1	3	0
3	3	1	3	0
4	0	3	3	0
5	0	2	1	3
6	0	3	2	2
7	0	2	1	3
8	3	0	2	2
9	1	2	1	3
Jim	—	—	1	3
James	1	3	—	—
Mean per Contact (in box)	0.0	2.5	3.0	0.0

Figure 6.2 Network Closure from Direct and Indirect Embedding

Three-step connections measure indirect structural embedding. For example, the "1" under "I" for Jim in the second row of the table in Figure 6.2 refers to persons 5 and 3 in the sociogram. Jim's connections to 2 through persons 4, 6, and 7 are 2-step connections. Jim's fourth contact, person 5, is not connected to person 2, but is connected to 3 who is connected to 2, so Jim has a 3-step connection to person 2 via person 5. In graph theoretic terms, I am looking for geodesics linking two people through one intermediary (direct structural embedding) or two intermediaries (indirect structural embedding). Since I want to know how indirect embedding adds to direct embedding, I only count distant connections in the absence of closer connections. For example, Jim is connected to person 6 who is connected to 3 who is connected to 2, which is a 3-step connection between Jim and person 2. However, Jim reaches 2 through 6 directly, so the table reports one 3-step connection (the 5–3–2 connection).

To the extent that direct structural embedding provides stability, I expect stability to increase with counts of 2-step connections. James illustrates direct structural embedding. I put a box around James' four contacts. He has three 2-step connections with each of his contacts. For example, the relationship between James and person 1 is embedded in their mutual connections to persons 2, 3, and 4. With all four contacts directly embedded in one another, there is no additional embedding recorded through indirect connections.

To the extent that indirect structural embedding adds to the stabilizing effect of direct embedding, I expect stability to increase with counts of 3-step connections that link contacts in the absence of more direct connection. Jim illustrates indirect closure. None of Jim's four contacts are connected to one another. Like the banker in Figure 2.2, Jim's contacts are only connected indirectly. For example, Jim's relationship with person 4 is embedded in three 3-step connections. Jim is indirectly connected to person 4 through his connection with person 5 (via 8 or 3). Jim is indirectly connected through person 6 (via 2, 3, or 8). Jim is indirectly connected through his connection with person 7 (via 2).

Reputation Stability

Given the substantial turnover in banker and analyst relations, and the large proportion of evaluation variance unique to individual relationships, I expected to see reputations bounce up and down from one year to the next.

Instead, reputation this year is a good predictor of reputation next year. The four levels of evaluation in Table 6.1 are scored in the organization as 1 to 4, then averaged for each employee to measure the employee's reputation with colleagues. An average evaluation of 1.0 indicates an employee consistently judged "poor" by colleagues. An average of 4.0 indicates an employee

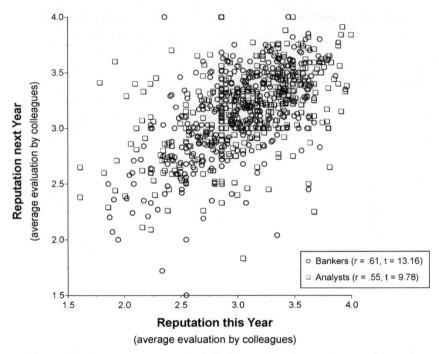

Figure 6.3 Despite the High Rate of Network Decay, Reputations Persist from One Year to the Next

consistently judged "outstanding." Figure 6.3 shows a strong association between reputation this year and reputation next year. There are people who dropped in reputation, and others who rose in reputation, but across the bankers and analysts on average—and for each population separately—reputation next year is clearly contingent on reputation last year (.56 correlation across the two populations, 15.3 t-test adjusted for repeated observations of the same people, P < .001; within-population statistics are given in Figure 6.3).

Intrigued by stable reputations in chaotic networks, I raised the issue over drinks with one of the senior people in the financial organization. He took on a puzzled look, then patiently explained to me that "of course" employee reputations are stable. They are the company's market index of employee quality. A good employee this year is a good employee next year, regardless of the colleagues with whom the employee works. Reputations are expected to go up and down a little depending on personalities and business opportunities, but good employees continue to be good employees, and weak employees are weeded out.

In other words, the division head had a human-capital explanation for reputation stability. Able people receive good evaluations. Weak people receive poor evaluations. Reputation is correlated over time because human capital continues over time, certainly between adjacent years.

I had a social-capital explanation. Colleague evaluations are based on limited personal experience mixed with the experiences of colleagues with whom work is discussed. The same is true of any colleague evaluation, whether bankers, consultants, products, or professors. The more connected the colleagues making their individual evaluations, the more likely their evaluations are in part formed by stories they have shared about the object being evaluated. In fact, their story-sharing activity is essential to the argument in the first paragraph of this chapter that closed networks constitute social capital.

The human-capital and social-capital explanations can be tested against each other. If individual ability is the reason for reputation stability over time, then stability should be independent of connections between colleagues. An able employee should receive good evaluations whether the colleagues who made the evaluations work together or work in separate parts of the organization. But if reputation stability is defined by colleagues sharing stories about the employee, then stability should be higher when colleagues are more connected because they are more likely to have shared stories about the employee.

Closure in the aggregate

The pattern in Figure 6.4 supports the social-capital explanation: Reputation stability increases with network closure. Closure is measured on the horizontal axis by the extent to which an employee is evaluated by connected colleagues. The measurement was illustrated in Figure 6.2. For each colleague citing an employee in a particular year, the number of mutual contacts is the number of people citing the employee that year and connected to the colleague by an evaluation. An employee's score on the horizontal axis in Figure 6.4 is the employee's average number of mutual contacts with evaluating colleagues (e.g., 0.0 for Jim and 3.0 for James in Figure 6.2). For the purposes of Figure 6.4, I rounded scores to the nearest of the eleven integer categories on the horizontal axis.

Reputation stability is measured on the vertical axis by a correlation between banker reputations in adjacent years.[3] The dashed line describes stability when

---

[3] The vertical axis is the correlation within a subsample around each employee. Rank order the employees present in two adjacent years by their average number of 2-step and 3-step connections with colleagues (the mean scores for Jim and James in Figure 6.2). The six employees above and below person i on the list are drawn as a subsample around person i. Person i's score on the vertical axis in Figure 6.4 is the correlation for the 13 people in the subsample between reputation this year and next year. I settled on subsamples of a dozen colleagues after testing alternatives. The association with closure in Figure 6.4 increases sharply through subsamples of size 4, 6, and 8 colleagues (decreasing sampling error), more slowly through subsamples of 10 and 12 colleagues, then little for larger subsamples. I took 12 as the inflection point. With subsamples of 13, I lose the first six and last six employees in the rank order.

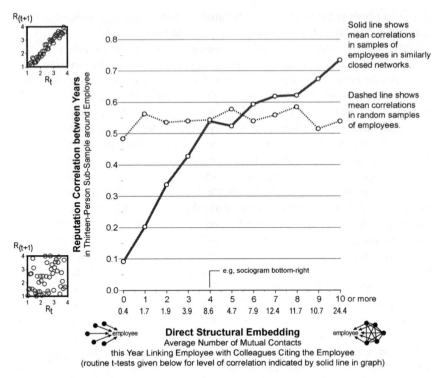

Figure 6.4 Closure and Reputation Stability from this Year to Next for the Bankers and Analysts

stability is measured independent of closure.[4] The dashed line is horizontal across the graph, showing that stability is roughly constant at each level of closure if a person at that level of closure is compared to a random sample of other employees.

However, when comparisons are made more precisely between employees at the same level of closure, I get the solid line in Figure 6.4—which shows stability sharply increasing with closure. The correlation between reputations in adjacent years increases from a .09 correlation for employees whose colleagues do not cite one another (zero closure), up to a .73 correlation for employees who share 10 or more mutual contacts with the colleagues evaluating them (high closure). Where colleagues evaluating an employee are strongly connected within a closed network, the employee's reputation

---

[4] For each employee, I drew a random sample of 12 other employees and correlated reputation scores for adjacent years across the 13 employees. The subsample size of 13 is arbitrary. I set the subsample size at 13 to match the subsamples of similarly embedded employees (see previous note).

continues over time. When the evaluating colleagues are disconnected, reputation quickly dissolves.

Consider two hypothetical employees who work well with ten colleagues this year. One works with colleagues segregated in the organization so they do not cite one another in the annual peer evaluations (illustrated by the sociogram at the bottom-left in Figure 6.4). That employee would be over the "0" on the horizontal axis in Figure 6.4. The second employee works with five colleagues who work together in one division and another five colleagues who work together in a second division (sociogram to the bottom-right in Figure 6.4). The second employee would be over the "4" on the horizontal axis.

Both employees do good work, but it is the second employee's work that will be remembered. The solid line in Figure 6.4 shows that an employee doing good work for colleagues not connected with each other can expect to be forgotten. The exact correlation expected between the employee's reputation this year and next year is given by the level of the solid line over the "0" on the horizontal axis. The correlation is indistinguishable from random noise.[5] The employees work with so many new contacts each year that their work is quickly forgotten—unless the people with whom they work talk to each other. For the second employee, the one who worked with two groups of connected colleagues, reputation has an expected correlation of .57 over time. What carries an employee's reputation into the future is people talking to one another about the employee.

Kinds of closure

Figure 6.5 shows the Figure 6.4 aggregate closure-stability association disaggregated for categories of bankers and analysts. Table 6.2 contains regression models predicting level of stability from closure and other variables. Zero-order associations are presented with partial effects holding the other predictors constant.[6] Routine standard errors are a heuristic here because the

---

[5] Test statistics are reported at the bottom of Figure 6.4. For example, there are 121 observations of employees who have an average of 3 mutual contacts with the colleagues evaluating them (20 employees in the first and second years, 42 employees in the second and third years, and 59 in the third and fourth years). Regressing reputation next year over reputation this year yields a coefficient of .432 across the 121 observations, with a standard error of .111 (adjusted for repeated observations of some employees over time), which yields the 3.9 t-test reported in Figure 6.4. I repeated the computation to get a test statistic for reputation stability in each of the other ten categories of network closure in the figure.

[6] One sign reversal warrants explanation. Stability is higher for bankers and analysts cited by many colleagues this year, but the partial effect in Table 6.2 for "Number of colleagues this year" shows a crowding effect of stability eroded by numerous colleague evaluations. Number of colleagues is highly correlated with direct structural embedding. The more colleagues who cite an employee, the more 2-step connections possible among the colleagues. There is a .84 correlation between "Number of colleagues this year" and "Number of positive 2-step connections" this year. Just holding constant the number of

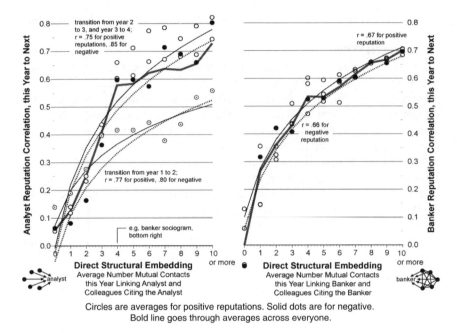

Circles are averages for positive reputations. Solid dots are for negative.
Bold line goes through averages across everyone.

Figure 6.5 Detail on Closure Stabilizing Reputation

sub-sample measure of employee reputation stability is computed from over-lapping samples of observations, so my reputation-stability scores are not independent observations (see footnote 4).

Closure and stability are clearly linked. The closure–stability association is lowest for analysts in the first year, when they began to participate in the peer evaluations, then highest for analysts in the last years, after they were a routine part of the peer evaluations. The difference between the bankers and analysts is substantial (−10.64 routine t-test for the lower association in first year), but the difference is negligible when the other factors in Table 6.2 are held constant (−10.64 t-test drops to 0.47), so I do not include the banker-analyst adjustment in Table 6.2.

The stability association with direct structural embedding is about the same as the association with indirect structural embedding. Both have strong associations in Table 6.2 holding the other constant along with the control variables.[7]

---

positive 2-step connections changes the strong positive association between stability and "Number of colleagues" to a strong negative association (routine t-test statistics of 23.6 versus −3.8). The multicollinearity is much less at the level of individual relations so I do not make much of the crowding effect in Table 6.2 in preference to raising it in the discussion of Table 6.4.

[7] I combined positive and negative 3-step connections together in Table 6.2 because they are so highly correlated when aggregated across an individual's relationships. There is a .92 correlation between positive 3-step connections and negative 3-step connections,

Table 6.2 Network Closure and Reputation Stability

Network this Year	Analysts		Bankers	
	Zero-Order	Partial	Zero-Order	Partial
Intercept	—	-.50	—	-.18
Risk year (2, 3, 4)	.11 (.01)**	.11 (.01)**	-.05 (.01)**	.02 (.01)
Number colleagues in risk year (/10)	.08 (.01)**	.01 (.01)	.09 (.01)**	.02 (.01)*
Relational Embedding				
Number colleagues this year (/10)	.10 (.01)**	-.02 (.01)**	.07 (.004)**	-.03 (.01)**
Number continuing colleagues (/10)	.15 (.01)**	-.01 (.01)	.11 (.01)**	.01 (.01)
Reputation this year (absolute score)	-.04 (.03)	-.01 (.02)	.02 (.02)	-.01 (.02)
Extreme reputation this year (dev. score)	-.02 (.02)	.02 (.01)*	-.02 (.01)	.03 (.01)*
Years reputation observed (1, 2, 3)	.12 (.01)**	.01 (.01)*	-.01 (.01)	-.01 (.01)
Direct Structural Embedding				
Number of positive 2-step connections	.12 (.004)**	.07 (.01)**	.11 (.01)**	.08 (.01)**
Number of negative 2-step connections	.13 (.004)**	.04 (.01)**	.10 (.01)**	.03 (.01)**
Indirect Structural Embedding				
Number of 3-step connections	.17 (.01)**	.074 (.01)**	.16 (.01)**	.07 (.02)**
Holds senior rank	.15 (.02)**	.026 (.02)	.11 (.01)**	-.01 (.02)
Percent colleagues at senior rank	-.002 (.0003)**	-.0004 (.0004)	.002 (.0002)**	-.0001 (.0003)
Percent colleagues in division	-.003 (.0006)**	-.0007 (.0003)*	.0004 (.0004)	-.0000 (.0002)
Percent colleagues in geographic region	-.002 (.0006)**	-.0002 (.0003)	.0002 (.0003)	-.0004 (.0002)*

Note: These are regression models predicting reputation stability from this year to next using network variables measured this year. Stability is measured for a person by the sub-correlation between reputation in adjacent years (see footnote 3). Connections 2-step and 3-step are log scores. There are 623 annual observations of analysts and 1179 annual observations of bankers. "Zero-Order" columns refer to models containing only a single row variable. Standard errors in parentheses are adjusted for autocorrelation between stability scores on the same person, but they are only a heuristic since routine statistical inference is not applicable for sub-sample correlations as a criterion variable. * P < .05 ** P < .001.

In other words, the banker in Figure 2.2 can expect the closure among his indirect contacts to improve the stability of his reputation from one year to the next. There is also a result in Table 6.2 corroborating the earlier characterization of bankers integrating across geography and analysts integrating across functions. Analyst reputation is less stable when it comes primarily from other analysts ("Percent colleagues in division"). Banker reputation is less stable when it comes primarily from colleagues in the same region ("Percent colleagues in geographic region").

The stability association with closure is consistent across positive and negative evaluations. Extreme reputations—in the sense of extremely negative or extremely positive—are more likely to persist into next year, but positive relations are no more or less likely to be stable than negative reputations. The hollow dots in Figure 6.5 indicate levels of stability in the reputations of people with above average reputations this year. The solid dots refer to stability in the reputations of analysts in the bottom 25 percent of analysts and bankers in the bottom 25 percent of bankers. The hollow and solid dots have very similar distributions. For example, Figure 6.5 shows that stability in banker reputation has a .67 correlation with closure for bankers with a positive reputation and a .66 correlation with closure for bankers with a negative reputation.

No trade-off between kinds of closure

Given stability effects from direct and indirect structural embedding, how do the effects work together? Figure 6.6 illustrates data patterns to be expected from three very different answers to the question. Horizontal and vertical axes in each graph are the same as axes in the previous two figures. Two lines in each graph show reputation stability increasing with closure in ego's immediate network when there is weak (dashed line) versus strong (bold line) closure among friends of friends just beyond the immediate network. The dashed line is identical in each graph. It is based on stability results for the bankers and analysts (discussed in a moment). The solid lines are hypothetical.

The possibility illustrated in Figure 6.6A is that direct and indirect closure make independent contributions to reputation stability. The graph shows reputation stability increasing with closure, but at a higher level when friends of friends are connected. I made this graph by copying the dashed line, pasting it in the graph at a higher level, then turning it into a solid line. The slopes of the solid and dashed lines in Figure 6.6A are identical.

and their respective correlations with the reputation stability measure in Table 6.2 are .63 and .63. There is nothing to distinguish the two kinds of 3-step connections aggregated across an individual's relations so I combine them in Table 6.2. I report them separately in Table 6.4 because they are less redundant at the level of individual relationships.

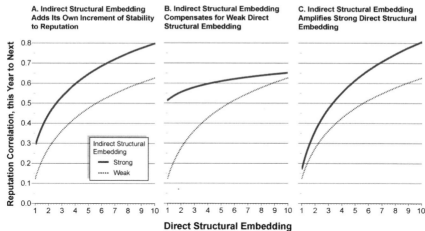

Figure 6.6 Possible Reputation–Stability Interaction Effects between Direct and Indirect Structural Embedding

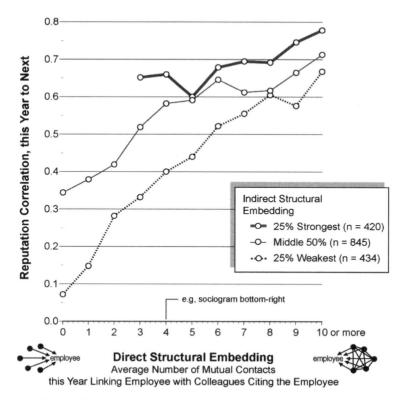

Figure 6.7 Detail on Interaction between Direct and Indirect Structural Embedding for the Bankers and Analysts

The graph in Figure 6.6B illustrates a negative interaction. Ego's reputation is unstable if ego's colleagues are disconnected—unless friends of the colleagues are connected, whereupon ego's reputation is almost as stable as it would be if the colleagues were densely connected. The pattern in Figure 6.6B would occur if closure among friends of friends could compensate for a lack of closure in ego's immediate network (illustrated by the banker network in Figure 2.2), but added no stability beyond what is already provided by extensive connections among ego's direct contacts.

The graph in Figure 6.6C illustrates a positive interaction. Ego's reputation is unstable if ego's colleagues are disconnected—regardless of connections among friends of the colleagues. With increasing closure among ego's colleagues, however, closure among colleague friends acts as a multiplier, increasing reputation stability beyond the level expected from closure within the immediate network around ego.

The actual association turns out to be the simplest of the three possibilities: Direct and indirect make separate, additive contributions to stability. The point is illustrated in Figure 6.7, which is a graph of reputation stability associated with direct structural embedding for three levels of indirect structural embedding. The three levels distinguish people whose friends of friends are weakly connected (dashed line), moderately connected (solid line), or strongly connected (bold line). "Weak" contains the analysts and bankers who were in the bottom quartile of indirect structural embedding, and "strong" contains those in the top quartile (where quartiles are defined within each year for analysts and bankers separately). Analysts and bankers are combined since reputation stability increases similarly with closure in the two populations, excluding the initial year of data on analysts.[8] The dashed line in Figure 6.7 shows that even when friends of friends are poorly connected, reputation stability increases sharply with closure in ego's immediate network, from zero stability when ego's colleagues are disconnected (zero on horizontal axis), up to strong stability when the colleagues are extensively connected (to the right on horizontal axis). The bold line in Figure 6.7 shows that when friends of friends are extensively connected, reputation stability increases with direct structural embedding at about the same rate as when friends of friends are disconnected, and ego is likely embedded in a closed network of direct contacts. On the first point, the bold line in Figure 6.7 runs parallel to the dashed line over most of the bold line.[9] On the second point, the bold line in

---

[8] I excluded the first year of data on the analysts since Figure 6.5A shows that transition from the first to the second year was clearly distinct from later transitions. I ran statistical tests including the few deleted analyst observations from the first year and reach the same conclusions. Standard errors are slightly larger since there is more variation within categories of direct structural embedding.

[9] Statistical tests for non-parallel slopes are negligible. Let Xhigh be a dummy variable distinguishing bankers and analysts with the strongest indirect structural embedding (bold line in Figure 6.7). Let Xlow be a dummy variable distinguishing bankers and

Figure 6.7 does not begin until ego has three mutual contacts among colleagues in his immediate network, and the average number of mutual contacts between ego and the people in his immediate network is high when friends of friends are strongly connected (average of 10.47 mutual contacts per colleague for the 420 ego observations in the Figure 6.7 "strong" indirect embedding category versus 4.86 for the 434 observations in the "weak" indirect embedding category, 19.37 t-test for the difference).

Network Decay

Closure's stabilizing effect can be traced down to the level of individual relationships. Table 6.3 reports hazard rates for decay. Of 16,505 relations cited in the first of the four years (first row of Table 6.3), 12,087 were not cited in the second year. In other words, of 16,505 relations at risk of decay during the first year, 12,087 did decay, so there is a .73 decay rate during the year. The surviving 4,418 relations were at risk of decay in the third year. Of those, 3,185 were not cited in the third year, which defines a .72 decay rate. The surviving 1,233 were at risk of decay in the fourth year. Of those, 666 were not cited, defining a .54 decay rate. A large number of new relations were reported in the second period (11,528), of which a large proportion decayed before the third period (9,355). Aggregating across time periods and survival durations, the 46,231 relations at risk of decay had a .73 decay rate, which is reported at the bottom of Table 6.3 just as it was reported at the bottom of Table 6.1.

The decay rates in Table 6.3 illustrate a baseline analogous to the "liability of newness" in population ecology (Hannan and Freeman, 1989:80). Relations decay over time, but more slowly in surviving relations. The decay process begins with people becoming acquainted as a function of random chance and exogenous factors. People who would not otherwise seek one another out can find themselves neighbors, colleagues in the same company, assigned to the same project team, or seated next to one another. It is rude not to strike up a relationship (see Feld, 1981, on the social foci from which relations emerge).

---

analysts with the weakest (dashed line). Compute interaction terms by multiplying Xhigh and Xlow times the level of direct structural embedding in ego's network (horizontal axis in Figure 6.7). Add the two interaction terms to each of the regression equations in Table 6.2 predicting reputation stability. Test statistics for the Xhigh and Xlow interaction terms predicting analyst reputation stability are .97 and −1.25 respectively (1.11 and −1.35 if I exclude the 95 observations on analysts in the first year). Corresponding test statistics for banker reputation stability are −1.45 and −.24 respectively. If I pool the bankers and analysts to have 1791 observations, the test statistics are −.26 and .36 respectively. All the test statistics are negligible, so I discuss in the text independent, additive effects from direct and indirect structural embedding.

The relations can be bridges to other groups when they result from events that bring people together from separate groups, events such as cross-functional teams, inter-department committees, or inter-organizational conventions and professional meetings. People in these relationships often discover that they do not enjoy one another, or cannot work well together, so they disengage in favor of more compatible contacts. The selection process in which new (hoped to be) compatible contacts replace existing (known to be) incompatible ones means that relations on average weaken and decay over time. There is a liability of newness because the longer a relationship has survived, the more likely that it connects people who have learned to appreciate one another, which increases the probability of the relationship continuing into the future. This is illustrated in Table 6.3 by the .73 decay rate in relations during the first year, and the .54 decay rate in relations that survived to a third year. Learning is more than an accompanist to selection processes. There is also learning from your current relationships to identify kinds of people with whom you are likely to be compatible. Whatever the average probability of a new relationship disappearing next year, that probability should be lower for people more experienced in the study population because experienced people have learned to identify partners with whom they can be compatible.

Thus, aging is a factor twice in decay functions. First is the age of a relationship, call it tie age, for which the liability of newness is evident from slower decay in older relationships. Second is the time that the person citing a relationship has spent in the study population (or in a specific role within the study population), call it node age, for which the liability of newness is evident from slower decay in relations cited by people with more experience.

Table 6.3   Decay in Colleague Relations

Years Observed (T)	Year in Which First Cited (P)	Relations at Risk[d]	Relations that Decay[e]	Decay Rate[f]
1	1[a]	16,505	12,087	.732
2	1[a]	4,418	3,185	.721
3	1[a]	1,233	666	.540
1	2[b]	11,528	9,355	.811
2	2[b]	2,173	1,247	.574
1	3[c]	10,374	7,147	.689
	Total	46,231	33,687	.729

Note: (a) This row describes colleague relations cited in the first year. (b) This row describes relations cited in the second year, but not in the first year. (c) This row describes relations cited in the third year, but not in the second. (d) These are the relations cited this year that are at risk of not being cited next year. (e) These are the relations at risk that were not re-cited. (f) This is column (e) divided by (d), in other words, the proportion of relations at risk that decayed.

Closure in the aggregate

Figure 6.8 shows the association between closure and stability in the banker and analyst relationships. Logit models in Table 6.4 predict the vertical axis in Figure 6.8 from the horizontal axes with various controls.[10] The point illustrated in Figure 6.8 is that closure is associated with more positive relations and relations are more robust to decay when embedded in closed networks, but closure stabilizes by protecting new and old relations differently.

The horizontal axes in Figure 6.8 distinguish relations this year by the number of mutual contacts between the two people connected by the evaluation. Measurement was illustrated in Figure 6.2, and sociograms at the bottom of Figure 6.8 illustrate here. The vertical axes show the state of the relationship next year. The upward-sloping lines in Figure 6.8A show the increasing probability of a positive evaluation next year between two people with mutual contacts this year. Downward-sloping lines in Figure 6.8B show the decreasing probability of decay in a relationship between people with mutual contacts this year.

Kinds of closure

Three variables in Table 6.4 show that relational embedding increases stability. The more positive the relationship this year, or the longer it has been reported in the peer evaluations, the more likely it will be positive next year and the more robust it is to decay. There is also a crowding effect related to the concentration effects that Uzzi has made familiar (e.g., Uzzi, 1996, 1999, see "positional measures" in Appendix B). A person only has so much attention. The more relationships a person has this year, the more prone is each to decay.[11]

---

[10] Two quick notes on the evidence in this section: Routine standard errors on the zero-order associations in Table 6.4 are not corrected for the multiple tests being made. They are presented as a heuristic to distinguish observable associations with stability. Second, bankers and analysts are combined. Relations to analysts are more negative ($-.385$ coefficient divided by .079 standard error yields a test statistic of -4.87, P < .001) and decay faster (4.76 logit test statistic, P < .001), but factors that predict next year's relation to an analyst similarly predict next year's relation to a banker, so I combined the two groups for this analysis.

[11] Continuing footnote 2, high turnover in relationships also makes the bankers and analysts an attractive research site because relational embedding is not be as influential as it would be in a population of people who work with the same colleagues over time. In other words, the bankers and analysts are nicely suited for studying the relative stabilizing effects of direct versus indirect structural embedding.

Direct structural embedding

Four variables in Table 6.4 show that direct structural embedding increases stability.[12] Holding relational embedding constant, the more often that you and I have positive relations with the same colleagues this year, the more likely that our relationship will be positive next year (.06 coefficient in Table 6.4, 5.16 test statistic) and the less likely our connection this year will decay (−.06 coefficient, −4.48 test statistic). Figure 6.8 shows that the closure effect is similar for people with positive and negative reputations (hollow and solid dots respectively). The effect is concentrated in positive 2-step connections (you and I like the same colleagues or dislike the same colleagues), but even negative 2-step connections slow decay (I dislike some of your friends).

The slower decay in embedded relations is consistent with other studies. Feld (1997) analyzes network data on 152 students enrolled in a small college at the beginning and end of their freshman year. Of 5,345 initial sociometric citations for recognition, 54 percent were observed again in the second survey, but the percentage increases significantly with mutual acquaintances. Krackhardt (1998) analyzes network data gathered over a semester on 17 sophomore college students living together. He too finds that a relationship is more likely

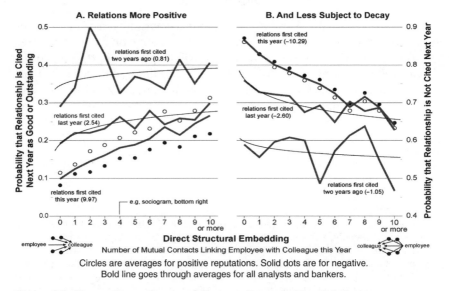

Figure 6.8 Closure Strengthens and Prevents Decay in New Relations

---

[12] I am using causal language here in keeping with the network theory of closure stabilizing social structures, but the empirical evidence is agnostic on causation. It is equally accurate to say that people who continue to work together accumulate mutual contacts.

Table 6.4 Network Closure, Positive Relations, and Decay

Network this Year	Positive Relation next Year		Relation Decayed next Year	
	Zero-Order	Partial	Zero-Order	Partial
Intercept	—	−5.05	—	2.79
Risk year (2, 3, 4)	.15 (.04)**	.09 (.05)	−.18 (.04)**	−.11 (.05)*
Marginals in risk year (/10)	.07 (.01)**	.09 (.01)**	−.09 (.01)**	−.10 (.01)**
Evaluated person is analyst (vs banker)	.12 (.06)	−.39 (.08)**	−.07 (.06)	.43 (.09)**
Relational Embedding				
Marginals this year (/10)	−.02 (.004)**	−.08 (.01)**	.01 (.01)*	.08 (.01)**
Positive relationship this year (1, 2, 3, 4)	.60 (.03)**	.58 (.03)**	−.18 (.02)**	−.13 (.02)**
Years relationship observed (1, 2, 3)	.46 (.04)**	.47 (.07)**	−.40 (.04)**	−.45 (.07)**
Direct Structural Embedding				
Number of positive 2-step connections	.09 (.01)**	.06 (.01)**	−.08 (.01)**	−.06 (.01)**
Number positive 2-step for new relations	.06 (.01)**	.06 (.01)**	−.06 (.01)**	−.05 (.01)**
Number of negative 2-step connections	.02 (.01)**	−.002 (.02)	−.07 (.01)**	−.03 (.02)
Number negative 2-step for new relations	−.01 (.01)	.06 (.02)*	−.05 (.01)**	−.08 (.02)**
Indirect Structural Embedding				
Number of positive 3-step connections	.05 (.003)**	.04 (.01)**	−.04 (.003)**	−.03 (.01)**
Number of negative 3-step connections	−.003 (.004)	−.03 (.01)**	−.003 (.003)	.03 (.01)**
Both people hold senior rank	.22 (.05)**	.02 (.05)	−.21 (.05)**	−.04 (.06)
Same division	.28 (.05)**	.10 (.08)	−.26 (.05)**	−.06 (.09)
Same geographic region	.40 (.04)**	.16 (.05)**	−.49 (.04)**	−.24 (.05)**

Note: These are logit models predicting a relation next year from network variables this year for people cited in both years. "Positive" predicts which of this year's relations are cited next year as good or outstanding. "New" relations are relations in their first year. "Decay" predicts which of this year's relations are not cited again next year. "Zero-Order" columns refer to logit models containing only a single row variable. Standard errors are adjusted for autocorrelation between citations from the same person and given in parentheses (chi-square statistics of 1166.0 and 827.5 for the "positive" and "decay" predictions with 15 d.f. and 27,364 observations). * P < .05 ** P < .001.

to continue when the two students have mutual friends. Similarly, Martin and Yeung (2006) focus on mutual friends as the factor predicting the persistence of relations over a twelve-year period. Using a portion of the data in this chapter, I too found that the banker peer evaluations which persisted over time were the ones embedded in networks of mutual colleagues (Burt, 2002).

A second pattern in the data is the shift from structural to relational embedding as a relationship ages. Positive relations become self-sustaining with time. I have data on four years of the banker relations so I can distinguish relations that are one, two, or three years old. Some relations are older still, but I do not know when each relationship started. Fortunately, relations change so quickly in this population that "this year" is the first year for most colleague relationships. The lines in Figure 6.8 labeled "relations cited this year" describe stability in relations first cited this year. They are new relationships. The lines labeled "relations cited last year" describe stability in relations that are two years old when at risk of decay next year. The lines labeled "relations cited last two years" describe stability in relations that are three years old when at risk of decay next year.

The lines of association in Figure 6.8 show two patterns. First, older relations are more stable. The line for three-year-old relations at the top of the left-hand graph shows a high probability of positive relationship next year. The line for three-year-old relations at the bottom of the right-hand graph shows a low probability of decay next year. These are the relational embedding effects captured in Table 6.4.

Second, the stabilizing effect of structural embedding decreases with the age of a relationship. The lines in Figure 6.8 for "relations cited this year" are steeper than the lines for "relations cited last two years." The interaction effects under "Direct Structural Embedding" in Table 6.4 capture this effect. Above and beyond the association between mutual contacts and stability in general, mutual contacts around a new relationship are associated with significantly more stability in the form of a more positive evaluation next year and higher resistance to decay next year. In short, structural embedding creates stability by carrying relations through the initial period of a relationship, when the risk of decay is highest.

Indirect structural embedding

Indirect structural embedding is also associated with stability. Indirect connections through friends of friends (as illustrated in Figure 6.2) add significantly to the stability associated with direct structural embedding. Regardless of how many people you and I know in common (direct structural embedding), for example, positive 3-step connections between us this year through friends of friends increases the odds of our relationship being positive next year (.04 coefficient in Table 6.4, 7.02 test statistic) and decreases the odds of decay (−.03 coefficient, −5.69 test statistic). In other words, the more that friends of my friends like the friends of your friends, the more likely that you and I will have a positive relationship next year, and the less likely our connection this year will disappear next year.

Strong indirect compensates for weak direct

Given significant stability effects from direct and indirect structural embedding, there is again the question of how direct and indirect work together to produce stability. Figure 6.9 is a detailed look at the closure link with stability in new relations, the relations for which closure most clearly strengthens and protects against decay. The vertical and horizontal axes in Figure 6.9 are the same as in Figure 6.8. The graph to the left shows the probability of a new relationship being cited next year as "good" or "outstanding," and the graph to the right shows the probability of the new relationship not being cited next year. The horizontal axis distinguishes relations by direct structural embedding, measured by number of mutual contacts between employee and colleague.

Compensation effect

Relations at each level of direct structural embedding are sorted in Figure 6.9 into three levels of indirect structural embedding measured by the number of positive connections between employee and colleague through friends of friends. "Weak" contains relations in the bottom quartile of indirect structural embedding, and "strong" contains relations in the top quartile (quartiles are defined within each year for analysts and bankers separately).

The separate effects of direct and indirect structural embedding are illustrated by the slope and relative heights of the lines in the graphs. For example, the dashed line in Figure 6.9A shows that even when indirect structural embedding is weak, the probability of a positive relationship next year increases with the number of mutual contacts between employee and colleague this year. The bold line is higher than the dashed line, illustrating the extent to which indirect structural embedding increases the probability of a positive relationship.

The lines not being parallel illustrate the interaction between direct and indirect. The gap between the lines in each graph is shaded to highlight the point. In Figure 6.9A, there is a large gap at low levels of direct structural embedding, and a small gap at high levels. Once stability is provided by direct structural embedding, there is little additional stability provided by indirect structural embedding (this is the compensation interaction illustrated in Figure 6.6B). The stability effect of indirect structural embedding is concentrated in relations where direct structural embedding is weak.

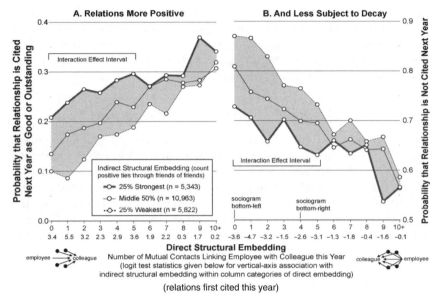

Figure 6.9 Detail on Closure Stabilizing New Relationships

Test statistics at the bottom of Figure 6.9A make the point more precisely. Consider the stability of bridge relations, that is, relations in which employee and colleague have no positive mutual contacts. The probability of a bridge relationship being positive next year increases by 108 percent across levels of indirect structural embedding distinguished by the dashed and bold lines (from .100 to .208). The 3.4 test statistic under "0" mutual contacts is from a logit equation predicting the odds of a "good" or "outstanding" relation next year from the number of positive 3-step connections between employee and colleague this year, holding constant the control variables in Table 6.4 (except time and the two interaction effects specific to first-year relations since all of the relations in Figure 6.9 are first-year relations). The 3.4 test statistic shows that indirect structural embedding significantly increases the odds of a new bridge relation being cited next year as "good" or "outstanding." Corresponding test statistics for relations at higher levels of direct structural embedding continue to show a statistically significant association with indirect connections—until the level reaches six. At six mutual contacts, indirect connections through friends of friends do not make a significant contribution (1.9 test statistic). The negligible contribution continues at eight, nine, and ten or more mutual contacts.

The same pattern occurs in the closure association with decay. The dashed line in Figure 6.9B shows how the odds of decay decrease as employee and colleague share more mutual contacts. The bold line is lower in the graph, showing lower odds of decay in relations embedded in numerous positive indirect connections through friends of friends. Here again, the lines are not parallel. The test statistics at the bottom of the graph show statistically significant decreases in decay from indirect connections through friends of friends— until the level of direct embedding reaches six or more. At six or more mutual contacts, indirect connections through friends of friends have no association with decay (-1.3 test statistic).

Conclusions

My summary conclusion is that closure creates an endogenous force for the status quo that secures and expands the boundary around a network, protecting new relations until they are self-sustaining, and doing so even for people only indirectly connected at the periphery of the network. More specifically, I draw four conclusions from the chapter.

No closure, no reputation

First, reputation stability depends on closure, increasing from completely unstable to stable in the span of a few mutual contacts (Figures 6.4, 6.5, and 6.7). In networks of colleagues who have little contact with one another, reputation this year has no correlation with reputation next year. Do the same work with interconnected colleagues, and reputation this year is a good predictor of reputation next year.[13] Also, it is striking to see stability

---

[13] This image of reputations persisting only if people discuss them has broader implications for information. Mayer-Schönberger (2009) argues that advancing technology has made remembering easy and forgetting difficult: "For millennia remembering was hard, and forgetting easy. By default, we would forget. Digital technology has inverted this." Not being able to forget has unattractive consequences, which Mayer-Schönberger explores to recommend public policy rules for the mandatory retirement of data. But does information live on because it is written or because it is discussed? The empirical results on analyst and banker reputations argue for the latter. Reputations only persist if discussed. Many a forgotten academic publication languishing in the library argues for the latter. It would be interesting to study citations to old articles before and after JSTOR made them so readily available. I enjoy searching the JSTOR archives as a way to discover the many things I did not know I did not know on topics closely related to topics familiar. This argues for Mayer-Schonberger's image of digital records giving information indefinite life. On the other hand, if discussion is what sustains life, then uncited old articles should continue to be uncited. If a publication previously ignored is brought back to life by someone citing it today, then closure predicts a social diffusion curve for the publication such that citations begin few and sporadic triggered by the initial citation, followed by a bandwagon of citations after the forgotten now-relevant publication has been discovered.

appear at such low levels of closure. This is reminiscent of Asch's (1951) laboratory results on conformity to a group standard: Reputation stability among the bankers and analysts increases from nothing to the full (aggregate) closure effect within four mutual colleagues.[14] And the closure effect is separate from quality of work measured by average colleague evaluation. The stability of positive and negative reputations increases similarly in Figure 6.5 with closure.

These results make it clear that individuals do not own their reputation. The possessive pronoun in "your reputation" refers to the subject of the reputation, not the owner. The people who own your reputation are the people in whose conversations it is built, and the goal of those conversations is not accuracy so much as bonding between the speakers (Burt, 2005: chap. 4). You are merely grist for the gossip-mill through which they strengthen their relationships with each other.

Lack of ownership has implications for managing reputation. First impressions are critical for the gossip chain they set in motion. Also, reputations do not emerge from good work directly so much as from colleague stories about the work. Good work completed for people who don't talk about it is work quickly forgotten. This is striking in Figures 6.4, 6.5, and 6.7, where banker and analyst reputations are no more stable than random noise if they work with colleagues who have no connection with one another. The key to building reputation is to close the network around colleagues talking to one another (known in word-of-mouth marketing as "building the buzz," e.g., Gladwell, 2000; Rosen, 2000).

---

[14] I do not wish to make too much of the analogy because it is only an analogy, but it is worth noting because analogy between the Asch results and the results reported here implies that the closure results for bankers and analysts could generalize to the many diverse situations in which Asch's results have been replicated and that Asch's laboratory methods could be a productive way to study closure's effect on stability. Asch (1951:188) reports the frequency with which subjects make errors in the direction of an obviously wrong peer opinion as the number of peers increases. He reports an average of 3.75 errors with 16 peers, 3.84 errors with eight peers, 4.20 errors with four peers, 4.00 errors with three peers, 1.53 with two peers, .33 with one peer, and .08 errors for people alone in the lab. Conformity increases quickly to three or four peers (after which the small lab became crowded). In Figure 6.4, there is a .09 correlation between reputations in adjacent years for people evaluated by colleagues with whom they share no mutual colleagues. Add one mutual contact and the correlation rises from .09 to .20, a 122% increase in stability. With two mutual contacts, the correlation rises from .20 to .34, which is a 70% increase. The marginal increases then begin to decline, to 26% for three mutual contacts, and 26% for four mutual contacts. After four mutual contacts, marginal increases are small. This is apparent in Figure 6.5 from the steep bold line for zero to four mutual contacts and the less-steep line thereafter.

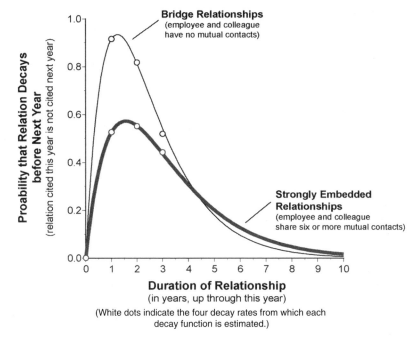

Figure 6.10 Closure Protects Against Decay, Especially in New Relationships

Closure reinforces status quo by protecting new relations from decay

My second conclusion is that closure's stabilizing effect is concentrated in new relations (Table 6.4). There is a division of labor over time between relational and structural embedding. By the third year of a relationship, mutual friends are less important than the strength of the relationship built up between the two people. The structural embedding provided by mutual friends is concentrated in protecting new relations from decay, which gives new relations in closed networks a survival advantage in becoming self-sustaining strong relations, thus reinforcing and expanding the status quo.

Summarizing the age-specific decay rates, Figure 6.10 describes decay across age for bridge versus embedded relationships. Age is defined by when a relationship is first cited in the annual evaluations. A relationship gets older as it continues to be cited. Each year of its existence, a relationship is at risk of decay in the form of not being cited next year. As a relationship ages across the horizontal axis in Figure 6.10, lines in the graph show the probability that the relationship will be gone next year. These are kinked-decay functions; the risk of decay increases quickly after colleagues first meet, peaks, then declines.[15]

The point illustrated is that closure primarily has its effect early in the relationship, when the risk of decay is greatest. The thin line in Figure 6.10 shows that the risk of decay in bridge relationships peaks at just after a year. A relationship is a bridge if there are no mutual contacts between employee and cited colleague. With six or more mutual contacts—a criterion of embedding strength taken for this study population from Figure 6.9—the relation is "strongly embedded" in a closed network around the employee. The bold line in Figure 6.10 shows that embedded relations have a longer honeymoon period, with decay risk peaking at one and a half years.[16] The gap between decay functions in Figure 6.10 shows that closure most protects against decay in the first year, slightly less in the second year, then little and less in older relationships. In other words, closure has its strongest effect protecting new relations from decay.

Relations in this population changed dramatically from year to year, so the decay functions in Figure 6.10 are probably higher than such functions in other populations. I expect three points about the functions to generalize:

---

[15] Banker and analyst relations are combined in Figure 6.10, as they were for the statistical analysis in Table 6.4 (see Burt, 2005:216, for similar functions describing decay in banker relations without the analysts). I use a two-parameter model to describe kinked decay: $r(T) = (aT)\exp(-T/b)$, where $r(T)$ is the risk of decay at time T, and a and b are parameters, b the time of the peak in decay risk (see Diekmann and Mitter, 1984; Diekmann and Englehardt, 1999:787). If detailed data were available through the first year, I would separate level, shape, and time of peak decay (e.g., Brüderl and Diekmann, 1995:162), but the two-parameter model is sufficient for illustration here. The decay functions were constructed in three steps: (1) Define rates of decay over time for the three categories of relations distinguished in Figure 6.10, holding constant the control variables in Table 6.4. For T equal one-, two-, and three-years duration, adjusted decay rates for bridge relations (no mutual colleagues) are .915, .817, and .519 respectively. For relations between people with six or more mutual colleagues the rates are .526, .551, and .442 respectively. I added one observation for new relations and assumed that etiquette would obligate people to continue a new relationship for at least half a day (0 decay rate for T equal to .5/365). (2) Weight the rates by observed frequencies. For example, for every bridge relation that survived through three years, there were 13.89 that survived through two years, and 194.78 that survived through one year. Many more relations must have decayed before the one-year marker, but for the purposes here, I set the frequency of half-day-old relations equal to the frequency of one-year-old relations. (3) Estimate parameters for the kinked-decay functions. I used a nonlinear fitting algorithm ("nl" in STATA) to estimate a and b in the two-parameter decay model from the four weighted observations for each function (T = 0, 1, 2, 3), and used the model to extrapolate decay in later years.

[16] Risk peaks are defined by the nonlinear model in the preceding footnote. For bridge relations, the estimate of parameter a is 2.055, and the estimate of b is 1.236 years, which puts the peak risk of decay at 14.8 months (1.236 times 12). For relations embedded in six or more mutual colleagues, the estimates of a and b are .999 and 1.558, which puts the peak decay risk at 18.7 months.

Decay decreases with closure, has a kinked functional form, and closure slows decay primarily by carrying relations through the initial period of a relationship, when the risk of decay is highest. With strong relations less subject to decay, and new relations between friends of friends more likely to survive to maturity, the existing structure is reinforced, increasing density within groups and deepening the structural holes between groups. In short, closure reinforces the status quo.[17]

Stability effect of closure spills over from neighbor networks

My third conclusion is that closure spills over between adjacent networks. The stability provided by closure in ego's immediate network is reinforced by closure within and across the networks around ego's neighbors. Expressed in network terms, indirect structural embedding enhances direct structural embedding. Ego's reputation is more likely to persist over time if ego is connected into the networks around her colleagues (3-step connections, Table 6.2). Ego's relationship with any one colleague is more likely to be positive next year and more robust to decay if the colleague's friends are connected to ego's other colleagues (3-step connections, Table 6.4). This can be termed "spillover closure" in that closure in neighbor networks spills over to affect stability in ego's network.

The relevance of indirect contacts to closure makes intuitive sense. Closure is about removing alternatives. The coordination-inducing stability benefits of closure depend on monopoly control over reputation. Structural holes in the network are backdoors through which deviants can escape, weakening the coercive pressure that reputation can exert (recall rancher Frank Ellis on pages 158–159 of this chapter). Thus, it is not surprising to find among the bankers and analysts that dense connections among friends of friends increase the stability of reputation and relations.

However, the relevance of indirect contacts to brokerage would also have made immediate sense. Being connected to well-connected colleagues would seem an obvious benefit in the mature capital markets in which the bankers and analysts work. Instead, connection to structural holes among friends of friends had no independent association with performance.

---

[17] The decay-embedding in the text has analogy at the level of organizations. For example, Stuart, Hoang, and Hybels (1999) show that a biotechnology start-up moves to IPO faster and earns higher valuation at IPO when it has alliances with companies that are central in the biotech network and hold patents often cited by other biotech companies. The beneficial effect of affiliation was most pronounced for the newest start-ups. I see analogy between new organizations embedded in a network and new relations embedded in a network. It is life chances of the newest additions that benefit most from the embedding, no doubt in some part because it is the newest additions that are most at risk of expiring. Whatever the reason, the stability benefit of structural embedding is strongest for the newest. In the case of banker and analyst relations, the benefit dissolves during the third year of a relationship.

The starkly different relevance of indirect contacts to brokerage and closure is a finding about which I want to be very clear. The evidence on interpersonal relations is summarized in Table 6.5. The industry buying and selling analyzed in Chapter 5 is put aside as an extreme of codified information flow. Each row of Table 6.5 corresponds to a model discussed in this or a preceding chapter in which the row criterion variable is predicted by a person's network of direct contacts, various control variables, and the person's network of indirect contacts.

The first six rows of Table 6.5, under "Brokerage Effects," are predictions from Chapters 3 and 4. For example, when I estimate compensation returns to brokerage for employees active in the Asia-Pacific launch of a new software product, I get the results in the first row of Table 6.5: A significant -2.7 t-test for compensation lost to network constraint among an employee's direct contacts, and a negligible -1.0 t-test for network constraint among indirect contacts (Table 3.1). Negative associations with network constraint are displayed in Table 6.5 as positive associations with brokerage.

The first four rows under "Closure Effects" are predictions from this chapter. For example, when I estimate the stability of analyst reputations in Table 6.2, I get a 12.0 t-test for the reputation-stability association with direct structural embedding and an 8.3 t-test for the association with indirect structural embedding.

The results in Table 6.5 show the consistency with which returns to brokerage are concentrated in direct contacts while closure has its stabilizing effect at further remove, through friends of friends as well as direct contacts. The first column of results in Table 6.5 contains test statistics for associations with the network of direct contacts. All are statistically significant. The second column contains test statistics for associations with the network of indirect contacts. The associations with closure are all statistically significant. The results for brokerage in the upper-right of Table 6.5 show no returns to brokerage among friends of friends.

Spillover difference could reflect differences in outcome or mechanism

The different results for brokerage and closure regarding indirect contacts carry two very different interpretations. One concerns the outcomes predicted. I used brokerage in Chapters 3 and 4 to predict performance measured as compensation, evaluation, and recognition. I used closure in this chapter to predict stability in terms of persistent reputation and a lack of network decay. Indirect contacts are a component in the network so they play a more obvious role in network stability than they play in individual performance. One could infer from Table 6.5 that indirect contacts are relevant to stability, but not to performance.

Or, the different results could be attributed to different mechanisms. Brokerage creates a vision advantage in selecting and synthesizing divergent opinion

Table 6.5 Brokerage and Closure Direct and Indirect Network Effects

	Statistical Test for Network of Direct Contacts	Statistical Test for Network of Indirect Contacts
Brokerage Effects		
Brokerage association with product-launch employee compensation (Table 3.1)	2.7	1.0
Brokerage association with supply-chain manager salary (Table 3.2)	3.4	1.6
Brokerage association with supply-chain manager annual evaluation (Table 3.2)	2.9	–.7
Brokerage association with quality of supply-chain manager best idea (Table 3.2)	4.2	.9
Brokerage association with HR compensation (Table 4.1)	4.4	.2
Brokerage association with banker compensation (Table 4.2)	3.4	1.5
Brokerage association with analyst election to All-America Research Team (Table 4.3)	3.2	–.2
Closure Effects		
Closure association with stable analyst reputation (Table 6.2)	12.0	8.3
Closure association with stable banker reputation (Table 6.2)	11.5	8.0
Closure association with decay in analyst relationships (Table 6.4)	–9.7	–4.0
Closure association with decay in banker relationships (Table 6.4)	–5.4	–3.1
Choice status association with banker compensation	4.9	3.5
Choice status association with analyst election to All-America Research Team	2.8	3.1

Note: These are test statistics for the association in the row with control variables held constant from the indicated tables. The status predictions in the bottom two rows are made with the same variables as the brokerage predictions in Table 4.2, Model C for the bankers, and in Table 4.3, Model C, for the analysts, except that the two brokerage variables in each prediction are replaced by corresponding status variables.

and practice. It affects the diversity of opinion and practice to which a broker is exposed. The effect is on the individual broker. Other people are unaffected, except indirectly through the broker's actions. In contrast, closure is about aligning neighbors. Closure creates a reputation cost that facilitates the task of coordinating work across people. It makes network members more attentive to their reputation with one another and protects them from the diversity of opinion and practice outside the network. With closure more about aligned neighbors, it would make sense to infer from the Table 6.5 results that indirect contacts are more relevant to enforcing alignment.

Difference in mechanism

The results in the bottom two rows in Table 6.5 support the second interpretation over the first. The results show performance returns to direct and indirect closure just as the results throughout this chapter have shown stability increases with direct and indirect closure.

At the level of individuals, direct and indirect centrality is a closure analogue to direct and indirect brokerage. People differ in the extent to which they individually contribute to closure. Some are more prominent, more central, in the network. There are benefits to being more central. More central people have more access to any resources in the network (e.g., see Coleman, 1966, 1972, on network centrality as "power," cf. Lin *et al.*, 1981; Mintz and Schwartz, 1981; Marsden, 1983; and Coleman, 1990:chap. 25, on the value of an individual's resources). Centrality is also signal. More central people are more visible to insiders and outsiders as the "best" people in the network (e.g., see Podolny, 1993, 2005, on network centrality as "status," signaling expert-endorsed quality).

In the bottom two rows of Table 6.5, I use individual differences in centrality to predict individual differences in performance for the bankers and analysts— the people used in this chapter to show how stability increases with closure.

Performance is measured as it was measured to estimate returns to brokerage: Banker compensation (Table 4.2) and z-score election recognition of an analyst (Table 4.3, Model C). I do not present coefficients for the prediction. Coefficients can be obtained from the means, standard deviations, and correlations in Tables E4 and E5 in Appendix E.

Predictors in the bottom two rows of Table 6.5 are the same as in Tables 4.2 and 4.3, but the network variables are different. The measures of direct and indirect network constraint in Chapter 4 are here measures of direct and indirect centrality. Centrality is measured by the number of people who cited you in the annual evaluation process (average 47.41 and 31.07 for the bankers and analysts respectively). To accurately distinguish levels of centrality, my count includes citations from everyone who participated in the annual evaluation process: The bankers and analysts in Figure 4.4, as well as employees at lower ranks and elsewhere in the organization. Indirect centrality is the average number of people who cited the people who cited you. Indirect is higher than direct on average because people often cited colleagues more central in the network (average 52.53 and 38.17 for the bankers and analysts). Number of citations received was introduced as "choice status" in early sociometry as an obvious and reliable way to identify the leaders in a group (Moreno, 1934:92–107; see Jennings, 1937, for detailed application over time). It is often discussed as network size or "degree" in contemporary network analysis (see Appendix B), but I discuss it here as choice status for the link to sociometry, and the link to contemporary business and sociology, in which centrality is often discussed as status following Podolny's (1993, 2005) influential discussion of it as a signal of market quality.[18] In measuring network centrality with choice status, I am assuming that people more often cited in the annual evaluations are people who contribute more to closing the network in their organization. This seems a reasonable assumption, which is corroborated by correlations between choice status and network constraint ($-.59$ and $-.73$ correlations in Appendix E between choice status and network constraint for the bankers and analysts, respectively). In other words, people whose networks bridge structural holes are more often acknowledged as colleagues.

The bottom two rows of Table 6.5 show performance increasing with both direct and indirect choice status. Bankers who are often cited in this year's evaluations, next year receive higher compensation than their peers (4.90 t-test,

---

[18] Direct and indirect choice status are combined in the eigenvector model typically used to measure network status (see footnote 10 in Chapter 2): direct choice status is in the sum of relations, and indirect choice status is in the weighting by the status of relation sources. Mehra *et al.* (2006) provide a recent eigenvector application analogous to the task in this chapter of measuring the extent to which a leader holds together the surrounding organization. For two reasons, I use choice status in the text instead of the eigenvector measure. First, I want to see the separate effects of direct versus indirect status as I have seen the separate effects for direct versus indirect network constraint and direct versus indirect embedding. I could have disaggregated the eigenvector measure into the two components (e.g., see Mizruchi *et al.*, 1986, on "derived" versus "reflected" centrality), but the meaning of the simple choice status measures is clear to a wider audience. Second, choice status captures most of the eigenvector measure. The eigenvector measure of status is correlated .81 with direct choice status for the analysts, and .95 for the bankers (based on the two annual panels of data on the analysts and the three panels on the bankers). By saying that choice status is the better measure for distinguishing direct from indirect effects, I am not saying that choice status is preferable to the eigenvector model elsewhere. In fact, the banker and analyst networks show the eigenvector superior to choice status as a summary index of status. Regressing the eigenvector measure across direct and indirect choice status shows statistically significant status variance attributed to indirect choice status: standardized regression coefficients of .91 and .10 for the bankers, .78 and .33 for the analysts (respective t-tests of 49.24 versus 7.76 for the bankers, adjusted for autocorrelation within individuals across three panels, and 14.88 versus 15.05 for the analysts, adjusted for autocorrelation within individuals across two panels).

where peers are defined by the control variables in Table 4.2). If the colleagues citing them this year are themselves often cited, compensation is higher still (3.51 t-test). Analysts who are often cited this year are significantly more likely to be elected next year to the All-America Research Team (2.79 t-test). If the colleagues citing them this year are themselves often cited, then the analyst's odds of being recognized in next year's election are significantly improved (3.14 t-test).[19]

These results correspond to the stability associations with closure and are consistent with the studies discussed in Chapter 2 that report positive spillover from high-status neighbors (Stuart, Hoang, and Hybels, 1999; Jensen, 2003) and negative spillover from low-status neighbors (Kang, 2008). I conclude that the importance of indirect contacts for closure, but not brokerage, is due to difference in the mechanisms responsible for closure versus brokerage effect, not to difference between the criterion variables used in this versus the preceding chapters. Closure effects spill over into adjacent networks. Brokerage effects do not.

Spillover closure promotes brokerage

My fourth conclusion from this chapter is that spillover closure is greater when there is little closure in ego's immediate network. Like water spilling from high pond into low, the stability effect of closure spills from networks where closure is high into adjacent networks where closure is low. Expressed in network terms, indirect structural embedding can compensate for weak direct structural embedding. The interaction is particularly interesting as an instance of spillover closure promoting brokerage by protecting bridge relations against premature decay.

The conclusion does not apply to all spillover closure and is not to be confused with the level of stability (discussed in the preceding section) that spillover provides regardless of closure in ego's immediate network. The stabilizing effect of spillover closure is primarily a level effect in that it occurs at high and low levels of direct. For example, the spillover effect on reputation is entirely a level effect: The effect of indirect structural embedding on reputation stability is consistent across the number of people that ego and colleague

---

[19] I tested for independent effects. Table 6.5 shows that direct and indirect status are each associated with performance holding the other constant. They are also each associated with performance ignoring the other (6.07 t-test for banker direct status ignoring indirect status, Model A in Table 4.2; 4.29 for banker indirect status ignoring direct status, Model B in Table 4.2; and 3.42 and 3.82 t-tests respectively for the analysts). I get inconsistent results on higher-order effects. I multiplied direct choice status times indirect and added the product to the predictions in the bottom two rows of Table 6.5. The interaction term adds nothing to the analyst prediction (0.96 t-test). There is a statistically significant interaction effect for the bankers. Above and beyond compensation expected from direct status and indirect status, there is an additional increment from being simultaneously high in direct and indirect status (3.88 t-test). Since I do not have a consistent result across the bankers and analysts, and the higher-order effect is not critical to my argument, I do not pursue the higher-order effect here.

know in common (Figure 6.7). However, the process is more complex in spillover closure preserving individual relationships. Spillover decreases as closure in ego's immediate network increases. The interaction effect only occurs with positive indirect connections through friends of friends, but it is clearly visible in the first year of a relationship (Figure 6.9).

Figure 6.11 puts the three structural-embedding effects into perspective. These summary graphs for kinds of relations correspond to the summary graph across all relations that was presented in Figure 6.10. The graph to the left, Figure 6.11A, describes decay in bridge relations, where ego and colleague have no mutual contacts. The graph to the right describes decay in relations strongly embedded in a closed network around ego (distinguished in this population, judging from Figure 6.9, as a relationship in which ego and colleague have six or more mutual contacts).

The effect of direct structural embedding is illustrated by comparing lines across the graphs. The thin line in Figure 6.11B is lower than the thin line in Figure 6.11A. The thick line in Figure 6.11B is lower than its counterpart in Figure 6.11A. In short, bridges decay faster. Direct structural embedding protects against decay (as already discussed with respect to Figure 6.10).

The two spillover-closure effects are illustrated: First, the thick lines in each graph are lower than the corresponding thin lines, illustrating the level of protection that indirect structural embedding provides against decay (as discussed in the preceding section).

Second, the thick and thin lines are further apart in Figure 6.11A, illustrating the greater protection that indirect provides when direct is weak. The second spillover effect is clearly modest relative to the other two illustrated in Figure 6.11. The other two effects are easy to see: The lines in Figure 6.11A are clearly

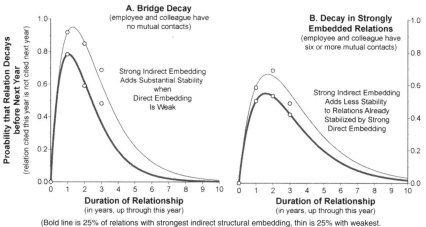

(Bold line is 25% of relations with strongest indirect structural embedding, thin is 25% with weakest. White dots indicate the four decay rates from which each decay function is estimated.)

Figure 6.11 Closure Protects Against Decay, Directly and Indirectly

higher than the lines in Figure 6.11B. The thin lines are clearly higher than the thick lines. In comparison, the interaction effect is not apparent from the lines in the graphs. It is more apparent from the data dots. In Figure 6.11A, for example, the decay rate for bridge relations in their first year is .92 for bridges embedded in indirect connections among friends of friends versus .78 for bridges with little or no indirect connections through friends of friends. The difference between the decay rates is an amount by which indirect structural embedding lowers the risk of decay in bridge relations (.14 = .92 − .78). The gap is smaller for relations strongly embedded in mutual contacts (.08 = .58 − .50 in Figure 6.11B). The gap is also smaller during the second and third years (respectively .16 and .07 for the strongly embedded relations in Figure 6.11B, versus .26 and .20 for bridges in Figure 6.11A).

Moreover, the visual clarity of the decay functions in Figure 6.11 belies their statistical ambiguity past year two—which could be obscuring the interaction effect. I am comfortable with the functional form of the decay functions in Figure 6.11, and I am certain about the early peaks in the functions because I have so many observations on relationships that are one year old. However, decay rates are so high in this population that I have relatively few observations on older relations. Of all 46,231 observations in Table 6.1, 83 percent are at the end of year one, 14 percent are at the end of year two, and 3 percent are at the end of year three. Three percent of so many observations is still a sizeable number (1,233 observations of three-year old relations), but older relations become rare within kinds of relations as in Figure 6.11. There are wide confidence intervals around the decay functions past year two. Note that the data dots in Figure 6.11 for one-year old relations are on the lines. Data dots for two-year old relations are right next to the lines. Data dots for three-year old relations are the most distant from the lines. Statistical estimates of the decay-function parameters give much more weight to the numerous first-year observations. There are so few observations at year three that year-three decay rates have little weight in determining the decay functions. If the year-three data dots are accurate (which I cannot know from the available data, but assume for a moment that they are), then the interaction effect would be much more apparent from decay functions forced to fit the year-three data because the data dots for year three in strongly embedded relations are so close together. The thick and thin lines in Figure 6.11B would be converging rapidly toward one another relative to the still-far-apart third-year data dots in Figure 6.11A for bridge relations.

I conclude that spillover closure probably does compensate for absent mutual contacts around a relationship. The interaction effect is at this point more intriguing than established. I would like to see the Figure 6.11 decay functions for a study population in which relations decay more slowly than is characteristic for the bankers and analysts, so I could see with confidence what the decay functions look like past the peak decay periods. Nevertheless, the evidence presented is sufficient to warrant studied attention to the interaction effect.[20] First, there is statistically significant evidence of the effect. Second, the effect is substantively consequential. It is a link between the social capital of brokerage and closure, grounding the growth and innovation provided by brokerage within the stability provided by closure. The relationship between you and I is by definition not a bridge if we have numerous mutual friends. Our relationship is a bridge when we know none of the same people. Without benefit of mutual contacts, bridge relations suffer a high rate of decay. However, bridge relations—and other relations only weakly embedded in mutual contacts—are precisely where indirect structural embedding has its interaction effect on stability. Indirect connections through friends of friends lower the risk of premature decay in bridges. Standing one step further back, local institutions such as schools, non-profit organizations, business groups and the like, provide indirect connections between friends of friends. The interesting question raised by the interaction between direct and indirect is how indirect structural embedding, probably through local institutions, sustains bridge relationships, and so promotes brokerage.

---

[20] In fact, one could speculate from the evidence that the three kinds of embedding measured in this chapter form a hierarchy with relational embedding at the top: Indirect structural embedding provides stability when direct structural embedding is weak (Figure 6.9). Direct structural embedding provides stability when relational embedding is weak (as in new relations), and when relational embedding is strong, there is little stability added by structural embedding (Figures 6.8 and 6.10). In a sentence, the relationship between close friends resists decay even if the friends have no mutual contacts, mutual contacts can preserve a weak relationship even if the contacts come from separate groups, and indirect connections through friends of friends can protect a weak relationship from decay, even if the relationship is a bridge between two people who have no contacts in common.

SEVEN

Mishpokhe, Not

THERE is a delightfully descriptive word in Yiddish, mishpokhe, that refers to people who are "one of us." The word is specifically about extended family, but it is popularly used to refer to people who are one of us. Rosten (1989:338) illustrates with Chase Manhattan Bank's advertising campaign built around the slogan "You have a friend at Chase Manhattan." In a window of the bank next to a Chase Manhattan branch there appeared a sign proclaiming "—BUT HERE YOU HAVE MISHPOKHE!"

This chapter is about people who are not mishpokhe, the outsiders who are not one of us. In other words, this chapter is about each of us at one time or another. No matter who you are, there are projects in which you are an insider, mishpokhe, and others in which you are an outsider. Example outsiders are an economist arguing the merits of his model to an audience of sociologists, an American pitching a venture to a French investor, a woman arguing the merits of a business policy to a sexist male, a baby-faced youngster proposing an acquisition to a seasoned pro.

Inside and Outside Brokerage

The distinction between insider and outsider is defined for insiders as clearly as the network is closed around them. Closure implies deep and nuanced knowledge about life inside the network (about the neighborhood, the local culture, the historical period) combined with a correspondingly deep ignorance about life outside the network (the monopoly aspect to closure that was highlighted by spillover effects in the previous chapter). Protection from the complexity and contradictions of life outside the network enables closure's reputation mechanism to focus insiders on one another, speeding them down the learning curve for their specialization.

Ignorance of life beyond the closed network is no barrier to strong opinion about the outside. Ignorance is more a lubricant for strong opinion. People unable to explain external events that affect them, turn to neighbors to discuss interpretations. As closure is simultaneously about dense relations within the network as well as a lack of relations beyond, discussion within a closed network is simultaneously about who we are as well as who we are not. It is often difficult to find articulate consensus about who we are. We muddle through with stories about who we are not. We take as data the vicarious experience of living through stories about an opinion or behavior that illustrates what it means to be "not us." Wannabe insiders seek out negative stories about outsiders to spread as a demonstration of commitment to the group and its values. Stories circulate, gathering emotional endorsements. Smiles, sighs, eyes too open, eyes too closed, eyes rolled over, shoulders up, fisted palms; so many ways to communicate emotional response to gossip's bid for status. The more closed the network, the thicker the surrounding crust of stories detailing instances of opinion and behavior that are "not us."

Particularly useful are stories about people like us whose opinion or behavior revealed them to be "not us." Frank Ellis in the previous chapter (pages 158–159) was unaffected by the gossip responsible for his negative reputation, but his gossiping neighbors were no doubt brought closer together by sharing stories of displayed distain for their former colleague. The sociology of the situation is that if we didn't know of unscrupulous colleagues, we would have to make them up. That is the essence of Durkheim's celebrated view on criminals as integral to people having a sense of community (Durkheim, 1893:102):

Never do we feel the need of the company of our compatriots so greatly as when we are in a strange country; never does the believer feel so strongly attracted to his co-religionists as during periods of persecution. Of course, we always love the company of those who feel and think as we do, but it is with passion, and no longer solely with pleasure, that we seek it immediately after discussions where our common beliefs have been greatly combated. Crime brings together upright consciences and concentrates them. We have only to notice what happens, particularly in a small town, when some moral scandal has just been committed. They stop each other on the street, they visit each other, they seek to come together to talk of the event and to wax indignant in common.

Durkheim's intuition is the touchstone for Erikson's (1966: chap. 3) analysis of the 1692 Salem witch trials as an example of insiders trying to maintain their sense of community by highlighting shared distain and abuse of people deemed witches on the periphery of the network (see Boyer and Nissenbaum, 1974, for explicit network data; Douglas, 1991, for analogy to medically unlikely outbreaks of leprosy). Particularly interesting is the connection between community values and the kind of behavior discussed as deviant (Erikson, 1966:23–27). Communities focused on property seem prone to incidents of theft. Communities focused on orthodox beliefs seem prone to incidents of heresy.

"Mobbing" is the contemporary office analogue to village witch hunts. The term is taken from studies of animal behavior. When a predator is discovered within a group of animals, individuals find strength in simultaneously attacking, or "mobbing," the predator. Workplace mobbing occurs when an individual is singled out for emotional abuse (Davenport, Schwartz, and Elliott, 1999). As insecure villagers were brought together and protected from Satan by mobbing the witch, insecure office workers are brought together and reassured of their worth by mobbing the target colleague. Following the witch analogy, two qualities should distinguish the colleague targeted by an office mob: living in a way different from others in the office, on the social periphery of the office (see Boyer and Nissenbaum, 1974, on the Salem villagers most likely to be accused of witchcraft).[1]

Where certain people are deemed outsiders, insiders are twice advantaged in proposing a course of action. Investors are more likely to believe they understand the meanings, intentions, and probable actions of someone like themselves. Reputation provides further assurance. It is easier for investors to trust someone like themselves to the extent that the person's reputation among us would be tarnished if investors were treated poorly. Outsiders have the same struggles as anyone else in bringing an idea to fruition, but they face the additional hurdle of convincing investors skeptical because of the outsider's youth, gender, nationality, or whatever other criterion makes a person suspect to insiders. Outsiders have to provide more detailed proposals because insiders feel less confident predicting an outsider's meanings, intentions, or future behavior. Outsiders have to provide greater assurance to compensate for the lack of a reputation cost that would lower the risk of insider trust.

The insider advantage creates at least four kinds of costs. Value available from brokerage with or by outsiders is less likely to occur. Second, outsiders disadvantaged in the informal organization of a company have an incentive to leave to find employment with a more compatible firm. The same leadership exercised elsewhere has a higher chance of success and lower probability of being credited to insiders. Third, the exit of able outsiders leaves behind less able outsiders, reinforcing insider stereotypes about outsiders being less able. Fourth, systematic departures by able outsiders sully the employer's reputation as an enterprise focused on performance.

Why this Chapter

My concern in this chapter is neither the phenomenon of finding common cause in shared distain for outsiders, nor the costs created by too severe a distinction between insider and outsider. I have elsewhere discussed reputations exaggerated by gossip echoing within closed networks (Burt, 2005: chap 4).

---

[1] This is a point that has always troubled me about Sutton's (2007) popular management book on making the workplace a more civil environment. Colorfully titled, *The No Asshole Rule*, Sutton's idea is to remove from the current workforce, and not allow into the workplace, those abusive people so often discussed as "assholes." I sympathize with Sutton's intent. Incidents of interpersonal abuse can have a dramatic negative effect on the workplace. I have watched too many senior people indulge themselves with public temper tantrums abusing weaker people. At the same time, I am mindful that "asshole" is a label, not a behavior. A policy that empowers colleagues to label one of their own an "asshole" opens the door to the insecurity-alleviating processes responsible for village witch hunts and office mobbings.

My concern here is an implication of the corrective action by which outsiders can work around the problem. The insider advantage is foundation for network diagnostics by which people being treated as outsiders can be identified. They are the people systematically denied the benefits of network brokerage. Insiders are people whose performance is enhanced when they connect across structural holes, as illustrated by the graphs in Chapters 2, 3, and 4. Outsiders are people whose performance suffers when they connect across structural holes— unless their connections are made in conjunction with an insider. Everyone needs sponsorship now and again. Outsiders are people whose success is systematically contingent on sponsorship. In the company to be analyzed in this chapter, the outsiders turn out to be women and young men. Race, geography, and kind of work are determined not to be criteria distinguishing outsiders.

The corrective action is relevant to this book because it seems to contradict the finding in Chapters 3 and 4 that "secondhand" brokerage provides no advantage. If brokerage among friends of friends provides negligible, secondhand, value, why is there such clear advantage to outsiders from affiliation with well-connected insiders? Classroom discussion seems to have a nose for this contradiction. The contradiction almost always comes up after students have had a chance to think about secondhand brokerage and outsider networks.

The seeming contradiction is one of those exceptions that proves the rule. How that is so is the subject of this chapter. I begin with the network diagnostics that indicate a diversity problem, as foundation for the evidence showing that affiliation with a network broker is a way for people deemed outsiders to overcome the problem.

Network Diagnostics Indicating a Diversity Problem

Network brokerage is a craft more than a commodity so benefits typically vary widely between individuals. For example, benefits vary with the kind of work a person does. The more unique the work, the more that ego has to figure out how to fit the work to the situation, so the more that performance depends on the information access and control benefits of bridging structural holes (Burt, 2005:156–162). Benefits also depend on other people accepting ego's brokerage, so another source of variation in benefits is whether ego is accepted as an insider or kept at arm's length as an outsider.

An instance of women treated as outsiders

Figure 7.1 contains graphs of associations between network constraint and early promotion to senior job rank for managers in a large American computer and electronics company. Company records on all managers in the four job ranks below vice president were combined with survey network data on a representative sample of 284 managers in the autumn of 1989 (Burt, 1992:118–126). Figure 7.1 contains data on men and women in the three job ranks below vice president (the top three job ranks of the four sampled). The managers were all employed in the same firm, but their firm was the size of a small city, scattered across separate parts of the country, and diverse corporate functions (sales, service, manufacturing, information systems, engineering, marketing, finance, and human resources). Since the 1989 survey, the company has been acquired, and its acquirer acquired, so this organization and its issues are ancient history. The lesson remains, perhaps more productive now that it is free of legal implications for the long-digested organization.

The vertical axis is early promotion. The company focused on promotions from within the company. A certain amount of time had to pass before people were ready for promotion to senior rank. How much time is a performance criterion in that certain people were promoted early to senior rank (see Merton's, 1984, theoretical analysis of the socially expected duration associated with time in a role, entry to the role, and exit; Burt, 1992:196–197, on using socially expected durations to measure competitive success). To distinguish early from late promotions, I used archival data on the managers to predict age

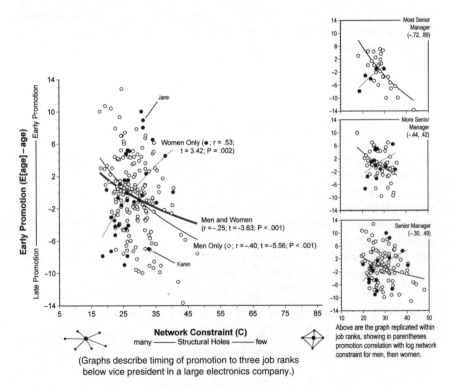

(Graphs describe timing of promotion to three job ranks
below vice president in a large electronics company.)

Figure 7.1 Returns to Brokerage Often Not the Same for Everyone

at promotion to current rank from a manager's kind of work (job rank and function), plant location, and personal background (education, race, gender, and seniority; see Burt, 1992:126–131, for details).[2] Expected age at promotion, E(age), is the average age at which a manager with a specific personal background is promoted to a specific rank within a specific function. Residuals from the regression prediction are the vertical axis in Figure 7.1. Early promotion is the difference between when a manager was promoted to current rank and the age at which similar managers on average are promoted to the same rank to do the same work: early promotion = E(age) – age. A score of –5.5, indicates a manager promoted five and a half years behind similar managers promoted to the same job. Managers promoted earlier than expected are at the top of the Figure 7.1 graphs.

The bold line in the large graph in Figure 7.1 shows that early promotion, on average, had a negative association with network constraint in the organization, indicating the usual advantage of a network that spans structural holes (cf., Figure 2.4). Network constraint varies across the horizontal axis of the graphs in Figure 7.1 with the extent to which a manager turned to one interconnected group of colleagues for kinds of relations (informal discussion and socializing, political support, advice, supervision; see Burt, 1992:121–126, for details on the network data used to measure constraint). Note that the network constraint scores are concentrated at the low end of the large graph (cf. Figure 2.4). These senior managers were all network brokers. They did not vary in whether their networks spanned structural holes so much as the extent to which their networks spanned holes. This organization was an early example of what would later be termed a "network" company. The orientation manual for new managers emphasized the importance of informal networks for collaboration. Culture was also evident in the labels assigned to deviants. Managers who did not invest in colleague networks were discussed in derogatory tones as "lone ranger" types.

The aggregate advantage of network brokerage in Figure 7.1 is a combination of two very different conditions. There is strong advantage for men. The thin solid line in the large graph shows an association with early promotion that is stronger than the average association (–.25 overall correlation is –.40 for men, –3.63 t-test overall increases to –5.56 for men). The dashed line shows the exact opposite association for women (.53 correlation, 3.42 t-test). With few women in the top three manager ranks (32 of the 202 managers in Figure 7.1), the aggregate network association with early promotion is based primarily on the advantages to men. Separating men from women shows that the women were not rewarded

---

[2] There is a significant promotion difference between men and women, reflecting company efforts to bring women into the senior ranks. The average woman is promoted three years earlier than a comparable man. The exact zero-order difference is 3.4 years (4.0 t-test), which is 3.1 years in a multiple regression holding constant the other variables in the age regression equation (3.9 t-test), and 2.8 years in the same regression excluding sample men older than the oldest women (3.8 t-test). Although women arrive at their senior ranks significantly earlier than comparable men, the network data show that the women arrive by a very different route.

for networks that spanned structural holes. In fact, they were punished. "Not rewarded" implies a negligible return to brokerage. What you see in Figure 7.1 is that the women with networks spanning structural holes were systematically late receiving promotions to senior ranks. The gender disadvantage is consistent across job ranks and company divisions. Details are given elsewhere (Burt, 1998a), but the small graphs in Figure 7.1 show the data within each of the three senior manager job ranks. In each graph, the solid line shows early promotions going to men with brokerage networks and the dashed line is reversed showing late promotions to women with brokerage networks.

A routine statistical test for the gender difference would be to test for level and slope adjustments to the association between network constraint and early promotion: $EP = \alpha + \beta \ln(C) + \gamma F + \delta X$, where EP is the early promotion variable on the vertical axis in Figure 7.1, C is the network constraint variable on the horizontal axis, F is a dummy variable distinguishing women (or some other category of people likely to be treated as outsiders), and X is the product of F times $\ln(C)$. Coefficient γ is a level adjustment measuring the amount by which women with $\ln(C)$ scores of zero would be promoted later than men (I say "would be" because there are no managers in this population with network constraint scores that low), and δ is a slope adjustment measuring the amount by which the network constraint delay on promotion is less for women. Estimates for Figure 7.1 yield t-tests of -5.20 for γ and 5.18 for δ. Women with extreme brokerage networks would be promoted significantly late, and network constraint hurt women's odds of early promotion significantly less than it hurt men's chances. The same equation with variable F distinguishing non-white managers yields t-tests of 1.37 for γ and -1.38 for δ. Both are statistically negligible. In this population of managers with primarily engineering backgrounds, race did not distinguish outsiders. Gender did. Women seem to have been systematically excluded from the benefits of network brokerage.

Broader Diagnostic Results

I tested gender and race as possible criteria distinguishing outsiders because those are criteria we often discuss. Ideally, a diagnostic should reveal categories of people treated as outsiders when the categories are not known in advance. I ran such a diagnostic, which turned out to be useful in broadening the criteria for outsiders beyond gender. The more general diagnostic is illustrated in Figure 7.2 using the network and early promotion data on all 284 managers who responded to the network survey.

Rank people by fit to the brokerage story

The first step in the diagnostic is to rank people by their fit to the network brokerage story. A person fits the story in either of two ways: performing well with a network that spans structural holes, or performing poorly with a closed network. The 284 sample managers are ordered across the horizontal axis in Figure 7.2 by their contribution to the negative correlation between early promotion and network constraint.

I use subsample correlations because they are so readily interpretable, but one could use any of a variety of scores based on residual deviation from the regression line. Subsample correlations are the basis for Tukey's jackknife statistic. Finifter (1972) continues to be a good introduction to subsampling used to generate statistical confidence. Let r be the aggregate correlation between network constraint and early promotion. Let r_i be the correlation when manager i is removed from the data. If a manager fits the brokerage story, excluding him or her from the data will weaken the negative correlation between early promotion and network constraint (r_i less negative than r). If the manager contradicts the brokerage story—by performing well with a closed network or performing poorly with a network that spans structural holes—then excluding him or her from the data will yield a stronger negative correlation (r_i more negative than r). The manager at rank one on the horizontal axis in Figure 7.2 is the manager who most contributed to the negative association between early promotion and network constraint across all 284 sample managers (maximum r_i-r).

The rank order is now defined, but as a descriptive indicator of how the network association with promotion changes across the rank order, I computed for each manager the correlation between early promotion and network constraint within subsamples of 21 managers (the manager plus the 10 next people higher in the rank order and the 10 next lower in the rank order). The

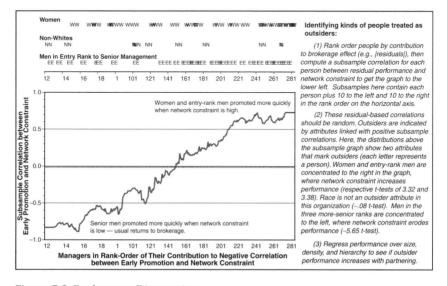

Figure 7.2 Exploratory Diagnostics

subsample correlation is the vertical axis in the graph at the bottom of Figure 7.2. The network-promotion correlation is severely negative across the 21 managers who most fit the brokerage story (−.84 correlation in the lower-left of the graph, −6.88 routine t-test). It increases to a high positive correlation for the 21 managers who least fit the brokerage story (.67 correlation in the upper-right of the graph, 4.22 routine t-test). The subsample size of 21 is arbitrary. Larger subsamples smooth away more individual differences. I settled on 21 after looking at variation in network constraint and the subsample correlation with early promotion for larger and smaller subsamples. The network-promotion correlation in small subsamples bounces up and down between adjacent subsamples because of subsample to subsample differences in the range of network scores.

The subsample correlations in Figure 7.2 increase steadily from left to right, showing no cluster of managers in which advantage is exceptionally concentrated or denied. If the benefits of network brokerage were concentrated in a small minority of managers, the correlations would increase sharply to the left of the graph. If a small group of managers were sharply distinguished as outsiders, then the correlations would remain low across the graph until they increased sharply toward the right of the graph.

Correlate personal attributes with rank order

Second, look for kinds of people concentrated at the bottom of the list. Estimation of the performance correlation with network constraint assumes that deviations from the correlation are random across individuals. The rank order in Figure 7.2 should be independent of personal attributes. An attribute concentrated toward the bottom of the rank order indicates that people with that attribute are systematically excluded from the benefits of network brokerage in the population being analyzed.

For example, each W at the top of Figure 7.2 represents a woman in the study population. The Ws are located by the corresponding woman's position in the rank order across the horizontal axis. Given the obvious gender difference in Figure 7.1, it is not surprising to see Ws concentrated to the right of the graph, among managers disadvantaged by network brokerage. Routine statistical inference implies that women are significantly lower in the rank order (3.32 t-test).

Each N at the top of Figure 7.2 represents a non-white manager in the rank order. The Ns are randomly distributed across the rank order, indicating that race is not a criterion distinguishing outsiders (−.08 t-test).

I searched through all the background variables available looking for personal attributes associated with brokerage. There was only one besides gender. The fourth job rank below vice president was a point of entry into senior management. Men in that entry job rank are the Es at the top of Figure 7.2.

They are concentrated to the right of the graph, among the managers denied the benefit of network brokerage (3.38 t-test). These were not young men by age, but they were the new guys in senior management. Like women, they were not rewarded for bridging structural holes. Unlike women, their careers were not delayed by brokerage so much as their returns to brokerage were negligible: The early promotion correlation with network constraint for the women in Figure 7.1 is .53 with a 3.42 t-test. For entry-rank men, the correlation is a negligible .11 and 0.88 t-test. I excluded entry-rank men from Figure 7.1 to highlight the gender difference with which I introduced the organization. It is now clear that men entering senior management ranks were also denied the benefits of network brokerage.

To say that a category of people is treated as outsiders does not mean that every person in the category is treated as an outsider. Women and entry-rank men are further down the rank order in Figure 7.2 (177 mean rank for women, 172 mean rank for entry-rank men, 121 mean rank for senior men), but not every woman was denied the advantage of network brokerage and some entry-rank men did well with a network spanning structural holes. There is a woman in Figure 7.1 who was promoted early to senior manager with a network that spanned structural holes (black dot with a 0.3 score on early promotion and 19.8 for network constraint; not much of an exception, but clearly a person not punished for having a low-constraint network). There were men promoted to the entry rank who got there early with a brokerage network (not presented in Figure 7.1 to highlight the gender difference; most extreme was promotion 4.8 years early with network constraint at 23.9). On average, however, women and entry-rank men were excluded from the benefits of network brokerage.

It might not seem a great shock to learn that men in senior job ranks are insiders while women and entry-rank men are outsiders, so it is useful to pause for a moment to reflect on the results. The diagnostic results show that women and entry-rank men in the study population were most at risk of being denied the benefit of network brokerage. The risk to women is more severe in that: (a) women's careers are delayed by network brokerage while entry-rank men merely enjoy no advantage from brokerage, and (b) men enter senior management as outsiders but are insiders for subsequent promotion while women remain outsiders for promotion to each rank (as illustrated by the small graphs by job rank in Figure 7.1).

There is also value in what the diagnostic results show about kinds of people not treated as outsiders. Apart from gender and entry-rank, no other measured attributes of managers, including race, is a criterion distinguishing outsiders. Moreover, women and entry-rank men might seem obvious candidates for outsider status, but they are not always outsiders. In other organizations, I have not found the distinction observed here in which entry-rank men are outsiders, and I have found one organization in which women were the insiders (Burt, 2000:403). Beyond the limited number of organizations on which I have network data, there are the many instances in which people assigned to a particular job have to battle as outsiders even though they would be readily accepted elsewhere as insiders (e.g., the cases of Paduka and George discussed later in the chapter).

More local diagnostic

The diagnostic can also be useful in detecting less traditional, finer-grain issues within organizations. Recall the supply-chain organization introduced in Chapter 3 (sociograms in Figure 3.6 and 3.7). I ran the network diagnostic on the organization. I found no evidence of gender, race, or age used as a criterion to distinguish outsiders. The organization was attractively open to leadership by all kinds of people. However, discussion with a colleague long familiar with the supply chain revealed an issue I had not considered. In the rank order of supply-chain managers, analogous to the rank order in Figure 7.2, my colleague noted a cluster of people at the bottom of the list who worked in the same city, and another cluster of people at the top of the list who worked in another city. The geographic regions corresponded to organizations run by two senior people. I had tested for region, but not as region corresponded to supervision by the two senior people. When I created attribute variables to distinguish people in the organizations run by the two senior people, there was a systematic tendency for one to have subordinates at the top of the rank order while the other's subordinates were at the bottom of the rank order.

It turned out that the person with subordinates at the top of the rank order was busy with other activities, which left subordinates to exercise their own leadership. Subordinates who ran a smooth operation were rewarded with positive evaluations and good salary increases. These subordinates tended to have networks that connected across groups in the company, which is how they managed to keep their operations running smoothly. Subordinates embedded in a closed network of colleagues were more often surprised by changing business demands and asked the boss for guidance or intervention. These closed-network subordinates were not rewarded. The result was a strong association between subordinate performance and network brokerage. The senior person running this organization was not paying much attention to the subordinates, but there was just enough attention paid to put out fires and grow an able group of new managers. Several subordinates in this organization rose to senior rank in the broader supply chain organization.

At the other extreme, the senior person with subordinates at the bottom of the rank order managed subordinates more closely. Rewards went to people who had been with the organization a long time. Subordinates were neither rewarded for brokering connections across groups, nor punished for building closed networks within their group. Almost none of the subordinates under this senior person rose to senior rank in the broader supply-chain organization, and the senior person was eventually relieved of command.

In sum, the network diagnostic illustrated in Figure 7.2 is useful for diagnosing the extent to which familiar categories of people—or company-specific categories of people—are being denied the benefit of network brokerage, which implies brokerage limited to a select group of insiders, and poor development of the leadership skills that employees will need for success at higher levels of the organization.

Hierarchy is the Active Ingredient

The implication of the story so far is that women in the study population would have been wise to build for closure, men would have been wise to build for brokerage, and men just entering senior management would have had to endure a period of suspicion from more-senior men before they were accepted as insiders. Before jumping to the conclusion that closure speeds promotion for anyone, I want to go deeper into the association with network constraint. As introduced in Chapter 2 (pp. 24–25), and explained in Appendix B (pp. 295–297), network constraint is composed of three network ingredients: size, density, and hierarchy. Access to structural holes is constrained when a person has very few contacts (size), contacts directly connected with one another (density), or contacts connected indirectly through a central person (hierarchy). Any of the three components could be responsible for a performance association with network constraint. Distinguishing the three components is a methodological distraction when describing the aggregate performance association with bridging structural holes. I now distinguish the three components to understand how constraint is an advantage for outsiders.

Karen and Jane

Figure 7.3 illustrates the point that will be nailed down in a moment with regression results across all of the managers. The figure contains sociograms and network scores for two women, Jane and Karen, identified in the Figure 7.1 graph. (Jane and Karen are pseudonyms.) The two women are at about the same level of network constraint on the horizontal axis in Figure 7.1, but Jane was promoted to the rank of senior manager 9 years earlier than other women like her while Karen was promoted to senior manager 7 years later than other women like her. Given similar levels of network constraint, what is different about the networks that could account for the wide difference in promotions for the two women?

Network constraint for the two women is presented in Figure 7.3 disaggregated down to contact-specific constraint scores. The network constraint index, C, is the sum of contact-specific scores (the c_{ij} in equation B1 in

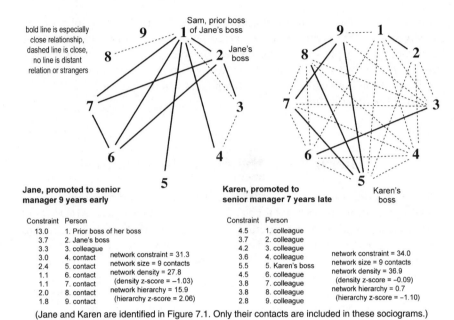

(Jane and Karen are identified in Figure 7.1. Only their contacts are included in these sociograms.)

Figure 7.3 Discovering Hierarchy

Appendix B).[3] For example, the contact first named in Karen's network survey posed 4.5 points of network constraint on Karen, the second posed 3.7 points, the third 4.2 points, and so on. Karen's nine contact-specific scores in Figure 7.3 sum across contacts to Karen's 34.0 score on the network constraint index. Similarly, the contact-specific scores for Jane sum to her 31.3 score on the network constraint index.

The networks around Jane and Karen are in some ways similar. The level of network constraint on both women is about the same; 31.3 and 34.0 points respectively, which puts them at about the same point on the horizontal axis in Figure 7.1. Both women cited nine contacts, so network size is the same for them. The average connection between Jane's contacts is slightly lower, but both Jane and Karen have about the average level of network density in this study population.

The two women differ on hierarchy. The hierarchy score for Jane's network is slightly more than two standard deviations above the population average. The

---

[3] To compute the network constraint and hierarchy scores for Jane and Karen, you need the strength of relations from each woman to their contacts. Karen felt equally close to each of her contacts. Jane felt close to her boss, less close to contacts six and seven, and especially close to her other six contacts. Quantitative scores for the survey responses are 1.00 versus .34 for especially close versus close relations between contacts, and 1.00, .69, and .37 for respondent–contact relations of especially close, close, and less close (Burt, 1992:287–288).

hierarchy score for Karen's network is slightly more than a standard deviation below average. The two women are on opposite extremes in the population distribution of network hierarchy scores.

Look down the list in Figure 7.3 of contact-specific scores for Karen. Density measures the average level of connection among a person's contacts and hierarchy measures the extent to which constraint is concentrated in one contact. Each of Karen's contacts poses about the same level of constraint. Her network hierarchy score is near zero. Karen has a network closed by dense connections among her contacts. The sociogram shows close relations between most of her contacts, augmented by especially close relations between some contacts, especially with Karen's boss. I know from the survey that Karen's network was concentrated in her immediate work group. Contacts 3, 4, 6, 7, 8, and 9 were all people who worked with Karen under her boss.

Jane's network involves the same number of contacts but has a broader reach. From the survey, I know that only two of Jane's nine contacts were from her work group: contact 3 and her boss, contact 2. Jane's other ties were essential sources of buy-in beyond her group (contacts 1, 4, 5, and 6), and more distant contacts who Jane cited as valuable sources of support and advice. Sam is the key to understanding Jane's network. (Sam is a pseudonym.) Sam was a sponsor for Jane.[4] Jane felt that she had received some good advice from Sam, but what she most appreciated were the introductions Sam made for her in the organization. Jane's boss maintained a good relationship with his prior boss, Sam. On her boss's recommendation, Jane represented her group in a project under Sam's direction. Sam was impressed with Jane and took her under his wing, brokering introductions to other senior people. Senior people dealing with Jane felt that they were dealing indirectly with Sam, which greatly simplified Jane's work with them. Look down the list of contact-specific scores for Jane. Sam poses a level of network constraint more than three times larger than the level posed by any of Jane's other contacts. The sociogram shows a few close relations, but many especially close relations with Sam and Jane's boss. Jane and Karen have similar levels of network constraint, but the constraint is for very different reasons. Karen's network is closed by dense interconnections among all contacts. Jane's network is closed by indirect connections through Sam.[5]

---

[4] Sponsor is my word, not Jane's. I telephoned Jane in 1993, four years after the original study, in the course of preparing the graphic in Figure 7.3 for an MBA course. I identified Jane and Karen from the sample data distributions because they nicely illustrated the hierarchy association with early promotion. I wanted more information on Jane to bring her to life for the business students. I called the telephone extension I had for Jane from the original study, and was transferred to her new number. I explained the nature of the call, and was graciously given a better understanding of Sam's role in her work at the time of the study.

[5] Continuing footnote 3, the concentration of Jane's network in Sam is increased by her especially close relationship with Sam, weaker relationship with her boss, and less close relationship with the two contacts especially close to her boss (contacts 6 and 7).

Generalizing the example

The bar charts in Figure 7.4 generalize the point illustrated by Karen and Jane and put it in the context of managers trying to diagnose their own networks. For Figure 7.4, I divided the managers into three qualitative network categories. Closed hierarchical networks are those with hierarchy scores that are average or higher in the population. Closed dense networks are non-hierarchical networks with constraint scores that are average or higher in the population. Broker networks are non-hierarchical networks with constraint scores below average.

The first panel in Figure 7.4 shows how early promotion varied across the three categories of networks. Senior men show the advantages expected of network brokerage. Early promotions went to senior men with broker networks. Late promotions went to senior men with networks closed by dense relations or network hierarchy. Continuous network measures yield the same conclusions. When I regress early promotion (the vertical axis in Figure 7.1)

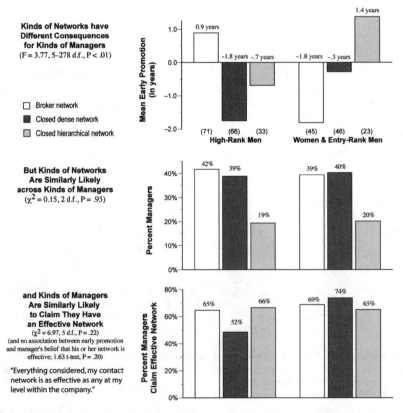

Figure 7.4 The Situation Can be Difficult to See

across the three component variables in network constraint, I get the following standardized multiple regression results for senior men (multiple correlation of .49): Early promotions went to senior men with larger networks (.27 coefficient for network size, 3.86 routine t-test). Late promotions went to senior men with networks closed by dense connections among contacts (−.43 coefficient for network density, −5.71 t-test), or networks of contacts connected indirectly through a central person other than ego (−.23 coefficient for hierarchy, −3.01 t-test). Results in other organizations also show the negative effect of network closure for insiders, sometimes from density alone, sometimes from both network density and hierarchy (Burt, 2000:378).

To the right in the first panel of Figure 7.4, the results on women and entry-rank men generalize the point illustrated by Karen and Jane. Closure is associated with early promotion for women and entry-rank men, but only closure by hierarchy. Networks closed by dense relations have no association with promotion for women or entry-rank men. And, as illustrated in Figure 7.1 for women, broker networks are associated with late promotion to senior manager rank. When I regress early promotion across the three component network variables, I get the following standardized multiple regression results for women and entry-rank men (multiple correlation of .37): Network size is irrelevant (−1.54 t-test). Network density is negligible (1.86 t-test). Network hierarchy has a strong positive association with early promotion (3.24 t-test). In other organizations, I find a similar effect concentration in network hierarchy for outsiders (Burt, 2000:403).

Diagnosis is difficult from inside the network

Given the networks associated with early promotion, one could expect that senior men would disproportionately build broker networks while women and entry-rank men built hierarchical networks. But company processes and the company emphasis on collaborative networks were powerful forces shaping networks. The second panel in Figure 7.4 shows that women and entry-rank men built the same networks built by senior men. In fact, the three categories of networks occur in similar proportions among every kind of manager in the study population.[6] This is interesting for observers who claim that kinds of people tend to build kinds of networks (e.g., women build closed networks while men build broker networks).

---

[6] The chi-square statistic for the second panel in Figure 7.4 shows that the three kinds of networks are independent of the distinction between senior men versus women and entry-rank men. The three kinds of networks are similarly independent of a distinction between men and women (4.10 chi-square, 3 d.f., P = .25), a distinction between people long with the firm in their function versus people more recently hired (1.22 chi-square, 3 d.f., P = .75), a distinction between the four job ranks (3.80 chi-square, 9 d.f., P = .92), and a distinction between eight functional areas (23.96 chi-square, 21 d.f., P = .30).

Even if the kind of network around a manager had been determined completely by the company and colleagues, a strategic manager should know whether his or her network is an asset or a problem. Senior men who had a broker network should have been pleased with their network since that is the network associated with early promotion for senior men. Women and entry-rank men with broker networks should have been displeased with their network since that is the network associated with late promotion for women and entry-rank men. The third panel in Figure 7.4 shows that the managers were quite poor at diagnosing their networks. Bars indicate the percentage of managers who said that their network was "as effective as any at my level within the company." The negligible test statistic in the figure shows that network evaluations were similar across kinds of networks and the insider–outsider distinction. Broker networks are the only kind associated with early promotion for senior men, but senior men with closed hierarchical networks were just as enthusiastic about their networks (about two-thirds of the men with either kind of network feel that their network is effective). Closed hierarchical networks are the only kind associated with early promotion for women and entry-rank men, but those with broker networks—the worst choice for these managers—were just as enthusiastic about their networks. If there is informed strategic behavior here, it is difficult to see. Kinds of networks had career implications for kinds of managers, but kinds of networks are randomly distributed across insiders and outsiders, and both were poor judges of whether their network was effective (as "effective" was reflected in early promotion).

Strategic Partners and Partner Networks

The key fact is that only one form of closure—hierarchy, not density—is associated with outsider success. The difference between the two kinds of closed networks is a partner who has access to structural holes.

Hierarchy indicates a partner with access to structural holes

The point is illustrated in Figure 7.5. Imagine that you are trying to broker connections among people who deem you an outsider. You find a well-connected insider willing to make introductions for you. The first sociogram in Figure 7.5 has you linked with that insider, who I will discuss as a partner, a strategic partner for the critical advantage provided to outsiders. The second sociogram in Figure 7.5 shows that your partner is connected across structural holes within the target environment. When your partner introduces you to his contacts, you end up with the hierarchical network displayed as the third sociogram in Figure 7.5. The network is hierarchical in that one of your contacts, the partner, indirectly connects your other contacts. You and your partner own the network jointly. Note that you only arrive at the hierarchical network when your partner connects across structural holes. If the partner's contacts are connected directly, you end up with a network of densely interconnected contacts—and networks closed by density are not associated with outsider success (top panel in Figure 7.4). In short, hierarchy indicates a network built around a partner who has access to structural holes.[7]

The partner has two effects. The first is a "framing" effect. Framing occurs when meaning derives in some part from the context in which an object, idea, or person is viewed. Affiliation with an established insider frames the outsider as a person who is not like other outsiders; this is an outsider acceptable to insiders, a "good" outsider. The partnership is also an implicit endorsement, carrying a reputation cost for the partner. If relations with the outsider sour, it would be to the detriment of the insider who brought the outsider in among us. If relations with the outsider turn out well, that too would reflect on the insider who made us aware of this terrific person. The essence of the partner role is to loan reputation to an outsider. The Rothschild anecdote I quoted in introducing this book is an example: asked to invest in a friend's new venture, it is said that the great man replied he would not invest, but he would walk arm-in-arm with his friend across the exchange floor. In short order, there would be investors to spare. The risk to reputation is not emphasized in the anecdote. Walking across the exchange floor too often with schemers who turned out to be con men would, in short order, destroy the great man's reputation.

The partner role is especially obvious when network brokerage crosses corporate or cultural boundaries. It is official in Japan. There are industry-specific directories of people available to help outsiders develop relations with Japanese firms.[8] The people in these directories are usually retired corporate executives who prefer the active life of consulting to life in a window seat. These people bring no technical skills, for they were too long at the top to know the technical details of their industry. They bring connections. Without the proper personal connections, outsiders don't do business in Japan. Corning Glass is a concrete illustration. Corning has a history of joint ventures that give Corning access to a market where the partner firm is established. Nanda and Bartlett (1990) offer illustrative examples in the United States and Europe, but

---

[7] On a methodological note, strategic partners are not captured by the measure of indirect network constraint used in Chapters 3, 4, and 5. Indirect network constraint measures the extent to which a manager is affiliated with network brokers, which seems analogous to the idea of strategic partners. However, mere affiliation is most closely analogous to the second sociogram in Figure 7.5; the sociogram of ego before relations have been established with the partner's contacts. After ego has established relations, the network is hierarchical as illustrated in the third sociogram in Figure 7.5.

[8] I am grateful to James E. Schrager for calling my attention to these directories. Professor Schrager's knowledge of them comes from their importance in his work arranging partnerships between American and Japanese firms through his firm, Great Lakes Consulting Group.

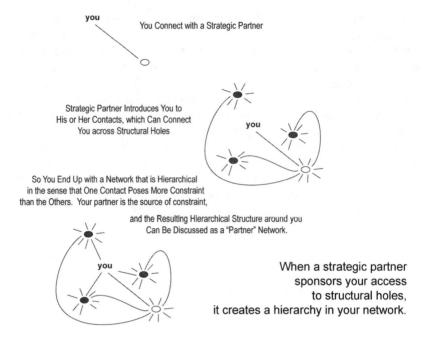

Figure 7.5 Hierarchy Indicates a Partner, Which Can be Strategic

I particularly enjoy their quote from a Corning executive commenting on the result of Corning's alliance with the Japanese firm Asahi (Nanda and Bartlett, 1990:14): "When our salespeople began calling on the Japanese TV set manufacturers, we felt as if a veil came over them when they dealt with us. Their relationships with their Japanese suppliers ran very deep, while they were very distant with us. Last week, Asahi people escorted me to a meeting with the worldwide TV tube manager of a large Japanese company and introduced me properly to him. We had extremely fruitful conversation. I wouldn't have even been able to meet him and discuss issues between us if it were not for the Asahi connection."

I am discussing the partner as strategic because of the association between hierarchy and outsider success. Strategic intent can originate with ego or the partner, but without knowing the origin of the hierarchical network around a manager, there is no sure indicator of strategic intent. In Figure 7.5, partner relations with contacts are the foundation for ego's relations. Alternatively, ego's relations could be the foundation. For example, I often see hierarchical networks around executive MBA students with the student's spouse playing the role of partner. The student is exposed to diverse new contacts in the program and those she enjoys she introduces to her husband. Ego's relations are foundation for the partner's relations. This program effect on conjugal networks is similar to the effect Bott (1957) reports for geographic mobility. When a married couple moves to a new town, new acquaintances close to either spouse are introduced to the other spouse. A hierarchical network emerges in which each spouse is partner to the other. Thus, non-strategic partners certainly exist. However, the systematic association in Figure 7.4 between hierarchy and outsider success implies that partners in the manager networks tended toward the strategic kind (again, allowing that the intent could originate with the manager or the partner).

Paduka and George

Bringing the concepts down to a more personal level, and expanding the range of examples, Figure 7.6 contains sociograms and network scores describing two men who have done well with strategic partners. The network data were obtained with the web-based survey instrument in Appendix A (see Figures A1 and A2), followed by discussion in workshops on business networks. I selected Paduka and George from the workshop participants because these two cases nicely broaden the range of strategic partner networks discussed in this chapter. To preserve confidentiality, the names are pseudonyms and the businesses are described in general terms.

To the left in Figure 7.6, Paduka is an entrepreneur who runs a successful manufacturing company. Paduka owns the company jointly with another man who is partner both in the usual legal sense of owning a large piece of the business and in the network sense of providing access. Look down the list

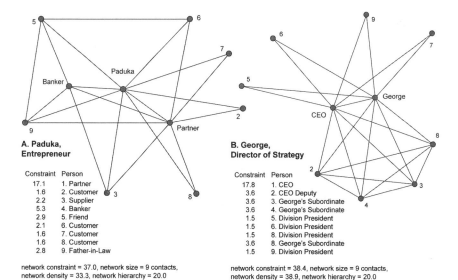

A. Paduka, Entrepreneur

Constraint	Person
17.1	1. Partner
1.6	2. Customer
2.2	3. Supplier
5.3	4. Banker
2.9	5. Friend
2.1	6. Customer
1.6	7. Customer
1.6	8. Customer
2.8	9. Father-in-Law

network constraint = 37.0, network size = 9 contacts, network density = 33.3, network hierarchy = 20.0

B. George, Director of Strategy

Constraint	Person
17.8	1. CEO
3.6	2. CEO Deputy
3.6	3. George's Subordinate
3.6	4. George's Subordinate
1.5	5. Division President
1.5	6. Division President
1.5	8. Division President
3.6	8. George's Subordinate
1.5	9. Division President

network constraint = 38.4, network size = 9 contacts, network density = 38.9, network hierarchy = 20.0

Figure 7.6 Two Example Partner Networks

in Figure 7.6 of contact-specific network constraint scores for Paduka. The partner poses more than three times the level of constraint posed by the next highest source. Paduka's network hierarchy score is high at 20.0 points. Jane's hierarchy score in Figure 7.3 was a lower 15.9 points, and that score was two standard deviations above average in the population of senior managers.

Paduka's partner has little to do with operations, but the business would not exist without him. Contacts 2, 6, 7, and 8 own retail stores through which the company sells its product. All four customers are long-term friends of the partner. Paduka feels that he has built up good relations with each of them, but they initially accepted contracts with Paduka on the strength of their relationship with the partner. More, the partner grew up with Paduka's father-in-law. It was the partner and father-in-law's joint endorsement to a banker with whom they had long-standing business that secured the loan for the company's initial funding. When Paduka started this business he was not an outsider in the sense of insiders being uncomfortable with his gender, race, or nationality. He was just another guy looking for an interesting business to run. The strategic partner distinguished Paduka as someone to whom the partner's contacts would do well to pay attention. All have done well with the venture.

To the right in Figure 7.6, George is the director of strategy in a moderate-size company organized into four divisions. George feels good about his contributions to the company in the two years since he joined: a successful acquisition in his first year that links two of the company divisions, and a new marketing campaign launched this year. The current CEO has run the company for a long time. He runs it with a strong hand. He met George at a social event, was impressed, brought George in for a couple months as a consultant, then created the full-time position George now holds. The sociogram in Figure 7.6 shows George and the CEO in a cluster composed of the CEO's deputy and George's three subordinates, who were company employees long before George joined. Beyond the staff cluster, George and the CEO are both tied to each division president, none of whom are close to the others, or anyone in the staff cluster. The list of contact-specific network constraint scores for George shows that the CEO is far and away the dominant source of constraint on George. Here again, George's network hierarchy score is high at 20.0 points.

George is twice an outsider. This is a company run by the same person for a long time with long-time employees. Long-term relations are routine in this company, so anyone new is a bit of an outsider, especially if they enter at a senior level. Youth is also an issue. The CEO is in his 60s and his four division presidents are within a decade of his age. At age 28 when he met the CEO two years ago, George is much younger than the people he advises on business strategy. Without the CEO's endorsement, it is not clear to George that he would have prospered in this position.

A third step in the network diagnostic

The link between hierarchy and a strategic partner sets up a third, elective, step to the network diagnostic in Figure 7.2. The first two steps identify kinds of people excluded from the benefits of network brokerage. This third step determines the operation of strategic partners. In thinking about the value of the third step, recall the evidence in Figure 7.4 showing how inadequate the managers were in diagnosing their own networks. Managers with networks beneficial to their situation were no more positive about their networks than managers with networks detrimental to their situation. The third diagnostic step is a rigorous way to determine whether strategic partners are operating in a study population.

The third step is to regress outsider performance across the size, density, and hierarchy components of network constraint to identify the active ingredient responsible for outsider success, as was done here in association with Figure 7.4. Systematic association between performance and hierarchy for a category of people indicates that success for those people depends on affiliation with a network broker, a strategic partner in the population. It is one thing for individuals to occasionally benefit from a partner's social connections—as did Paduka and George. It is another thing for a category of people to consistently depend on partners for success. Since partnering is a strategy through which suspect outsiders get access to the benefits of network brokerage, a category of people for whom success depends on partnering is a category of people deemed suspect. The fact that women and entry-rank men in Figure 7.4 fell behind when they brokered connections on their own, and moved ahead when they worked with a partner, corroborates the diagnosis of a diversity problem in the organization, and confirms the operation of strategic partners for outsiders lucky enough to have them. A practical next step in managing the diversity problem would be to ensure the availability of strategic partners until the kind of people deemed outsiders have been absorbed into the organization as another kind of insider.

Conclusion

In ostensible contradiction to the findings on secondhand brokerage, people can benefit from affiliation with network brokers. However, the benefit is limited to a specific category of people—people deemed outsiders. In fact, the benefit provides a network diagnostic for identifying the kinds of people deemed outsiders in a population. The usual association between performance and network brokerage is reversed for outsiders. Outsiders with networks that span structural holes are punished in the sense that their evaluations are less positive relative to peers, their compensation is lower, and their promotions come later. The outsiders are not being punished for having good ideas, if in fact insiders ever listen to their ideas. Nor are they punished for having relations outside, if in fact insiders are ever privy to the outsider's relations. Outsiders are being punished for making a claim to insider status, for being so presumptuous as to suggest how insiders should think or behave. Strategic partners provide a route around the problem. Outsider access to the benefits of network brokerage is indirect, through a strategic partner who frames the partnered outsider as unlike the stereotype of outsiders, using the partner's reputation as an endorsement.

The key research result is the particular form of network closure associated with outsider success: it is hierarchy, not density. Hierarchy results when a manager affiliates with a network broker who makes introductions to the broker's contacts (Figure 7.5). The resulting network is rich in structural holes with the manager's access to them underwritten by the partner. A manager partnering with someone in a network of densely interconnected contacts ends up a member of the dense network, and density is not associated with outsider success. The fact that outsider success is keyed to hierarchy highlights a similarity between insider and outsider: They both benefit from access to structural holes. They differ in how they access the benefit. Access is direct for insiders; in fact, they are punished for relying on partners for their access (negative effect of hierarchy on early promotion for senior men in Figure 7.4). Access is indirect for outsiders. The positive correlation between network constraint and outsider success is a reduced-form coefficient. It is the combination of a strong relation to a partner and a broker network around the partner. The two factors combine to define a high-constraint hierarchical network around the manager. Within the manager's hierarchical network, partner access to structural holes provides competitive advantage. Whether a manager has direct access to structural holes as an insider, or indirect access as an outsider through the broker network borrowed from a partner, the manager enjoys competitive advantage to the extent that he or she has access to structural holes.

Codicil to the broader story

In one sense, this chapter is little more than an interesting codicil to the broader story about the network structure of social capital. Outsiders are typically a minority in a population, so they can be ignored in estimating average returns to network brokerage. As illustrated by the bold regression line in Figure 7.1, men in the top three senior manager ranks below vice president greatly outnumbered the women, so performance had the usual negative association with network constraint when estimated across senior managers. However as illustrated by the thin solid regression line in Figure 7.1, the returns to brokerage were more clear and more substantial in this organization when women were analyzed separately. In other words, network analysts have an incentive to run the network diagnostics to test for outsiders if only to remove outsiders so as to better see brokerage effects unobscured by the distortion of poor returns to outsider brokerage.

Essential feature of contemporary business

In another sense, this chapter is essential to understanding contemporary business because global operations mean everyone is more exposed to people about whom they have held stereotypes. We are asked more often than ever before to collaborate with kinds of people we could have, and would have, avoided in the past. Whether you are on the inside working to facilitate the integration of outsiders into the organization, or on the outside pitching to people who have trouble accepting ideas from people like you, the solution is affiliation with network brokers who can act as strategic partners. Strategic partners are defined by their network, not their job rank. Access to structural holes is correlated with job rank (people in higher job ranks tend to have more access), but it is not identical (there are senior people embedded in dense networks of interconnected colleagues). More, the network diagnostic goes beyond identifying broad categories of people deemed outsiders. Instead of distinguishing broad categories of people by attributes such as age, gender, or race, then treating everyone with the same attributes as equivalent, the analysis indicates the extent to which individual people are excluded from the benefits of network brokerage (Figure 7.2). Outsider status is keyed to the social situation of an individual, not to the individual's attributes. Anyone can be an outsider in their particular situation, including senior white males. Defining diversity at the level of individuals—all individuals, regardless of age, gender, race, or any other broad category—is a powerful shift in the analysis of diversity problems.[9]

---

[9] It would not be unreasonable to say that the rigor with which diversity problems are addressed by the network diagnostics is also a powerful shift away from the anecdotes and convenience samples that so often guide diversity policy. At the same time, there is a vibrant industry of earnest people proposing practical ways to manage diversity so that firms can benefit from the full potential of employee collaborations. I have avoided practical issues in this chapter for two reasons: it would distract from my main purpose in the chapter, and I could not do justice to the breadth of work available on practical issues. On the first point, my purpose here is to show that returns to outsider affiliation with network brokers do not contradict my conclusion that secondhand brokerage offers negligible advantage to managers. That purpose can be met without discussing diversity policy. Moreover, a network process that explains behavior in multiple populations can require population-specific policy to manage the process in any one population. I cannot speak with the same authority about diversity policy in its variety as I can speak about network diagnostics for detecting diversity problems. Policy discussion I leave to clinical work elsewhere. Eagly and Carli (2007) offer broad review, with Roth (2007) a quick update on continuing issues on Wall Street. For quality discussion of contemporary views, I often rely on the non-profit organization, Catalyst (www.catalyst.org).

The shift in perspective also highlights the dangers of living too long in the shadow of strategic partners. I concluded in Chapter 4 that emotional and cognitive skills are enhanced as a by-product of brokering connections across structural holes. The skills to be expected as a by-product of sponsored broker-age are more passive; learning how to fit into the partner's frame of mind, acting effectively on partner interests. With time, living in the shadow of partners can be expected to wither a person's ability to independently detect and develop new ideas. Under a big tree only mushrooms grow.

Beyond skill atrophy, there is a danger of sponsored outsiders coming to accept their second-class citizenship as deserved. I mentioned in Chapter 4 the learned helplessness that can result from prolonged dependence on a stronger person, citing Peterson, Maier, and Seligman (1993). The phenomenon here is more specific and more subtle, resulting from differential exposure to gossip. A nice example is provided by Elias and Scotson (1965, especially chap. 7). They describe gossip enforcing a status boundary between adjacent neighborhoods in an English suburb (also see Gluckman, 1963, on gossip used to maintain group exclusivity, and Fine, 1996, on "reputation entrepreneurs" who define a person's negative place in history by circulating derogatory stories uncon-tested by the person's supporters). The two neighborhoods, discussed as the "Village" and the "Estate," were similarly working class with respect to the usual socioeconomic metrics of occupation, education, and type of housing. Yet the Village was recognized in both neighborhoods as socially superior to the Estate. The Village had been established a generation before the Estate, and some families in the Village were second generation so they were "old fam-ilies" relative to people in the Estate. Age was not the immediate explanation for the status order. The explanation lay in the social network that had devel-oped with age (Elias and Scotson, 1965:94):

In the closely-knit neighborhood of the Village gossip flowed freely and richly through the gossip channels provided by the differentiated network of families and associations. In the loosely-knit and less highly organized neighborhood of the Estate the flow of gossip was on the whole more sluggish. Gossip circuits were shorter and often not linked to each other. Even neighbouring families quite often had no or only slender gossip links. There were more barriers to gossip communication.

Stories about people in the Estate—about their domestic abuse, excessive drink, lost jobs, unruly and wayward children—were a staple in Village gossip, reinforcing Village social cohesion with vivid illustration of Village superiority over people in the Estate. Elias and Scotson (1965:93) wrote of the Villagers:

. . . while supporting and praise-gossip played their part in the stream of gossip which never stopped running through the gossip channels in the Village, they were mixed with, and inseparable from, gossip items with the opposite emotional colour, with rejecting and blame-gossip. On a rough estimate the latter seemed to play a much larger part as ingredients of the gossip stream than the former. . . . Blame-gossip appealed more directly to the gossiper's sense of their own righteousness. But it also provided the pleasure of being able to talk with others about things which were forbidden, which one should not do.... That one gossiped about it with others was proof of one's own blamelessness. It reinforced the community of the righteous. The group blame meted out to those who had broken the rules had a strong integrating function. But it did not stand on its own. It kept alive and re-inforced already existing group links.

Curiously, Estate residents seemed unable to escape the stigmatizing effect of Village gossip (Elias and Scotson, 1965:101):

A good deal of what Villagers habitually said about Estate families was vastly exaggerated or untrue. The majority of Estate people did not have "low morals"; they did not constantly fight with each other, were not habitual "boozers" or unable to control their children. Why were they powerless to correct these misrepresentations? Why could they be put to shame if a Villager used in their presence a humiliating code word, symbol of their lower status such as "rat alley"? Why could they not shrug it off or retaliate with an equally massive flood of insinuations and distortions?

Elias and Scotson attribute Estate acceptance of their second-class citizenship to four factors: (a) Estate residents had continuing contact with Village residents, (b) were undeniably residents of the Estate by dint of where they lived, (c) shared the values of the Village in terms of which it would be shameful to behave in the manner described in the gossip about certain Estate people, and (d) were, because of their exclusion from the Village gossip network, more familiar with people in the Estate who fit the gossip stereotypes than they were familiar with Villagers who fit the stereotypes. As Elias and Scotson (1965:101–102) explain:

The majority of the Estate people could not retaliate because, to some extent, their own conscience was on the side of the detractors. They themselves agreed with the Village people that it was bad not to be able to control one's children or to get drunk and noisy and violent. Even if none of these reproaches could be applied to themselves personally, they knew only too well that it did apply to some of their neighbors. They could be shamed by allusions to this bad behavior of their neighbors because by their living in the same neighborhood the blame, the bad name attached to it, according to the rules of affective thinking, was automatically applied to them too. In their case, as in so many others, blemishes observable in some members of a group were emotionally transferred to all members of the group. The rejecting gossip of the Village, all the open or whispered expressions of reproach and contempt leveled against the Estate people, had power over them, however decent and orderly they were in their own conduct, because part of themselves, their own conscience, agreed with the Villagers low opinion of their neighbourhood. It was this silent agreement which paralysed their ability to retaliate and to assert themselves.

Translated into relations between insiders and outsiders, the four factors making an outsider prone to accepting second-class citizenship as deserved are: (a) continuing contact with insiders, (b) identification as an outsider by unambiguous attributes such as skin color, gender, age, credentials, or costume, (c) values similar to insiders about proper, admired, and detested behavior, and

(d) more knowledge about fellow outsiders than about the population of insiders. The four factors should be familiar to anyone proud of their heritage who has spent time living as an outsider among insiders. The result can manifest as the "imposter syndrome" in which a successful person believes himself to be an imposter in the sense that he does not deserve the success he has achieved (e.g., Clance and Imes, 1978; Kets de Vries, 2005). This is a second danger of living too long in the shadow of strategic partners: one's confidence can wither in the face of derogatory insider gossip uncontested.

Exception that proves the rule

My goal for this chapter is less sophisticated than the above discussion. Outsiders are an exception that proves the secondhand-brokerage rule. The exception follows from the results in Chapters 3 and 4: If brokerage among friends of friends provides negligible value, why is there such tremendous advantage to outsiders from affiliation with network brokers?

Resolution begins by recognizing that the outsider advantage from affiliation with a network broker is not a vision advantage enhancing the outsider's emotional or cognitive skills. Strategic partners do not create advantage by affecting ego.

Resolution concludes by recognizing that partners create advantage by making ego more acceptable to insiders. The partner is a mutual contact—an element of network closure—that reassures insiders asked to trust the outsider. As evidence of closure inducing trust, the positive effect of strategic partners does not contradict the negligible returns to secondhand brokerage in Chapters 3 and 4. The positive effect is an instance of the trust and alignment returns to closed networks documented in Chapter 6.

Part III

EXPLORING IMPLICATIONS

EIGHT

Bent Preferences

D RIVEN by the evidence of local and personal processes in the preceding chapters, I speculate in this chapter on the role individual people play in the process by which network structure constitutes social capital. This is the question of agency: How much do individuals matter relative to the social structure around them? The question's neglect in contemporary network analysis has been noted from a variety of perspectives (e.g., Emirbayer and Goodwin, 1994; Baum and Rowley, 2008; Kilduff and Krackhardt, 2008). With some exceptions, much of the social capital research on performance and network structure reads as though performance springs directly from structure. The phrase "as though" warrants emphasis. Everyone knows that people are the source of action. Measured networks are only the residue of how people have spent time together up to the moment a network is measured. However, agency has often been put aside to focus on describing the performance association with network structure. Even in this book, with its emphasis on local and personal processes, I made it all the way to this final chapter without mentioning agency.

Networks certainly affect what people can do in the sense that certain people are advantaged while others are hindered. Such effects have been described in the preceding chapters. However, networks also affect what people want to do, what they see as valuable. How much of the performance association with networks is due to differences in network advantage versus network-induced differences in seeing or seizing network advantage? Action that seems worthwhile to one person can seem trivial, even status eroding, to another person. Are networks the performance factor to manage, or would it be more effective to manage incentives to act on network advantage? Network advantage is worthless until someone acts on it.

Agency in Networks

I begin with the usual solutions. There is no agency in the preceding chapters. People were drawn by brokerage opportunities into enhanced performance. People were pushed by closure into collaborative alignment. The agency question has not been ignored in these analyses, but it has been put aside in the usual two ways: it has been assumed away, and it has been held constant.

Assume it away

Agency can be put aside if it is coincident with opportunity. This solution to the agency question has been used in formal models and empirical research. Formal models of network dynamics address intuitions about aspects of social capital such as contacts exercising monopoly power to erode the returns to brokerage (Reagans and Zuckerman, 2008), or everyone striving to bridge structural holes (Ryall and Sorenson, 2007; Buskins and van de Rijt, 2008). The agency question is resolved by assuming that ego develops every opportunity and is motivated to increase the opportunities available, subject to a budget constraint of limited time or resources. To know who acts on network advantage, you only need to know who has network advantage. Thus, agency is not a variable in the analysis; it can be put aside.

Clarity and generality are the attractions of assuming that agency is defined by opportunity, but desperately wrong is another feature to the assumption. Managers often fall below the performance potential of their network. The usual data display of residual performance across levels of network advantage has a triangular distribution (e.g., Burt, 1992:37, for suspicion; Burt, 2005:37, for illustrative data displays). High performance often occurs with high advantage, and rarely occurs with low advantage. However, low performance often occurs with both high and low advantage. In other words, many people in brokerage positions do not derive advantage from their position. A variety of explanations are possible, but whatever the reason, it is clear that people are not equal in benefiting from the opportunities provided by the network around them.

The assumption can seem less strident when embedded in data. Imagine that the network structure around a person indicates personal preference. People adapt to the network around them. They also learn, editing the network to personal taste. There is evidence that even a little network training can produce substantial improvements in learning new networks as well as the usual performance metrics indicating network advantage (Janicik and Larrick, 2005; Burt and Ronchi, 2007). Whatever the etiology of the network around a person, the person is motivated to act on the advantage provided by the kind of network to which they have adapted and contributed. Motivation need not be measured directly because it is already measured by data on the network (Burt, 1992:34–36; 2005:47–50). The result is the same as assuming agency away; agency can be put aside to focus on performance associations with network structure.

Hold it constant

A more direct solution to the agency question is to measure individual differences to hold them constant when predicting performance. To a degree, this is generic in social capital research. People differ in their ability to act on network advantage. Some are better educated. Some have more experience. Some hold higher job rank, or work in a more prosperous region. Therefore, individual differences in capability are held constant when measuring performance relative to peers, as illustrated in Figure 2.4. A manager is well paid, for example, to the extent that his or her compensation is higher than managers with the same education and experience, in the same kind of work, job rank, organization, location, and so on.

Beyond individual differences in capability are differences in motivation. Two people equally *able* to act on network advantage can have distinct *inclinations* to act; one drawn to it, another repelled. Inclination to act on network advantage has been attributed to individual personality, and more broadly, to culture. A familiar culture story is Weber's (1905) thesis that Protestant beliefs encouraged capitalism by making entrepreneurial behavior righteous. If I had network data from the Reformation, I would infer from Weber's argument that people more Calvinist in their beliefs would be more likely to act on network advantage. In a related vein, Xiao and Tsui (2007) argue that network brokerage is inconsistent with Chinese social norms, and show a lack of returns to brokerage in the job ranks on which they have data. Burt, Hogarth, and Michaud (2000) compare senior managers in a pair of French and American engineering firms. The French networks are based on long-standing friendships that rarely spanned the boundary of the firm, while the Americans build from work relations that often reached outside the firm. Differences in the etiology of network connections notwithstanding, performance in both firms is associated with networks that span structural holes.

A familiar personality story is McClelland's (1961) thesis that the early formation of a need to achieve is a personality factor significant for later entrepreneurial behavior. I infer from the argument and research evidence that people raised insecure in their childhood would have a need to achieve that would predispose them to act on network advantage, resulting in them having performance metrics higher than peers. In a related vein, Anderson (2008) shows that managers with what he terms a high "need for cognition" are more likely to take advantage of the information advantages of the network around them. Mehra, Kilduff, and Brass (2001) argue that managers high on a personality index of self-monitoring are more likely to act on network advantage. Self-monitoring is a tendency to match one's speech and behavior to the situation—the way I behave here would be inappropriate over there. Mehra, Kilduff, and Brass report scores in self-monitoring higher for people whose networks more often span structural holes (also Oh and Kilduff, 2008), and show that performance increases with both network brokerage and self-monitoring.

I expect to see much more research adding personality and culture variables to network predictions of performance because the predictions are often successful, the predictions typically do not pay attention to agency, and it is interesting to talk about kinds of people prone or averse to action. However, it will be difficult to produce general theory from the research. The issue is not quality. The research to date has been of good quality and the strategy of measuring individual differences is attractive for its burden of proof. The null hypothesis can be cleanly rejected. The problem is the many alternatives that could reject the null hypothesis. The requirement for empirical evidence that is the strategy's strength is also its weakness. Numerous measures of personality could be added to the performance prediction, barriers to entry for new measures are easily breached, and the organization-specific data typically used to estimate performance returns to network structure are prone to idiosyncratic correlations inconsistent across research projects. So many individual differences could be held constant. Holding constant a particular favorite cannot provide a general solution to the agency question.

Endogenous agency

The "assume it away" and "hold it constant" solutions treat agency as exogenous in that individuals come to their current network with agency predetermined. The "assume it away" solution has people a priori motivated to act on whatever network advantage occurs, or motivated to act on whatever their network is configured to provide. The "hold it constant" solution measures the personality or cultural dispositions an individual brings to their network.

The lack of returns to secondhand brokerage implies endogenous agency. I concluded in Chapter 4 that brokerage seems not to be beneficial for the information it provides so much as it is beneficial as a forcing function for the cognitive and emotional skills required to manage communication between colleagues who do not agree in their opinion or behavior. The cognitive and emotional skills produced as a by-product of bridging structural holes are the proximate source of competitive advantage. This interpretation implies endogenous agency in that agency is in some part determined by network context.

The exogenous–endogenous distinction with respect to agency is analogous to the person–situation distinction that followed Walter Mischel's (1968) review of personality measurement (Mischel, 2004, is an efficient port into subsequent research). The gist of the review is that personality measures vary so much for a person across situations that it is difficult to believe that the person has a personality in the form of emotional and behavioral traits independent of situation. A person can be aggressive in some situations, passive in others. A person can be depressed in some situations, elated in others. As Mischel (1968:146) put it: "With the possible exception of intelligence, highly generalized behavioral consistencies have not been demonstrated, and the concept of personality traits as broad predispositions is thus untenable."

One way to reassert that personality is exogenous to situations is to say that personality measures contain random error, so reliable measurement requires repeated measures. In a widely cited article, for example, Epstein (1979) reports on college students making daily records of their strong feelings and behaviors. There is low reliability between daily records (correlations under .3), but high reliability between measures averaged across multiple days (correlations over .7). People who feel happy today, for example, cannot be predicted to feel that way tomorrow (one-day reliabilities of −.03 and .22, Epstein, 1979:1107), but people who feel happy across several days are likely to feel that way across several other days (.92 reliability for average across 15 odd-number days with average across 15 even-number days, Epstein, 1979:1107).

Personality does not have to be exogenous to affect outcomes. Instead of averaging personality scores across situations, Mischel and Shoda (1995) propose contingency theories of personality in which the personality manifest in a situation depends in some part on the situation. At work, Susan is passive. At home, she is not. The "*if* this situation, *then* that personality" statements that result make sense in terms of capturing personality–situation interactions. Looking back on the search for consistency as evidence of personality, Mischel (2004:13) reflects: "In retrospect, the intuition of consistency turns out to be neither paradoxical nor illusory: It is linked to behavioral consistency but not the sort for which the field was searching for so many years, and it was found by incorporating the situation into the search for invariance rather than by removing it."

With respect to social capital research, however, "if situation, then personality" variables only deepen the empiricist weakness of the "hold it constant" solution to the agency question. There are a great many existing and possible personality measures, any of which can be proposed as a control in a social capital prediction. The range of legitimate control variables is the empiricist weakness discussed above in the "hold it constant" solution. Different studies can be expected to report different results for different measures in different organizations. Add situational adjectives, and those many personality measures become each cross-classified by the many distinctions that can be made between situations, increasing by a power the controls to consider in a social capital prediction.

I take a related, but distinct, approach. Rather than build situational variation into personality theory, I model people and situations separately, then let agency emerge from people reacting to situations. Assuming that ego is more likely to act on opportunities that provide clear benefit, one way to answer the network agency question is to model how benefit is perceived in network context. I want a solution to the agency question that is close to the ground in the sense that it can guide and be subject to empirical research at the same time that the solution provides general description across populations and levels of analysis. I want a solution that can be productive at the intersection of economics, psychology, and sociology; something consistent with substantive research in psychology and sociology, while capable of being used as a primitive term in formal models exploring network applications of economic reasoning (e.g., Jackson, 2008). The course I have in mind is in the spirit of what Hedström (2005) describes as analytical sociology, with its emphasis on "the actual mechanism at work." I draw on all three faces of social psychology (House, 1977): I draw on psychology to model people in terms of a function from psychophysics that has been shown to describe the stimulation people feel in response to actual stimulation. I draw on sociology to model the situation as a social network. I draw on symbolic interaction to describe how people use others in the situation as a frame of reference.

The result is a model of the mechanism by which ego's preferences are bent by the surrounding network. Bent preferences are evaluations shaped by social comparisons. Ego evaluates what she has, or what is proposed, in comparison to what she already has and what people like her, her network peers, have. She feels happy, or drawn to act, depending on her evaluation. More specifically, bent preferences are in two ways a subset of possible results from social comparison. First, they have a specific functional form inferred from the functional form of intra-personal evaluations observed in psychophysics research. Second, they emerge within a reference group severely constrained by social network analysis defining the extent to which each of the individuals in the network around ego serves as a "like me" peer with respect to whom social comparisons are made.

With respect to the three reference disciplines, the bent preferences model would fall under the relative income hypothesis in economics, social comparison theory in psychology, and reference group theory and the concepts of relative advantage and deprivation in sociology. My training in sociology will be clear in the forthcoming pages, but here and in Appendix G, I make an effort to sketch links to work in all three disciplines. I can do no more than sketch links. Each link I made revealed to me three or four others next to be made in an expanding web of related work. I only know enough now to be sure that there are interesting links to be made into each of the three disciplines.

I refer to the bent preferences model as an exercise in social psychology because the model predicts a psychological state from the social context in which the state occurs. Thus, the model is social psychology of the classical kind in which the social is a causal factor in ego's psychological state, versus contemporary work in which the social is merely an object subject to intra-personal perception (Greenwood, 2004). At the same time, in keeping with contemporary social psychology, the model makes the social a causal factor without positing a transcendental group mind. Ego is merely assumed to make inter-personal comparisons just as she makes intra-personal comparisons. Without speculating about a group mind, and without assuming that ego knows the preferences of her peers, a variety of hypotheses are implied by the way ego makes social comparisons that give social context a causal role in her evaluations, thereby defining a social psychology of network agency.

Fair warning: Argument here is more formal than the arguments in the preceding chapters. The empirically verified precision with which psychophysics describes stimulus–response means that I can speak with more precision about agency than I could discuss performance in the earlier chapters. I take advantage of the available precision. The math involved is modest, but it is sure to irritate some readers I wish to reach. My only excuse is that when a little math accurately captures a key mechanism, it is worth extra effort to use the math to track down clear, testable implications to better understand the mechanism. I feel empowered by the available math closely tethered to familiar data, but I only retain key bits in the text, relying on footnotes for asides to the reader interested in more detail.

Perception in Network Context

Consider ego evaluating alternative courses of action. Allow, for the sake of argument, that the resources relevant to ego's choice can be measured on a single dimension. Complex stimuli can be addressed after evaluation is linked to network context, but for the moment allow a single dimension. The stimulation dimension could be money, people, time, or any other resource. Whatever the resource, ego's felt resources, what she feels she has, is a subjective evaluation of what she actually has. Evidence from psychophysics shows that physical stimulation, x, translates into felt stimulation, u, by a power function:

$$u = \kappa \, x^{v}, \tag{1}$$

where κ and v are parameters to be estimated (Greek letters will reference parameters). Stevens (1975) provides examples and a review of work leading to equation (1), with interim reviews available in journal archives (Stevens, 1957; 1970). Unless otherwise indicated, illustrative estimates for the exponent v are taken from Stevens (1957:166; 1970:1045; 1975:15).[1]

---

[1] The power function in equation (1) is widely cited as a benchmark, but also has its critics. Most relevant to the discussion here, Stevens' evidence for the function was obtained by individuals evaluating magnitudes with respect to a single reference point (so differences in the function at different reference points are ignored, see Steingrimsson and Luce, 2006:17–19, for illustration) and fitting the function to evaluations averaged across individuals, rather than fitting the function to individual responses directly (so Stevens' method did not provide a direct test of the power function). More sophisticated criticism of the power function with respect to ratio measurement and signal detection are beyond the scope of this chapter, though it is reassuring to read that Luce's (Luce, 2002:520) more sophisticated treatment "sharply limits the form of the psychophysics function to either a power function or something that for most of the range closely approximates a power function." Regardless, the precision of the psychophysics power function is well ahead of the precision with which network mechanisms are defined and measured. I begin with the simplicity of equation (1), in no way preempting future moves to more sophisticated psychophysics when and if significant substantive results emerge with the bent preferences model derived from equation (1).

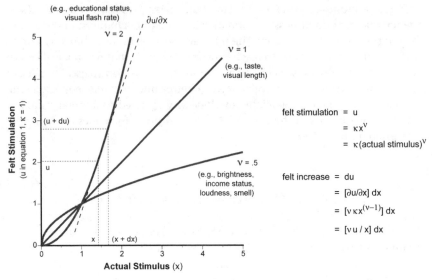

Figure 8.1 Psychophysics of Marginal Evaluation: Translating Actual Stimulus into Felt Stimulation

The association described by equation (1) is illustrated in Figure 8.1. One possibility is that ego's felt resources increase linearly with actual resources (e.g., the straight line in Figure 8.1 for v equal 1). For example, when the subject in a psychophysics experiment is presented with a line and asked to describe its length, there is a linear association between the length of the line displayed and the reported length of the line.

Felt resources are often assumed to increase more slowly than actual resources, which happens when the exponent v is a fraction between zero and one. An example from psychophysics research is the .3 to .7 exponent obtained for people evaluating the loudness of a sound. Low volumes are overestimated. Differences between high volumes are underestimated. A fractional exponent corresponds to the familiar assumption of marginal decreasing utility; increasing stimulation yields decreasing effect. A thousand dollars is a lot of money for someone who has very little. It is less impressive for someone who has many thousands. Hamblin (1971:433) reports estimates of v for people evaluating the status associated with increasing levels of annual income. Hamblin's estimates are about .5, showing that the largest felt increases in status come from unit increases at low levels of income (e.g., the line in Figure 8.1 for v equal .5).

If the exponent is greater than one, then ego's felt resources increase faster than her actual resources. For example, the exponent is 3.5 for people evaluating the strength of an electric shock administered through their fingers.

Small shocks are difficult to identify. Differences between strong shocks are overestimated. Educational status is a more familiar example: Hamblin (1971: 432) reports exponents of about two for the association between educational status and years of education (e.g., the line in Figure 8.1 for v equal 2). An additional year of education generates more status for a college graduate than it does for someone with an elementary school education. Ego is perceived to be better educated when she is familiar with that state-of-the-art business process, can discuss that recent article in the *Wall Street Journal*, or can explain how to do that much-abused new calculation.

Marginal evaluation

Equation (1) implies that evaluations are made at the margin of what ego currently has. The raise ego feels from an increase in her salary (du), equals the salary increase (dx) multiplied by the rate at which ego feels increase at her current salary ($\partial u/\partial x$):

$$\begin{aligned}
du &= (\partial u/\partial x)\ dx, \\
&= (v\kappa\ x^{(v-1)})\ dx, \\
&= (vu/x)\ dx.
\end{aligned}$$

The partial derivative in parentheses defines felt increase benchmarked against x, ego's current condition. Dashed lines in Figure 8.1 illustrate the calculation. For ego on the horizontal axis at resource level x, generating on the vertical axis a felt level of resource u, the increase dx increases ego's felt level of resource by du to a higher level u+du. The idea that ego evaluates an increase in resource against what she currently has is the familiar idea of marginal evaluation. There is no absolute good or bad, high or low. Such adjectives are meaningful relative to a benchmark, which in psychophysics has been ego's current condition.

Marginal interpersonal evaluation

Evidence for the power function in equation (1) comes from people making evaluations when they are alone in a psychophysics laboratory. Imagine another person in the lab, a person socially similar to ego such that ego views the other person as "like me" (Laumann, 1965). Based on the history of research on peer influence discussed in Appendix G, I expect ego to make evaluations that take into account the other person. More, with no other evidence to go on, I expect ego to use the other person as a frame of reference in the same way that she uses herself as a frame. According to equation (1), ego making an evaluation feels an increase in x as a function of her current level x_i, as described by the partial derivative displayed above in parentheses, here displayed in brackets with u referring to ego and x_i referring to ego's current level of x:

$$\left[\frac{\nu u}{x_i}\right],$$

The analogy for interpersonal comparison is that ego brings person j into the evaluation by performing the same marginal calculation with respect to the other person, imagining how things would feel if ego were in the other person's situation:

$$\left[\frac{\nu u}{x_j}\right], \tag{2}$$

which is a marginal evaluation for ego stated with respect to resources x_j held by the other person. There is no assumption in equation (2) that ego knows what the other person feels. Ego is not assumed able to look into her neighbor's soul to understand the neighbor's preferences, implicit or expressed. Ego is only assumed able to imagine what it would be like to have what her neighbor has, to have the neighbor's budget, to have the neighbor's subordinates, to have the neighbor's salary, to imagine herself in her neighbor's position.

The mechanism in equation (2) is not limited to neighbors with whom ego speaks. Communication is symbolic rather than behavioral. Symbolic communication is familiar from a school of sociology established in the early 1900s with the work of Cooley, Mead, and Thomas (e.g., Collins, 1994: chap. 4). The interpersonal comparison in equation (2) has ego putting herself in the roles of other people, from which a generalized other emerges to guide ego in her own opinion and behavior (Mead, 1934:154–155). More significant for economic sociology, equation (2) is a way for interpersonal influence to reach wordlessly across the structural holes in a network. Equation (2) does not require that ego has direct, or indirect, or any contact with the person in whose position she puts herself. Ego only needs to be aware of the other person and have a sense, accurate or not, of the person's current resources. The critical element that enables and makes likely the interpersonal comparison is ego perceiving the other person to be "like me" such that the other person is a frame of reference for ego's own evaluations.

Bent preferences

Let w_{ij} be a proportional measure of the extent to which person j plays such a role in i's evaluations ($0 \leq w_{ij} \leq 1.0$, $\Sigma_j w_{ij} = 1.0$). I use network structure to define the w_{ij} below, but for the moment, allow that w_{ij} is the extent to which person i sees person j as "like me" such that w_{ij} measures the proportional weight person j carries in i's evaluation. In the absence of evidence requiring something more complicated, I model ego's marginal evaluation as a weighted average across the N people in the network around ego:

$$\frac{\partial U}{\partial x_i} = w_{i1}\left[\frac{vu}{x_1}\right] + w_{i2}\left[\frac{vu}{x_2}\right] + \ldots + w_{ii}\left[\frac{vu}{x_i}\right] + \ldots + w_{iN}\left[\frac{vu}{x_N}\right]. \tag{3}$$

I use upper-case U to distinguish this evaluation from the u in equation (1). Equation (3) simplifies to equation (1) if ego is alone with no peers (w_{ii} equals 1.0), or if ego and her peers are receiving the same level of stimulus ($x_j = x_i$ for all j for whom w_{ij} is nonzero). The network evaluation in equation (3) contains an element for ego using herself as a frame of reference, and a sum of elements describing ego using each other person j as a frame of reference. Integrating equation (3) provides a network model analogous to the psychophysics model of individuals making evaluations in isolation:

$$U = \left(w_{ii} + \sum_j \phi\, w_{ij}\left[x_i/x_j\right]\right)\kappa\, x_i{}^\nu, \tag{4}$$

where ego i is excluded from the sum across peers (j $\neq$ i), I have ignored the integration constant, and ϕ is a parameter that dampens resources felt relative to peers (parameter ϕ is a fraction equal to $\nu/(\nu+1)$, that increases toward 1.0 as ν increases).[2] Defined by equation (4), ego's felt level of resource increases with her actual resource (x_i) and the ratio of that to whatever each peer has (x_i / x_j).

---

[2] I do not elaborate on the dampening parameter ϕ in the text because I do not need it to reach the hypotheses to be presented. The parameter is created by my extrapolation from intrapersonal evaluation in equation (1) to interpersonal evaluation in equation (2). Holding network structure and peer j's resources constant during ego's evaluation (i.e., constant w_{ij} and x_j), the integral of equation (3) with respect to increasing ego resource, x_i, contains two kinds of elements summed in equation (4), one for ego's comparison to herself:

$$\kappa\, w_{ii}\int\left[\frac{\nu x_i{}^\nu}{x_i}\right] = w_{ii}\,\kappa\, x_i{}^\nu,$$

and N–1 elements in a network size N for ego's comparison to each other person j:

$$\kappa\, w_{ij}\int\left[\frac{\nu x_i{}^\nu}{x_j}\right] = \kappa\, w_{ij}\left[\frac{\nu x_i{}^{(\nu+1)}}{(\nu+1)x_j}\right] = \phi\, w_{ij}\left(x_i/x_j\right)\kappa\, x_i{}^\nu,$$

where peer j is each person other than ego i. Because I replaced ego resource, x_i, with peer j's resource, x_j, in the denominator of equation (2), the interpersonal comparison does not simplify as cleanly as the intrapersonal comparison implicit in equation (1). I end up with a multiplier $\nu/(\nu+1)$ in the interpersonal comparison, which I put aside as the dampening parameter ϕ. I could have dropped ϕ from equation (4) and worked backward to find a derivative that would imply a ϕ-free version of equation (4). That would put the ϕ complication in equation (3) instead of equation (4). I prefer, and it is no more than personal preference at this point, to leave the ϕ complication in equation (4) for two reasons: First, to simplify the argument from intrapersonal evaluation (equation 1) to interpersonal evaluation (equations 2 and 3), and second, because my use of the integral in equation (4) is rudimentary at this stage of theory development. Having specified the dampening parameter ϕ, however, it merits brief explanation for its potential substantive meaning beyond a mathematics place-keeper ignored in the hypotheses to be

I will refer to U as a bent preference, and equation (4) as a bent preferences model. Equation (4) describes evaluation bent by the surrounding network in which it occurs.

Bent preferences preserve the psychology of marginal evaluation. Equation (4) is identical to equation (1) for evaluations made in isolation. For ego alone, all w_{ij} equal zero, except w_{ii} which equals one, so equation (4) reduces to $U = \kappa\, x_i^{\nu}$, which is the power-function psychophysics model in equation (1).

For evaluations made in a social context, bent preferences broaden motivation to include other people. Sherif's (1935) early experiments on peer pressure showed that people in isolation resort to their personal history as a frame of reference to guide them through difficult evaluations, but they use peers as a frame of reference when peers are available (more detail is in the first few pages of Appendix G). To what extent would implementing the new business practice put me ahead, or behind, people like me? The idea that people understand themselves through comparison to others is the concept of relative advantage and deprivation, discussed as reference group theory in sociology (Stouffer *et al.*, 1949; Merton and Rossi, 1957; Merton, 1957; Stouffer, 1962), social comparison theory in psychology (Festinger, 1954), and the relative income hypothesis in economics (Duesenberry, 1949; Leibenstein, 1950).[3] The concept of relative deprivation emerged just after World War II from research conducted under Samuel Stouffer while he was a sociology professor at the

---

discussed in the text. The dampening parameter measures the extent to which ego with peers feels that she has less resource than she would if she were alone; her felt resources are dampened down from what they would be if she were alone. This is illustrated in Figure 8.3 by the solid lines lying below the dashed line in Figure 8.3A until ego exceeds her peers by more than a unit of resource. The point is illustrated in Figure 8.3B by the solid lines crossing the dashed line when ego's peers are still a unit of resource below what ego has. The ratio of ν to $(\nu+1)$ is larger when ν is less than one, so dampening parameter ϕ will most affect evaluations subject to marginally decreasing utility.

[3] Social comparison in psychology is similar in metaphor to reference group theory in sociology, which is not surprising because they developed together during a period of frequent cross-reference between sociology and psychology, the golden age for social psychology (House, 1977, 2008; Sewell, 1989; Greenwood, 2004; Pooley and Katz, 2008). More specifically, the person who created social comparison theory, Leon Festinger, led the earlier research (Festinger, Schachter, and Back, 1950) so warmly cited in the influential Columbia University research by Lazarsfeld, Katz, Coleman, and colleagues on opinion leaders and diffusion, which together with Stouffer's *American Soldier*, provided the foundation for Merton's theoretical work in sociology on reference groups—all of which is foundation for my treatment in this chapter of social context creating bent preferences. Kindred economic theory emerged at the same time on a separate track. The relative income hypothesis and its component effects have a great deal to say about population implications of social comparison when it occurs, but little to say about the situations in which social comparison is unlikely, so I draw few results from that work for this chapter (primarily from Frank, 1985, but see Appendix G, p. 335, "Corresponding developments in economics").

University of Chicago, serving as Director of the Research Branch, Information and Education Division of the US Army (more than 200 questionnaires used to interview more than half a million soldiers between December 8, 1941 and the end of the war). Stouffer was recruited to Harvard right after the war to run the Laboratory for Social Relations, where he and colleagues produced a final report, *The American Soldier*, in which the concept of relative deprivation was a recurring theme. Stouffer *et al.* (1949:125, italics in original) describe wide differences in soldier attitudes as a preface to introducing the concept: "To help explain such variations in attitude, by education, age, and marital condition, a general concept would be useful. Such a concept may be that of *relative deprivation* . . . The idea is simple, almost obvious, but its utility comes in reconciling data, especially in later chapters, where its applicability is not at first too apparent. The idea would seem to have a kinship to and, in part, include such well-known sociological concepts as 'social frame of reference,' 'patterns of expectation,' or 'definition of the situation.' Becoming a soldier meant to many men a very real deprivation. But the felt sacrifice was greater for some than for others, *depending on their standards of comparison.*" Research is now available on questions such as how comparisons are made, with whom, and toward what end (e.g., Hyman and Singer, 1968; Frank, 1985; Suls and Wheeler, 2000; Walker and Smith, 2002; Guimond, 2006; Buunk and Gibbons, 2007; Greenberg, Aston-James, and Ashkanasy, 2007). The model in equation (4) is consistent with evidence in *The American Soldier* (Burt, 1982:195–198), but the power of the model lies in a precise definition of relative advantage and deprivation in terms of network context. Before discussing how context defines peers, I illustrate the expected peer effect on ego.

Relative advantage

Figure 8.2 describes ego feeling relative advantage. The vertical axis describes how ego feels about her resources increasing while peer resources are fixed. For this illustration, I put measurement metrics aside by setting the stimulus-specific constant κ to one. In addition, assuming knowledge in organizations is analogous to education, I use the exponent of two that Hamblin (1971) reports for people evaluating the status associated with years of education. As a benchmark, the dashed line in Figure 8.2 describes ego alone. The dashed line in Figure 8.2 is identical to the upward-sloping line in the Figure 8.1 psychophysics results for an exponent v equal to two.

The heaviest solid line in Figure 8.2 describes the simplest social situation, ego and one peer such that ego and the other person have equal weight in one another's evaluations. The line is defined by the following expression: $.5\, x_i^2 + .5\, (.66)\, x_i^3$, which is equation (4) with parameters and scores inserted for the example ($\kappa = 1$, $v = 2$, $x_j = 1$, $w_{ij} = .5$), and x_i is ego's resource level. The first term in the expression is from ego's evaluation with respect to her own

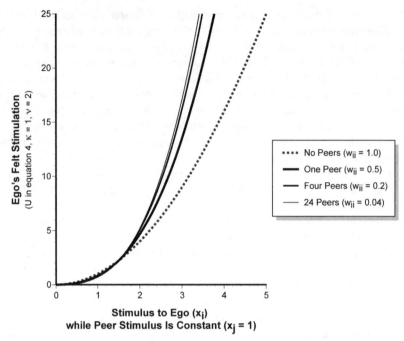

Figure 8.2 Feeling Relative Advantage

resources. The second term is from ego putting herself in her peer's situation. The bold solid line rises faster than the dashed line, showing the extent to which ego feels satisfied with her resources because she has more than her peer. Whatever the intrinsic value of your resources, there is an element of satisfaction in having more than other people like you. You can feel like a big frog if you find a suitably small pond. The other solid lines in Figure 8.2 show what is to be expected in larger groups. The lines are higher than the bold solid line, but they do not increase ego's felt advantage in proportion to the number of peers exceeded. The largest increase in relative advantage happens when ego shifts from being alone to being with one other person, as when ego is pitted against a single competitor.

Returning to the initial research in *The American Soldier*, racial differences in soldier attitudes are often cited as an example of relative advantage. On average, African-American soldiers in 1943 were less satisfied than White soldiers with military life. Whites were more likely to say that the war was as much their personal responsibility as anybody's, the war was being fought for the right of free speech for everyone, everyone was being given a fair chance to participate in the war effort, or the military police treat soldiers fairly (Stouffer *et al.*, 1949:507ff.). However, African-American soldiers stationed in the South were more positive about military life, especially if they grew up in the South. Stouffer and his colleagues (1949:563) interpret this in terms of relative advantage: "Relative to most Negro civilians whom he saw in Southern towns, the Negro soldier had a position of comparative wealth and dignity. His income was high, at least by general Southern standards. Moreover, in spite of the Army carryover of many civilian practices of segregation, the Negro soldier received treatment more nearly on an equality with the white soldier than the treatment of the Negro civilian in the South as compared with the white civilian."

Relative deprivation intensity

Figure 8.3 describes ego feeling relative deprivation. Dashed lines describe evaluations independent of peers (equation 1), and solid lines describe evaluations affected by their network context (equation 4).

The graph to the left, Figure 8.3A, shows ego catching up with peers. This is the same social situation as in Figure 8.2 except I increased the resources held by peers from one to three units. Solid lines below the dashed line in Figure 8.3A show that ego with less than her peers makes ego feel as though she has less resource that she would if she were alone (the dampening effect of peers, see footnote 2). There is a comparable interval of relative deprivation in Figure 8.2, but it is difficult to see because it is condensed into the interval between zero and

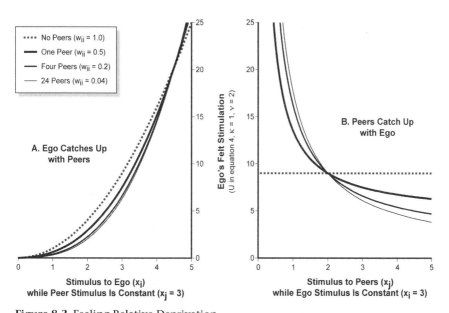

Figure 8.3 Feeling Relative Deprivation

one (note the dashed line slightly above the solid for ego resource less than one unit). Reversing the familiar colloquialism, this is a small frog in a big pond. A person with a good college education can feel intimidated in an office full of people with M.B.A. degrees and doctorates.

Figure 8.3B shows how ego feels as good things happen for peers. The dashed line is horizontal because ego in isolation is unaffected by what happens for peers. The solid lines describe ego's misery as peers who were below her, catch up, and surpass her. The heaviest solid line in the graph describes ego with one peer. The line is defined by the expression: $4.50 + 8.91/x_j$, which is equation (4) with scores and parameters for the example inserted ($\kappa = 1$, $\nu = 2$, $x_i = 3$, $w_{ij} = .5$), and x_j is the peer's resources.

Ego feels intense loss as peers catch up. Ego suffers no actual loss, but she feels loss. She loses something she felt she had. The severity of the felt loss results from evaluation based on a ratio of ego to peer resources. Whatever ego has feels like a lot when her peer has very little (x_i feels big when divided in equation 2 by a very small x_j). That inflated feeling of worth, bulging from comparison to a less-fortunate peer, evaporates quickly as good things happen for the peer (ratio x_i/x_j drops quickly as x_j increases from near-zero).[4] Highway driving provides a familiar example. You are driving on the highway and a car comes up out of nowhere to pass you. The approaching car makes you feel as though you have slowed. Academic life provides a specialized example. The first person in a cohort of sociology graduate students who publishes a paper in the *American Journal of Sociology* has an intense feeling of accomplishment. That feeling is eroded when a weak member of the cohort soon thereafter publishes a paper in the journal. The merit of the earlier publication is unchanged, but its felt significance is diminished.

Numerous instances of relative deprivation emerged in *The American Soldier.* An example close to contemporary life in organizations is education and promotion. It is not surprising to see that soldiers with more education were more likely to be promoted, or that soldiers who advanced more slowly relative to others of equal longevity were more critical of promotion opportunities (Stouffer *et al.*, 1949:246ff). However, soldiers with more education were more negative about their opportunities for promotion. Why would the people who have more opportunity feel that they have less opportunity?

Table 8.1 contains illustrative data (Stouffer *et al.*, 1949:250–258).[5] The table summarizes sample noncommissioned officers, noncoms, expressing their

---

[4] The partial derivative of what ego feels she has (equation 4) with respect to increasing peer resources (x_j) is a negative ratio of ego's resources to peer resources: $\partial U/\partial x_j = -\kappa\, \phi\, w_{ij}\, x_i^{(\nu+1)}\, x_j^{-2}$, so ego's felt deprivation is more severe to the extent that the peer is similar to ego ($w_{ij} > 0$), and increasing from below ego ($x_j < x_i$, which is the interval to the left in Figure 8.3B where the solid lines descend most steeply).

[5] I offer the illustrative data in Table 8.1, and the original text of Stouffer's explanation, because the original text can be difficult to obtain (Stouffer, 1962, is another source for key bits of relative deprivation evidence from the full study). Statistics

Table 8.1 People with the Better Chances of Promotion are More Negative about Promotion

Opinion of Promotion Chances	Military Police, High School or College (n = 241)	Military Police with Less Education (n = 165)	Air Corps, High School or College (n = 152)	Air Corps with Less Education (n = 70)	Loglinear Z-Score Opinion Link with	
					Education	Military Police
Percent Positive	27	58	19	30	−5.93	4.32
Percent Neutral	53	34	47	49	1.43	0.19
Percent Negative	20	8	34	21	3.98	−3.87
Total	100%	100%	100%	100%	—	—
Percent at Higher Rank	34	17	55	47	—	—

Note: These are *American Soldier* sample noncommissioned officers in the two services during 1944 who have been in the Army for one to two years answering the question, "Do you think a soldier with ability has a good chance for promotion in the Army?" Column percentages and loglinear z-score test statistics are given. Positive response is "A very good chance." Negative responses are "Not much of a chance" or "No chance at all." Neutral responses are "A fairly good chance" or "Undecided" (see footnote 5 for test statistics and explanation of combined responses). High education is high school graduate or some college. Low education is less than high school graduate.

opinion of promotion chances. Noncoms here are corporals and sergeants. Longevity is held constant by only considering soldiers who have been in the Army for one to two years. The soldiers in Table 8.1 most likely to be positive about their promotion chances were low-education Military Police (58 percent positive, 8 percent negative). The soldiers most likely to be negative were high-education men in the Air Corps (19% positive, 34% negative). Loglinear z-score test statistics in Table 8.1 show that the opinion associations with education and service branch are statistically significant beyond a .001 level of confidence.

In contrast to soldier opinion, the truth about promotion opportunities can be seen in the extent to which enlisted soldiers held noncommissioned officer rank. Within the sample enlisted men from among whom the noncoms in Table 8.1 were drawn, 39.9 percent of high-education enlisted men were noncoms (versus 23.0% of low-education men; 5.45 loglinear z-score for the education association with noncom rank), and 25.6 percent of the sample enlisted men in the Military Police were noncoms (versus 52.6% in the Air Corps; −9.62 loglinear z-score for the lower odds of an MP noncom rank).

Educated enlisted men in the Air Corps had the best chances for promotion to noncom rank. Why were they the most likely to express negative opinions about their promotion chances? Stouffer and his colleagues (1949:251–253) answered the question in terms of exposure to relative deprivation. Begin with the promotion chances of a high-education enlisted man in the Military Police:

The chances of his being a noncom were 34 out of 100, based on the proportions of noncoms in the sample at this time. If he earned the rating, he was one of the top third

---

reported in this and the next paragraph are based on loglinear models of frequencies computed from percentages and respondent numbers in a graph in *The American Soldier* based on opinions expressed by sample enlisted men numbering 628 noncommissioned officers (in Table 8.1) and 1,379 other enlisted men (privates and privates first class; Stouffer *et al.*, 1949:252). I began with frequencies for the original four-way tabulation: opinion (four categories), by education (as in Table 8.1), by service branch (as in Table 8.1), by rank (noncom versus other enlisted). I ran a saturated loglinear model of the frequencies to identify strong interactions. The two opinion responses combined as negative in Table 8.1 were combined in the original study. The two responses combined as neutral in Table 8.1 had similarly negligible loglinear associations with the other three variables, so I combined them as a single category. Higher-order interactions with rank were also negligible, so I eliminated them from the model (11.13 chi-square statistic for all 2,007 sample men, 6 d.f., P = .08). This is the loglinear model providing the 5.45 and −9.62 z-score test statistics in the text for education and service-branch associations with noncom rank (so the association between rank and education is holding constant service branch and the association between rank and service branch is holding constant education). I only present the noncommissioned officers in Table 8.1 as illustrative data because relative deprivation was more apparent among the noncoms than the other enlisted men. The only statistically significant interactions were two-way, so I eliminated the three-way interactions among opinion, education, and service branch (4.03 likelihood ratio chi-square across the 628 noncoms, 2 d.f., P = .13). This is the loglinear model that provides the z-score test statistics in Table 8.1.

among his fellows of equal educational status. If he failed to earn the rating, he was in the same boat with two thirds of his fellows with equal schooling. Contrast him with the Air Corps man of the same education and longevity. The chances of the latter's being a noncom were 56 in 100, based on the proportions in this sample at this time. If he had earned a rating, so had the majority of his fellows in the branch, and his achievement was relatively less conspicuous than in the MP's. If he had failed to earn a rating, while the majority had succeeded, he had more reason to feel a sense of personal frustration, which could be expressed as criticism of the promotion system, than if he were one of two thirds in the same boat, as among the MP's.

The process would work in the same way among the less educated. In both the Military Police Branch and the Air Corps, the promotion chances of the less educated were inferior to the chances of others. In the MP sample, only 17 per cent of the less educated were noncoms; in the Air Corps sample, the corresponding figure was 47 per cent. An MP who did not complete high school would feel unusually rewarded compared with others in his outfit in becoming a noncom; one who remained a private had so much company that he hardly could view discrimination against him as a reflection on his personal competence. In the Air Corps, those with ratings had almost as much company as those who remained privates—with less room for personal satisfaction over comparative achievement and more room for dissatisfaction over comparative failure to climb the status ladder.

The more-likely promotions for high-education men in the Air Corps meant that they were the men more exposed to feelings of relative deprivation when left behind by promoted colleagues (the steep segment to the Figure 8.3B bold line describing relative deprivation). More exposure meant more negative feelings, which were observed as more negative opinion of the promotion process.

An implication for organizations more generally is that some people would be willing to work for low pay and little opportunity for promotion to avoid the pain of relative deprivation. Here again is the big frog in a small pond phenomenon in which ego prefers to be central in a peripheral organization rather than peripheral in a central organization. Frank (1985: chaps. 3–5) argues that many people are willing to exchange cash income for the status of deference from colleagues. His evidence on flattened pay schedules is relevant to Stouffer's analysis. Imagine a graph in which the vertical axis is pay (e.g., dollars per month an individual receives in compensation) and the horizontal axis is performance (dollars per month the individual produces). Plot by pay and performance employees doing the same kind of work in an organization. A regression line through the data describes a pay schedule for the work. If employees were paid for what they produce, the line would have a slope of one; the highest paid employee would be proportionally the highest performing employee, and so on. Observed pay schedules typically have slopes less than one; they are flatter than would be expected in a perfectly competitive market. Flattened pay schedules can be explained in various ways. Frank focuses on people exchanging pay for status (Frank, 1984: Figure 2; 1985: Figure 3.3). In exchange for deference from colleagues, high performers are willing to receive less pay than would be appropriate to compensate their high performance.

Low performers are willing to give deference to colleagues in return for receiving higher pay than would be appropriate for their low performance. Frank presents illustrative evidence on upstate New York car salesmen, Ithaca real estate brokers, and chemistry professors at Cornell University (respectively Frank, 1984: 556, 558, and 562; 1985: 63, 67, and 73). Such conditions can persist because they protect employees from the negative emotions displayed by Stouffer's Air Corps soldiers: Feelings of relative deprivation are less likely where pay differs less between employees doing the same work.

There is a positive note to relative deprivation: As a peer's good fortune erodes ego's felt fortune, peer misery creates relative advantage (Wills, 1981, on downward comparison, and Nachman, 1986; Portmann, 1999, on schadenfreude, referring to unanticipated delight in the suffering of another). From serious illness (e.g., Taylor, Wood, and Lichtman, 1983; Tennen, McKee, and Affleck, 2000), to personal attractiveness (e.g., Brown *et al.*, 1992), to performance on exams (Friend and Gilbert, 1973), we all feel better when our position at the end of the line is changed by someone getting in line behind us.

Relative deprivation duration

Beyond cross-sectional description, the bent preference model implies that feelings of relative deprivation are short-lived. The bold line in Figure 8.3B decreases quickly, then continues with much slower decrease once ego's peers have surpassed her.[6] A bubble of hubris from felt advantage is painfully burst by the success of a lesser peer followed by a rapid diminution of pain from good things continuing to happen for the peer. To continue the highway analogy about being passed by another car, your felt speed is little affected by a passing car after the car is well into the pack ahead of you.

Grinblatt, Keloharju, and Ikäheimo (2008) present evidence that illustrates the brevity of relative deprivation. For residents in a densely populated area of Finland during 1999 through 2001, Grinblatt and his colleagues combine detailed data from tax records and car purchases. They construct measures of car purchases by ego's closest neighbors, and use those measures to predict ego's own car purchase. The research question: How does ego react to the relative deprivation of neighbors coming home in newly purchased cars? Neighbor purchases significantly increase the probability that ego will buy a car, but the effect has a strikingly short duration. The effect is strongest during the two days following neighbor purchases, with a weaker but still substantial

---

[6] The second derivative of equation 4 with respect to increasing peer resources (x_j) is positive, $\partial^2 U / \partial^2 x_j = 2\kappa \, \phi \, w_{ij} \, x_i^{(v+1)} \, x_j^{-3}$, so the partial derivative in footnote 4 becomes less negative as j's resources continue to increase, which means that ego's felt deprivation becomes less severe.

effect for a week or two, and no effect thereafter (Grinblatt *et al.*, 2008:744–745). In fact, Grinblatt and his colleagues (2008:750) do not believe that keeping-up-with-the-Joneses envy is a feasible interpretation of their neighbor effects because the effects are so transitory: "it is difficult to explain how quickly the social influence of those nearest neighbors decays. Envy is a more persistent emotion." On the contrary, envy is a bent preference of short duration (baring the possibility of ego and peer resources somehow held in painful balance for a period of time). The theoretical prediction illustrated in Figure 8.3B is that the relative deprivation of falling behind the Joneses is a discomfort intense but transitory. That prediction is consistent with the intense, short-lived neighbor effects reported by Grinblatt and his colleagues.

Relative deprivation in mix and sequence

Evidence on the diffusion of opinion and behavior was an early justification cited for what I here discuss as bent preferences (Burt, 1982:198–211; 1987): Ego failing to keep up with opinion and behavior adopted by peers experiences relative deprivation, which encourages ego's adoption. Felt deprivation was argued to be an emotional kick in the pants to get ego on board with her peers. Illustrative evidence is discussed in Appendix G.

The emotion driving adoption is more than deprivation alone. Ego's motivation to act is a shifting mix of the relative advantage and deprivation illustrated in Figures 8.2 and 8.3. Adoptions by ego's peers can be expected to create a feeling of relative deprivation. Each adoption by a peer is a deprivation shock to ego. Repeated shocks create a sense of falling behind one's peers. On the other hand, early adoption of what becomes a popular opinion or practice can trigger a feeling of relative advantage. People who adopt before their peers enjoy a resource not yet held by their peers—an effect beyond whatever felt benefits are expected from adoption. The tension for ego debating whether to adopt as a new opinion or behavior spreads is between diminishing opportunity for relative advantage, and increasing feeling of deprivation. If ego adopts early, she enjoys the advantage of having something her peers do not and she avoids the deprivation associated with delayed adoption. The risk is to look foolish if peers do not adopt later. If ego postpones her adoption to see how peers respond to it, adoption carries less risk, less relative advantage, and cumulating relative deprivation threatens ego with a sense of being left behind.

Now allow that multiple opinions and behaviors diffuse simultaneously where ego's status is a function of being up to date with opinion and behavior popular among peers. Emotions can be expected to cycle through a three-stage sequence: Ego causes relative deprivation in her peers by displaying a new opinion or behavior that gives her status among her peers (Figure 8.3). Ego experiences relative advantage over her peers as they defer to her expertise on the new opinion or behavior (Figure 8.2). Ego experiences relative deprivation when a peer displays some new opinion or behavior that increases the peer's status relative to ego (Figure 8.3). The third-stage pain of relative deprivation is ego's motivation to look for something new to display that re-establishes her status, thereby re-initiating the sequence.

The sequence characteristic of a group can be intense, or mild, depending on the magnitude of felt advantage and deprivation across the three stages, and the speed with which people move through the stages. The more quickly people move from one fashion to the next, then the more frenetic the search for new status-enhancing opinion and behavior to display. With respect to magnitude, ego accustomed to a certain level of positive stimulation can be expected to look for new opinion or behavior able to provide a feeling of relative advantage as strong as last time. For a person like me, is this new project significant, worthy, a reasonable way to spend time, or a status-eroding waste of my time? Larger magnitudes of relative advantage and deprivation mean wider swings between manic and depressive. The greater the advantage in stage one, the more pain when it dissolves away in stage three.

Intense sequence is illustrated metaphorically by Veblen's (1899) concept of a leisure class—a group of people wasting resources on conspicuous consumption with the goal of attaining "the esteem and envy of one's fellow men."[7] In the sequence of advantage and deprivation just described, stage one provides

---

[7] I quote the "esteem and envy" phrase from Veblen's chapter 2, on pecuniary emulation, in which he introduced the motivation responsible for leisure-class conspicuous consumption and leisure described in his chapters 3 and 4. In credit to Veblen's imagery, I initially used the phrase "Veblen sequences" to refer to the sequenced feelings of relative deprivation and advantage described here. However, I found Veblen's text difficult; robust to point estimate of what he was trying to say. Fine (1994) offers a sociology of reactions to Veblen's text, quoting as one view (p. 467) satirist H. L. Mencken: "It is difficult to imagine worse English, within the limits of intelligible grammar." Uncertain about Veblen's exact meaning, I put in the text a bent-preferences version of the motive mix I thought was responsible for conspicuous consumption, and acknowledged Veblen in this footnote for inspiration. I am not the first to behave so. I was led back to Veblen by efforts within the relative income hypothesis to capture so-called "Veblen" effects. Leibenstein (1950) used the term to describe a nonfunctional demand response to a price decrease. More people are expected to be interested in buying a product when the product's price decreases. But if potential buyers are repulsed by an infusion of lower-price buyers, then a drop in price can trigger a drop in demand (Leibenstein, 1950:202). Such an event seemed to happen in the market for luxury goods in the early 1990s (*Economist*, 1992). Bagwell and Bernheim (1996:349–350) are certainly correct in saying that Veblen was not talking about consumer responses to price, as Leibenstein assumes. Veblen described people interested in a product to the extent that it confers status on people who own the product. Price is a secondary consideration; the status-conferring capacity of a product is eroded when too many people own the product, as can happen at lower prices. Bagwell and Bernheim (1996) work to capture their own version of Veblen effects defined by the increased price ego is willing to pay for a status-enhancing product versus a functionally equivalent product at lower cost. As

envy, stage two provides esteem, and stage three is the emotional jolt that launches a new sequence. Such a sequence is not peculiar to the upper-middle class that so irritated Veblen. The same story could be told about a clique of indolent teenagers whose primary worry is looking cool, as they move from one pop song to another, from this cause to that, from that fashion to another. The story can be told equally well about fashion in business practice. Abrahamson (1996:255) summarizes nicely: "Many management fashion setters—consulting firms, management gurus, business mass-media publications, and business schools—compete in a race to define which management techniques lead rational management progress. Fashion setters who do not participate successfully in this race, . . . will be perceived as lagging rather than leading management progress, as being peripheral in the business community, and as being undeserving of societal support."

Nor need the sequence be played out in different groups with respect to the same status-enhancing opinion or behavior. The something that triggers advantage or deprivation—the resources x in equation (4) in terms of which the effects are defined—can come from any source. Origins do not matter. What matters is the effect with respect to ego's peers. In this group, ego trumps peers by wearing the latest fashion worn by celebrity entertainers. In the group over there, status is about familiarity with the new technology. In the next group over, status is about admiring words received from a wise colleague. In that other group, status is about driving an expensive car, putting in an expensive kitchen, or living in an expensive house. Whatever the relative advantage provided by displaying an opinion or behavior, the advantage disappears as others adopt the display. Local fads and fashions are to be expected. As peers catch up with what was new, ego hunts for the next something new that can again provide the buzz of relative advantage.

In sum, ego's preference on a question need not be permanently bent; it can bend this way and that in predictable sequences. Bent preferences therefore can be difficult to study directly without sequence data (such as the real-time car purchase data studied by Grinblatt, Keloharju, and Ikäheimo, 2008). It is not clear what an average survey response would mean on an opinion affected by sequenced relative advantage and deprivation since people respond from their unique, personal stages in the sequence. The recourse is to study bent preferences indirectly by comparing characteristics of social contexts in which

---

I re-read Veblen's text, I found myself increasingly in sympathy with Leibenstein's decision to not try to capture what Veblen meant, focusing instead on a kindred phenomenon one can model. As Leibenstein (1950:202–203) so gently described his decision: "Although the theory of conspicuous consumption as developed by Veblen and others is quite a complex and subtle sociological construct we can, for our purposes, quite legitimately abstract from the psychological and sociological elements and address our attention exclusively to the effects that conspicuous consumption has on the demand function."

sequences are likely to be more versus less intense (e.g., Stouffer's comparison of the Military Police versus the Air Corps).

Network fear hypothesis: new frame on feelings of loss versus gain

In defining the frame of reference through which ego evaluates alternative actions, the surrounding network creates pressure on ego to take action. Ego is lured to action by the prospect of moving ahead, as illustrated in Figure 8.2. Ego is pushed to action by fear of falling behind, as illustrated in Figure 8.3. Note from the shape of the graphs in Figures 8.2 and 8.3 how much steeper is the felt drop from falling behind relative to the gain from moving ahead. The felt gain provided by relative advantage is less intense than the felt loss induced by relative deprivation. In other words, network pressure on ego to act is less about the lure of gain, than the fear of loss. Figures 8.2 and 8.3 together illustrate the following hypothesis about the fear created by the social network around ego: *The feelings of loss as peers overtake ego are more severe than the feelings of gain in overtaking peers, but the feelings of loss fade as peers continue to do well.* The first part of the hypothesis is defined by the relative rates at which ego is affected by increases in her resources versus those of a peer, and is illustrated by the steep descent of the solid lines in Figure 8.3B as good things happening for a peer bring the peer's resources up toward ego's level. The second part of the hypothesis is defined by the decreasing negative effect on ego's felt resources with continued peer success (footnote 6), and is illustrated in Figure 8.3B by the solid lines decreasing more slowly after ego is surpassed by her peers.

Figure 8.4 illustrates the hypothesized effect in a situation used in Figure 8.3: the stimulus-specific constant is put aside by setting it to one ($\kappa = 1$), ego has one peer ($w_{ij} = .5$), and the resource being evaluated is analogous to educational status ($\nu = 2$). The vertical axis is ego's felt change from a half-unit resource increase. The top solid line in Figure 8.4 shows ego's felt gain at different levels of ego resource on the horizontal axis when the peer's resources are fixed at three units.[8] Felt gains from an increase in resource are small when

---

[8] Ego's felt change, dU, from a change in her resources, dx_i, is defined in two terms by multiplying dx_i times the partial derivative in equation (3): $dU = (\partial U/\partial x_i) \, dx_i = ([w_{ii} \, \nu \, \kappa \, x_i^\nu / x_i] + [w_{ij} \, \nu \, \kappa \, x_i^\nu / x_j]) \, dx_i$. The first term describes ego's evaluation of the change using her own situation as a frame of reference. The term is the expression for du displayed just below equation (1) in the text, here weighted by w_{ii}. The second term describes how ego's evaluation is affected by the change in x_i changing ego's situation relative to the peer. If good things happen for ego such that a gain in x_i moves ego ahead of her peer, the second term enhances ego's felt increase in resources, as illustrated by the solid line lying above the dashed line at the top of Figure 8.4. The solid line is defined by substituting the example values into the above equation ($dx_i = .5$, $w_{ii} = w_{ij} = .5$, $\nu = 2$, $\kappa = 1$, $x_j = 3$, with x_i increasing along the horizontal axis).

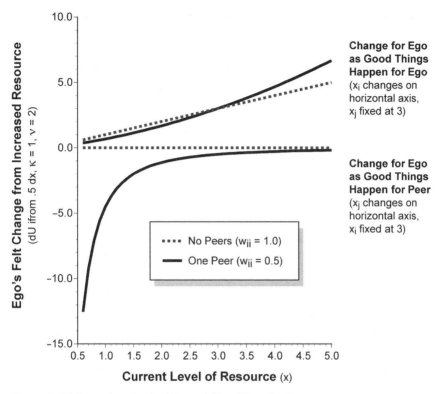

Figure 8.4 Illustration for the Network Fear Hypothesis

ego has little. Relative advantage is illustrated by the bold line expanding above the dashed line after ego surpasses her peer. The lower solid line in Figure 8.4 shows ego's felt loss at her peer's gain when ego's resources are fixed at three units.[9] The bold line shows severe feelings of relative deprivation as good things begin to happen for the peer. A half-unit increase for the peer at one current unit of resource elicits a felt loss for ego of -4.52 units. As the peer continues to do well past ego, subsequent gains have little effect on ego. For example, a half-unit increase for the peer at five current units of resources (and ego is back at three units) elicits a felt loss for ego of only $-.18$ units.[10]

---

[9] Ego's felt change, dU, from a change in the peer's resources, dx_j, is defined by multiplying dx_j times the partial derivative $\partial U/\partial x_j$ in footnote 4. The line at the bottom of Figure 8.4 is defined by replacing parameters and variables with their example values ($dx_j = .5$, $w_{ii} = w_{ij} = .5$, $v = 2$, $\kappa = 1$, $x_i = 3$, with x_j increasing along the horizontal axis).

[10] The predicted difference between loss and gain increases with the exponent v. The exponent is set to two for Figure 8.4. At higher values, there is larger difference between the solid lines in Figure 8.4. With v set to three, for example, ego's felt gain at one unit of

Turning to empirical evidence, the hypothesis is illustrated by car crashes in professional racing. Bothner, Kang, and Stuart (2007) analyze the probability that a NASCAR driver will experience a car crash during a race as a function of competitors crowding above and below the driver. Under the assumption that "a crash is more likely if a driver attempts risky maneuvers on the track," the incidence of car crashes is an indicator of the pressure a driver feels during a race (Bothner, Kang, and Stuart, 2007:211). That pressure can come from crowding ahead or behind the driver. Drivers earn points according to their finishing position in a race. The season champion is the driver with the most points from races run during the season. Bothner, Kang, and Stuart (2007:219) measure the crowding around a driver in a race by the number of competitors that the driver could surpass in the rankings if the driver did really well in the race (crowding above), and the number that could surpass the driver if they did really well in the race (crowding below). The potential gain from a race depends on crowding above the driver. If the competitors ahead of a driver are far ahead, there is no crowding above, and little potential gain for the driver from pushing hard in this race. But if there is a cluster of competitors just ahead of the driver (crowding above), he has an incentive to make that little bit of extra effort in this race to pass a couple of them, and move ahead in the rankings. The potential loss from a race depends on crowding below the driver. If the competitors behind the driver are way behind, it will be difficult for any of them to move ahead of the driver, whatever their performance in this race. On the other hand, if there is a cluster of competitors just behind the driver, he is at risk of one or more of them making that little bit of extra effort in this race to pass him, which could move him lower in the rankings. The research question is whether crowding around a driver increases the incidence of a car crash, and if yes, which kind of crowding is more associated with car crashes—crowding ahead of the driver, or crowding behind? Bothner, Kang, and Stuart (2007:225–228) show that crowding in the rankings around a driver before a race does increase the probability that the driver will crash his car during the race, and the effect is entirely from crowding below. Consistent with the network fear hypothesis, drivers are much more pushed to risky maneuvers by the possibility of being overtaken (loss), than they are drawn to risky maneuvers by the possibility of overtaking others (gain).

The network fear hypothesis is a bridge between the sociology of networks and the psychology of felt loss and gain. The prediction is that differences between felt loss and gain are contingent on the network structure around the

---

resource from a half-unit increase resource is 1.0 and ego's felt loss from her peer at one unit gaining a half unit is −15.19. The felt loss is more severe than the .67 versus −4.52 displayed in Figure 8.4 and mentioned in the text. Felt gain when the peer is ahead is dampened by ϕ in equation (4). Fractional exponents ν dampen the solid line at the top of Figure 8.4 to below the corresponding dashed line. Ego's felt loss from an overtaking peer remains negative when the peer is below ego, so the network fear hypothesis remains true, but with smaller difference expected between feelings of loss and gain.

perceiver. The hypothesis could be tested with psychophysics experiments in which ego's felt stimulation is monitored as ego and alter stimulation are manipulated. It would be interesting to test the hypothesis with the same experiments (extended to manipulate peer stimulus) used to document Kahneman and Tversky's prospect-theory finding that people are more sensitive to loss than gain (Kahneman, Slovic, and Tversky, 1982; Kahneman and Tversky, 1984). If the loss-felt-more-than-gain finding familiar from prospect theory turns out to be a bent preference as predicted by the fear hypothesis, then the finding is not a psychological feature of people so much as it is a feature of the social situation in which they find themselves. Such a re-framing of the finding could be a productive new bridge between economic sociology and behavioral economics. Expected variation within and between people generates my next hypothesis.

Network Defines Peers

Bent preferences are not yet defined. Ego in equation (4) is motivated by the pull of relative advantage, and the push of relative deprivation, but relative to whom? Who is "like me" in a network? The question has been answered in the past by studying network conditions associated with two people, ego and a peer, expressing similar opinion and displaying similar behavior. Two criteria have emerged: connectivity and equivalence.[11]

---

[11] An argument can be made for leaving peers defined in a general, intuitive way. Interesting hypotheses can be derived without having to muck about in the empirical details of peer criteria. I needed no peer criterion to define bent preferences in equation (4), to numerically illustrate the feelings of relative advantage and relative deprivation that peers can elicit (Figures 8.2 and 8.3), or to define the network fear hypothesis. Component effects for the relative income hypothesis in economics are typically defined without specifying a peer criterion because the criterion is not needed to derive hypotheses about aggregate market behavior (see Appendix G, "Corresponding developments in economics"). Reasonable precedent notwithstanding, here are at least two reasons to move beyond an intuitive criterion for peers: First, we can do better. Network analysis makes it possible to define peers in a rigorous way grounded in theory and empirical research. Second, consequential empirical test requires it. Without a concrete definition of ego's peers, social comparison theory such as the bent preferences model in equation (4) is robust to empirical research. With peers only defined intuitively, empirical evidence failing to support the theory is easily attributed to an incorrect definition of peers. If the author had selected the appropriate reference group, he would have seen the evidence of social comparison. Robust to empirical research is twice a misery. Believers continue to endorse the theory as-is despite contradictory empirical evidence, and non-believers continue to ignore the theory despite corroborating evidence. No evidence can convince die-hard opposition, but there are always people whose curiosity can be sparked by compelling evidence. In short, social comparison theory such as the bent preferences model in equation (4) is as informed and empowered by empirical research as it is clear in defining the peers against whom social comparison is made. Fortunately, advances in network analysis provide clear alternative definitions of peers.

Connectivity is the traditional criterion, and follows from the discussion of network closure in Chapter 6: A peer is someone strongly connected to ego, directly and through mutual friends. Such a pair of people would be high on the closure measures used in Chapter 6 (e.g., the horizontal axes in Figure 6.8). The argument for a connectivity criterion is that by talking to one another, ego and her peer shape one another's opinion of objects, people, and behaviors for which there is no one obvious interpretation. The stronger the connection between people, the more likely they trust one another, the more likely the socializing communication between them, and so the more likely they express similar opinion and display similar behavior.

Equivalence is traditional where competition has been discussed, but it was not widely used in network analysis until the 1970s. I begin with the most concrete form of equivalence, structural equivalence. Two people are structurally equivalent to the extent that they have similar relations with other people. They need not be connected directly, but they seek out relations with the same other people and are sought out by the same other people. The argument for an equivalence criterion defining peers is competition: people engaged in relations with the same other people could replace one another in those relations. Equivalent people are expected to benchmark against one another for how to be more attractive in their relations. The more equivalent two people are, the more likely they benchmark against one another, and so the more likely they express similar opinion and display similar behavior.

Connectivity versus structural equivalence

It will be convenient here and later to have a concrete example. The sociogram of a hypothetical organization is displayed in Figure 8.5. The organization contains managers and four functional groups. Lines indicate reporting relations and correspond to a one in the displayed adjacency matrix. As in earlier sociograms, physical distance in Figure 8.5 indicates strength of connection. People connected directly are next to one another. People connected indirectly through intermediaries are separated (e.g., the six-link indirect connection between persons 12 and 15 puts them on opposite sides of the space).

Figure 8.6 is a multidimensional scaling of structural equivalence distances in the organization. Two people are close together in Figure 8.6 to the extent that they have identical relations with the same contacts. Structural equivalence between i and j is measured by a distance, call it d_{ij}, which increases as each person k in a population has different relations with i and j, for example:

$$d_{ij}^2 = \Sigma_k(z_{ik} - z_{jk})^2 + \Sigma_k(z_{ki} - z_{kj})^2, \quad i \neq k \neq j \tag{5}$$

where z_{jk} is the strength of connection from j to k. Distance d_{ij} is zero when i and j have identical relations with everyone else in the organization. There are

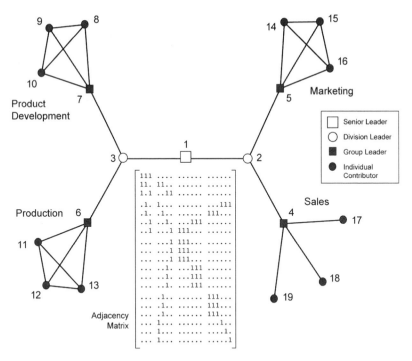

Figure 8.5 A Hypothetical Organization

subtleties to measuring structural equivalence, subtleties debated in the 1980s, but for the purposes here, I discuss distance simply as the Euclidean distance in equation (5).[12] The distances used to generate Figure 8.6 are given in Table F3 in Appendix F.

---

[12] For this illustration, I traced indirect connections from the direct connections in Figure 8.5, used a simple fixed decay weighting to define the relational measures z_{jk}, and computed Euclidean distances using equation (5), excluding self-relations. The indirect connections are given in Table F1 of Appendix F. The derived z_{ik} are given in Table F2. Note that direct connections equal 1.0, two-step connections are .5, three-step connections are .5 squared, four-step connections are .5 cubed, and so on. Structural equivalence distances are given in Table F3. For details on measuring structural equivalence, see a general introduction to network analysis, such as Wasserman and Faust (1994: chap. 9), or online Hanneman and Riddle (2005: chaps. 12–13). Since relations are symmetric in Figure 8.5, either the row or column sums in equation (5) would be sufficient to capture relative distance between people. Including both terms in equation (5) doubles distance squared so it has no effect on the multidimensional scaling in Figure 8.6. I keep the row–column distinction in equation (5) because the distinction between relations sent (row) and received (column) can be substantively significant when relations are not symmetric as is the case in some of the empirical evidence presented in Appendix G.

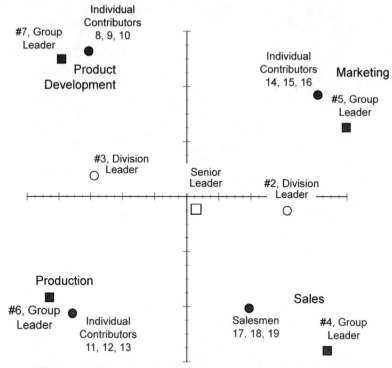

This is a multidimensional scaling of the structural equivalence distances in Table F3 (Kruskal stress = .048)

Figure 8.6 Spatial Map of Structurally Equivalent Peers in the Hypothetical Organization

No contest when the criteria agree

The spatial display of connections in Figure 8.5 is in many ways similar to the spatial display of equivalence distances in Figure 8.6. In both, there are clusters corresponding to the four functional groups, sales, marketing, production, and product development. Individual contributors are close together within their group. For example, the three individual contributors in marketing (persons 14, 15, and 16) are on top of one another in Figure 8.6 because they have identical relations to everyone in Figure 8.5 and identical relations from everyone. The senior leader is in the center of Figure 8.5 because she has the strongest connections on average to everyone else. She is at the center of Figure 8.6 because she has a pattern of relations similarly distant from everyone else's. On either side of the senior leader are the division leaders, each on the side of the space with the people each division leader supervises. The division leader to the right in Figure 8.5, person 2, is on the right because his connections with people in marketing and sales are stronger than his connections to people in production and product development. Further removed are the group leaders, each close to the groups they supervise.

The only structurally equivalent people in the organization—the individual contributors in each functional group—are with one exception strongly connected directly and indirectly. Structurally equivalent people often have direct connections with one another. When they do, equivalence and connectivity define the same peers for ego, so there is no need to decide between the criteria. This is illustrated by three of the four functional groups in Figure 8.5, and can be seen in the Washington network of leading lobbyists during the early 1990s (Figure G3 in Appendix G).

Deciding to use the equivalence criterion

A choice has to be made when the two criteria contradict one another. Contradiction occurs in either of two situations. Two people who are strongly connected to each other can be structurally nonequivalent if they have very different relations with other people, ego connected into one group, and the other person connected into a different group. Such connections are the bridge relations essential to brokerage. Second, two people who do not speak with one another can be structurally equivalent if they have identical relations with everyone else. The salesmen in Figure 8.5 are an example. The salesmen have no connection to one another. They are only connected to the head of sales, person 4. By connectivity, each salesmen in Figure 8.5 talks exclusively with the head of sales so the head of sales would be their network peer under the connectivity criterion. By structural equivalence, the salesmen take one another as peers because they are similarly connected to the head of sales and disconnected from everyone else. Under the equivalence criterion, the salesmen would be expected to benchmark against one another.

The communication and competition justifications for connectivity and equivalence respectively can each be stretched to interpret the other criteria, but neither justification fits the other criterion so well as it fits its own. Competition is a rude interpretation of interpersonal influence between strongly connected people. Socializing discussion cannot account for interpersonal influence between structurally equivalent people who do not speak with one another.[13]

---

[13] One could argue that structurally equivalent people not connected directly can influence one another indirectly through their mutual contacts. The argument is not compelling. Indirect connection is weaker than direct connection. If socializing communication through indirect connections is responsible for the similarity between structurally equivalent people not directly connected, then there should be evidence of even closer similarity between structurally equivalent people who do talk to one another directly. Instead, equivalent people are similar whether connected directly, indirectly, or not at all, and nonequivalent people are dissimilar regardless of connectivity (see footnote 10 in Appendix G).

Appendix G contains argument and evidence for my decision to use equivalence to define peers. The material is important to explain my choice, but it is not essential to understand the forthcoming two hypotheses derived from my choice, so I put the material in an appendix. The gist of the material is that I find more evidence of equivalence than connectivity. Equivalence was implicit in early research on interpersonal influence and peer pressure (see "Equivalence Implicit in Early Research" in Appendix G), structurally equivalent people display similar opinion and behavior regardless of their connectivity, and structurally nonequivalent people display dissimilar opinion and behavior regardless of their connectivity (see "Across the Populations" in Appendix G). Beyond supporting equivalence over connectivity, evidence supporting the equivalence criterion fits well with the interpersonal marginal evaluation process implicit in equation (2). Ego does not have to communicate directly with a peer to be in competition with the peer, and so affected by the peer's condition. Ego only has to be aware of the peer, and be able to imagine herself in the peer's situation.

Intrepid broker hypothesis

Let the w_{ij} network weights in equation (4) be defined by structural equivalence. I will give an exact definition shortly, but for the moment allow that ego i's w_{ij} increase as d_{ij} decreases. The point I want to highlight is that people can differ greatly in the extent to which they have peers. Within the simple organization displayed in Figure 8.5, for example, structural equivalence clearly defines peers only for the individual contributors. With peers more clearly defined for certain people, relative deprivation is more clearly a threat for those people, which implies a contingency hypothesis that distinguishes people more subject to the network fear hypothesis.

Structurally unique people

Figure G7 in Appendix G shows that structural equivalence is more obvious, so the pain of relative deprivation and fear of it is more severe, in populations of small, clearly differentiated groups. These groups can be closed-network groups like the individual contributors in marketing in Figure 8.5, or sets of people like the salesmen in Figure 8.5 who do not speak with one another but are structurally equivalent by dint of their similar relations with others.

Either way, brokers stand apart. The leaders in Figure 8.5 are all network brokers. They connect otherwise disconnected people and each leader's pattern of relations is unique such that none has a structurally equivalent peer. Leaders in the organization each have a unique pattern of relations that puts them alone in their own unique location in the Figure 8.6 spatial map of structural equivalence distances. They are not alone in terms of sensory deprivation. Such people have full calendars. They are alone in bearing unique responsibilities that give them no obvious peers—defined by structural equivalence—as a frame of reference for social comparison. The leader relation patterns in Figure 8.5 are not equally different in Figure 8.6, but they are each unique to an individual leader. The point is discussed in detail in Appendix G with respect to evidence of brokers being less likely to have structural-equivalence peers (Figure G7), and the link between network complexity and peer pressure: the more complex the network, the less clearly peers are defined by structural equivalence, and the weaker the competitive pressure of relative deprivation aligning peers.

Hypothesis

A lack of structural-equivalence peers frees brokers from the competitive pressure of structural equivalence, so brokers are less subject to the pain of relative deprivation, and therefore more free to evaluate a new idea or practice for its merit. In other words, the dashed lines in Figures 8.2 and 8.3 describe network brokers and the solid lines describe people with network peers.

People who have no peers only experience their own resources. The flat dashed line in Figure 8.3 shows the lack of relative deprivation. That leaves the upward-sloping dashed line in Figure 8.2 as the only foundation for evaluating alternative actions. Such are the brokers.

People with peers experience their own resources, and evaluate what they have relative to the resources held by peers. Peers create the solid lines in Figures 8.2 and 8.3. Relative advantage is possible, but relative deprivation is a risk severe and painful. The risk of relative deprivation is concentrated in two kinds of people: People in groups that correspond to closed networks (such as three groups of connected individual contributors in Figure 8.5), and people who have little to do with one another but have similar relations with other people (such as the salesmen in Figure 8.5, or more generally, people who are satellites to the same superior or more popular group).

If agency in networks is motivated by the interpersonal evaluations described by the bent preferences model, then fear of failure should motivate brokers less than it motivates people in closed networks (or anyone for whom peers are obviously defined by structural equivalence). I discuss the implication as a hypothesis about brokers appearing intrepid, a contingency variation on the network fear hypothesis: *When evaluating a new idea or practice, network brokers are—relative to people with obvious peers—more motivated by the lure of gain and less troubled by a fear of failure.*

The hypothesis does not distinguish kinds of people prone to social comparison. It is about kinds of situations that make social comparison difficult to avoid. It is natural to focus on kinds of people because that is where the hypothesized outcomes are manifest. For example, to illustrate his discussion of competition and emotional energy, Collins (2004:123) uses a photo of two women in a foot race, one passing the other. The woman passing is looking straight ahead. The woman passed is glancing over at the person passing her. The caption: "Winner focuses on the goal, loser focuses on the winner." The situation resembles the highway driving example discussed earlier in which ego is passed by a car speeding up from behind, or Bother, Kang, and Stuart's (2007) results on NASCAR accidents associated with the threat of being over-taken. The situation does not predispose everyone equally to social compari-son. The person in front would have to turn her head to make social comparisons. The person in second place has an obvious social comparison with the person passing her. I would like to see a photo of the racing women a minute earlier. Did the women passing ever glance over at the woman she was about to pass?

Gibbons and Buunk (1999) provide broader evidence. Consistent with Col-lins' photo caption, Gibbons and Buunk believe that individuals are not equally prone to social comparison: "...the need to compare oneself with others is phylogenetically very old, biologically very powerful, and recogniz-able in many species. However, we believe that the extent to which people do so varies, perhaps considerably, from one individual to the next. That belief led to the efforts described in this article to develop a scale assessing individual differences in comparison orientation (CO)." Gibbons and Buunk's index distinguishes people for the extent to which they make social comparisons.[14] Across thousands of people, Gibbons and Buunk (1999:133–134; Buunk and Gibbons, 2006:17–19) find that the individuals prone to social comparison have three qualities: They are more self-conscious, reflective about themselves in the presence of others. They are more empathetic, interested in the behavior

---

[14] In the interest of replication with situational data, here are the six core items that Gibbons and Buunk (1999:137) say stand alone as an index that has .92 correlation with the full index (response is on a five-point scale from disagree strongly to agree strongly): (1) "I often compare how my loved ones (boy or girlfriend, family member, etc.) are doing with how others are doing." (2) "I always pay a lot of attention to how I do things compared with how others do things." (3) "If I want to find out how well I have done something, I compare what I have done with how others have done." (4) "I often compare how I am doing socially (e.g., social skills, popularity) with other people." (5) "I am not the type of person who compares often with others." (6) "I often compare myself with others with respect to what I have accomplished in life." The parenthetical expressions in items (1) and (4) are appropriate to the college students so often asked to complete the scale, but might be deleted or edited for organization research. Gibbons and Buunk (1999:142) use the following instructions: "Most people compare themselves from time to time with others. For example, they may compare the way they feel, their opinions, their abilities, and/or their situation with those of other people. There is nothing particularly 'good' or 'bad' about this type of comparison, and some people do it more than others. We would like to find out how often you compare yourself with other people. To do that we would like to ask you to indicate how much you agree with *each* statement below, by using the following scale."

and opinion of others. They are more likely to feel depressed and negative, about events and about themselves.

The three correlates are consistent with the intrepid broker hypothesis: people with obvious network peers have more difficulty avoiding social comparison with peers, so they are more self-conscious about themselves in public, more alert to how others feel, and more at risk of painful relative deprivation.

However, the hypothesis says that the correlates result from comparison; they are not predispositions to it. Instead of certain people being prone to social comparison, structural equivalence make comparison obvious for certain people, which increases the risk of relative deprivation for those people, which is a negative experience. Causation moves out of the individual, into the situation. If you change the situation, you can change the risk of relative deprivation, and so alleviate the negative feelings induced by relative deprivation. Measures of social comparison, such as Gibbons and Buunk's, will be interesting to study across kinds of networks.[15]

Meanwhile, the intrepid broker hypothesis is offered for future research. It has a felt reality from the situations in which people seem most concerned about looking foolish to their peers. Beyond face validity, I have two bits of research evidence that give me confidence in the hypothesis.[16]

Brokers are opinion leaders

First, network brokers show less evidence of the peer pressure associated with structural equivalence. On average, structurally equivalent people express

---

[15] Such study will require more subtlety than it might seem. The intrepid broker hypothesis does not say that brokers are less likely to make social comparisons; it says that structural equivalence provides less obvious peers for brokers to compare themselves to. Measures of comparison orientation, such as the measure proposed by Gibbons and Buunk, will be high when a broker compares herself to others, whether those others are structurally equivalent peers or role equivalent peers (as predicted below by the network identity hypothesis).

[16] The intrepid broker hypothesis is only one of many that can be generated from the idea that structurally unique people are less exposed to the competitive pressure of peers. A familiar example is that peer pressure reduces the returns to network brokerage—the more peers working a job, the greater the competitive pressure on people in the job, so the lower the average returns to brokerage for people in the job (Burt, 1997, 2005:156–162). Baron and Pfeffer's (1994) article on the social psychology of organizations and inequality is interesting to read in parallel to this chapter. They too make use of social comparison for motivation, but do not limit the comparison process to a particular form (as is done in equations 2 and 4). They too discuss comparison within to a frame of reference, but do not limit the frame to a particular criterion other than by their examples in which job title is often the criterion (as is done with structural equivalence in equation 6; see Ingram and Yue, 2008:276–280, for still broader criteria). By being less precise about how comparison works, and more general in its implications, Baron and Pfeffer cover a broader range of intuitions than is covered here. Those intuitions are each potentially fruitful to explore as bent preferences.

similar opinions and display similar behavior, while nonequivalent people display dissimilar opinion and behavior. Summary evidence is given in Figure G6 in Appendix G. However, the same figure shows consistent evidence of ideas and behavior being contagious between connected people who are only weakly equivalent to another. Group and division leaders are examples in the Figure 8.5 organization. The salesmen to the east in Figure 8.6 are not structurally equivalent with their head of sales (person 4) or their division leader (person 2), but are more equivalent to both than they are to people in production or product development (the other side of Figure 8.6). The head of sales and division leader are not equivalent to the salesmen, but are somewhat equivalent. Such people are "near peers." Near peers are almost peers to ego, but not quite. They have relations in common with ego at the same time that they have relations different from ego's. Figures G5 and G6 show that contagion between near peers depends on connectivity: the stronger ego's connection with a near peer, the more likely that ego's opinion and behavior resembles the opinion or behavior of the near peer. The near peers through whom opinion and behavior spreads through connections turn out to be network brokers (Table G1), and correspond to the opinion leaders widely familiar from mass media research conducted in the 1950s at Columbia University by Elihu Katz, Paul Lazarsfeld, and Robert Merton (pages 354–356 in Appendix G). Information enters a group by connectivity through network brokers as opinion leaders, then spreads within the group by competitive pressure between structurally equivalent people. As long as brokers are a minority relative to the number of people in closed groups, structural equivalence on average predicts where ideas and behaviors are similar (as illustrated for managers in Figure G2, lobbyists in Figure G3, and doctors in Figure G4). However, for the few opinion leaders, those network brokers who connect across groups, connectivity is the key to contagious ideas and behaviors. In short, and as predicted by the intrepid broker hypothesis, brokers are less subject to the peer pressure otherwise evident between structurally equivalent people.

Brokers display emotion

A second bit of evidence consistent with the intrepid broker hypothesis is the tendency for network brokers to display emotion in proposing ideas to senior management.

Brokerage and good ideas

My evidence comes from the ideas proposed by the supply-chain managers in Chapter 3. The network story on good ideas is that network brokers are connected to more varied sources of information and are therefore at higher risk of detecting and developing good ideas—by moving best practice from one group to another unfamiliar with the practice, or by seeing new combinations across segregated groups. The story was illustrated in Chapter 3. Figure 3.8A showed that brokers enjoyed compensation higher than peers. Figure 3.8B showed that brokers were more likely to receive the highest performance evaluations. To the point here, Figure 3.8C showed that brokers were more likely to express good ideas, as judged by senior management. Summarized in the original report (Burt, 2004:349): "people who stand near the holes in a social structure are at higher risk of having good ideas." More specifically (Burt, 2004:388–389): "People with connections across structural holes have early access to diverse, often contradictory, information and interpretations, which gives them a competitive advantage in seeing and developing good ideas. People connected to groups beyond their own can expect to find themselves delivering valuable ideas, seeming to be gifted with creativity. This is not creativity born of genius; it is creativity as an import–export business.... Across the clusters in an organization or market, creativity is a diffusion process of repeated discovery in which a good idea is carried across structural holes to be discovered in one cluster of people, rediscovered in another, then rediscovered in still others—and each discovery is no less an experience of creativity for people encountering the good idea." The brokerage–creativity link has been illustrated in a variety of ways (Burt, 2005:66–78, for review). Hargadon and Sutton (1997:716) provide an ethnographic account of the brokerage responsible for creativity in the leading American design firm, IDEO (cf. Obstfeld, 2005): "This firm exploits its network position, working for clients in at least 40 industries, to gain knowledge of existing technological solutions in various industries. It acts as a technology broker by introducing these solutions where they are not known and, in the process, creates new products that are original combinations of existing knowledge from disparate industries." Uzzi and Spiro (2005: 447) describe the success of Broadway musicals in terms of bridges across clusters of production teams, guided by the image, "that creativity is spurred when diverse ideas are united or when creative material in one domain inspires or forces fresh thinking in another." There is the early work on scientists in R&D labs showing that scientists more active in communicating across organizational boundaries were also more active in keeping up with professional journals (Allen and Cohen, 1969:17; see Tortoriello and Krackhardt, forthcoming, for network analysis), and recent work on brokerage and creativity inferred from the scope and detail of patent data such as Fleming, Mingo, and Chen's (2007) authoritative evidence on inventors with densely interconnected collaborators being less likely to file patents that are new combinations of patent categories (cf., Rosenkopf and Nerkar, 2001, at the organization level on boundary-spanning patents; Hsu and Lim, 2006, on knowledge bridging indexed by an organization filing patents that cite patents in other categories).

Emotion and good ideas

There is reason to suspect that emotions play a role in the link between creativity and brokerage. There is a general case for emotion operating as a social lubricant. The argument is articulated in Turner and Stets' (2005) broad theoretical review, in Barsade and Gibson's (2007) and Eifenbein's (2007) reviews of affect in organizations, and in Baron's (2008) discussion of affect in the entrepreneurship process. The argument is illustrated with examples such as flight attendants selected and socialized to maintain an upbeat tone with passengers (Hochschild, 1983), bill collectors socialized to convey a tone of urgency with "a hint of irritation" (Sutton, 1991), bank customers echoing back the emotions displayed by bank tellers (Pugh, 2001; cf. Barsade, 2002, for an experimental manipulation, with both Pugh and Barsade showing that positive emotion displayed in an encounter elicits more positive evaluations of the encounter), up to the extreme of flexible emotion manipulation techniques employed by actors and directors (Orzechowicz, 2008). Each of these roles—flight attendant, bill collector, bank teller, actor—involves brokerage in the sense that ego is an interface between groups. Brokerage roles, or brokerage components in otherwise non-brokerage roles, are a productive site for emotion research because tensions can run high when inconsistent or contradictory interests meet.

Given potential tension, it is sometimes a virtue to be seen as a neutral honest broker. Emotion is sometimes most apparent from the personal control required to conceal the emotion. Medical students have to learn to suppress feelings of desire or disgust during intimate exams. A way to maintain affective neutrality is to focus on the procedure, the sequence, the details (Smith and Kleinman, 1989). To avoid echoing back the anger of irate passengers, a flight attendant pretends "something traumatic has happened in their lives" (Hochschild, 1983:25).

On the other hand, emotion can facilitate brokerage in that people can be brought together through appeals to sentiments deeper than tactical coordination issues and positive emotion is associated with the recombinant kind of creativity that network analysts attribute to brokerage.

In a forerunner to work later discussed as the positive psychology movement (Fredrickson, 1998; Seligman and Csikszentmihalyi, 2000; Seligman *et al.*, 2005), Isen, Daubman, and Nowicki (1987:1123) showed that even a modest amount of positive affect can enhance creativity (Amabile *et al.*, 2005, offer field-research corroboration with daily emotion data recorded over an average 19-week period from 222 employees in 26 project teams from seven firms in three industries). Isen, Daubman, and Nowicki assigned college students at random to teams in one of four treatments. In the baseline treatment, each team is seated at a table in front of a wall corkboard and given a box containing a candle, tacks, and matches. The team is given ten minutes to solve the following task (Isen, Daubman, and Nowicki, 1987:1123): "affix the candle to the corkboard in such a way that it will burn without dripping wax onto the table or the floor beneath."

The required element of creativity is to make use of the box containing the candle, tacks, and matches: tack the box to the corkboard and use it as a platform for the candle. In the facilitated display treatment, the box is presented with candle, tacks, and matches outside the box, which makes the box more obviously a component in the task. In the positive film treatment, the task is preceded by having the students watch five minutes of a video containing humorous production errors edited out of two popular television shows. A quick paper-and-pencil test shows that the video created positive emotions in the students. After watching the film, students began the task as in the baseline. The same sequence happened in the neutral film treatment except the video was five minutes of a math film.

The task is not trivial. Students in the baseline condition are rarely successful (2 of 15 succeed, 13%). The simple hint of displaying the box as a component rather than a container, reverses the odds (19 of 23 succeed, 83%).

Almost as much success occurs when positive emotions are induced in the students before they begin the task (9 of 12 succeed, 75%). The success was not due to the video itself because students shown the neutral video were no more likely to succeed than the students in the baseline condition. Isen and colleagues show similar results in other studies with other creative tasks (e.g., making unique and varied word associations, Isen *et al.*, 1985), and show that success is not due to aroused emotions because arousing negative emotions does not increase success (Isen, Daubman, and Nowicki, 1987). They (1987:1130) conclude: "the impact of positive affect on creative problem solving is that good feelings increase the tendency to combine material in new ways and to see relatedness between divergent stimuli."

Emotion and brokerage

The psychological image of recombinant creativity is strikingly similar to the sociological imagery used in network studies of creativity. Positive emotion might work together with brokerage. For example, positive emotion could give ego the energy to act on brokerage opportunities. Collins (2004: chap. 3) has an image of ego accumulating "emotional energy" from repeated ritual interactions with other people (bring energy to an interaction ritual, it ricochets off the other people and comes back amplified), which creates in ego feelings of confidence and solidarity among colleagues. Those feelings can be essential to successful brokerage. As Cross and Thomas (2008:62) quote an executive: "You have to be energizing to get people to listen to your idea to begin with, and certainly energizing to get them to help you implement it or accept it."[17]

---

[17] There is evidence that brokers are a source of emotional energy (and see Csermely, 2008, for an intriguing analogy between network brokers as the active centers in proteins). Rob Cross kindly provided illustrative network data on energy and information

To see emotion and brokerage together as they are associated with good ideas, I coded the content of the texts in which the supply-chain managers described their best idea. Recall that each manager was asked to describe his or her best idea for improving the supply-chain organization, and could respond with up to 2000 characters. There are obvious limits to the data. Emotions are more easily displayed in conversation than in written text, and there is very little text available here. Even limited text can be informative, however, given the known performance association with networks around the managers.

Figure 8.7 contains results. The graphs in Figure 8.7 correspond to the graphs in Figure 3.8: an outcome variable on the vertical axis, network constraint across the horizontal axis distinguishing networks that bridge structural holes (low constraint) from closed networks (high constraint), and data averaged within levels of network constraint to simplify the graph (statistics are based on the individual-level data).

A manager's idea is coded for its emotion content on the vertical axes in Figure 8.7. Content is measured with word counts. Word counts are a shallow form of content analysis, but attractive for clarity and reliability. In addition, correlations with significant psychological phenomena give an element of construct validity to the word counts produced by the software used here.[18] Pennebaker, Mehl,

---

ties in a small organization of 125 people. On a web network survey, people were asked to cite their sources of work information and cite colleagues who were energizing or de-energizing. On average, people cited 32 sources of information, 25 energizing people, and 7 de-energizing people. Here are correlations between the number of citations a person received and network constraint computed from the person's network of information contacts:

Cites for energizing colleagues	1.00			
Cites for de-energizing colleagues	−.14	1.00		
Cites for information	.78	.30	1.00	
Ln (network constraint)	−.70	−.24	−.78	1.00

Strong negative correlations with network constraint show that brokers tended to be cited as sources of information and energy. If I divide network constraint at its median to distinguish brokers (bottom 50% of network constraint), the average broker was cited as energizing by 35.1 colleagues while non-brokers were cited by 15.9 colleagues. Brokers were cited as de-energizing by 7.5 colleagues on average, while non-brokers are cited by 5.9 colleagues. If I hold constant the fact that brokers were cited more often for all kinds of relations, the probability that a broker was cited for energy by someone citing the broker for any reason is .62 (versus .53 for non-brokers) and the probability of a contact citing the average broker as de-energizing is .13 (versus .20 for non-brokers). Measuring energy by the probability of energy between existing colleagues, non-brokers were more likely to be cited as de-energizing. Measuring energy in terms of the number of colleagues affected, brokers were disproportionately a source of energy.

[18] I used output from the word-counting program, LIWC (for Linguistic Inquiry and Word Count). Kahn *et al.* (2007) present results on the validity of the program's word counts measuring positive and negative emotion. The program is available from the authors—James W. Pennebaker, Roger J. Booth, and Martha E. Francis—for Windows and Macintosh operating systems. Enter LIWC in your browser, and you will see the home page from which the program can be downloaded.

and Niederhoffer (2003) review research showing that the words we use reveal emotions and expressing them has therapeutic effect. Relative to people telling the truth, for example, liars are more likely to use negative words, less likely to use self-references, and less likely to use qualifiers such as but, except, or without (Newman *et al.*, 2003). Recently unemployed professionals who write about their thoughts and emotions surrounding the job loss gain a sense of control over the traumatic event, and find new employment more quickly, relative to people who avoid emotional issues or do not write at all (Spera, Buhrfeind, and Pennebaker, 1994). The therapeutic effect of writing about emotional stress was consistent with an earlier study in which students who used more emotion words in writing for a period about traumatic events, later showed decreased blood pressure, fewer illness visits to the university health clinic, and improved blood-test measures of immune-system function (Pennebaker, Kiecolt-Glaser, and Glaser, 1988). The word-count software works from a dictionary of word characteristics. As a text is read, counts are made of characteristics in the text. For example, the following sentence contains four positive words and no negative words: "The *smiling* manager walked *happy* in the *bright, sunny* day." The output measures of positive and negative emotion would be 40 percent and 0 percent respectively. Here is the same sentence with negative words replacing the positive so the output measures of positive and negative emotion would be 0 percent and 40 percent respectively: "The *sad* manager walked *depressed* in the *dull, gloomy* day."

Figure 8.7 shows a strong association between emotion and brokerage. Brokers offer longer descriptions of their best ideas (Figure 8.7A), and those words are more likely to express emotion (Figure 8.7B).

The emotion expressed is both positive and negative. Brokers are not prone to positive or negative emotions so much as are prone to both. Create two binary variables: a manager can use positive words in his or her idea proposal (yes, no), and can use negative words in the proposal (yes, no). Create a four-fold table by crosstabulating the two variables.

The white dots in Figure 8.7C show the managers in the positive-only cell of the four-fold table (yes positive, no negative). The dots form a horizontal band across the top of the graph: About half of the idea proposals contained only positive words. The proportion does not increase or decrease with network constraint. Brokers and people in closed networks were equally likely to offer positive-only descriptions.

White squares in Figure 8.7C show the managers in the negative-only cell of the four-fold table (no positive, yes negative). The squares form a horizontal band across the bottom of the graph. Only 5 percent of the managers proposed an idea using negative words without positive words. Again, the low frequencies of such proposals across network constraint in Figure 8.7C shows that both brokers and people in closed networks were equally unlikely to offer negative-only descriptions.

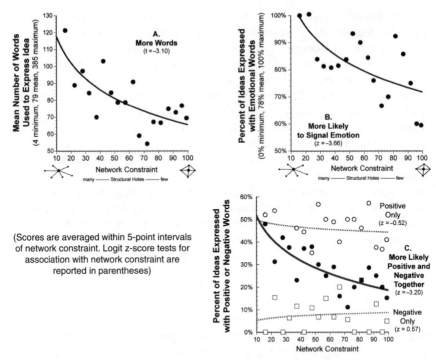

Figure 8.7 Brokers Are More Expressive in Pitching Ideas

What distinguishes brokers from people in closed networks is the tendency for brokers to mix positive and negative words when proposing an idea (yes positive, yes negative). The solid dots in Figure 8.7C show positive and negative emotions more likely in the idea proposals from network brokers.[19]

---

[19] My efforts to replicate this result elsewhere emphasize to me that the intrepid broker hypothesis is not about brokers being emotional so much as it is about people being less likely to display emotion when they are at risk of looking foolish relative to clearly defined peers. I have replicated the Figure 8.7 results in an electronic assembly company in which managers were asked to explain why a recent initiative failed. Brokers were more likely to display positive and negative emotions in their explanations. However, I did not see the same results among students in Chicago's executive M.B.A. program. The students are a couple decades past college and have typically done well in their careers. During the 2007/08 academic year, I ran a clinical workshop on social capital in which students in Chicago, London, and Singapore were asked as one of the workshop exercises to briefly describe their best idea for improving the value of their business (just as the supply-chain managers were asked for Figure 8.7). Everyone displayed positive and negative emotion in their description, leaving no association with network variables. My interpretation was that the workshop was an environment in which it had become safe to display emotion. The interpretation is self-serving, but consistent with the intrepid broker hypothesis. If there is no fear of looking foolish relative to network peers, non-brokers are no less likely than brokers to display emotion.

Whatever the reason for the mixed emotions in broker proposals, mixed emotions are not associated with value. Brokers in the supply-chain organization were more likely to propose what senior management deemed a good idea. The correlation is displayed in Figure 3.8C and statistically significant against alternative explanations in Table 3.2. I took the three emotion variables in Figure 8.7C (positive-only, mixed positive and negative, versus negative-only), and added them as predictors to the idea-value prediction in the last column of Table 3.2. None of the three improved the prediction. Idea value continues to be higher for network brokers (−4.12 t-test for network constraint, versus the −4.34 in Table 3.2). Idea value is independent of the proposal being positive-only (1.32 t-test), negative-only (−1.24 t-test), or a mix of positive and negative (0.49 t-test). I get the same lack of association between idea value and expressed emotion if I add to the prediction a binary distinction between any emotion words in a proposal versus none (0.77 t-test), any positive words versus none (1.84 t-test), any negative words versus none (−1.16 t-test), the proportion of words in the proposal that are emotion words (1.91 t-test), the proportion positive (1.75 t-test), or the proportion negative (−0.31 t-test).[20]

---

[20] Although not related to the value of an idea, mixing positive and negative emotions in broker proposals could be strategic. Preliminary ambiguity can improve the odds of successful action. Ego ambiguously signals interest, alter ambiguously signals acceptance, then ego and alter can move to concrete action with a lower risk of embarrassment. Leifer (1988) describes this action foreplay as "local action." A command can put ego in a powerful or an impotent role depending on whether or not the command is obeyed. It is wise to have a sense of how people will respond to the command before you issue it. Local action is a personal repertoire of ambiguous behaviors that can be taken to signal interest in a role, or acceptance if another occupying a role, should events develop in that direction; otherwise the behaviors can equally well be taken as random social activity. Specifically, local action refers to behavior "that, ex ante, leaves open a range of roles and, ex post, does not prove inconsistent with any role that might be claimed later" (Leifer, 1988:868). Padgett and Ansell (1993) provide a substantively rich illustration of local action in describing how Cosimo d'Medici rose to power by keeping his interests ambiguous, playing one family against another, so he could seize on advantages as they arose; a strategy that Padgett and Ansell (1993:1263–1265) term "robust action." Returning to the supply-chain managers proposing ideas, brokers could be engaging in local action when they mix positive and negative emotions in their proposals. Mixing positive and negative keeps their interests ambiguous until events take a clear direction. Such behavior is possible, though it seems too manipulatively clever for this population of relatively open, middle-class folks. Also, ambiguity could be maintained by mixing positive and negative within sentences, but emotion content at the sentence level is not ambiguous. Emotion is clearly positive or negative within sentences, but rarely both. When I divide the texts into sentences, and predict emotions in a sentence, the association with mixed emotions disappears (logit test-statistic in Figure 8.7C changes from a significant −3.20 to a negligible 0.52). Brokers were unambiguously positive or negative within sentences. From this bit of evidence, and a sense of the kind of people the managers were, I infer that the more likely broker use of emotions reflects broader exposure to positive and negative possibilities with any idea and lower social inhibitions to displaying emotion.

With a wider range of emotions expressed by brokers, and those emotions irrelevant to the value of the idea proposed when the network around the speaker is held constant, I conclude that displayed emotion is style more than manipulation. Brokers are exposed to a wider diversity of opinion and practice, so they can see positive and negative aspects to any proposal, and they are not afraid to display those aspects as positive and negative. These results are consistent with psychological research reporting a correlation between good ideas and positive affect, but extend the research by showing that the correlation disappears when the network around ego is held constant. The results are consistent with sociological research reporting a correlation between good ideas and brokerage, but extend those results by showing that brokerage is accompanied by displays of emotion, both positive and negative.[21] Returning to the reason for presenting the results in this chapter, the results are consistent with the intrepid broker hypothesis: Network brokers are more likely to display emotion in proposing ideas to senior management.[22]

---

[21] There is a further implication. Figure 8.7 describes people proposing ideas. The other side of the coin is seeking and acknowledging ideas from colleagues. Menon and Pfeffer (2003) argue that managers prefer to get advice from outsiders, rather than from colleagues within the company, because advice from a peer implies that the peer is superior, which is status eroding for the advice seeker. People who seek advice from inside the organization are seen as less attractive on a variety of dimensions including creativity and competence (Menon and Pfeffer, 2003:508; Menon, Thompson, and Choi, 2006:1136–1137). The status erosion associated with seeking advice internally is an example of relative deprivation, which is less likely for network brokers. Therefore, the intrepid broker hypothesis not only implies that network brokers will express more emotion when proposing ideas to senior management, they will be also more likely to seek and acknowledge ideas from colleagues.

[22] The qualification "in proposing ideas to senior management" picks up two variables likely to matter in future research testing the intrepid broker hypothesis. First, "proposing ideas" refers to a discussion topic sufficiently novel such that proper opinion on it is ambiguous. Such topics are most subject to peer pressure (see Appendix G), so they are the topics on which broker opinion will be most liberated from the peer pressure people with obvious peers, such as people in closed networks. I expect people in closed networks to display emotion after they understand what their group deems the proper emotion to display. Second, "to senior management" refers to an intimidating audience. I have elsewhere shown that gossip echoes within a closed network to amplify positive and negative opinions (Burt, 2005: chap. 4). The echo can sustain within the closed network of a cult or clique strong opinion at odds with the outside world. Having a strong feeling, however, does not mean that the feeling gets expressed to outsiders. With respect to Figure 8.7, and continuing the point in footnote 19 about fear of looking foolish relative to peers, the survey request for a best idea put closed-network managers in a difficult situation: As managers, they should have an idea to express, but their lack of experience outside their closed network gave them grounds to be concerned about looking stupid or foolish relative to peers. The safe course was to say nothing, which was the most common response from closed-network managers (Burt, 2005:69).

Aside on motivation in teams

For this exploratory discussion, built on the lack of returns to secondhand brokerage in the initial chapters, I focus on brokers as less subject to relative deprivation. I could instead focus on the people more subject to relative deprivation, the people with peers clearly defined by structural equivalence. Viewed in terms of who is more subject to network fear, the hypothesis is about crowding. Ego crowded by numerous peers is at high risk of relative deprivation, so fear of relative deprivation is more likely among people crowded by peers. I used this imagery in discussing Bothner, Kang, and Stuart's (2007) NASCAR race results as support for the network fear hypothesis.[23] Ego can be crowded in two ways by peers. The peers can be satellites structurally equivalent to ego by dint of their similar relations to outsiders and lack of relations with each other, or the peers can be group members structurally equivalent to ego by dint of their similar relations outside the group and strong relations with one another. The second form of crowding has special business relevance because crowding within a group corresponds to high-performance teams.

I mentioned in Chapter 1, and discussed in Chapter 6, how network closure provides advantage by creating a reputation cost for deviant opinion and

---

[23] More than an alternative metaphor for the hypothesis, crowding offers an alternative network measure for the hypothesis. Numerous peers means many people engaged in relations with ego's contacts, so network weights w_{ij} would be high for peers j, leaving self-weight w_{ii} low. In other words, $1 - w_{ii}$ is a measure of crowding around ego, varying from zero to one with the extent to which ego i is crowded by numerous peers. The intrepid broker hypothesis can be stated as a hypothesis about crowding: When evaluating a new idea or practice, people more crowded by peers ($1 - w_{ii}$ closer to one) are more troubled by fear of failure. Crowding between structurally equivalent peers has precedent in ecological theory: McPherson (1983) on two organizations crowding one another to the extent that they draw membership from the same social categories, Hannan and Freeman (1989:103–104) on organizations crowding one another to the extent that they are dependent on the same resources (also used in network theory, Burt, 1992:208–225), or Podolny, Stuart, and Hannan (1996) on two technologies crowding one another to the extent that they cite the same precedent patents. Unlike the ecological precedents, crowding here is a social psychological phenomenon. Crowding around ego is defined in the ecological precedents by measures of actual overlap between ego and peer relations. For example, Podolny, Stuart, and Hannan (1996:666) compute overlap coefficient α_{ij} as the proportion of technology i precedent patents that are also cited by technology j, then measure crowding around technology i as the sum of α_{ij} across other technologies j. In the bent preferences model, the network weights defining peers, and so crowding, are based on social perceptions of overlap (discussed below and illustrated in Figure 8.8). The network around ego can give her a feeling of being crowded for one evaluation at the same time that she feels independent in another evaluation. The empirical question is whether reactions to crowding are better predicted by actual or perceived crowding. Judging from the empirical results discussed in Appendix G, the need to distinguish perceived from actual crowding will increase with the complexity of the network around ego.

behavior. As connections close the network, people are more informed about one another, and use one another as a frame of reference for social comparison. Reputations emerge. People wary of news reaching colleagues that might erode their reputation in the network are careful to behave well (which lowers the risk of trust within the network) and work to keep up with their colleagues (which lowers cost within the network by increasing the quality and quantity of work and decreasing the need for a supervisor to monitor individual behavior). Closure's advantage is manifest as enhanced collaboration, productivity, and stability that speed a group down its learning curve (see Burt, 2005:93–166, for review and diverse examples).

Reputation cost was left an intuition in the previous discussion. By common sense, the cost is a diminution of social standing, a loss of face, a feeling of letting people down, a feeling of not contributing your fair share. Reputation is a benchmark that floats with contributions from peers. They put in more, you have to put in more—or deal with your own and others' feeling that you are not contributing your share.

I can now be more specific about reputation cost. The motivation induced by fear of reputation cost is the motivation induced by fear of relative deprivation, and indexed by the downward-sloping curves in Figure 8.3B. People anticipate the pain of falling behind and avoid it. More, the labor and monitoring efficiencies associated with reputation-driven alignment are enhanced by such anticipation since people afraid are drawn to others similarly afraid (Schachter, 1959). An engineer on a project team expressed the sentiment as follows: "Since Jim is killing himself; I mean he's here every night until three in the morning. I'd almost feel guilty if I wasn't working so hard." Guilt about not doing your part is reinforced by intense monitoring. Barker (1993) describes how monitoring changed when a small company shifted from a traditional chain of command to self-management within teams. Barker (1993: 418) asked employees how control practices in the new environment were different from practices in place before. One employee complained that (Barker, 1993:408), "he felt more closely watched now than when he worked under the company's old bureaucratic system. He said that while his old supervisor might tolerate someone coming in a few minutes late, for example, his team had adopted a 'no tolerance' policy on tardiness and that members monitored their own behaviors carefully." As the employee summarized (Barker, 1993:408): "Now the whole team is around me and the whole team is observing what I'm doing."

Analogy between relative deprivation and the reputation mechanism by which network closure provides advantage is useful in at least three ways. First, the analogy makes more precise how the reputation cost induced by closure is felt (the downward sloping curves in Figure 8.3B), and the conditions under which it is felt (clearly defined network peers, as happens when the people in a team feel strongly connected with each other and special in some way that separates them from people outside the team).

Second, the analogy brings to mind alternative lines of research on the intrepid broker hypothesis. For example, Frank (1985) describes the flattened pay schedules that would result from people trading income for status among colleagues, which I cited earlier as an instance of people avoiding the pain of relative deprivation that afflicted Stouffer's Air Corps soldiers. In fact, Frank adumbrates the intrepid broker hypothesis when he links flattened pay schedules to dense networks (1984: 552, proposition 2; 1985: 51, Figure 3.4): "In firms in which co-workers perform their tasks independently of one another, one's rank among one's co-workers should matter less than it does in a firm in which interactions among co-workers are more extensive.... An important implication of the theory of markets for local status is that wage schedules will be flattest in those firms in which co-workers interact most intensively." The intrepid broker hypothesis says that people in closed networks are, relative to network brokers, more motivated by fear of relative deprivation. One manifestation of that fear should be flattened pay schedules, with performance compensation extended beyond pay to include status symbols such as job titles, fringe benefits, and colleague deference (Frank, 1985:91–94). In other words, if pay schedules are flatter in closed networks (where relative deprivation would otherwise be more severe), and reputation in a closed network is responsible for the greater productivity of high-performance teams, then high-performance teams should have flatter pay schedules.

Third, the analogy has practical significance for managing closed-network teams to generate advantage. Expressed in terms of the downward-sloping curves in Figure 8.3B, the pain of sliding down the curves is less motivating than the threat of sliding down the curves. The way the curves flatten out as good things continue to happen for peers that have left ego behind implies a resignation at having been left behind that I assume would result in ego becoming truculent, disinterested, and eventually withdrawing. To avoid the disinterest and withdrawal expected from being left behind (flat segments of the bold lines in Figure 8.3B), the pain of relative deprivation (steep segments of the bold lines) should be spread around so everyone gets a taste without experiencing a disproportionate share, and should be reversed quickly with praise or appreciation for previous contributions. In short, managing a closed network to generate its potential for collaboration and efficiency turns on maintaining a tension about pending relative deprivation. Brokerage is easier in that advantage turns on a constant search for productive variation. Relative to brokerage, managing closure is a balancing act that drives alignment by maintaining tension about who will next experience relative deprivation.[24]

---

[24] The balancing act required to elicit the potential advantage of a closed network is another window on the strategic ambiguity that Leifer (1988) discusses as local action, and Padgett and Ansell (1993) discuss as robust action. See footnote 20. Balance also links back to Mayer-Schönberger's (2009) discussion of forgetting (see footnote 13 to Chapter 6). Relative deprivation is a brief, intense effect illustrated in Figure 8.3B by the

Perception Defines the Network

I have assumed that equivalence distance is like physical distance in that there is only one distance between two people. I relax the assumption in this section. Equivalence is an evaluation, and like other evaluations, equivalence as it is perceived is subject to bent preference distortion.

Network weights defined

My assumptions in the previous section that brokers are relatively free from network peers, and that peers are defined by structural equivalence, was based on evidence reviewed in Appendix G of peer pressure between structurally equivalent people.

There is a complication I did not introduce in the previous section because it was not needed to state the intrepid broker hypothesis: To see the evidence of structural equivalence defining network peers, I had to distinguish structural equivalence as it exists from equivalence as it is felt. I do not mean that ego cannot see the similar relations with the same people measured by distance d_{ij} in equation (5). I mean that actual structural equivalence need not be relevant in the same way to all of ego's evaluations.

The shift from actual to felt equivalence is a straightforward application of the psychophysics model linking felt to actual stimulation. Begin with d_{ij} in equation (5) as the actual structural equivalence distance from ego i to some person j.[25] Let $dmax_i$ be the maximum observed distance from ego. Then $(dmax_i - d_{ij})$ measures the extent to which ego is more structurally equivalent to j than she is to others, and ego's felt equivalence to j can be measured by replacing stimulus x in the psychophysics model (equation 1) with the actual equivalence between ego and j:

$$\kappa \, (dmax_i - d_{ij})^v,$$

---

bold line sharply decreasing as a peer overtakes ego then flattening out as good things continue to happen for the peer. The flattened segment of the bold line is ego forgetting the pain and getting on with her life. The pain cannot be forgotten if colleagues engage in schadenfreude gossip about the event, thereby ensuring a persistent pain for ego only alleviated by getting away from the colleagues. The closed network that defines a high-performance team increases the risk of painful relative deprivation at the same time that gossip within the team can neutralize the capacity team members would otherwise have to forget the pain.

[25] It is a leap to treat structural equivalence distance as if it were a concrete stimulus. People differ in their network skills and measured distance is subject to error. For example, distance is usually based on sociometric citations, which are subject to recall errors and social insecurities. Perhaps future work will define an epistemology distinguishing object-ive versus felt equivalence. Here, I treat the distance defined by network data as an objective reality subject to ego's interpretation. My motivation is empirical, not theoretical: Transforming objective equivalence d_{ij} into felt equivalence w_{ij}, generates evidence of peer pressure in Appendix G that is not visible without the transformation.

which, when converted to a proportion, is a measure of network weight w_{ij} for the bent preferences model in equation (4):

$$w_{ij} = \frac{(dmax_i - d_{ij})^v}{\Sigma_j (dmax_i - d_{ij})^v},$$
(6)

The network weights defined by equation (6) are positive fractions that sum to one for ego i across everyone in the network ($0 \leq w_{ij} \leq 1$, $\Sigma_j w_{ij} = 1$). Weight w_{ij} equal to zero says that person j is irrelevant to ego's evaluation. Weight w_{ij} close to one says that ego's evaluation is greatly affected by how it would feel if ego were person j.

Network horizon

The ($dmax_i - d_{ij}$) metric in equation (6) says that differences are negligible between people at the horizon of the network around ego (that is to say at $dmax_i$ distance from ego). People on and past the horizon are irrelevant to ego's perception. Perceived equivalence varies between people close to ego. It would be equally reasonable to define perceived equivalence in terms of the d_{ij} directly, with zero distance defining peers and perceived distance differing at far removes from ego. I use a horizon as the fixed point of irrelevance because ego identically indifferent to distant contacts seems more likely than ego identically close to proximate contacts.[26]

My frame of reference for the horizon imagery here is the related work by Noah Friedkin and Diederik van Liere. Friedkin (1983) discusses interpersonal influence in terms of a horizon of observability referring to the length of indirect connection past which there is no social control from monitoring the other person's opinion and behavior. Friedkin (1983:65ff.) reports tight horizons around selected University of Chicago and Columbia University academics. Awareness extends to friends of friends, but it is much weaker than with direct contacts. Connections longer than friends of friends are irrelevant. In other words, the interpersonal control possible through closure can extend to friends of friends (as reported in Chapter 6 for the analysts and

---

[26] A more Newtonian alternative to ($dmax_i - d_{ij}$) would be to express proximity as the reciprocal of distance, say as $1 / (d_{ij} + 1)$. This variable would equal one for ego and her structurally equivalent peers, then fractions for everyone else. Sorenson has used this metric to advantage in describing businesses clustering in geographic space (Sorenson and Audia, 2000:434; Sorenson and Stuart, 2001:1570). Another option would be to have proximity go fractional past a threshold of distance away from ego: $D / (d_{ij} + 1)$ where D is a threshold distance beyond which ego pays little attention. Many alternatives satisfy the goal of having more discriminating perception distinguish levels of close equivalence to ego rather than levels of extreme nonequivalence. Equation (6) will do until there is evidence for an alternative.

investment bankers), but friends of friends define the horizon. Van Liere, Koppius, and Vervest (2008) report on a series of inventive laboratory experiments with middle managers and M.B.A. students showing that brokerage is contingent on a person's network horizon (see van Liere, 2007, for more detail and corroborating evidence). People able to see more of the forming and dissolving connections among others in the business simulation are more successful in building a brokerage network.

The primary difference to my use of the horizon imagery here is that I am not using horizon to refer to what ego can see, merely what ego deems relevant from what she can see. Van Liere, Koppius, and Vervest (2008:602) define the network horizon around a firm as "the number of firms and their relationships that the focal firm knows to exist in an interfirm network." In contrast, the gist of the story here is that exponent v in equation (6) tightens or expands the horizon for ego's frame of reference across the known surrounding network.

Exponent v shifts the horizon

Like the focus on a microscope, exponent v can be increased to zoom in on a more narrow set of ego's peers as her frame of reference. Actual structural-equivalence distance from ego does not change. What changes is how ego feels about actual distance. A high value of the exponent makes finer the distinctions between people close to ego as it makes more coarse the distinctions between distant people. In the extreme, high values of the exponent can make everyone outside ego's closest peers reduce to a single broad category of "them." Recall the cartoon map on the cover of the *New Yorker* magazine (March 29, 1976) that represented fine-grain distinctions within Manhattan, a narrow band called Jersey on the other side of the Hudson, followed by the rest of the country packed into a small, desolate area between Mexico and Canada, followed by a condensed Pacific Ocean that ended on the horizon at China, Japan, Russia. A high exponent v underlay that caricatured New Yorker's frame of reference. Baron and Pfeffer (1996:195) offer more everyday illustration using the third edition of the U.S. Department of Labor's *Dictionary of Occupational Titles*. The classification categories were constructed by psychologists, resulting in a variety of occupation titles within psychology and a great lumping-together of titles in other social sciences: 37 base and related occupation titles in psychology, 13 titles in economics, 9 in sociology, 7 in anthropology, and 2 in political science.

More specifically, Figure 8.8 illustrates the equation (6) link between actual and felt equivalence. Actual distance d_{ij} is on the horizontal axis. Felt equivalence w_{ij} is on the vertical axis. The graph to the left, Figure 8.8A, displays actual distance and felt equivalence for salesman 19 in the Figure 8.5 organization. Distances from salesman 19 to each person in the organization are given in the bottom row of Table F3. The three salesmen are separated by zero

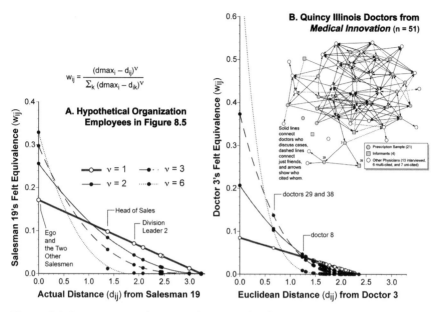

$$w_{ij} = \frac{(dmax_i - d_{ij})^v}{\Sigma_k (dmax_i - d_{ik})^v}$$

A. Hypothetical Organization Employees in Figure 8.5

— v = 1   — v = 3
— v = 2   — v = 6

Head of Sales

Division Leader 2

Ego and the Two Other Salesmen

Salesman 19's Felt Equivalence (w$_{ij}$)

Actual Distance (d$_{ij}$) from Salesman 19

B. Quincy Illinois Doctors from Medical Innovation (n = 51)

Solid lines connect doctors who discuss cases, dashed lines connect just friends, and arrows show who cited whom.

Prescription Sample (21)
Informants (4)
Other Physicians (13 interviewed, 6 multi-cited, and 7 uni-cited)

doctors 29 and 38

doctor 8

Doctor 3's Felt Equivalence (w$_{ij}$)

Euclidean Distance (d$_{ij}$) from Doctor 3

Figure 8.8 Exponent v Tightens Ego's Frame of Reference

distance. They are completely equivalent. The next closest person is the head of sales, at a distance of 1.38, followed by division head 2 at a distance of 1.90, and so on. The people most nonequivalent to the salesmen are the group heads under the other division head (persons 6 and 7 at distance 3.23). With exponent v equal to one, the w_{ij} in equation (6) defining each person as a potential peer to salesman 19 are as follows: .06, .07, .01, .10, .04, .00, .00, .01, .01, .01, .01, .01, .01, .04, .04, .04, .17, .17, and .17. Salesman 19 takes the other two salesmen as peers (persons 17 and 18), followed to a lesser extent by the head of sales (person 4), followed by the division head of sales and marketing (person 2) and the senior leader (person 1). These scores are the white circles on the bold line in Figure 8.8A. Felt equivalence w_{ij} decreases linearly with increasing observed structural-equivalence distance d_{ij}.

The other lines in the graph show higher exponent values tightening ego's frame of reference. With the exponent set to one, the network weight between salesmen is .17, and for the head of sales is .10. Salesmen have 170 percent more weight than the head of sales. Increase the exponent to two, and more weight shifts from the head of sales to the other salesmen. Salesmen have 305 percent more weight. Increase the exponent to three, and the ratio increases to 500 percent. (Table F4 in Appendix F contains network weights for each person in the Figure 8.5 organization with exponent v set to three.) Increase the exponent to six, and almost no weight is given to the head of sales. Only salesmen define one another's frame of reference. For some evaluations—such as "Did I receive a good bonus?"—social comparison can be limited to a narrow circle of people exactly like me.

I was driven to distinguish felt equivalence from actual equivalence by empirical research on interpersonal influence in complex networks. In a network that is simple in the sense that it is composed of groups within which relations are symmetric and dense, and between which relations are rare, actual structural equivalence clearly defines network peers (e.g., the lobbyists in Figure G3 in Appendix G). In a network that is complex—in the sense that people are connected by long asymmetric indirect connections so group boundaries are difficult to distinguish, everyone is a little bit structurally equivalent to everyone else, so it is difficult to distinguish network peers from actual equivalence (e.g., the doctors in Figure G4 in Appendix G, some of whom are discussed in the next paragraph). The exponent v in equation (6) tightens the frame of reference around ego to focus on her one or two closest network peers, which then reveals the evidence of interpersonal influence between structurally equivalent peers.[27]

The graph to the right in Figure 8.8 illustrates the exponent v tightening a frame of reference in a complex network. The graph describes felt and actual structural equivalence for a doctor in a network of physician advice and discussion. The data were obtained in the early 1950s from physicians in Quincy, Illinois. Quincy was one of the four cities studied by Coleman, Katz, and Menzel (1966) in their *Medical Innovation* report on social factors affecting when doctors begin to prescribe a new antibiotic. The data are discussed in Appendix G (pages 346ff.). The point here is that the Quincy sociogram in Figure 8.8 is more complex than the organization in Figure 8.5. It is difficult to see group boundaries in the Quincy sociogram. The graph in Figure 8.8B shows actual and felt equivalence for doctor 3 (who can be found to the south in the sociogram). Doctors 29 and 38 are the most structurally equivalent to doctor 3, then there is a space after which other doctors follow in quick proximity to one another. Higher values of the exponent v more clearly distinguish network peers 29 and 38 from the other doctors in Quincy.[28]

---

[27] Operationally, when the average opinion of ego's structurally equivalent peers is computed from network weights defined by actual structural equivalence in a complex network, there is a regression to the mean. Everyone is a little bit equivalent to everyone else, so everyone contributes to everyone else's frame of reference. Specifically, y* in equation G1 in Appendix G has low variance relative to variance in observed individual opinion or behavior, y. The low variance in y* created by putting too many people in ego's frame of reference obscures the correlation between y* and y.

[28] Distinguishing felt from actual structural equivalence also allows for broader frames of reference. When the exponent v in equation (6) is less than one, network differences are suppressed, so felt differences in equivalence are less than actual differences. An example would be the banding together of scientists from different disciplines in the 1980s to oppose Congressional budget cuts to basic research. Values of v larger than one exaggerate network differences so felt differences in equivalence are larger than actual differences. An example is the distinction between two scientists competing for the same

Network identity hypothesis

The distinction between felt and actual structural equivalence allows ego to expand or tighten her frame of reference as appropriate for a particular evaluation. That flexibility is necessary to see the evidence in complex networks of structurally equivalent people using one another as peers. As ego tightens her frame of reference to identify peers in a complex network, she risks losing her frame of reference. I'm different from Sheila for this reason. I'm different from Bob for that reason. Continue drawing finer and finer distinctions, and ego eventually becomes unique. The question of who is "like me" eventually gets answered "no one."

The dissolving frame of reference around ego is indexed by the self-weight, w_{ii}, defined by equation (6). For ego isolated from other people, w_{ii} equals one and all other w_{ij} for ego i equal zero, so the bent preference model in equation (4) simplifies to the model in equation (1) describing an individual alone in a psychophysics lab. For ego in a network that contains network peers structurally equivalent to ego, those peers provide a frame of reference for ego's evaluations, w_{ij} for peer j is nonzero and w_{ii} is less than one. As the exponent v in equation (6) increases to limit the frame of reference around ego's closest peers, more weight is given to ego's own situation. This is illustrated in Figure 8.8 by levels of felt equivalence over zero distance. Distance d_{ii} always equals zero. Using the equivalence metric in equation (6), increasing the exponent v tightens ego's frame of reference to people closer to ego, but especially heightens the weight given to ego herself and anyone completely equivalent to her.

Consider the three salesmen in the Figure 8.5 organization. With the exponent v equal to one, each salesman and his two colleague salesmen has a weight of .17. The bold line in Figure 8.8A crosses the vertical axis at .17. Increase the exponent to two, and the self-weight increases to .26 (solid thin line in Figure 8.8A), then to .30 for an exponent of three (dashed line), then to .33 for an exponent of six, at which point the three salesmen alone define 99 percent of one another's frame of reference (dotted line).

Compare the vertical axes for the two graphs in Figure 8.8. The self-weight for doctor 3 in the Quincy physician network increases much more than the self-weight increased for salesman 19 in the hypothetical organization. With the exponent v equal to three, doctor 3's self weight is .37, and it is off the chart when the exponent is set to six. The Quincy network is more complex, so no one is exactly equivalent to any one else, and a higher exponent that more

---

senior professorship. In normal times, and by most observers, such competitors would be seen as similar in most respects. In trying to resolve a choice between the two professors as alternative candidates for a position, much ado is made of small differences between them. Exponents less than one can be expected among people pursuing collective goods of benefit across groups. I do not make much of fractional exponents here because I have not found a study population in which the exponent defining network peers had to be less than one.

clearly distinguishes a doctor's network peers simultaneously makes the doctor dramatically unique.

The distinction between felt and actual structural equivalence adds a new layer to the story about brokers being less subject to relative deprivation. The intrepid broker hypothesis is based on brokers having a unique pattern of connections in a network, so structural equivalence does not define an obvious set of network peers, which provides a freedom from the competitive pressure of relative deprivation. The distinction between felt and actual structural equivalence clarifies why the brokers in the physician networks are so much more unique than the brokers among the lobbyists and managers (Figure G7): the physician networks are more complex, so they require a higher exponent v to distinguish network peers, which makes everyone more unique (and the weak evidence of peer pressure is silent witness to the lack of clearly defined peers for the physicians, Figure G4).

The distinction between felt and actual structural equivalence introduces a new question: How does ego manage the self-reliance foisted upon her when trying to identify suitable network peers by limiting her frame of reference to a narrow set of people? Network brokers are relatively free from the competitive pressure of structural equivalence because they are less likely to have peers obviously defined by structural equivalence. That freedom can be an incentive for some people sometimes to be a broker, but everyone feels the need sometimes for a social frame of reference to make sense of ambiguous data and events. Is this a good idea? Do I look good? Is this job opportunity a good move for me? Answers to these questions are a matter of opinion, not fact. Certain answers come from evaluating data within a social frame of reference. When a structurally unique ego feels that an evaluation is too important to resolve within the limits of personal experience, ego looks around for a frame of reference, for a benchmark against which data can be evaluated. For brokers, the lack of an obvious frame of reference defined by structural equivalence means that a frame has to be found in more abstract images of social structure. Where the intrepid broker hypothesis describes correlates of the freedom provided brokers by their lack of structural peers, the following network identity hypothesis describes corrective moves expected from brokers when they feel the need for social comparison: *The lack of an obvious frame of reference for brokers results in them being less guided by structural equivalence in identifying peers (including claims that they have no peer), and therefore more dependent on abstract images of social structure in which broker peers are more obvious.* As with the intrepid broker hypothesis, I leave this third hypothesis to future research. However, a few comments on lines of attack would be useful to flesh out the hypothesis.

Brokers break frame

I expect brokers to be less guided by structural equivalence in identifying peers, ceteris paribus, because structural equivalence provides brokers a less clear definition of network peers. Of course, brokers are connected beyond their local group, but many of those contacts beyond their local group are no more than contacts. Brokers are free to benchmark against peers inside a frame of reference broadly defined (other people in the same discipline) or narrowly defined (other people in the same discipline in this firm, in this office). The network identity hypothesis prediction is that brokers more often break out of the frame defined by structural equivalence.

One empirical test would be to run the usual contagion analysis of peer opinion affecting ego opinion to see whether the opinions of brokers are less well predicted by structurally equivalent peers. That is the evidence in Figure G6 in Appendix G. Brokers are disproportionately involved in the near-peer relations in which connectivity rather than structural equivalence defines contagious opinion and behavior.

A second empirical test would be to ask people who they see as their competitors. Brokers should more often name competitors with whom they are not structurally equivalent. For example, Porac et al. (1995:214) surveyed heads of Scottish knitwear firms asking them to identify on a roster of the firms those firms that they considered to be competitors in the sense "that they were often considered during the past 18 months when setting prices, developing products, and marketing their knitwear." Porac and his colleagues predict competitor citations from market segments defined by product and company variables that lead people to see two firms as competitors. The more closely a

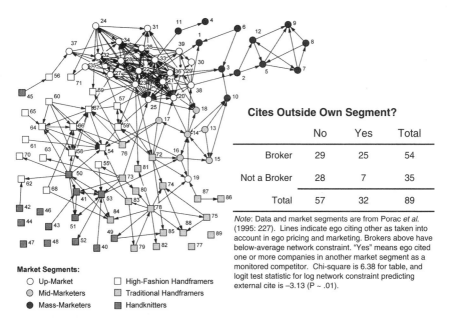

Cites Outside Own Segment?

	No	Yes	Total
Broker	29	25	54
Not a Broker	28	7	35
Total	57	32	89

Note: Data and market segments are from Porac *et al.* (1995: 227). Lines indicate ego citing other as taken into account in ego pricing and marketing. Brokers above have below-average network constraint. "Yes" means ego cited one or more companies in another market segment as a monitored competitor. Chi-square is 6.38 for table, and logit test statistic for log network constraint predicting external cite is −3.13 (P ~ .01).

Market Segments:

○ Up-Market □ High-Fashion Handframers
◑ Mid-Marketers ▨ Traditional Handframers
● Mass-Marketers ▨ Handknitters

Figure 8.9 Sociogram of Scottish Knitwear Competitors

firm fits into a market segment, the more often it was cited as a competitor within the segment.[29]

Figure 8.9 provides more concrete illustration of the network identity hypothesis using the citation data provided by Porac *et al.* (1995:227). There are 89 people in the sociogram. An arrow goes from ego to the head of a firm cited as a competitor that ego considers in his own firm's pricing, products, and marketing. Six market segments distinguished by Porac *et al.* are indicated by shading and shape in the sociogram. The table in Figure 8.9 shows that most managers only monitor other firms in their market segment (57 of 89, or 64 percent, only cite competitors within their own market segment). I computed network constraint scores from the citation data and divided the managers into below-average versus average-or-higher network constraint. Brokers in the Figure 8.9 table are managers with constraint scores below average. Brokers relative to non-brokers are twice as likely to benchmark against companies outside their own market segment (25 of 54 citations, 46%, versus 7 of 35 citations, 20%).[30]

Role equivalence provides frame

Coming at the network identity hypothesis from another direction, I expect brokers to make more use of abstract role analogies. In the absence of network peers clearly defined by structural equivalence, peers can be found by identifying with a role that allows comparisons across situations. "I see myself as a mother to this organization." "I see myself as the guard dog for this project." Identifying with a role allows for social comparison outside a situation that does not provide a clear frame of reference. As a mother to this organization, which of my current choice options would be the choice of a good mother? As

---

[29] The results are reported in Porac *et al.* (1995:219–221). The specific effect to which this sentence refers is the negative association between a company that fits poorly into a market category (AVGDIS) and the tendency for the company to be cited as a competitor by others in the category (RIVIN).

[30] This is only an illustration. The network data defining structural equivalence distance are the competitor citations used as a criterion variable. Ideally, network data on buying and selling would distinguish brokers and define market boundaries around structurally equivalent producers, both of which would be used to predict who cites whom as a competitor. Also, controls in the original report are not included here. There are nuances to consider in theory (Porac and Thomas, 1990; Hodgkinson, 2005). There are analogies to pursue. For example, Porac, Wade, and Pollock (1999) show that CEO compensation is benchmarked primarily against compensation within a company's primary industry (which is consistent with common sense and the structural equivalence definition of industries), but there are conditions under which comparisons systematically occur beyond the industry frame of reference. Those frame-breaking comparisons are more likely from network brokers. These issues notwithstanding, Figure 8.9 illustrates the point that network brokers looking to benchmark against peers are more likely (than non-brokers) to break out of the frame of reference defined by structural equivalence.

a guard dog for this project, how do the obligations of that role guide my choice between current options?

Beyond colloquial labels, I expect brokers to make more use of role equivalence to define peers. Role equivalence is an abstract form of structural equivalence. People are structurally equivalent to the extent that they have similar relations with the same people. People are role equivalent to the extent that they have similar relations with people similarly involved in relations. Directors in two divisions supervise different people, so they cannot be structurally equivalent, however, they can be role equivalent.

A brief example will suffice to show role equivalence clearly defining network peers in situations where structural equivalence does not. Figure 8.10 is a spatial display of role equivalence in the hypothetical organization in Figure 8.5. Role equivalence distance is computed as described in Appendix G (see equation G2), and the distances for Figure 8.10 are given in Table F3 in Appendix F.

Compare the role-equivalence space in Figure 8.10 to the structural-equivalence space in Figure 8.6. The two division leaders are on opposite sides of the

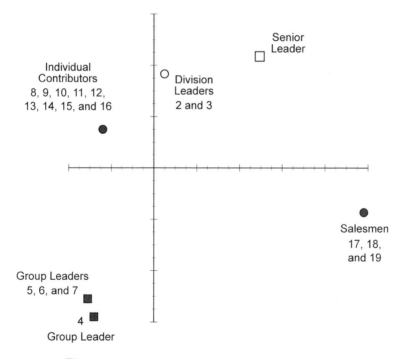

This is a multidimensional scaling of the role equivalence distances in Table F3 (Kruskal stress = .004)

Figure 8.10 Spatial Map of Role Equivalent Peers in the Hypothetical Organization

space in Figure 8.6 because they supervise entirely different people. However, the division leaders are similarly network brokers to identical organizations of people below them, so the division leaders are role equivalent in Figure 8.10. In a situation where structural equivalence provides no peer, role equivalence provides an intuitively appropriate frame of reference—as a division leader, my natural peer for social comparison is the other division leader.

Group leaders are clustered together in the southwest corner of Figure 8.10. Group leaders 5, 6, and 7 are role equivalent. They are piled on top of one another in Figure 8.10 and separated by zero role-equivalence distance in Table F3. They each supervise a densely connected group of individual contributors, and report up to a division leader. Because they supervise different individuals, the group leaders are separated into the four corners of the structural equivalence space in Figure 8.6. Because they supervise similar organizations and connect up similarly, they are role equivalent. Subtle differences in roles are also captured. The head of sales, group leader 4, is a little apart from the other group leaders because he supervises a disconnected group of individual contributors. The lack of connections between salesmen makes the head of sales a group-leader role different from the group-leader role in the other three functions. Here again, role equivalence provides the group leaders an intuitively appropriate frame of reference in a situation where structural equivalence does not.

Role equivalence does not provide a peer to the senior leader. Only one person in the organization plays the role of senior leader. Having come up through the roles of group and division leader, assume the senior leader has developed the cognitive skill required to define peers by role equivalence in lieu of structural equivalence. The senior leader can be expected to abstract his role in the organization so he can make social comparisons to senior leaders playing the same role in other organizations. Once network structure is abstracted into a role, it can be compared to similar roles anywhere.

Figure 8.10 also illustrates an important trade-off between the concrete conditions of structural equivalence and the abstract conditions of role equivalence. Individual contributors all have a frame of reference unambiguously defined by structural equivalence. Their network peers are the other individual contributors in their function. The four structural-equivalence clusters of individual contributors in Figure 8.6 reduce to two role-equivalence clusters in Figure 8.10. The three salesmen are both structurally equivalent and role equivalent. They form a cluster to the east in Figure 8.10. However, the three clusters of individual contributors in the other functions are clustered together as role equivalent to the northwest in Figure 8.10. The individual contributors in the other functions are role equivalent in that they all have strong relations with interconnected colleagues, and a strong relation with a group leader who is broker to the rest of the organization. However, the individual contributors outside sales do not have to use role equivalence to identify network peers. A perfectly clear frame of reference is provided by structural equivalence. More, the frame of reference provided by structural equivalence is simpler; it involves social comparisons within function. Role equivalence implies that comparisons across functions are as likely as comparisons within function.

The network identity hypothesis is conditional. Structural equivalence does not provide a social frame of reference for people who are brokers between groups. People in senior job ranks often play such a role, but more generally, structurally unique people include anyone who is the sole bridge from one group to another. Such people will not find a social frame of reference in structural equivalence. To the extent such a person wishes to have a social frame of reference for an evaluation, I expect them to rely on role equivalence more than structural equivalence.

Where structural equivalence does provide a clear definition of network peers, I expect people to rely on structural equivalence more than role equivalence because structural equivalence is more concrete and less demanding intellectually. It is less demanding because—as a special case of role equivalence—it requires social comparison with fewer people. Figure 8.10 shows that the individual contributors in marketing, production, and product development are role equivalent. That is a lot of people in different functions, many of whom will be unknown to ego, and none of whom counts very much toward ego's evaluation (even with the exponent set to three, each role-equivalent peer counts only 8 percent of ego's frame; see Table F5). Social comparison across many people, each counting a little, seems an unlikely mental calculation. I suspect that ego will select a subset of peers to make the task manageable. Structural equivalence provides a manageable, less subjective, frame of reference by focusing on people who compete for the same relationships.

Empirical tests here are the same as the ones discussed above in the section on brokers breaking frame. One empirical test would be to run the usual contagion analysis with role equivalence defining network peers instead of the structural equivalence definitions discussed in Appendix G. Broker opinions predicted less well by the average opinion of structural-equivalence peers should be better predicted by the average opinion of role-equivalence peers. A second empirical test would be to follow the Porac *et al.* example in Figure 8.9 of asking ego she sees as her competitors. Where structural equivalence clearly defines network peers, those peers should be named as competitors. For brokers and other structurally unique people for whom structural equivalence does not clearly define peers, the named competitors should be predicted less well by structural equivalence and better predicted by role equivalence.

Summary

I have argued that perceptions are bent by feelings of relative advantage and relative deprivation defined by the network around the perceiver. The link between felt and actual stimulus was taken from psychophysics. Concepts of structural and role equivalence in sociology provided context. Together, they imply the bent preferences model in equation (4) from which I derived the three broad hypotheses around which I organized this chapter.

First, the motivation that networks create is disproportionately about fear, specifically, fear of falling behind peers. In defining the frame of reference through which ego evaluates alternative actions, the network around ego creates pressure to act. Ego is lured to action by the prospect of moving ahead and pushed to action by fear of falling behind. The bent preferences model predicts that the push is stronger than the pull; the network pressure on ego to act is less about the lure of gain, than the fear of loss. The following *network fear hypothesis* is implied: The feelings of loss as peers overtake ego are more severe than the feelings of gain in overtaking peers, but the feelings of loss fade as peers continue to do well.

Second, networks differ predictably in the intensity of fear they generate. The difference between felt loss and gain predicted by the first hypothesis is larger for people with more obvious peers. With peers defined by a network criterion of structural equivalence, more obvious structural equivalence makes falling behind peers more obvious, which ensures the pain, and so fear, of relative deprivation. Network brokers are relatively unique within their networks. There is often no one structurally equivalent to a broker. Brokers having no structurally equivalent peers are free from the competitive pressure of peers, so they are less subject to the pain of relative deprivation, and therefore more free to evaluate and espouse something new for its benefits. An *intrepid broker hypothesis* is implied as a contingency variation on the network fear hypothesis: When evaluating a new idea or practice, network brokers are more motivated by the lure of gain, and less troubled by a fear of failure.

Where the second hypothesis describes correlates of the freedom provided to brokers by their lack of peers, the third describes corrective moves expected when brokers feel the need for a social frame of reference. Freedom from the competitive pressure of structural equivalence is an incentive to be a broker, but everyone at one time or another needs a social frame of reference to make sense of ambiguous events. The question, "Who is like me?" sometimes needs to be answered, presupposing an answer to the identity question, "Who am I?" For brokers, the lack of obvious peers means that a social frame of reference has to be found in more abstract images of social structure, implying a *network identity hypothesis*: Brokers are less guided by structural equivalence in identifying peers (including claims that they have no peer), and are more likely to be guided by abstract images of social structure in which broker peers are more obvious.

This chapter is a break from the past in bringing agency to center stage in network theory. Consistent with the past, the focus on agency comes at the request of empirical research: The evidence in the preceding seven chapters implies that closure operates through local processes and brokerage operates through personal processes. There is no evidence of global processes. Social capital remains a phenomenon local and personal despite technological advance. How the local and personal operate, with what consequence, are questions that move now to center stage.

Appendices

A
Measuring the Network

This task involves creating one or more tables of relations between people or groups in a study population. There are variations from the usual, but the typical output is a table of people down the rows by people across the columns, in which the cell where row i crosses column j is a measure of the strength of connection from person i to person j. I will refer to that cell as variable z_{ij}, a variable that increases with the strength of connection from i to j. Quality network data are available from archives, such as the z_{ij} in Chapter 5 that measure the dollars of goods sold by industry i to industry j (not to mention the varied network data available as joint involvements in archival records). It is a fortunate break when interpersonal data are available as a by-product from normal company operations, such as email traffic, or job applications, or, as in Chapters 4 and 6, annual peer evaluations in which z_{ij} is employee i's acknowledgement and evaluation of working with employee j. Peer evaluations are an under-utilized asset. They are a subjective judgment in that only relations deemed worthy of acknowledgement are cited. They are unobtrusive with good response rates in that everyone knows that the data are a consequential, but routine, process in company operations. Companies typically average elements in a column of the table to record the peer evaluation of an employee, then discard the data. Those discarded data contain a wealth of productive information on the informal organization of the company and the social capital of each person in it.

I usually end up measuring the network with a survey. When I find that archival data are not available on a population, I go through four steps to measure the network: define the study population, run a network survey, check for selection bias, complete the network with perceived relations. Marsden (1990, 2005) provides comprehensive review of network measurement. With respect to web-based surveys in particular, I strongly recommend Vehovar *et al.* (2008) when designing the instrument. They experiment with alternative formats for name generators and interpreters, among other things showing an expected effect of graphic layout (multiple name boxes increases the number of names elicited), and respondents are more likely to continue when name interpreters are listed by question (respond about each contact for one interpreter, then move on to the next interpreter and respond to each contact). At the current time, there are no generally accepted standards for network surveys as there are for opinion surveys more generally. Item conventions, wording effects, order effects, selection biases, scaling and the like are still largely a matter of personal wisdom and experience—which varies considerably between people selling network analysis. I do not propose what follows as optimum. It is what I have found to be simple and productive. I draw illustration from the product-launch, the supply-chain, and HR populations because details on them are readily available in the text.

The measurement process can be completed in a day, or require a few weeks, depending on population boundaries, response rates, and name difficulties. For example, the network of supply-chain managers was measured quickly because I had a definitive roster of who was in the study population, people responded quickly to the initial survey invitation and follow-up reminder, I was familiar with English naming conventions, and I had direct access to everyone involved. Measuring the network required only a few days. It was quite another story for the product-launch network. It was not clear who was in the population because the product-launch was a new layer imposed on existing structures. Response was delayed because people invited to the survey were not sure that their part-time contribution to the product launch warranted the bother of completing the survey. Alphabets, names, and naming conventions varied in unfamiliar ways across Japan, Korea, China, India, Australia, and the many ASEAN countries between India and Australia. I had to rely on the HR staff for assistance much more than usual, and the HR staff itself had a long chain of indirect connections to the regional clusters in the product launch network, as illustrated in Figure 3.1. Measuring the product-launch network required a month.

Population boundary

The study population has vertical and horizontal boundaries. The vertical concerns the job ranks to include. The horizontal concerns are the organizational groups, or silos, to include. Neither boundary decision is final. This step is just to define core people who should be included in the study population. These people will be asked to name the people with whom they discuss their work. If those named colleagues come from lower ranks, the population can be "snowballed" into lower ranks. If those named colleagues come from other divisions, the population can be "snowballed" into the other divisions.

The key to the vertical boundary is to include all job ranks in which people are in large part the authors of their jobs. They are expected to find ways to create value with their work. In lower job ranks, where people are told what to do, their networks have less to do with performance differences than with differences in personal taste (Burt, Jannotta, and Mahony, 1998). Among the supply-chain managers, for example, the lowest two managerial ranks show little benefit of social capital while the upper three ranks show strong and increasing benefit (Burt, 2004:371).

The key to the horizontal boundary is to include all groups that have a direct effect on the issue under study. The network of supply-chain managers was being mapped to learn how they were organized and where they tied into the surrounding organization. The horizontal boundary was drawn around anyone who was a manager in the supply-chain. There were no often-named discussion partners outside the supply-chain organization, so the population boundary remained supply-chain managers. The product-launch network was more complicated. The network was being mapped to learn where coordination was strong and where it might need to be facilitated or encouraged. At the center of the study population were 87 employees targeted for study by the launch director. The 87 employees included 14 people on the leadership team plus 73 direct reports to the people on the leadership team. The 87 people received an email explanation of the survey and directions to the online survey. The initial invitation was followed by two reminder messages, yielding 70 completed interviews, which included everyone on the leadership team. The social network connecting the 87 people involved chains of command through people elsewhere in the company and discussion relations with colleagues adjacent to the target population. Another 98 completed interviews resulted from inviting to the survey other employees working below the targeted people. Another 115 people, employees who were invited to the survey but did not respond, were added to the network because they were cited as contacts by two or more survey respondents. This so-called "snowball sampling" expanded the network to include people who provide indirect connections around the target population.

Network survey

There are two kinds of questions on a network survey: name generators and name interpreters. Generators elicit the names of contacts: "Who is your boss?" "With whom do you most often discuss company policy?" "Who are essential sources of support for your job?" Name generators have the general form: "Who do you _____?" Selecting name generator items involves filling in the blank. There is no limit to the words you can use to fill in the blanks. Respondent patience and design elegance are the limiting factors. My two baseline questions are to ask for the boss and key discussion partners. Responses to the two questions are sufficient to map the formal and informal organization of a study population.

I used four name generators in the product-launch survey. Figure A1 contains two of the name generators. These are screen shots of the items as they appeared on the survey webpage. Respondents come to the survey after receiving an invitation (typically by email) from the senior person or people sponsoring the survey. The invitation states the purpose of the survey, assures confidentiality of individual responses, and states whatever feedback will be provided on the survey results (typically a workshop in which interested participants can discuss the results). There is a screen preceding Figure A1 that contains a welcome message that re-states the three points in the invitation. The survey begins with the respondent identifying himself or herself by name and email address. The email address is important in case names and nicknames become an issue later. The boss is named, then the respondent is asked to name seven or eight people with whom the respondent has had "the most frequent and substantive work contact." The organization was large so full names were elicited to facilitate later identifying the contacts. There were some additional questions asked (items 2, 3 and 4 are not listed in Figure A1). After describing a "change that would most increase the value of the business in which you work," respondents were asked to name a person whose support would be essential to making the idea happen and the name of a colleague with whom the respondent had discussed the idea (if the idea had been discussed with a colleague). A maximum of eleven contacts could have been cited in the survey. Nine respondents named the maximum. Five named only one. On average, respondents named 7.9 contacts.

Network Diagnostic Survey

What is the first and last name by which you are most likely to be listed by colleagues citing you as someone with whom they work? (e.g., John Smith)	Your Name: _____ (required) Your Email Address: _____ (required)

1. Who is your immediate supervisor? (person most responsible for your annual review and initial salary-promotion recommendations) Please enter the person's first and last name, then the approximate years for which you have known the person, and the typical frequency with which you have direct contact with the person (not email lists).	Name (enter full first and last name, e.g., John Smith)	Years Known	Contact Frequency
	_____	☐	About Once a Week ▾

5. More generally, who are the seven or eight people with whom you have had the most frequent and substantive work contact over the last six months? Limit yourself to people with whom you have had direct contact (not email lists). Include any of the people you named above if they qualify under the "most frequent and substantive contact" criterion. And once more, please enter first and last names, then the approximate years for which you have known each person, and the typical frequency with which you have direct contact with the person.	Name (enter full first and last name, e.g., John Smith)	Years Known	Contact Frequency
	_____	☐	About Once a Week ▾
	_____	☐	About Once a Week ▾
	_____	☐	About Once a Week ▾
	_____	☐	About Once a Week ▾
	_____	☐	About Once a Week ▾
	_____	☐	About Once a Week ▾
	_____	☐	About Once a Week ▾
	_____	☐	About Once a Week ▾

Figure A1 Survey Network Name-Generator and Name-Interpreter Questions

After a name is generated, there are two name interpreters in Figure A1: For approximately how many years have you known the person? How often do you have direct contact with the person? Years are entered directly. Frequency is a drop-down menu distinguishing four options: "almost every day," "about once a week," "about once a month," or "less often." In small study populations with concrete boundaries, the survey can be simplified by listing everyone in the population and going straight to name interpreters. Given a list of everyone in a remote office, for example, people could be asked to indicate the frequency of their contact with each person on the list. This "roster" method has virtues. The disadvantage is that it will not reveal the variable extent to which people are connected outside the people put on the roster.

The final name-interpreter item is a matrix asking about relations between cited contacts. The item is given in Figure A2. There is a matrix at the bottom of the screen. The matrix contains one row and column for each person the respondent named. Figure A2 shows the matrix for a respondent who named five contacts. The respondent is to

5. This final question asks for your view of connections among the people you named. Please don't quit here. You are almost finished. The people you cited in the previous page are listed in the table below. The task is to select a letter indicating your view of the connection between each pair of people, where

"Often" means that, to your knowledge, the two people speak often with one another such that they are probably familiar with current issues in one another's operations.

"Some" indicates that you know only that the two people sometimes talk to one another, such that they have some familiarity with current issues in one another's operations.

"Rare" indicates, again as best you know, that the two people speak infrequently or not at all to one another.

"Difficult" indicates that, for reasons that could be no fault of either person, there has been difficulty in coordinating work between the two people.

For example, if you named three people (Jose, John, and Jody) who speak often with one another and haven't had difficulty coordinating their work when they should, the table would look like this:

Jose A
O   John S
O   O   Jody Y

If you named four people (Jose, John, Jody, and Wen) where Jose and Jody are closely connected, Jose and John have had difficulty coordinating their work, and the others rarely speak to one another, the table would look like this:

Jose K
D   John S
O   R   Jody Y
R   R   R   Wen Q

HERE IS THE TABLE WITH NAMES OF YOUR CONTACTS ON THE DIAGONAL. People are listed with the default that they speak often. **USE THE PULL-DOWN MENUS IN THE CELLS TO INDICATE YOUR VIEW OF THE CONNECTION BETWEEN EACH PAIR OF PEOPLE.** If you wish to change or add names, hit your browser's "BACK" button, edit your citations on the previous page, and return here to describe the network.

Click the SUBMIT button to save all your data.

Figure A2 Survey Network Name-Interpreter Matrix Question

click on the cell between each pair of cited contacts to indicate whether connection between the contacts is "often," "some," "rare," or "difficult." The response categories are explained in the text above the matrix.

Figures A1 and A2 define a simple survey. The network survey used with the HR employees in Chapter 4 contained many more items. There were a dozen name generators (qualifying phrases deleted and bank name replaced by "[bank]"):

1. From time to time, most people discuss important matters with other people, people they trust. The range of important matters varies from person to person across work, leisure, family, politics, whatever. The range of relations varies across work, family, friends, and advisors. If you look back over the last six months, *who are the three or four people with whom you discussed matters important to you?*

2. Consider the people with whom you like to spend your free time. Over the last six months, *who are the three people you have been with most often for informal social activities such as going out to lunch, dinner, drinks, visiting one another's homes, and so on?*

3. Turning to your formal job description, *who would be considered your primary HR manager?*

4. In your opinion, *who is the most promising of the people you supervise?*

5. Thinking of your job in more general terms, success usually requires the support of colleagues and contacts well beyond the formal job description. Suppose you were moving to a new job and wanted to leave behind the best network advice you could for the person moving into your current job. *Who are the three or four people you would name to your replacement as essential sources of support for success in your job?*

6. *Of the many [bank] employees with whom you have worked, who has been the most difficult?*

7. Considering all your personal contacts within [the bank], *who are your most valued contacts in the sense that they have been the most important to your accomplishments?*

8. *Is there anyone who could have been one of your most valued contacts, but for one reason or another the relationship never developed?*

9. If [the bank] were going through a re-organization, and you could select someone to represent your interests on the subcommittee deliberating the re-organization of HR, *who would you select?*

10. Suppose you learned that you are one of two finalists being considered for promotion to an attractive job assignment. Suppose further that the other finalist is a [bank] employee. *Who would be your best guess to be the other finalist in competition with you for the promotion?* This isn't a question about tension between people. It is a question about the [bank] labor market.

11. If you decided to find a job with another firm, *who are the two or three people with whom you would most likely discuss and evaluate your job options?* These could be people inside [the bank], or outsiders such as family, friends, or people at other firms.

12. Now that you have a list of contacts, please give it a quick scan. *Is anyone significant missing? Is there someone without whom your job would be much more difficult, or someone without whom you would be much more effective?*

Respondents were then asked how close they were to each named contact, how often they spoke with each contact, how long they had known each contact, and how each contact was connected to the others (the matrix question in Figure A2). It was a long questionnaire that required almost an hour to complete. There was a strong center to the HR organization (Figures 4.1 and 4.2), so people were patient with a long questionnaire. I would not attempt such a questionnaire in a decentralized study population— especially since I now know that I get the bulk of the network information likely to be useful in an organization diagnosis from the simple questions in Figures A1 and A2. I know this by mapping the extent to which responses to multiple network items provide the same names.

Figure A3 is a network content "map" distinguishing kinds of relationships cited by the HR respondents. The map begins with a rectangular matrix of binary data. Each row describes a respondent's relationship with a contact. A "1" in a column indicates that the respondent has the column kind of relationship with the row contact. The 219 HR respondents cited a total of 2,863 contacts, so the data file for the map in Figure A3 contained 2,863 rows and 23 columns, one column for each kind of relationship distinguished in the map. The solid dots refer to the above dozen name generators and the

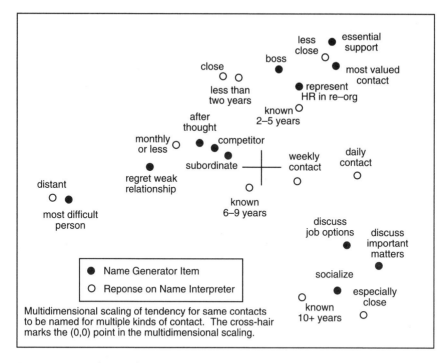

Figure A3 Spatial Map of HR Network Contents

hollow dots refer to responses on name interpreter items. The map results from combining the data columns where they are similar. Of the many ways one could go about the task, Figure A3 is a multidimensional scaling of Jaccard coefficients between the columns (using the STATA default option for multidimensional scaling). Two kinds of relations are close together in the map when the same people were named for both kinds of relations. For example, "most difficult person" refers to contacts named as the person who "makes it most difficult for you to do your job." The word "distant" (located next to "most difficult person") refers to the closeness name interpreter in which some of a respondent's cited contacts were people from whom the respondent felt "distant." The two kinds of relations, "distant" and "most difficult person," are close together in the map because the same contacts were named on both items; people who made a respondent's job difficult were often people from whom the respondent felt distant.

The pattern in Figure A3 is something I now expect to see in detailed network surveys (cf. Burt, 2005:52, for almost identical patterns in an American electronics company and a French chemical company). The east–west axis is an evaluative axis on which negative relations are to the left, positive to the right. The north–south axis is a contrast between personal relations at the bottom and work relations at the top. There are nuances captured by the detailed name generators, but the boss and work discussion items in Figure A1 provide much of the positive content on the right. The dozen name generators in Figure A3 generated a median eight contacts per employee in the HR organization. The items in Figure A1 generated a median of six contacts in the product-launch network and seven contacts in the supply-chain organization. What will not be captured by the items in Figure A1 are negative relations (network content to the left in the Figure A3 map). Data on negative relations require an explicit question about colleagues who make work difficult (see Labianca, Brass, and Gray, 1998; Labianca and Brass, 2006).

Selection bias

As responses come in, the data can be analyzed for selection bias. Two issues: Are the people responding representative of the study population? Are there additional people who should be invited into the survey? If people not initially in the survey are named by multiple respondents as a discussion partner, the outsiders are part of the informal organization and can be invited to the survey. If certain groups are not responding, they can be encouraged with special attention.

Non-response should be random across the network. If it clusters, in the sense that a disproportionate number of people in a certain area of the network are not responding, then non-response can be a diagnostic indicator of a problem.

Consider Figure A4. Lines in Figure A4 indicate that one of the two connected people supervises the other and kinds of work are distinguished by symbol shapes (see Figure 3.1). Symbol shading distinguishes people by their participation in the survey: 168 respondents (dark grey dots), 17 people in the target population who did not respond to the survey (black dots), and 115 snowball-sample contacts beyond the target population who were

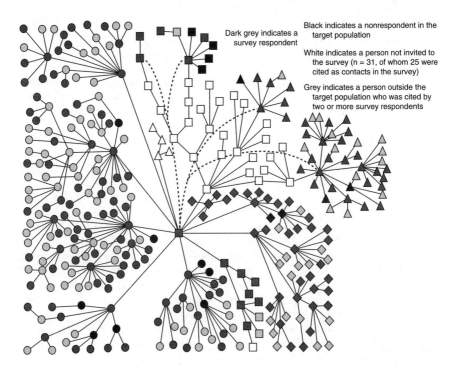

Figure A4 Survey Network Response

invited to the survey but did not respond (grey dots). As in Figure 3.1, white dots indicate the 31 administrative people outside the survey population. The scatter of dark grey dots across the sociogram is visual evidence of survey respondents scattered across the study population, providing network data on each organization in the product launch. If there is any group not taking the survey seriously, it is the finance group at the top of the sociogram. Finance contains the largest concentration of black dots. The indifference is not a serious issue, however, since the non-responders are few and the product launch depended on sales people more than accountants.

I have seen clustered non-response indicate two kinds of serious problems in other networks. One is non-response from a key stakeholder group. For example, it would have been a problem for the product launch if non-response had been concentrated in one of the regional clusters. A second kind of serious problem is more unique to informal organizations. When an initiative depends on a charismatic person to recruit employees to the initiative, non-response can cluster around the periphery of the charismatic person's reach. Non-response clustered on the periphery of a network is an indicator that the network will have difficulty growing and will survive only as long as the central person's energy.

With respect to selection bias more generally, Table A1 shows that the survey respondents represent the kinds of people in the product-launch population. A high proportion of the target population completed the survey (70 of 87, or 80%), but a smaller proportion responded from lower job ranks (98 of 213, or 46%). With the low response rate at the outer reaches of the study population, it is important to know that the people who responded are not a biased sample. I used employee characteristics to distinguish people who responded to the survey (dark grey dots in Figure A4) from people who did not

Table A1   Predicting Response to the Network Survey

Northeast Cluster	−1.97	(1.33)
Northern Cluster	−2.55	(1.29)
Southern Cluster	−2.17	(1.30)
Western Cluster	−1.74	(1.36)
Southeast Cluster	−2.46	(1.27)
Compensation (z-score)	.54	(.34)
Annual Evaluation (z-score)	−.19	(.17)
Job Rank (individual contributor)	−.08	(.20)
Job Rank (manager)	−.56	(.35)
Age	−.01	(.03)
Female	−.06	(.35)
Sales Function	−.65	(.39)
Years with Company	−.03	(.04)
Regional Headquarters	.38	(.70)
In the Target Population	1.85	(.49)**

Note: These are logit coefficients predicting which employees responded to the network survey. Clusters are Asia-Pacific regions, distinguished in Figure 3.2. The cluster of 31 administrative people in the network but not in the product launch (white symbols in Figure 3.1 and Figure A4) were not eligible to respond to the survey and are excluded. The contrast group is the administrative hub at the center of the Figure 3.2 sociogram. Standard errors are in parentheses (* $p < .05$, ** $p < .001$).

(black and grey dots in Figure A4). The employee characteristics include whether the employee was in the target population, geographic cluster, job rank, age, gender, years with the company, years in the employee's current job, annual compensation, and most recent performance evaluation. Response is independent of every tested employee characteristic, except one: People in the target population—the people central to the product launch who received two reminders to respond—were significantly more likely to respond (3.1 z-score test statistic, P < .01). Otherwise, no kind of employee is more represented in the survey than other kinds of employees.

Perceived relations

With caution, respondent perceptions of relations between cited contacts can be used to flesh out the network around non-respondents. The 168 survey respondents in the product launch cited 1,327 contacts and reported on 4,985 relations between their cited contacts. The more often two people were cited together, the more respondent perceptions I have on the relationship between the two people. For example, the most-often described relationship is between the head of one of the five regional organizations and one of his lieutenants. Fourteen respondents cited both people as contacts. All 14 reported that the two people "often" speak with one another. In fact, when the head of the regional organization responded to the network survey, he did cite the lieutenant as a discussion partner.

The empirical question is how often observed discussion citations correspond to respondent perceptions of relations between cited contacts. The results in Table A2 answer the question. For example, there are 16 relationships on which I have five or more reports that the two people "often" speak to one another, and most of the relations are cited for discussion in the survey (14 are cited, which is 87.5% of the 16 five-report relations). A discussion citation occurs between two people when one or both of the people cited the other as someone with whom they discussed their best idea for improving the value of their business or as someone with whom they often discuss their work. The data in Table A2 are limited to reports on relations between pairs of people in which one or both the people responded to the survey (citations between non-respondents cannot occur) and both people are in the network of 331 displayed in Figure 3.1 (I made no effort to trace contacts cited by one respondent).

The results in Table A2 show that the odds of a discussion relation between two people is high if two or more respondents report that the two people speak "often" and no respondent says that contact between the two people is "rare" or "difficult." Only reports of "often" are associated with discussion citations. Reports of anything less than "often" are associated with decreased odds of a discussion citation.

I used the above results to extrapolate beyond respondent relations. Across the 1,535 relations in Table A2, I estimated a logit equation in which discussion citations were predicted from supervision and the number of respondents reporting each level of connection in Table A2. I then used the logit equation to predict the probability of a discussion citation in each of the 1,906 relations for which one or more respondents reported their perception of the relationship. The logit coefficients are given in the note to Table A2. Parentheses in each cell contain the average probability of a discussion citation as predicted by the logit model. The pattern of predicted citations across the cells of Table A2 follows the pattern of observed citations (e.g., 87.5% observed citations in the upper-right corner of

Table A2 Perceptions of a Relationship and the Probability of Discussion Citation

Respondent Perception of the Relationship:	Number of Respondents Reporting on the Relationship						
	None	One	Two	Three	Four	Five or More	Total
"Often"	9.6 (750, .11)	40.1 (511, .39)	56.2 (169, .56)	67.8 (59, .63)	70.0 (30, .81)	87.5 (16, .92)	29.1 (1535)
"Some"	31.4 (1132, .31)	23.4 (363, .23)	19.4 (36, .19)	0.0 (4, .15)	—	—	29.1 (1535)
"Rare"	38.7 (1058, .39)	8.2 (449, .09)	4.4 (23, .02)	0.0 (5, .00)	—	—	29.1 (1535)
"Difficult"	30.9 (1442, .31)	1.1 (91, .01)	0.0 (2, .00)	—	—	—	29.1 (1535)

Note: Rows distinguish kinds of respondent reports on the relationship between two cited contacts. Columns distinguish number of reports. Cells give the percent of cell relations cited for discussion in the network survey. Parentheses contain the number of relations on which the row kind of report was made with the column frequency, and the average logit probability of a discussion citation between two people (the logit coefficients are 1.06 for a reporting relation between the two people, .45 for each report of "often," −.26 for "some," −.65 for "rare," and −1.83 for "difficult"). Tabulation is based on the 1,535 relations in which one or both people responded to the survey (so their relationship could have been cited for discussion in the survey).

Table A3 Perceptions of a Relationship and the Strength of Discussion Citation

Respondent Perception of the Relationship:	Insider Report on Strength of Relationship				
	"Distant"	"Less Close"	"Close"	"Especially Close"	Total
"Especially Close"	11 (−2.17)	18 (−3.08)	54 (−1.24)	240 (10.99)	323
"Some Connection"	66 (.69)	120 (1.34)	250 (.74)	298 (−3.98)	734
"Rare/Distant"	56 (2.56)	99 (3.30)	176 (1.04)	135 (−9.72)	466
Total	133	237	480	673	1,523

Note: Rows distinguish kinds of respondent reports on the relationship between two cited contacts. Columns distinguish reports made by either of the two people in the reported relationship. Cells are the frequency of column relations reported as the row relationship. Parentheses contain unadjusted loglinear test statistics showing the extent to which observed frequencies exceed the frequencies expected if perceptions were independent of insider reports. Tabulation is based on the 1,523 relations in which one or both people responded to the survey (so their relationship could have been cited by one or the other in the survey).

the table corresponds to the high .92 predicted probability of a discussion citation). Dichotomizing the predicted probabilities at .5 to identify connections with better than a fifty-fifty chance of being cited for discussion, I have a total of 415 predicted discussion citations in the network, which brings to 1,034 the total number of discussion relations in the network: 330 reporting relations between boss and subordinate (the 331st person is the CEO and deemed to report to himself), another 585 relations cited in the survey for discussion without supervision (171 of the 756 cited discussion relations were with the boss, leaving 585 discussion relations beyond the boss), and a final 119 perceived relations between colleagues reported in the survey to "often" speak with one another.

The HR employees were asked to distinguish how close they felt to each of their contacts, so instead of scaling a perceived relationship by how often it was cited (columns in Table A2), I can scale by how often it was cited as strong (columns in Table A3). There are three rows in Table A3 because the HR questionnaire only distinguished three categories of perceived relationship: especially close, rare or distant, and something between those extremes. Loglinear effects within the table show that perceptions of "especially close" are only associated with insider reports of "especially close" (10.90 z-score versus negligible or negative association with other categories). The category of "close" is separate in that it has negligible association with other categories; it is neither especially close nor distant. "Some connection" is definitely not "especially close," but neither is it associated with any other categories. "Distant" and "less close" are similarly not "especially close" and similarly associated with perceptions of "rare/distant."

Applying a one-dimension loglinear association model to Table A3 yields the scale values plotted in Figure A5 (Goodman, 1984; .92 for "especially close," −.24 for "some connection," −.67 for "rare/distant" down the rows, and .98 "especially close," −.13 for "close," −.46 for "less close," −.40 for "distant" across the columns).

Perceived and cited "especially close" relations stand so far apart from other relations that perceived "especially close" relations can be added as maximum-strength relations while all other relations are ignored as weak.

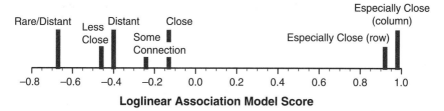

Figure A5 Loglinear Association Scores for Table A3

At the same time, there are many "close" and "less close" cited relations and they can be valuable bridge relations ("strength of weak ties"), so I used a continuous measure of relationship strength. I normalized the association-model scores to vary from zero for no relation to 1.0 for an especially close relation (relation strength equals [association score – min]/[max – min], where min is the minimum association-model score and max is the largest): 1.00 for an "especially close" cited relation, .96 for an "especially close" perceived relation, .33 for a "close" cited relationship, and so on. This preserves the distinctions in relation strength and adds 103 relations to the network (of 731 perceived relations among the people in Figure 4.1, 628 were already in the network as direct citations).

B
Measuring Access to Structural Holes

Structural holes are opportunities to broker connections between people. Access to structural holes indicates your opportunities to broker connections. When everyone you know is connected with one another, you have no opportunities to make connections. When you know a lot of people disconnected from one another, then you have opportunities to make connections between people otherwise disconnected, connections in terms of coordination between the disconnected people, and connections in terms of ideas or resources derived from exposure to contacts who differ in opinion or the way they behave. In this, access to structural holes can be said to measure the extent to which a manager's network gives him a vision advantage in detecting and developing opportunities, the extent to which the network puts him at risk of productive accident. This appendix is about the access people have to structural holes. Industry access is discussed in Chapter 5 as an extension of the discussion here.

"Opportunities" should be emphasized in these sentences. None of the network measures to be discussed index brokerage behavior. They index opportunities for brokerage. There are reliability, cost, and precedence reasons to measure brokerage opportunity instead of behavior, as discussed around Figure 2.4 in Chapter 2. Reasons notwithstanding, measuring brokerage behavior by its opportunities rather than its occurrence has implications, again as discussed in Chapter 2.

The implication relevant to this Appendix is that three brokerage terms are used as synonyms in current practice. I want to be clear about it to avoid confusion when the measures are discussed: Access to structural holes is discussed as synonymous with brokerage opportunities, both of which are discussed as synonymous with brokerage. All three terms are about the advantage created when connections are made between disconnected people, connections in terms of coordination between the disconnected people, or connections in terms of ideas or resources derived from exposure to contacts who differ in opinion or the way they behave.

Bridge counts

Bridge counts are an intuitively appealing measure. The relation between two people is a bridge if there are no indirect connections between the two people through mutual contacts. Associations with performance have been reported measuring brokerage with a count of bridges (e.g., Burt, Hogarth, and Michaud, 2000:Appendix; Burt, 2002).

Constraint

I measure brokerage opportunities with a summary index, network constraint which measures the extent to which a manager's time and energy are concentrated in a single group of interconnected colleagues—which means no access to structural holes (Burt, 1992: chap. 2):

$$C_i = \Sigma_j \ c_{ij}, \ i \neq j \tag{B1}$$

where C_i is network constraint on manager i, and c_{ij} is a measure of i's dependence on contact j:

$$c_{ij} = (p_{ij} + \Sigma_q p_{iq} p_{qj})^2, \ i \neq q \neq j \tag{B2}$$

where p_{ij} is the proportion of manager i's network time and energy spent on contact j, $p_{ij} = z_{ij} \ / \ \Sigma_q z_{iq}$, and variable z_{ij} measures the strength of connection between contacts i and j, so the contact-specific constraint c_{ij} varies from 0 to 1 with the extent to which i's network time and energy is directly (p_{ij}) or indirectly ($\Sigma_q p_{iq} p_{qj}$) spent on colleague j. Connection z_{ij} measures the lack of a structural hole so it is made symmetric before computing p_{ij} in that a hole between i and j is unlikely to the extent that either i or j feels that they spend a lot of time in the relationship (strength of connection "between" i and j versus strength of connection "from" i to j; see Burt, 1992:51). Network constraint, as the sum of c_{ij}, measures the extent to which the manager's network of colleagues is like a straightjacket around the manager, limiting his or her vision of alternative ideas and sources of support. I multiply scores by 100 to discuss integer levels of constraint. The calculation is illustrated in Figure B1.

Network constraint varies with three network dimensions: size, density, and hierarchy. Constraint on a person is high if the person has few contacts (small network) and those contacts are strongly connected to one another, either directly (as in a dense network), or through a central, mutual contact (as in a hierarchical network). The index, C, can be written as the sum of three variables: $\Sigma_j (p_{ij})^2 + 2\Sigma_j p_{ij}(\Sigma_q p_{iq} p_{qj}) + \Sigma_j (\Sigma_q p_{iq} p_{qj})^2$. The first term in the expression, C-size in Burt (1998a), is a Herfindahl index measuring the extent to which manager i's relations are concentrated in a single contact. The second term, C-density in Burt (1998a), is an interaction between strong ties and density in the sense

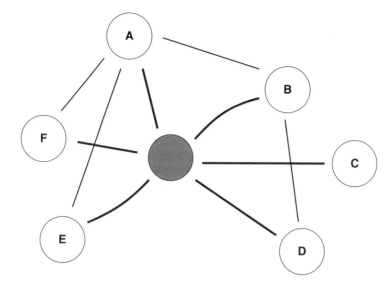

Network constraint measures the extent to which your network time and energy is concentrated in a single group. There are two components: (direct) a contact consumes a large proportion of your network time and energy, and (indirect) a contact controls other people who consume a large proportion of your network time and energy. The proportion of i's network time and energy allocated to j, p_{ij}, is the ratio of z_{ij} to the sum of i's relations, where z_{ij} is the strength of connection between i and j, here simplified to zero versus one.

$$c_{ij} = (p_{ij} + \Sigma_q \, p_{iq} p_{qj})^2 \quad q \neq i,j$$

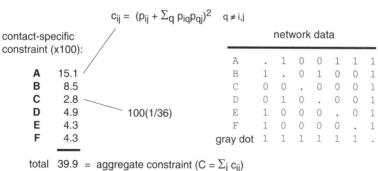

contact-specific
constraint (x100):

		network data
		A . 1 0 0 1 1 1
A	15.1	B 1 . 0 1 0 0 1
B	8.5	C 0 0 . 0 0 0 1
C	2.8	D 0 1 0 . 0 0 1
D	4.9	100(1/36)	E 1 0 0 0 . 0 1
E	4.3	F 1 0 0 0 0 . 1
F	4.3	gray dot 1 1 1 1 1 1 .

total 39.9 = aggregate constraint (C = $\Sigma_j \, c_{ij}$)

Figure B1 Computing Network Constraint

that it increases with the extent to which manager i's strongest relations are with contacts strongly tied to the other contacts. The third term, C-hierarchy in Burt (1998a), measures the extent to which manager i's contacts concentrate their relations in one central contact. See Burt (1992:50ff.; 1998a:Appendix) and Borgatti, Jones, and Everett (1998) for further discussion of the components in network constraint.

Size

Network size, N, is the number of contacts in a network. In graph-theory discussions, the size of the network around a person is discussed as "degree." Isolates, that is, people with no contacts, are a special case discussed below. For non-zero network size, other things equal, more contacts mean that a manager is more likely to receive diverse bits of information from contacts and is more able to play their individual demands against one another. Network constraint is lower in larger networks because the proportion of a manager's network time and energy allocated to any one contact (p_{ij} in equation B2) decreases on average as the number of contacts increases.

Density

Density is the average strength of connection between contacts: $\Sigma\, z_{ij}\, / \, N^*(N-1)$, where summation is across all contacts i and j. Density is sometimes discussed as a proportion because in studies limited to binary network data (people are connected or not), the average strength of connection between contacts equals the proportion of contact pairs connected. Dense networks are more constraining since there are more connections ($\Sigma_q p_{iq} p_{qj}$ in equation B2). Connections between contacts increase the probability that the contacts know the same information and eliminate opportunities to broker information between contacts. Dense networks offer less of the information and control advantage associated with spanning structural holes. Density is only one form of network closure, but it is a form often discussed as closure. Contacts in a dense network are in close communication so they can readily enforce sanctions against individuals who violate shared beliefs or norms of behavior.

Hypothetical networks in Figure B2 illustrate how constraint varies with size, density, and hierarchy. Relations are binary and symmetric in Figure B2. The graphs display relations between contacts. Relations with the respondent are not presented. The first column contains sparse (minimum density) networks. No contact is connected with other contacts. The second column of the figure contains maximum-density networks. Every contact has a strong connection with each other contact. At each network size, constraint is lower in the sparse-network column.

Hierarchy

Density is a form of closure in which contacts are equally connected. Hierarchy is another form of closure in which a minority of contacts, typically one or two, stand above the others for being more the source of closure. The extreme is to have a network organized around one contact. For people in job transition, such as MBA students, that one contact is often the spouse. In organizations, hierarchical networks are often built around the boss.

Hierarchy and density both increase, but in different ways, the indirect connection component in network constraint ($\Sigma_q p_{iq} p_{qj}$ in equation B2). Where network constraint measures the extent to which contacts are redundant, network hierarchy measures the extent to which the redundancy can be traced to a single contact in the network. The central contact in a hierarchical network gets the same information available to the manager and cannot be avoided in manager negotiations with each other contact. More, the central contact can be played against the manager by third parties because information available from the manager is equally available from the central contact since manager and central contact reach the same people. In short, the manager whose network is built around a central contact runs a risk of playing Tonto to the central contact's Lone Ranger. Network constraint increases with both density and hierarchy, but density and hierarchy are empirically distinct measures and fundamentally distinct with respect to social capital because it is hierarchy that measures social capital borrowed from a partner (the central point in Chapter 7).

The Coleman-Theil inequality index has attractive qualities as a measure of hierarchy (Burt, 1992:70ff.). Applied to contact-specific constraint scores, the index is the ratio of $\Sigma_j \, r_j \, \ln(r_j)$ divided by $N \ln(N)$, where N is number of contacts, r_j is the ratio of contact-j constraint over average constraint, $c_{ij}/(C/N)$. The ratio equals zero if all contact-specific constraints equal the average, and approaches 1.0 to the extent that all constraint is from one contact. Again, I multiply scores by 100 and report integer points of hierarchy.

In the first and second columns of Figure B2, no one contact is more connected than others, so all of the hierarchy scores are zero. Non-zero hierarchy scores occur in the third column of Figure B2, where one central contact is connected to all others who are otherwise disconnected from one another. The hierarchy can be seen in the relative levels of constraint posed by individual contacts. Contact A poses more severe constraint than the others because network ties are concentrated in A (cf. contact A in Figure B1). The Coleman-Theil index increases with the number of people connected to the central contact (the difference between minimum and maximum constraint is larger in larger hierarchical networks). Hierarchy is 7 in the third column of Figure B2 for the three-contact hierarchical network, 25 for the five-contact network, and 50 for the ten-contact network. This feature of hierarchy increasing with the number of people in the hierarchy turns out to be important for measuring the network advantage of outsiders because it measures the volume of a strategic partner's network (Chapter 7), which strengthens the hierarchy association with performance (Burt, 1998a:Table 1).

Note that constraint increases with hierarchy and density such that evidence of density correlated with performance can be evidence of a hierarchy effect (as illustrated in Chapter 7). Constraint is high in the dense and hierarchical three-contact networks (93 and 84 points respectively). Constraint is 65 in the dense five-contact network, and 59 in the hierarchical network; even though density is only 40 in the hierarchical network. In the ten-contact networks, constraint is lower in the dense network than the hierarchical network (36 versus 41), and density is only 20 in the hierarchical network. Density and hierarchy are correlated, but distinct, components in network constraint.

Betweenness

Freeman's (1977; 1979) betweenness index is an intuitively appealing measure. The index is a count of, or ratio of possible, monopoly opportunities for brokerage. If you know two disconnected people, then you have one opportunity to broker a connection between people. If you know four people disconnected from one another, then you have six opportunities to broker a connection between people. Where a structural hole is defined to occur when two people are disconnected, then betweenness is a count of the structural holes to which a person has monopoly access.

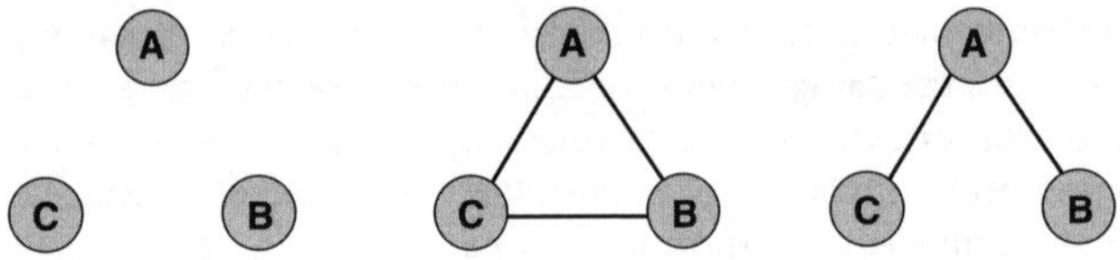

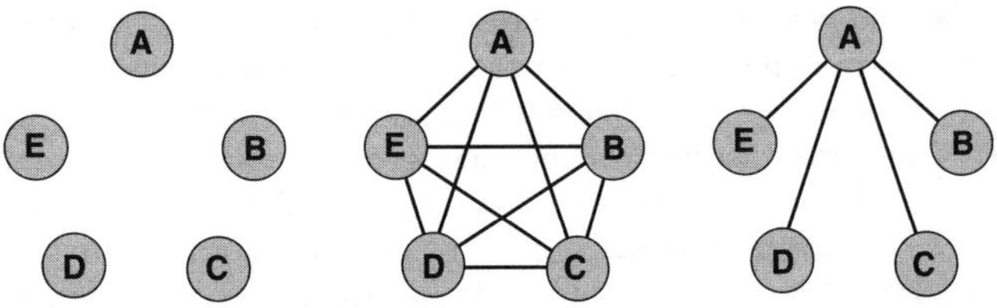

	Sparse Networks	Dense Networks	Hierarchical Networks
Small Networks			
size	3	3	3
density	0	100	67
hierarchy	0	0	7
constraint	33	93	84
from:			
A	11	31	44
B	11	31	20
C	11	31	20
Larger Networks			
size	5	5	5
density	0	100	40
hierarchy	0	0	25
constraint	20	65	59
from:			
A	4	13	36
B	4	13	6
C	4	13	6
D	4	13	6
E	4	13	6
Still Larger Networks			
size	10	10	10
density	0	100	20
hierarchy	0	0	50
constraint	10	36	41

NOTE — Network scores other than size are multiplied by 100.

Figure B2 Network Size, Density, Hierarchy, and Constraint

In the network around the manager in Figure 2.1, for example, there are two indirect connections between contacts 1 and 3, one through contact 2 and the other through the manager. Since one of the two shortest paths between 1 and 3 goes through the manager, the manager has one half of an opportunity to broker the connection between 1 and 3. That is his only brokerage opportunity. Half of a brokerage opportunity divided by the three connections possible among three contacts means that the manager has the betweenness score of .17 reported in Figure 2.1.

There are $N(N - 1)/2$ possible opportunities for brokerage between pairs of N contacts. The banker in Figure 2.1 is in a position to broker 23 connections between colleagues. Divided by the 28 connections possible among eight contacts, the banker has a betweenness score of .82, which says that he very nearly has a monopoly on all brokerage opportunities in the network (until the banker network is extended in Figure 2.2 to include indirect connections).

The index does not distinguish brokerage opportunities to which a person has direct access versus opportunities to which the person has indirect access. A brokerage opportunity between two of your close friends has the same weight in the index as a brokerage opportunity between two strangers far away in the network. Betweenness was introduced to describe centrality in small, five-person task groups in laboratory experiments (Freeman, 1977). Distant contacts were not an issue. When the index is applied to even modest-size populations such as the ones analyzed in this book, it can include opportunities in the index that are probably unrealistic to include— especially given the results in Chapters 3 and 4 showing that returns to brokerage are limited to opportunities among direct contacts (as was the case in the five-person task groups in which betweenness was initially measured). I am not describing a problem with the index. I am describing a caution in its use. Ideally, betweenness would be computed for the immediate network around a person, then for indirect contacts further removed.

The special case of isolates

An isolate is a person who has no contacts in a network. When asked to name the people with whom they discuss their work, for example, isolates name no one and no one names them. In fact, virtually everyone at a managerial rank discusses their work with someone, but that someone could be a relative, a bartender at a favorite pub, a subordinate who did not make it into the study population, or some other colleague who did not make it into the study population. People can have a local circle of discussion partners at the same time that they are isolated within management. I use the term "isolate" in the specific network sense of the term.

Isolates pose a unique problem for certain measures of brokerage. Network size is unambiguously zero. A count of bridge relations is unambiguously zero. Betweenness as a count of brokered relations is unambiguously zero. However, measures of "average" relationship such as network density, or network constraint, are undefined. When N is zero, there is no average.

One way to proceed is to eliminate isolates by research design. For example, reporting relations are included among discussion relations in three study populations analyzed in this book. Since everyone reports to someone, no one is an isolate. Snowball sampling is another way to go. Two study populations in this book, the investment bankers and the analysts, are define by snowball sampling. A banker or analyst is only included in the study population when they cite or are cited by colleagues. The supply-chain population was defined by response to a network survey, augmented by snowball sampling to include contacts cited by two or more of the survey respondents. The respondents all named discussion partners and the additional contacts were only included if they were cited, so there would be no isolates even without reporting relations being included among the discussion relations. There were in fact a large number of supply-chain managers in the company who were isolated from other supply-chain managers (Burt, 2004), but the isolates were ignored for this analysis.

In general, populations defined by a non-network criterion—all students in a classroom, or all managers in an organization—will contain isolates. If isolates are included in the analysis, they have to be assigned density or constraint scores in keeping with the network concept being measured. If performance is being predicted from access to structural holes (as in Chapters 3 to 5), then each isolate is a closed network unto him or herself. Having no access to structural holes, isolates correspond to density and constraint scores of one. Assigning constraint scores of one to isolates is also consistent with the strong correlation between network size and the log of constraint (e.g., −.86 in the product-launch network, −.77 across the supply-chain managers, −.87 in the HR organization, −.70 across the bankers, −.76 across the analysts). On the other hand, if stability and trust are being predicted from social regulation within a closed network (as in Chapter 6), then each isolate, like a hermit, is free from social regulation. Neither constrained nor supported by a surrounding network of colleagues, isolates correspond in social regulation to density and constraint scores of zero. A moral here is that, if isolates are included in an analysis of social capital, it is wise to test effect robustness by adding to any prediction a dummy variable distinguishing isolates.

Indirect network constraint

The network around each of a manager's direct contacts poses some level of constraint and opportunity, on the contact directly, and on the manager indirectly through the contact. I measure indirect network constraint by aggregating constraint in networks around each of the manager's contacts,

$$IC_i = \Sigma_j \, \delta_{ij} C_j, \; i \neq j \tag{B3}$$

where C_j is direct network constraint on contact j (equation B1), and δ_{ij} is a weight for pooling contact networks. There is low indirect constraint on a manager connected to brokers (low C_j scores average to a low IC_i score). A manager subject to low indirect constraint is connected to colleagues whose networks are rich in brokerage opportunities, through whom the manager has indirect access to structural holes.

I tried measuring indirect network constraint as the arithmetic average across a manager's contacts ($\delta_{ij} = 1/N$, where N is the number of the manager's contacts). This is the measure on the horizontal axis of Figure 4.5. I also tried the constraint on the manager's boss, under the assumption that the chain of command is the primary source for opportunities ($\delta_{ij} = 1$ for manager's boss, 0 for all other contacts; Figure 4.6), and constraint on the manager's best-connected colleague, under the assumption that every contact need not be a source of opportunity, but you need at least one ($\delta_{ij} = 1$ for the contact with the lowest network constraint, which means the largest, least redundant, network; 0 for all other contacts; Figure 4.7). These three aggregations yield the same result: strong zero-order association with performance and negligible partial association.

More sophisticated measures could be productive in other study populations, however, the simple arithmetic average is strongly correlated with more sophisticated measures in the manager populations studied here (also see Table 5.1 for tests with alternatives predicting performance, and Table E6 in Appendix E for correlations among the alternatives). For example, I computed indirect constraint as the weighted average of constraint with weights proportional to the constraint posed by each contact. The 1/N weight for alter j in the arithmetic mean is replaced with c_{ij}/C, where c_{ij} is the level of constraint posed on ego i by alter j and C is the network constraint score for ego. This weighting emphasizes the networks around the direct contacts who most constrain ego. The weighted measure of indirect network constraint is correlated with the arithmetic mean .84, .78, .97, and .95 respectively for the analysts, bankers, managers, and the product-launch employees. I also tried weighting inverse to c_{ij} to emphasize networks around the contacts most likely to be bridges. Again the weighted measure is strongly correlated with the arithmetic mean and yields the same associations with performance.

Average within ignores across

Indirect constraint on ego measured by average constraint on alters has two properties to note for future research. First, it does not measure total indirect constraint. The total has two components: a component defined by connections within the network around each alter, and a component defined by connections across the networks around each alter. Averaging constraint scores across alters captures the first component plus some unknown portion of the second component (larger portion to the extent that the contacts for one alter are the same for other alters). The difference is illustrated in Figure 6.1b, where person 1 is part of a group separate from persons 2 and 3. Constraint is high within the network around each of ego's three contacts, but lower in the combined network across the three contacts.

I feel comfortable averaging within contact networks because within-neighbor network constraint measures the extent to which each neighbor has no direct access to structural holes and returns to brokerage are concentrated in direct access. Moreover, Model F in Table 5.1 shows that where there is brokerage spillover from neighbor networks—between industry networks—the results with total indirect constraint are similar to the results with indirect constraint averaged within contact networks. Total indirect constraint adds negligible prediction to indirect constraint averaged within contact networks. As a further check, I ran some tests with the product-launch and supply-chain managers. These are the populations most balkanized into subgroups, so connections across networks would be most likely in these populations to be valuable for coordinating information across the networks. I created a "total indirect network constraint" measure, TC, analogous to the measured used in Model F in Table 5.1 so I could add ln(TC) to the predictions in Chapter 3 to see whether something important had been lost by ignoring connections across neighbor networks. For each manager with M indirect contacts, I constructed an (M,M) matrix of connections among the indirect contacts, and computed network constraint from equation (B1) as if the manager had a connection with each of the M indirect contacts. The more interconnected the indirect contacts, the higher the total indirect network constraint on the manager. This measure of total indirect network constraint includes constraint from connections within the network around each of the manager's contacts, plus constraint from connections across the networks. Across the product-launch managers, ln(TC) is correlated .45 with the log average indirect constraint measure used in the text and adds negligible prediction to the performance equations in Table 3.1 (−1.02 t-test for compensation, .75 for z-score annual evaluation). Across the supply-chain managers, ln(TC) is correlated .57 with the log average indirect constraint measure used in the text, and adds negligible prediction to the performance equations in Table 3.2 (−1.62 t-test for compensation, .01 for annual evaluation, and −1.79 for value of best idea). These results for total indirect network constraint are not equally negligible, but they are similar to average indirect constraint in being negligible, and all pale in comparison to the strong performance associations with direct network constraint. In short, there is no evidence of spillover missed by ignoring connections across neighbor networks to focus on structure within the networks.

Unproductive if pushed too far

A second property to note for future research is that the average-alter measure can be unproductive in describing distant alters. Specifically, where each person in a population can reach every other person by some number of intermediaries, each person is indirectly constrained by N−1 alters (everyone else in the population) and indirect constraint averaged across all alters equals the population average excluding ego. In such a population, as alters further removed are included in alter averages, variance in indirect constraint decreases and the correlation between direct and indirect constraint approaches negative one.

Illustrative results are given in Table B1 for the bankers in Chapter 4. The first column is the length of the path distance from ego to alters included in the network around ego, the second column is the standard deviation of indirect constraint, and the third column is the correlation between direct and indirect network constraint. The first row is the measure used in Chapters 3 and 4: Indirect constraint is the average network constraint on ego's direct contacts (alters one step distant from ego). The bottom row corresponds to the longest path distance, which in the banker population is 5 steps. As the network around ego expands to include more distant alters (down the rows), the indirect-constraint standard deviation decreases and the correlation between direct and indirect constraint approaches negative one. I am comfortable with alter averaging in this book because indirect constraint is limited to direct contacts and direct contacts are few relative to the number of people in each study population. In other populations, convergence could be an issue to consider. Ceteris paribus, the convergence to negative one will be faster in smaller, more-connected populations.

Table B1 Average Constraint from Increasingly Distant Alters

Maximum Path Distance to Averaged Alters	Standard Deviation in Indirect Constraint	Correlation between Direct and Indirect Constraint
1	4.68	.31
2	1.51	−.09
3	.92	−.52
4	.25	−.76
5	.11	−1.00

Positional measures

Gathering data on relations between contacts complicates a routine survey (Figure A2 in Appendix A). Inter-contact data are the most difficult and time-consuming survey network data to obtain. It is tempting to leave them out of the survey. There is the further incentive that useful work on social capital can be published that does not take into account ties between contacts. For example, Meyerson (1994) predicts executive salary in a selection of Swedish firms from a count of an executive's sociometric contacts outside the firm, and the proportion of the cited relations that are strong. Executives with stronger ties outside the firm enjoy higher salaries. Uzzi (1996) predicts failures among New York apparel contractors from distributions of business across contacts. Failure is less likely for contractors who have an exclusive business relationship with a preferred partner.* Baum, Calabrese, and Silverman (2000) predict the performance of biotechnology start-ups from the diversity of the start-up's alliance network at founding. Alliances are sorted into nine categories according to the alliance partner (e.g., non-rival biotechnology firm, government laboratory, marketing company, etc.) and a start-up has a diverse network to the extent that it has alliances equally in all nine categories (Baum *et al.*, 2000:276–277). This is diversity distinct from the image of spanning structural holes. For example, a start-up that has alliances with five non-rival biotechnology firms that do not have alliances with one another has a network that spans structural holes between the alliance partners (network constraint score would be 20, as illustrated in the first column of Figure B2), but the start-up would be coded by the Baum *et al.* measure as having zero network diversity because all five partners are the same kind of partner (non-rival biotechnology firm). Measurement complications notwithstanding, the brokerage

---

* Uzzi's measures warrant comment because the work is so engaging but the measures can be understood to measure the extent to which relations are embedded in dense networks, whereupon their association with survival would be misinterpreted. The measures are computed from data that describe contractor sales of apparel components to manufacturers who assemble and market finished clothing (Uzzi, 1996:696). Two measures Uzzi discusses as embeddedness are associated with contractor survival (a third, "social capital embeddedness," a dummy variable distinguishing contractors affiliated with a business group, has negligible association with survival). Uzzi (1996:686, italics in original) begins with an exclusive contractor–manufacturer tie; "The degree to which a firm uses embedded ties to link to its network is measured with the variable *first-order network coupling*." The variable is a Herfindahl index of concentration (sum of squared proportions) measuring the extent to which all of a contractor's sales are to a single manufacturer (Uzzi, 1996: Eq. 1). The other network variable (Uzzi, 1996:687) measures the average extent to which the contractor (focal firm) is the only contractor selling to its manufacturers (network partners); "*Second-order network coupling* measures the degree to which a focal firm's network partners maintain arm's length or embedded ties with their network partners." The variable is a Herfindahl index measuring the extent to which all of a manufacturer's purchases are from the contractor, averaged across the manufacturers to which the contractor sold goods (Uzzi, 1996: Eq. 3). The two Herfindahl indices are associated with contractor failure: failure is less likely to the extent that a contractor sells exclusively to a single manufacturer, and the manufacturers to which it sells only buy from that contractor. Thus my summary statement in the text that failure is less likely for contractors that have an exclusive business relationship with a preferred partner. Relations between manufacturers and between contractors are unknown, so there is no measure of the density and hierarchy of the network in which contractor–manufacturer relations were embedded. Uzzi's (1996) results are conceptually the same as, though substantively more detailed than, Meyerson's (1994) and Gabbay's (1997) results showing how important it is to span a structural hole with a strong, reliable relationship. The structural hole from which Uzzi's contractors and manufacturers profit is the division between people who make garment components and people who assemble the components into clothing.

concept is robust: Baum *et al.*'s network diversity measure does well predicting start-up differences in patent production (Baum *et al.* 2000:283). There has even been productive work at the radical extreme of measuring social capital without network data. Belliveau *et al.* (1996) infer relations from background similarities between people, as do Ancona and Caldwell (1992a) and Reagans and Zuckerman (2001) in their suggestive work on the external networks of teams (though Reagans, Zuckerman, and McEvily, 2004, build on Reagans and McEvily, 2003, to show the enhanced performance prediction that network data can add to predictions from team demography). Leana and Pil (2006) measure school social capital with teacher opinions about information sharing, trust, and shared goals within the school to report a correlation between high student test scores and positive teacher opinions. Perhaps most widely known is Coleman's (1988; 1990:590–597) analysis of social capital in which he infers network closure from family demography (children in families with two parents and few children have more closed networks), family mobility (children who have lived in the same neighborhood all their lives have more closed networks), and school (children in Catholic and other religious private high schools have more closed networks).

Inferences about social capital can be made in the absence of data on relations between contacts if data are available on the positions contacts hold in the broader social system beyond the network under analysis. People who occupy the same position in the broader social system are exposed to similar ideas, skills, and resources, and so are to some extent redundant contacts. They are redundant by structural equivalence (see Figure 8.5 in Chapter 8 for numerical illustration). Therefore, social capital can be inferred from the positions to which a person is connected. This is the foundation for positional measures of social capital (see Lin, Fu, and Hsung, 2001; van der Gaag, Snijders, and Flap, 2008, for methods review, and see Lin and Erickson, 2008, for recent applications to questions of access, trust, and inequality).

Positional measures are defined in two steps. The first step sorts potential contacts into categories according to their position in some broader social system. For example, contacts in different occupational statuses have access to different resources (Laumann, 1966; Lin, Ensel, and Vaughn, 1981; Lin and Dumin, 1986; Erickson, 1996), relations in broken homes are different from relations in intact families (Coleman, 1990), people long with the firm are different from new hires (Ancona and Caldwell, 1992a; Reagans and Zuckerman, 2001), contacts inside a firm are different from contacts outside (Meyerson, 1994), contacts in one division or function of a company are different from contacts in another (Ancona and Caldwell, 1992b; Hansen, 1999), contacts in one academic school of thought are different from contacts in another (Collins, 1998), alliances can be distinguished by kind of alliance partner (Baum, Calabrese, and Silverman, 2000; Powell, White, Koput, and Owen-Smith, 2005), or positions can be inferred from patterns of interaction (Walker, Kogut, and Shan, 1997). This first step for positional measurement is akin to the name generators in survey network data. Contacts are elicited for kinds of relationships by name generators and research design involves selecting an appropriate set of generators. Here, contacts are elicited for kinds of positions and research design involves selecting an appropriate set of positions.

The second step asks people about their connection with each position. Specific contacts are sometimes known, but often not. Nan Lin has been a leading advocate for positional measures of social capital, and offers an example survey item in which positions are defined by an assortment of occupations from high to low socioeconomic status (Lin, 2001:18): "Here is a list of jobs (show card). Would you please tell me if you happen to know someone (on a first-name basis) having each job?" If the respondent knows more than one contact in a category, he or she is asked to "think of the one person whom you have known the longest (or the person who comes to mind first)." When a respondent answers "yes," there are follow-up questions asking how long he or she has known the contact, the nature of the relationship with the contact, and so on. Often-used positional measures of social capital are the heterogeneity of contacts (number of occupations is akin to number of bridges assuming that contacts in different occupations are non-redundant, see Erickson, 1996; 2001, for two productive applications) and "upper reachability," which is the highest status in which the respondent has a personal contact.

This is not the place to offer a critique of positional measures, though a rigorous comparison of positional and network measures would be welcome. What can be said by way of summary critique is that positional measures have at least two virtues: An obvious one is that they are inexpensive: it is easy and quick for a survey respondent to provide the data. Second, they generate results. The primary disadvantage of positional measures is not a defect so much as a risk: positional measures are leveraged against the accuracy of the first step, the delineation of positions. For example, scholars outside the United States follow Lin's lead in using positional measures of social capital based on translated American occupational categories. Such use poses no problems as long as the American categories correspond to structurally equivalent contacts in the application country. However, if there is structural variation within a category (e.g., lawyers whose clients are major corporations might have access to resources different from those to which personal injury lawyers have access, or professors at a nationally prominent university differ in some ways from professors at a community college), then the assumption that contacts are redundant within positions is violated and the inference from positional contact to social capital is unclear. A strength of Walker, Kogut, and Shan's (1997) analysis is that they study structural equivalence to identify positions in terms of which their study population is stratified before computing positional measures.

It might seem that positional measures are hopelessly flawed by their lack of data on the relations between contacts. Positional measures cannot distinguish the columns in Figure B2; a sparse network is the same as a clique, and both are the same as a hierarchical network. However, turn the situation around and consider Figure B2 in light of positional distinctions. If a manager cited the three contacts at the top of the middle column and they were all three from the same segment of a company, then the manager indeed would have no social capital as is implied by the network constraint scores. But what if each contact worked in a different function, or a different division, or in a different company? Then the dense network among them would reinforce the strength of their bridge relationships with one another and the manager would be, in contrast to the high constraint score, rich in social capital. Recall the successful manager in Figure 2.2 whose closed network coordinated leaders in three divisions of the company.

C
Measuring Analyst Accuracy

I follow Phillips and Zuckerman (2001) in measuring the relative accuracy of analysts: the extent to which an analyst's earnings forecasts were more accurate than forecasts by other analysts covering the same company. I use data from the I/B/E/S Detailed History

File for each of the two years concluded with an *Institutional Investor* election, dating each forecast by the point at which its accuracy would be known (e.g., a forecast published in December 1997 about annual earnings as of June 1998 would be assigned to 1998). Analyst forecasts of company earnings per share (EPS) are listed in the I/B/E/S data with actual earnings so the magnitude by which an analyst forecast was wrong for company f can be measured as (cf. Phillips and Zuckerman, 2001:410): $ABSDIF_{ift} = $ | Actual EPS_{ft} − Forecast EPS_{ift} |, which is the absolute difference between the actual annual ESP for firm f in year t and analyst i's forecast of the company's annual ESP. To hold constant differences between the companies covered by different analysts, the following z-score measures accuracy relative to other forecasts on the same company: $Z_{ift} = (MABSDIF_{ft} - ABSDIF_{ift})/SDABSDIF_{ft}$, where $MABSDIF_{ft}$ is the average $ABSDIF_{ift}$ for analysts j forecasting firm f's EPS in year t, and $SDABSDIF_{ft}$ is the standard deviation of their forecasts. To measure analyst i's accuracy during year t, I averaged the Z_{ift} across firms f during year t for analyst i's annual earnings forecasts made within six months of the company announcing its actual earnings. An accuracy z-score of zero indicates an analyst for whom I found no forecasts more or less accurate than forecasts from other analysts covering the same companies. Positive z-scores indicate an analyst for whom I found forecasts closer to actual earnings than the forecasts from other analysts covering the same companies.

I have three notes on the accuracy measure. The first concerns the time interval in which accuracy is measured. Table C1 shows the rate at which forecasts became more accurate closer to a company announcing its actual earnings. The I/B/E/S data list an average of 141,773 annual-earnings forecasts per year from 1996 through 1999. For each forecast made by any analyst in the two years of the I/B/E/S data under study here, I computed the Z_{ift} accuracy measure described in the text for analyst i forecasting the annual earnings of firm f during year t. I divided the number of days between forecast date and the date of announced earnings by 30 to assign forecasts to a month, distinguished by the rows in Table C1. Forecasts made less than 30 days before announced earnings are in the "Same Month" row at the top of the table. Forecasts made more than 360 days before announced earnings are in the "Eleven or More" row at the bottom of the table. Variation in forecasts (last column) is consistent across the rows, but the center of the distribution, the average analyst forecast, becomes more accurate closer to announced earnings (middle column). Accuracy is highest for forecasts made during the month in which earnings were announced (.65 z-score). Accuracy decreases with length of time in longer-range forecasts to a minimum in forecasts made a year before earnings were announced (−.53 z-score). The pattern is the same for both of the two years under study here, it is the same for US companies versus companies elsewhere, and there is no tendency for forecasts on US firms to occur earlier or later than forecasts on companies outside the US. Note the shift from below-average to above-average accuracy during the sixth month before announced earnings—which encourages following Phillips and Zuckerman (2001) in measuring analyst accuracy with forecasts made six months before announced earnings, and is the reason for the non-zero mean accuracy in Table E5 in Appendix E (accuracy in the text is based on forecasts six months before announced earnings and the above table shows that forecasts in that interval are above-average accurate). Some analysts tended to make forecasts closer to announced earnings, so they were on average more accurate in their forecasts, which could affect the accuracy association with election recognition. I computed the average time interval between

Table C1 Analyst Accuracy by Time between Forecast and Announced Earnings

Months between Earnings Forecast and Announced	Z-Score Accuracy (mean Z_{ift})	Z-Score Accuracy (sd Z_{ift})
Same Month	.65	1.00
One	.54	.94
Two	.47	.88
Three	.40	.82
Four	.28	.83
Five	.12	.82
Six	.05	.82
Seven	−.08	.86
Eight	−.23	.89
Nine	−.34	.90
Ten	−.43	.95
Eleven or More	−.53	.99

forecast and announced earnings for each analyst, each year (mean is 3.77 months before announced earnings with a standard deviation of 3.29 months), and re-estimated Models B and D in Table 4.3 with average time interval held constant. Election associations with network constraint in Models B and D are not affected: Test statistics for election recognition eroded by direct network constraint are −2.97 and −2.89 in Models B and D respectively, and indirect network constraint continues to have no association with election recognition (−0.14 and −0.90 test statistics).

A second note concerns averaging across forecasts to characterize an analyst's accuracy. The measure in the text gives equal weight to each company on which an analyst makes forecasts. To consider a more sophisticated alternative, I computed accuracy as an average weighted by company prominence—on the intuition that investors are more likely to notice analyst accuracy in forecasts about more prominent companies. Instead of the simple average in the text ($\Sigma_M Z_{ift}[1/M]$, where M is the number of forecasts being averaged), I computed a weighted average ($\Sigma_M Z_{ift}[RF/RI]$, where RF is the number of forecasts made by any analysts on firm f during year t, and RI is the total number of forecasts made by any analysts on the firms in the M forecasts). For example, imagine an analyst who made two forecasts, one about company A and one about company B, where there were 44 forecasts from other analysts about company A and 4 forecasts from other analysts about company B. The accuracy measure in the text would give equal weight to the analyst's two forecasts (M = 2). The weighted average would give nine times more weight to the analyst's forecast about company A (RF = 45 for company A, RF = 5 for company B, RI = 50 for the analyst). I suspect that analysts make more forecasts about prominent companies, whereupon an unweighted average is self-weighting for company prominence, because the weighted and unweighted measures are correlated .96 for the analysts, and I obtain the same predictions in Table 4.3 with either measure. I only report the simpler unweighted measure in the text.

A third note concerns analysts unlisted in the I/B/E/S data. I tried a measure more sophisticated than the simple dummy variable used in the text ("Published Forecasts"). The more sophisticated measure treated unlisted analysts as the low end of a continuum that increased with the visibility of the companies on which an analyst made forecasts.

Let N_{ft} be the number of forecasts in the I/B/E/S data predicting the annual earnings of firm f during year t. Let $N(i)$ be the average of N_{ft} for firms f on which there was a record in the I/B/E/S data of a forecast on firm f from analyst i during year t. $N(i)$ equals zero for unlisted analysts. It increases above zero as analyst i covers companies on which many analysts publish many forecasts. The more forecasts made about the companies an analyst covers, the more visible the analyst's companies in the sense of warranting the attention that went into the many forecasts. I added $N(i)$ to Model D in place of the dummy variable "Published Forecasts" at the bottom of Table 4.3. I get the same results reported in the table: analysts who covered more visible companies were more likely to be elected to the All-America Research Team and there were no election associations with accuracy or indirect network constraint. If I re-estimate the models for only the analysts located in the I/B/E/S data, or if I return the dummy variable distinguishing unlisted analysts, there is no election association with analyst differences in the visibility of the companies they covered. Test statistics for Model D in Table 4.3 are 0.95 for $N(i)$ and 2.73 for the dummy variable "Published Forecasts" at the bottom of the table distinguishing unlisted analysts, versus 2.69 for $N(i)$ when the dummy variable is not included in the model. In short, the aspect of the more sophisticated measure that is associated with election recognition is the aspect captured by the dummy variable in the text distinguishing analysts who could not be matched to forecasts in the I/B/E/S data.

D
Industry Networks

Network constraint in Chapter 5 is defined by a 2% business criterion, and by company size approximations to four-firm concentration ratios in non-manufacturing industries. This appendix contains evidence for those two decisions.

Bounding the immediate network

The immediate network around an industry in Chapter 5 contains its direct suppliers and customers. Beyond them are the industry's indirect suppliers and customers. In theory, the immediate network consists of a producer industry plus every other industry with which it has business. How much business qualifies? For the 1992 benchmark input–output table, the Department of Commerce rounded dollar flows to the nearest million dollars. If a million dollars is the criterion in the 403-industry table, then the immediate network around an average manufacturing industry would contain 87.2 other industries as suppliers or customers, varying from a minimum of 16 to a maximum of 375. In the 1987 input–output table, dollar flows are rounded to the nearest $100,000. The 1987 table contains more non-zero dollar flows (56,763 among the 403 industries versus 43,472 in the 1992 table). The difference between the tables is almost entirely small dollar flows in 1987 that would not round up to a million dollars for the 1992 table (13,742 dollar flows in the 1987 table are .5 million or less). Using the $100,000 minimum dollar flow as a criterion, the immediate network around an average manufacturing industry would contain 122.3 other industries as suppliers or customers, varying from a minimum of 23 to a maximum of 400, which is almost every one of the other 402 industries in the table.

I prefer not to use "any business" as the criterion for inclusion in the immediate network around an industry. There would be inconsistency between the 1987 and 1992 tables, and immediate networks would be large, leaving little of the economy for the extended network. Large networks in a small population produce extended networks that regress to the population mean since each extended network quickly includes every node in the population (see Table B1 for illustration with the investment bankers).

Table D1 shows how industry network size would vary with five alternative boundary criteria: any buying or selling with the industry, 1 percent of industry buying and selling, 2 percent, 5 percent, and 10 percent. Criteria are expressed as percentages of producer buying and selling as is usual in studies of resource dependence. Dollar amounts large for one industry can be trivial for another.

Table D1 shows that the primary difference between 1987 and 1992 is in the small transactions and that even a small limit on what qualifies as business brings network size down to a practical number of supplier and customer markets that a manager could be expected to monitor. If immediate networks are limited to industries with which producers conduct at least one percent of their buying and selling, the immediate networks around manufacturing industries in 1987 average 16.6 other industries as suppliers or customers, varying from a minimum of 4, up to a maximum of 34. Network size is about the same in 1992. Increasing the criterion to two percent cuts network size in half; averages of 9.3 and 8.8 respectively in 1987 and 1992. Increasing the criterion to five percent halves the networks once again to reach average sizes of 4.2 and 4.1 in 1987 and 1992.

Table D1 Defining the Immediate Network

Criterion for Inclusion in the Immediate Network around Producer Industry	Year	Average Percent of Business in the Network (%)	Smallest Network	Average Network	Largest Network
Any Producer Buying or Selling	1987	100.0	24	121.34	399
	1992	100.0	17	86.31	375
One Percent of Producer Business	1987	84.3	4	16.56	34
	1992	82.1	4	16.90	31
Two Percent of Producer Business	1987	73.9	2	9.30	19
	1992	73.5	3	9.18	17
Three Percent of Producer Business	1987	66.8	2	6.50	13
	1992	66.2	2	6.29	12
Five Percent of Producer Business	1987	56.7	1	3.97	8
	1992	56.3	1	3.85	8
Ten Percent of Producer Business	1987	40.7	0	1.71	5
	1992	40.4	0	1.73	4

Note: These are counts for the 361 manufacturing industries. Percent of business in the network is the sum of p_{ij} that exceed the criterion, where p_{ij} is the percentage of producer buying and selling transacted with industry j. Each of the other 402 input–output sectors is a potential supplier or customer. Producer industry is not included in the counts.

Business is clearly concentrated in a few key supplier and customer industries, with smaller but substantial amounts of business conducted in other industries. The substantial amounts are indicated in Table D1 by the percent of business included in the networks. Even a low criterion of one percent excludes from the industry networks 17 percent of producer business on average (84.3% of producer business in 1987 is included in the one-percent networks, 82.1% of business in 1992). To cast a broad network, my instinct was to use a one-percent criterion. Networks would be a manageable size and roughly similar in 1987 and 1992, while retaining a high level of producer business. However, it is not clear that all those small one-percent transactions need to be included in the network.

Given the lack of a clear boundary criterion for the immediate network around an industry, I estimated effects in the baseline network model for four alternative criteria—one percent, two percent, three percent, and five percent—to determine where the boundary should be drawn.

The results are presented in Table D2. I draw three conclusions from the results. First, the negative effect of rivalry within the industry is stable across all the alternatives. The coefficient is consistently about negative five and a half with a standard error of about one and a half.

Second, the 2 percent criterion seems to me to be the right criterion to define the immediate network around industries in Chapter 5. The results for 2 percent in Table D2 are about the same as the results for the more extensive 1 percent criterion, and slightly stronger than the slightly more restrictive criteria of 3 percent and 5 percent. Given substantial producer business excluded from the networks by a two-percent criterion (about a quarter of producer business on average), I tested for industry differences in the amount of business excluded, and report in Chapter 5 that controlling for the percent of producer business included in an industry's network adds nothing to the Table 5.1 predictions.

Third, after defining the boundary of a network, I normalize connections to the relative proportion of business transacted within the network. The four models to the left in Table D2 use p_{ij} normalized to sum to one across all production industries in the economy. The four models to the right in Table D2 use p_{ij} normalized within the immediate network around an industry: $p_{ij} = p_{ij} / \Sigma_k p_{ik}$, $i \neq j$, where the sum is across all industries k in the immediate network excluding industry i itself. This assumes that the connections most relevant to the focal industry are the connections within its immediate network, not connections across the economy. Normalizing within the immediate network is exactly what is done with manager networks defined by survey network data, so I am comfortable using the same operationalization with industry networks to obtain stronger network effects. The final result is that the 2% column to the right in Table D2 is the baseline network model used in Chapter 5 (model A in Table 5.1).

Non-manufacturing

Aggregation is not an actionable issue for the manufacturing industries in Chapter 5 because I use the most detailed input–output categories available. Non-manufacturing categories and a measure of producer organization within the categories are taken from an unpublished report in which structural equivalence between detailed input–output

Table D2 Baseline Model Predictions of Price–Cost Margins for Alternative Boundaries around the Immediate Network

Criterion Business for Inclusion in the Immediate Network:	Dollar Flows Normalized across the Whole Economy				Dollar Flows Normalized within Immediate Network			
	1%	2%	3%	5%	1%	2%	3%	5%
Log(100 − O)	−5.58** (1.45)	−5.60** (1.45)	−5.66** (1.47)	−5.57** (1.44)	−5.56** (1.42)	−5.42** (1.41)	−5.33** (1.41)	−5.17** (1.41)
Log(C)	−2.31** (.62)	−2.03** (.56)	−2.06** (.64)	−1.61** (.43)	−4.22** (.75)	−4.39** (.80)	−3.79** (.80)	−3.37** (.77)
1987	2.33** (.40)	2.33** (.40)	2.40** (.40)	2.31** (.40)	2.50** (.40)	2.38** (.41)	2.30** (.41)	2.36** (.41)
Intercept	40.72	40.29	40.34	39.37	47.13	48.41	47.37	46.29
R²	.12	.12	.11	.12	.16	.15	.14	.14

Note: These are ordinary least-square regression equations predicting non-negative price–cost margins in manufacturing industries corresponding to unique four-digit SIC categories in 1987 and 1992 (N = 632). Log(100 − O) measures the constraint of severe competition between producers in an industry (O is the four-firm concentration ratio). Network constraint C measures dependence on concentrated supplier-customer industries. Standard errors (in parentheses) are corrected for autocorrelation across repeated observations of same industry ("cluster" option in STATA). * P < .05 ** P < .001.

categories was used to test the boundaries around US Department of Commerce aggregate categories (Burt, 1998b).

The 42 non-manufacturing industries from the 1998 report are listed at the end of this appendix, in Table D3. The first nine industries describe agriculture, mining, and construction. The nine correspond to aggregate categories in the 1987 printed benchmark input–output table. For example, the first row of Table D3 lists data on the "Livestock and livestock products" industry in 1987. The row lists year, "1987," then a concentration score of "0.538" explained in a moment. The column labeled "N" in Table D3 lists the number of detailed input–output categories combined in each aggregate category. The "Livestock and livestock products" industry contains four detailed categories in 1987: 10100 "Diary farm products," 10200 "Poultry and eggs," 10301 "Meat animals," and 10302 "Miscellaneous livestock." Detailed categories within each aggregate category are published with the input–output tables (Lawson and Teske, 1994:93–97; Lawson, 1997:58–62). Identification codes for each industry are listed in the column labeled "ID" in Table D3. The final column contains the industry name (followed in parentheses by SIC categories combined in the aggregate category, also published with the benchmark tables).

The other 33 industries in Table D3 are subdivisions of, or combinations across, the 27 aggregate distribution and service sectors distinguished in the 1987 and 1992 benchmark input–output tables. In theory, detailed categories combined in an aggregate category have nearly identical patterns of buying and selling. Detailed categories with similar patterns of buying and selling are "structurally equivalent" in network terminology (see Figure 8.5 in Chapter 8 for numerical illustration). Where the structural equivalence analysis of buying and selling among detailed categories revealed segregated clusters within an aggregate category, I divided the aggregate category down to separate categories for the different clusters. The Department of Commerce distinguished 77 aggregate categories in the benchmark input–output tables just before the 1987 table, then 88 aggregate categories in the 1987 and 1992 benchmark tables. The 88 aggregate categories were revised to 123 in the structural equivalence analysis. The revised industry categories have more reliable boundaries and higher construct validity (Burt, 1998b): Structural equivalence within industry categories increases across the three partitions (65.7% on average for the 77 categories, 70.1% for the 88 categories, 78.4% for the 123 categories). Variation in price–cost margins is increasingly between, rather than within, industries across the three partitions (48.9% between industries for the 77 categories, 49.8% between for the 88 categories, 71.1% between for the 123 categories).

The ID codes in Table D3 show where Department of Commerce categories were expanded. Identification codes follow the convention used by the Department of Commerce, and are the codes with which non-manufacturing industries are identified in the source network data available on my university research website. The initial two digits are the industry ID in the Department of Commerce 77-category partition. For example, "65" is the transportation industry. A capital letter following a digit indicates an industry expanded from the 77-category partition. For example, the transportation industry was expanded by the Department of Commerce for the 1987 benchmark input–output table to distinguish five industries: railroads (65A), trucking and warehousing (65B), water transportation (65C), air transportation (65D), and a residual category of pipelines, freight forwarders, and travel agents (65E). Where there is no capital letter following the digit, the category continued unchanged from the initial 77-category partition. For example, industry 67 continued to be radio and TV broadcasting. Finally, a lower-case letter at the end of an ID number in Table D3 marks an industry expanded from the 88-category partition. For example, the residual transportation category contained a pipeline industry (65Eb) with a pattern of buying and selling distinct from the pattern for freight forwarders and travel agents (65Ea).

I tried three measures of concentration in non-manufacturing. For each, I computed a network constraint variable based on four-firm concentration in the manufacturing industries and a concentration approximation in the 42 non-manufacturing industries, then estimated a network constraint effect in the baseline network model.

The first alternative was approximations based on company size distributions as used in previous research and described in Chapter 5. These data yield the estimates reported in Chapter 5 for the baseline network model (the 2% column to the right in Table D2, model A in Table 5.1), reproduced here as a reference point:

$$PCM = 48.41 - 5.42 \text{ Log} (100 - O) - 4.39 \text{ Log} (C) + 2.38 \text{ D87},$$
$$(1.41) \qquad\qquad (.80) \qquad\qquad (.41)$$

which generates a squared multiple correlation of .15, a -3.83 t-test for the negative effect of rivalry within the industry, and a -5.47 t-test for network constraint from industry suppliers and customers.

Second, I tried network constraint assuming that non-manufacturing industries (farming, mining, construction, services, and distribution) are so full of competitors that concentration in non-manufacturing can be treated as zero. I get the following estimates for the baseline model:

$$PCM = 48.41 - 5.42 \text{ Log} (100 - O) - 4.39 \text{ Log} (C) + 2.38 \text{ D87},$$
$$(1.41) \qquad\qquad (.80) \qquad\qquad (.41)$$

which generates a squared multiple correlation of .09, a -3.41 t-test for the negative effect of rivalry within the industry, and a negligible -1.21 t-test for network constraint.

Third, I tried an approximation more sophisticated than the one based on company size. The unpublished report provides a measure of producer organization in 1987 and 1992 (Burt, 1998b:Table 3) from which I derived scores in non-manufacturing analogous to the concentration ratios in manufacturing.

"Effective organization" (EO) was introduced to measure how well competition within an industry, as competition affected profits, was captured for organization research by traditional concentration data (Burt, *et al.* 2002). EO scores are obtained by reversing the baseline network model. Instead of predicting price–cost margins from O and C as measures of industry structure, the observed price–cost in an industry and its dependence weights on other sectors are held constant (i.e., the data provided by an input–output table are held constant), and producer concentration in each industry is obtained numerically so as to align observed profit margins with the level expected from industry structure. In industries where margins are higher than expected, producers are "effectively" more organized than they appear to be. Such industries tend to be regional markets (versus national) or subject to government regulation (Burt et al., 2002). For example, there are numerous hotels operating in the United States, but only one down the street from your business, so your local hotel can enjoy profits higher than would be expected from the number of hotels operating nationally. In industries where margins are lower than expected from observed industry structure, producers are "effectively" less organized than they appear to be, which is primarily correlated with imports increasing the level of competition within an industry above the level implied by concentration among American producers (Burt *et al.*, 2002).

Using EO scores to approximate concentration in non-manufacturing, I get the following estimates for the baseline model:

$$\text{PCM} = 46.78 - 5.16 \text{ Log } (100 - O) - 3.26 \text{ Log } (C) + 2.19 \text{ D87},$$
$$(1.47) \qquad\qquad (1.13) \qquad\qquad (.40)$$

which generates a squared multiple correlation of .11, a -3.50 t-test for the negative effect of rivalry within the industry, and a -2.89 t-test for network constraint from industry suppliers and customers. The one change I made to the EO scores was to adjust them to a metric comparable to the four-firm concentration ratios in manufacturing. EO scores average .551 in 1987, and .535 in 1992, across the 80 aggregate manufacturing industries distinguished in Burt (1998b). Four-firm concentration ratios average .395 in 1987, and .405 in 1992, across the 361 detailed manufacturing industries analyzed in Chapter 5. To convert the non-manufacturing EO scores in Burt (1998b:Table 3) to a scale comparable to the manufacturing four-firm concentration ratios used in Chapter 5, I multiplied EO scores in non-manufacturing by .717 in 1987 and .757 in 1992 (mean EO in manufacturing divided by mean four-firm concentration in manufacturing).

The network constraint effect in the above equation based on the EO approximation to O in non-manufacturing is significantly negative, but weaker than the effect estimated with size-based approximations, so I returned to the size-based approximations for the analysis in Chapter 5 and report them in Table D3 in the column labeled "O."

Table D3 Aggregate Non-Manufacturing Industries

Year	O	N	ID	Aggregate Input–Output Industry (SIC codes)
1987	0.538	4	1	Livestock & livestock products (*019, 0251–3, 0211–14, *0219, 024, *0259, 0271–3, *0279, *029)
1992	0.627	4		
1987	0.639	13	2	Other agricultural products (011, 013, 016, 017, 018, *019, *0219, *0259, *029)
1992	0.667	13		
1987	0.626	2	3	Forestry & fishery products (081, 083, 097, 091)
1992	0.667	2		
1987	0.369	2	4	Agricultural, forestry, & fishery services (0254, *0279, 071–2, 075–6, 078, 085, 092)
1992	0.560	2		
1987	0.417	3	5–6	Metallic ores mining (iron, copper & other; 101–4, 106, *108, 1094, 1099)
1992	0.303	3		
1987	0.620	1	7	Coal mining (122–3, *124)
1992	0.690	1		
1987	0.681	1	8	Crude petroleum & natural gas (131–2, *138)
1992	0.700	1		
1987	0.580	5	9–10	Nonmetallic minerals mining (141–2, 144, 145, 147, *148, 149)
1992	0.584	5		
1987	0.272	5	11–12	Construction (15, 16, 17, *108, *124, *138, *148, *6552)
1992	0.239	15		
1987	0.347	2	65A	Railroads & related services (40, 41, 474)
1992	0.375	2		
1987	0.342	1	65B	Motor freight transportation & warehousing (421–3)
1992	0.312	2		
1987	0.173	1	65C	Water transportation (44)
1992	0.345	1		
1987	0.335	1	65D	Air transportation (45)
1992	0.328	1		
1987	0.408	2	65Ea	† Freight forwarders & travel agents (472–3, 478)
1992	0.496	2		

(continued)

Table D3 (Continued)

Year	O	N	ID	Aggregate Input–Output Industry (SIC codes)
1987	0.694	1	65Eb	† Pipelines (except natural gas; 46)
1992	0.740	1		
1987	0.525	1	66	Communication (except radio & TV; 481–2, 484, 489)
1992	0.581	2		
1987	0.522	1	67	Radio & TV broadcasting (483)
1992	0.646	1		
1987	0.582	1	68A	Electric services (utilities; 491, 4931)
1992	0.632	1		
1987	0.577	1	68B	Gas production & distribution (utilities; 4922–5, 4932, 4939)
1992	0.664	2		
1987	0.007	2	68C	Water & sanitary services (494, 4952–3, 4959, 496–7)
1992	0.475	2		
1987	0.395	1	69A	Wholesale trade (50, 51)
1992	0.406	1		
1987	0.499	1	69B	Retail trade (52–7, 59)
1992	0.592	1		
1987	0.301	3	70A	Finance (60, 61, 62, 67, excluding 6732)
1992	0.516	3		
1987	0.477	1	70Ba	† Insurance carriers (63)
1992	0.548	1		
1987	0.663	1	70Bb	† Insurance agents (64)
1992	0.703	1		
1987	0.704	1	71A	Owner-occupied dwellings (—)
1992	0.747	1		
1987	0.644	1	71Ba	† Real estate agents (65, excluding 6552)
1992	0.680	1		
1987	0.717	1	71Bb	† Royalties (—)
1992	0.757	1		
1987	0.411	1	72A	Hotels & lodging places (701–4)

(continued)

Table D3 (Continued)

Year	O	N	ID	Aggregate Input–Output Industry (SIC codes)
1992	0.475	2		
1987	0.402	6	72B	Personal & repair services (except auto; 721–6, 729, 762–4)
1992	0.518	6		
1987	0.388	1	73A	Computer & data processing services (737)
1992	0.467	1		
1987	0.466	1	73Ba	† Legal services (81)
1992	0.542	1		
1987	0.449	1	73Bb	† Engineering services (871)
1992	0.529	1		
1987	0.197	2	73BC	† Management, accounting, & testing services (872, 873, 874, 89)
1992	0.483	3		
1987	0.462	6	73Ca	† General business services (7331, 732, 7334, 7338, 734–6, 7381–3, 7389, 769)
1992	0.567	6		
1987	0.507	1	73Cb	† Photographic services (7335–6, 7384)
1992	0.647	1		
1987	0.425	1	73D	Advertising services (731)
1992	0.526	1		
1987	0.339	1	74	Eating & drinking places (58)
1992	0.412	1		
1987	0.446	3	75	Automotive repair & services (751–3, 7542, 7549)
1992	0.491	3		
1987	0.419	8	76	Amusements (781–4, 791–3, 7941, 7948, 7991–3, 7996–7, 7999)
1992	0.547	8		
1987	0.342	4	77A	Health services (074, 801–3, 8041–3, 8049, 805–6, 807–9)
1992	0.453	6		
1987	0.223	11	77B	Educational & social services (6732, 821–4, 829, 832–3, 835–6, 839, 84, 861–6, 869, 8733)
1992	0.408	11		

Note: Data are explained in the text. Asterisk indicates that partial SIC category is in the row industry. Dagger (†) indicates a row industry disaggregated from a broader input–output category.

E Means, Standard Deviations, and Correlations

Table E1 Product-Launch Employees

	Mean	Standard Deviation	1	2	3	4	5	6	7	8	9	10	11	12
Direct Network Constraint	3.79	.48	—	-.063	-.469	.229	.394	-.571	-.263	.011	-.190	-.091	-.170	-.539
Indirect Network Constraint	3.66	.31	-.093	—	-.020	-.074	-.054	-.027	-.134	.058	-.036	.186	-.129	-.207
Compensation	.00	1.00	-.430	-.037	—	.101	-.328	.694	.374	-.168	.423	-.080	.233	.520
Annual Evaluation	.00	1.00	-.229	-.074	.101	—	-.091	.133	-.055	-.073	-.047	.009	.088	.133
Job Rank (Ind.)	1.57	1.48	.350	-.039	-.298	-.091	—	-.749	-.044	.008	-.186	-.052	-.077	-.421
Job Rank (Mgr.)	.96	1.34	-.472	-.033	.627	.133	-.760	—	.369	-.237	.172	.091	.186	.664
Age	38.65	6.91	-.228	-.125	.407	-.055	-.057	.402	—	-.087	.027	.331	.111	.325
Female	.29	.46	.019	.008	-.192	-.073	-.011	-.222	-.122	—	.148	-.001	-.024	-.189
Sales Function	.41	.49	-.113	-.027	.391	-.047	-.130	.077	-.051	.140	—	-.244	.017	.254
Years with Company	5.37	4.27	-.020	.089	-.147	.009	-.031	.065	.283	.065	-.277	—	-.047	-.020
Regional HQ	.09	.28	-.134	-.126	.277	.088	-.051	.143	.092	-.015	.030	-.065	—	.146
Targeted by Study	.30	.46	-.463	-.199	.453	.133	-.338	.561	.364	-.129	.159	.001	.131	—

Note: Moments below the diagonal are computed across 258 employees, except the correlations with annual evaluations, which are computed across 182 employees. Correlations above the diagonal are computed across the 182 employees for whom evaluations were available. Network constraint is the log of constraint. The two performance variables are measured as z-scores. The job-rank variables distinguish four levels of individual contributors (Ind.) and four levels of managers (Mgr.).

Table E2 Supply-Chain Managers

	Mean	Standard Deviation	1	2	3	4	5	6	7	8	9	10	11	12	13	14
Direct Network Constraint	4.03	.47	—													
Indirect Network Constraint	3.89	.40	.230	—												
Salary	.00	1.00	-.574	-.394	—											
Annual Evaluation	.00	1.00	-.301	-.114	.338	—										
Idea Value	.00	1.00	-.329	-.165	.312	.109	—									
Job Rank	1.95	1.42	-.584	-.411	.904	.336	.308	—								
Age	49.17	7.33	-.057	-.082	.149	-.141	.037	.102	—							
College Degree	.67	.47	-.246	-.218	.424	.175	.203	.461	.002	—						
Graduate Degree	.31	.46	-.202	-.189	.316	.088	.158	.351	-.102	.094	—					
Minority	.36	.48	.117	.014	-.170	.072	-.025	-.168	-.102	-.216	-.103	—				
High-Tech Businesses	.32	.47	.030	-.035	.090	.015	.018	.007	.002	.055	-.026	.062	—			
Low-Tech Business	.07	.26	.033	.034	-.127	-.078	.055	-.069	.016	-.027	.076	.059	-.190	—		
Regional HQ	.15	.36	-.112	-.100	.182	.146	.039	.133	.028	-.029	-.018	.252	.363	-.092	—	
Corporate HQ	.17	.37	-.114	-.028	.343	.047	.095	.296	-.059	.176	.082	-.131	.068	.015	-.189	—

Note: Correlations are computed across 455 survey respondents. Network constraint is the log of constraint. The three performance variables are measured as z-scores.

Table E3 HR Employees

	Mean	Standard Deviation												
Direct Network Constraint	3.57	.61	—											
Indirect Network Constraint	3.63	.33	.365	—										
Total Compensation	.00	1.00	-.439	-.259	—									
Bonus	.00	1.00	-.453	-.236	.945	—								
Job Rank (Ind.)	.80	1.11	.235	.160	-.448	-.325	—							
Job Rank (Mgr.)	1.76	1.30	-.332	-.245	.762	.590	-.644	—						
Evaluation Positive	.31	.47	-.151	-.103	.200	.154	-.033	.150	—					
Evaluation Average	.53	.50	-.013	.002	-.038	-.017	-.009	.007	-.714	—				
Years with the Firm	6.86	6.71	-.321	-.283	.380	.390	-.141	.296	.091	.032	—			
Minority	.60	.46	.187	.251	-.116	-.133	.055	-.138	-.143	.056	-.164	—		
Corporate HQ	.52	.50	-.254	-.386	.123	.125	-.141	.101	.062	.002	.053	-.296	—	
Field Office	.19	.40	.191	.340	.036	-.024	-.030	.037	-.006	-.035	-.193	.538	-.507	—

Note: Correlations are computed across 283 HR employees. Network constraint is the log of constraint. Compensation is measured as a z-score to indicate relative annual compensation. The job-rank variables distinguish three levels of individual contributors (Ind.) and four levels of managers (Mgr.).

Table E4 Investment Bankers

	Mean	Standard Deviation	1	2	3	4	5	6	7	8	9	10	11
Direct Network Constraint	2.18	.63	—										
Indirect Network Constraint	2.06	.43	.457	—									
Annual Compensation	.00	1.00	-.345	-.195	—								
Annual Bonus Only	.00	1.00	-.351	-.194	.998	—							
Senior Job Rank	.81	.40	-.138	-.039	.323	.301	—						
Peer Evaluation	3.05	.52	-.185	-.066	.286	.299	-.119	—					
Seniority	8.67	6.56	-.189	-.034	.262	.254	.171	.074	—				
Minority	.14	.34	.125	-.036	-.047	-.043	-.072	.024	-.060	—			
US Headquarters	.58	.49	.073	-.016	.159	.161	.061	.009	.161	.164	—		
Status	47.41	30.15	-.586	-.332	.368	.371	.119	.166	.111	-.049	.070	—	
Colleague Status	52.53	13.21	-.320	-.560	.222	.220	.021	.023	-.018	.017	.049	.270	—

Note: Means and correlations are computed from annual data pooled across three years (469 observations). Network constraint is the log of constraint. Compensation is measured as a z-score within each year to indicate relative annual compensation. Status is the number of people who evaluated a banker in the annual 360 evaluations. Colleague status is the average number of people who evaluated the people who evaluated the banker.

Table E5 Analysts

	Mean	Standard Deviation	1	2	3	4	5	6	7	8	9	10	11	12	13
Direct Network Constraint	2.11	.70	—													
Indirect Network Constraint	1.75	.48	.554	—												
All-America Team	.00	1.00	-.353	-.301	—											
Senior Job Rank	.90	.31	-.210	-.172	.051	—										
Peer Evaluation	3.06	.35	-.272	-.132	.300	.065	—									
Seniority	7.31	6.69	-.209	-.172	.084	.014	.071	—								
Minority	.20	.40	-.021	-.129	.099	.076	-.041	-.019	—							
US Headquarters	.57	.50	-.214	-.248	.269	-.091	.341	.331	.158	—						
Office in the US	.61	.49	-.262	-.302	.331	-.063	.447	.320	.176	.893	—					
Forecast Accuracy	.25	.39	-.126	-.212	.157	.060	-.054	-.031	.039	-.049	-.024	—				
In I/B/E/S Data	.60	.49	-.199	-.243	.263	.135	-.171	-.172	.059	-.291	-.236	.526	—			
Status	31.07	16.61	-.727	-.331	.270	.188	.206	.060	.009	.043	.062	.074	.160	—		
Colleague Status	38.17	12.29	-.321	-.762	.280	.201	-.047	.100	.176	.054	.134	.278	.365	.307	—

Note: Means and correlations are computed from annual data pooled across two years (351 observations). Network constraint is the log of constraint. The performance variable, election to the All-America Research Team, is for each year an analyst's highest rating from *Institutional Investor* (4 for election to first team, 3 for second team, 2 for third team, 1 for runner-up, 0 for not being named). Status is the number of people who evaluated an analyst. Colleague status is the average number of people evaluating the people who evaluated the analyst. The performance variable is measured as a z-score for each year (criterion variable for Model E in Table 3.3).

Table E6 Industries

	Mean	Standard Deviation									
Price–Cost Margin (PCM)	16.89	9.46	—								
1987	.50	.50	.121	—							
Log(100–O)	3.99	.50	-.271	.009	—						
Log(C)	2.52	.55	-.237	.009	-.061	—					
IC1: Unweighted Average	2.25	.37	-.240	-.055	-.116	.377	—				
IC2: Weighted Average	2.17	.48	-.187	-.037	-.191	.396	.838	—			
IC3: Percent Low	3.70	.80	.230	.034	.145	-.508	-.644	-.770	—		
IC4: Percent High	1.63	1.53	-.205	-.040	-.134	.335	.784	.815	-.571	—	
IC5: Extended Network	1.02	.29	-.227	-.039	-.035	.619	.333	.451	-.533	.408	—

Note: Means and correlations are computed across non-negative price–cost margins in the 320 manufacturing industries corresponding to unique four-digit SIC categories in 1987 and 1992 (N = 632). All variables are measured as log scores, except price–cost margins and the dummy variable distinguishing observations in 1987. Criterion to be a supplier-customer is 2% of industry business (see discussion of Table D2 in Appendix D). Log(100 − O) measures the constraint of rivalry between producers in an industry (O is the four-firm concentration ratio). Log(C) measures the network constraint of dependence on concentrated supplier-customer industries (Eq. 1 in Chapter 5). Indirect network constraint measures are discussed in the text around Table 5.1 in the chapter: IC1 is unweighted indirect network constraint on industry, IC2 is weighted average indirect network constraint on industry, IC3 is percent industry business with low-constraint supplier-customer industries, IC4 is percent industry business with high-constraint supplier-customer industries, and IC5 is total network constraint across indirect supplier-customer industries.

F Network Weights for the Organization in Figure 8.5

Table F1 Path Distances

	1	2	3	4	5	6	7	8	9	10	11	12	13	14	15	16	17	18	19
1	–	1	1	2	2	2	2	3	3	3	3	3	3	3	3	3	3	3	3
2	1	–	2	1	1	3	3	4	4	4	4	4	4	4	4	2	2	2	2
3	1	2	–	3	3	1	1	2	2	2	2	2	2	2	2	4	4	4	4
4	2	1	3	–	2	4	4	5	5	5	5	5	5	5	5	3	3	3	1
5	2	1	3	2	–	4	4	5	5	5	5	5	5	5	5	3	3	3	3
6	2	3	1	4	4	–	2	3	3	3	3	3	1	1	1	5	5	5	5
7	2	3	1	4	4	2	–	1	1	1	1	1	3	3	3	5	5	5	5
8	3	4	2	5	5	3	1	–	1	1	1	1	4	4	4	6	6	6	6
9	3	4	2	5	5	3	1	1	–	1	1	1	4	4	4	6	6	6	6
10	3	4	2	5	5	3	1	1	1	–	1	1	4	4	4	6	6	6	6
11	3	4	2	5	5	3	1	1	1	1	–	1	4	4	4	6	6	6	6
12	3	4	2	5	5	3	1	1	1	1	1	–	4	4	4	6	6	6	6
13	3	4	2	5	5	1	3	4	4	4	4	4	–	1	1	4	4	4	4
14	3	4	2	5	5	1	3	4	4	4	4	4	1	–	1	4	4	4	4
15	3	4	2	5	5	1	3	4	4	4	4	4	1	1	–	4	4	4	4
16	3	2	4	3	3	5	5	6	6	6	6	6	4	4	4	–	1	1	2
17	3	2	4	3	3	5	5	6	6	6	6	6	4	4	4	1	–	1	2
18	3	2	4	3	3	5	5	6	6	6	6	6	4	4	4	1	1	–	2
19	3	2	4	1	3	5	5	6	6	6	6	6	4	4	4	2	2	2	–

Note: Cell (i,j) is the shortest number of links required to connect the person in row i to the person in column j.

Table F2 Strength of Relations (Z_{ij})

	1	2	3	4	5	6	7	8	9	10	11	12	13	14	15	16	17	18	19
1	1.00	1.00	1.00	.500	.500	.500	.500	.250	.250	.250	.250	.250	.250	.250	.250	.250	.250	.250	.250
2	1.00	1.00	.500	1.00	1.00	.250	.250	.125	.125	.125	.125	.125	.125	.500	.500	.500	.500	.500	.500
3	1.00	.500	1.00	.250	.250	.500	.500	.063	.063	.063	.063	.063	.063	.125	.125	.125	.125	1.00	1.00
4	.500	1.00	.250	1.00	.500	.125	.125	.063	.063	.063	.063	.063	.063	.250	.250	.250	.250	.125	.125
5	.500	1.00	.250	.500	1.00	.125	.125	.063	.063	.063	.063	.063	.063	.250	.250	.250	.250	.125	.125
6	.500	.250	.500	.125	.125	1.00	.500	.250	.250	.250	.250	.250	.250	.063	.063	.063	.063	.500	.500
7	.500	.250	.500	.125	.125	.500	1.00	.250	.250	.250	.250	.250	.250	.063	.063	.063	.063	.500	.500
8	.250	.125	.063	.063	.063	.250	.250	1.00	1.00	1.00	1.00	1.00	1.00	.031	.031	.031	.031	.125	.125
9	.250	.125	.063	.063	.063	.250	.250	1.00	1.00	1.00	1.00	1.00	1.00	.031	.031	.031	.031	.125	.125
10	.250	.125	.063	.063	.063	.250	.250	1.00	1.00	1.00	1.00	1.00	1.00	.031	.031	.031	.031	.125	.125
11	.250	.125	.063	.063	.063	.250	.250	1.00	1.00	1.00	1.00	1.00	1.00	.031	.031	.031	.031	.125	.125
12	.250	.125	.063	.063	.063	.250	.250	1.00	1.00	1.00	1.00	1.00	1.00	.031	.031	.031	.031	.125	.125
13	.250	.125	.063	.063	.063	.250	.250	1.00	1.00	1.00	1.00	1.00	1.00	.031	.031	.031	.031	.125	.125
14	.250	.500	.125	.250	.250	.063	.063	.031	.031	.031	.031	.031	.031	1.00	1.00	1.00	1.00	.125	.125
15	.250	.500	.125	.250	.250	.063	.063	.031	.031	.031	.031	.031	.031	1.00	1.00	1.00	1.00	.125	.125
16	.250	.500	.125	.250	.250	.063	.063	.031	.031	.031	.031	.031	.031	1.00	1.00	1.00	1.00	.125	.125
17	.250	.500	.125	.250	.250	.063	.063	.031	.031	.031	.031	.031	.031	1.00	1.00	1.00	1.00	.125	.125
18	.250	.500	1.00	.125	.125	.500	.500	.125	.125	.125	.125	.125	.125	.125	.125	.125	.125	1.00	.500
19	.250	.500	1.00	.125	.125	.500	.500	.125	.125	.125	.125	.125	.125	.125	.125	.125	.125	.500	1.00

Note: Cell (i,j) measures the strength of the relation from row i to column j. Strength varies from zero to one as a function of path distance (shorter connections are stronger relations).

Table F3 Structural and Role Equivalence Distances (d_{ij})

	1	2	3	4	5	6	7	8	9	10	11	12	13	14	15	16	17	18	19
1	—	.10	.10	.26	.24	.24	.24	.14	.14	.14	.14	.14	.14	.14	.14	.14	.13	.13	.13
2	1.64	—	.	.16	.15	.15	.15	.07	.07	.07	.07	.07	.07	.07	.07	.07	.23	.23	.23
3	1.64	2.81	—	.16	.15	.15	.15	.07	.07	.07	.07	.07	.07	.07	.07	.07	.23	.23	.23
4	2.34	1.76	3.34	—	.04	.04	.04	.13	.13	.13	.13	.13	.13	.13	.13	.13	.39	.39	.39
5	2.34	1.76	3.34	2.60	—	.	.	.11	.11	.11	.11	.11	.11	.11	.11	.11	.37	.37	.37
6	2.34	3.34	1.76	3.71	3.71	—	.	.11	.11	.11	.11	.11	.11	.11	.11	.11	.37	.37	.37
7	2.34	3.34	1.76	3.71	3.71	2.60	—	.11	.11	.11	.11	.11	.11	.11	.11	.11	.37	.37	.37
8	2.52	3.39	3.39	3.63	3.63	2.83	2.83	—	.	.	.	.	.	.	.	.	.27	.27	.27
9	2.52	3.39	3.39	3.63	3.63	2.83	2.83	.95	—	.	.	.	.	.	.	.	.27	.27	.27
10	2.52	3.39	3.39	3.63	3.63	2.83	2.83	.95	.95	—	.	.	.	.	.	.	.27	.27	.27
11	2.52	3.39	3.39	3.63	3.63	2.83	2.83	2.89	2.89	2.89	—	.	.	.	.	.	.27	.27	.27
12	2.52	3.39	3.39	3.63	3.63	2.83	2.83	2.89	2.89	2.89	2.89	—	.	.	.	.	.27	.27	.27
13	2.52	3.39	3.39	3.63	3.63	2.83	2.83	2.89	2.89	2.89	2.89	2.89	—	.	.	.	.27	.27	.27
14	2.52	3.39	2.15	.95	.95	3.63	3.63	3.44	3.44	3.44	3.44	3.44	3.44	—	.	.	.27	.27	.27
15	2.52	3.39	2.15	.95	.95	3.63	3.63	3.44	3.44	3.44	3.44	3.44	3.44	3.44	—	.	.27	.27	.27
16	2.52	3.39	2.15	.95	.95	3.63	3.63	3.44	3.44	3.44	3.44	3.44	3.44	3.44	3.44	—	.27	.27	.27
17	2.08	2.99	1.38	2.46	3.23	2.99	2.99	2.99	2.99	2.99	2.99	2.99	2.99	2.42	2.42	2.42	—	.	.
18	2.08	2.99	1.38	2.46	3.23	2.99	2.99	2.99	2.99	2.99	2.99	2.99	2.99	2.42	2.42	2.42	2.42	—	.
19	2.08	2.99	1.38	2.46	3.23	2.99	2.99	2.99	2.99	2.99	2.99	2.99	2.99	2.42	2.42	2.42	2.42	2.42	—

Note: Cell (i,j) measures the distance between the persons in row i and column j. Structural equivalence distance is below the diagonal. Role equivalence distance is above the diagonal. A period "." indicates zero distance (complete equivalence).

Table F4 Structural Equivalence Weights (W_{ij})

	1	2	3	4	5	6	7	8	9	10	11	12	13	14	15	16	17	18	19
1	.91	.04	.04	.	.06	.	.	.07	.	.	.	.	.	.03	.03	.03	.05	.05	.05
2	.08	.57	.	.06	.	.	.	.	.	.	.	.	.	.03	.03	.03	.05	.05	.05
3	.07	.07	.60	.	.01	.06	.06	.	.	.	.	.	.	.	.	.	.	.	.
4	.03	.07	.	.50	.01	.	.	.	.	.	.	.	.	.01	.01	.01	.12	.12	.12
5	.02	.06	.01	.01	.40	.	.	.	.	.	.	.	.	.16	.16	.16	.01	.01	.01
6	.02	.	.06	.	.	.40	.01	.16	.16	.16	.	.	.	.	.	.	.	.	.
7	.02	.	.06	.	.	.01	.40	.16	.16	.16	.	.	.	.	.	.	.	.	.
8	.01	.	.02	.	.	.16	.16	.28	.28	.28	.	.	.	.	.	.	.	.	.
9	.01	.	.02	.	.	.16	.16	.28	.28	.28	.	.	.	.	.	.	.	.	.
10	.01	.	.02	.	.	.16	.16	.28	.28	.28	.	.	.	.	.	.	.	.	.
11	.01	.02	.02	.	.	.11	.11	.	.	.	.28	.28	.28	.	.	.	.	.	.
12	.01	.01	.02	.	.	.11	.11	.	.	.	.28	.28	.28	.	.	.	.	.	.
13	.01	.01	.02	.	.	.11	.11	.	.	.	.28	.28	.28	.	.	.	.	.	.
14	.01	.02	.	.	.	.	.	.	.	.	.28	.28	.28	.28	.28	.28	.	.	.
15	.01	.02	.	.	.	.	.	.	.	.	.28	.28	.28	.28	.28	.28	.	.	.
16	.01	.02	.	.	.	.	.	.	.	.	.28	.28	.28	.28	.28	.28	.	.	.
17	.01	.02	.	.06	.	.	.	.	.	.	.	.	.	.	.	.	.30	.30	.30
18	.01	.02	.	.06	.	.	.	.	.	.	.	.	.	.	.	.	.30	.30	.30
19	.01	.02	.	.06	.	.	.	.	.	.	.	.	.	.	.	.	.30	.30	.30

Note: Element w_{ij} is the proportional extent to which i's situation is frame of reference for i's perception (for structural equivalence distances in Table F3 and $v = 3$). A period "." indicates a weight smaller than .005.

Table F5 Role Equivalence Weights (W_{ij})

	1	2	3	4	5	6	7	8	9	10	11	12	13	14	15	16	17	18	19
1	.45	.09	.09	.	.	.	.	.03	.03	.03	.03	.03	.03	.03	.03	.03	.03	.03	.03
2	.01	.25	.25	.	.	.16	.16	.04	.04	.04	.04	.04	.04	.04	.04	.04	.04	.04	.04
3	.01	.25	.25	.	.	.16	.16	.04	.04	.04	.04	.04	.04	.04	.04	.04	.04	.04	.04
4	.	.01	.01	.	.16	.16	.16	.03	.03	.03	.03	.03	.03	.03	.03	.03	.03	.03	.03
5	.	.01	.01	.	.16	.16	.16	.03	.03	.03	.03	.03	.03	.03	.03	.03	.03	.03	.03
6	.	.01	.01	.	.16	.16	.16	.03	.03	.03	.03	.03	.03	.03	.03	.03	.03	.03	.03
7	.	.01	.01	.	.16	.16	.16	.03	.03	.03	.03	.03	.03	.03	.03	.03	.03	.03	.03
8	.	.01	.01	.	.	.	.	.08	.08	.08	.08	.08	.08	.08	.08	.08	.08	.08	.08
9	.	.01	.01	.	.	.	.	.08	.08	.08	.08	.08	.08	.08	.08	.08	.08	.08	.08
10	.	.01	.01	.	.	.	.	.08	.08	.08	.08	.08	.08	.08	.08	.08	.08	.08	.08
11	.	.01	.01	.	.	.	.	.08	.08	.08	.08	.08	.08	.08	.08	.08	.08	.08	.08
12	.	.01	.01	.	.	.	.	.08	.08	.08	.08	.08	.08	.08	.08	.08	.08	.08	.08
13	.	.01	.01	.	.	.	.	.08	.08	.08	.08	.08	.08	.08	.08	.08	.08	.08	.08
14	.	.01	.01	.	.	.	.	.08	.08	.08	.08	.08	.08	.08	.08	.08	.08	.08	.08
15	.	.01	.01	.	.	.	.	.08	.08	.08	.08	.08	.08	.08	.08	.08	.08	.08	.08
16	.	.01	.01	.	.	.	.	.08	.08	.08	.08	.08	.08	.08	.08	.08	.08	.08	.08
17	.	.01	.01	.	.	.	.	.08	.08	.08	.08	.08	.08	.08	.08	.08	.08	.08	.08
18	.	.01	.01	.	.	.	.	.08	.08	.08	.08	.08	.08	.08	.08	.08	.08	.08	.08
19	.	.01	.01	.	.	.	.	.08	.08	.08	.08	.08	.08	.08	.08	.08	.08	.08	.08

Note: Element w_{ij} in row i, column j, is the proportional extent to which column j's situation is frame of reference for row i's perception (for role equivalence distances in Table F3 and $v = 3$). A period "." indicates a weight smaller than .005.

G Defining Network Peers

I use structural equivalence to define network peers in Chapter 8 (equation 5), claim that brokers have less obvious network peers (intrepid broker hypothesis), and claim that brokers are more likely to move up from structural to role equivalence (network identity hypothesis). This appendix contains argument and evidence for the treatment in Chapter 8.

Connectivity mechanism: Socialization

A foundation was laid with Muzafer Sherif's (1935; 1936) experiment on social norms among college students at Columbia University.[1] The study involved a psychophysics experiment with a stimulus selected for its ambiguity. Students were asked to judge the distance moved by a point of light projected from 15 feet away in a dark room. The point of light was stationary, but appeared to move because of random noise in human sight combined with the lack of visible reference points in the dark room (autokinetic effect, Sherif, 1936:91–92).

When students were alone and asked to evaluate the extent to which the point of light moved, evaluations converged toward a standard for each person; less than one inch for some students, over seven inches for others, with 3.3 inches the average across individuals (Sherif, 1936:102–103). As Sherif (1936:97) quotes from participants, the lack of a reference point made the evaluation difficult (e.g., "It was difficult to estimate the distance the light moved because of the lack of visible neighboring objects") so people relied on their prior evaluations as the best available frame of reference (I "compared with previous distance"), which resulted in different individuals converging on different standards.

When Sherif's students made evaluations in groups of three, group standards emerged. Individual evaluations quickly converged to a group standard consistent across the individuals in the group, and the group standard persisted when the subjects returned later to repeat the experiment alone. Zucker (1977) took up the persistence result to show that the arbitrary group standard could be expected to persist for a dramatically longer period of time if evaluations were embedded in a simple organizational routine (from persistence across seven sessions in Sherif's design to persistence beyond 38 sessions if the group standard is embedded in a simple organizational routine, Zucker, 1977:735).

Outside the lab, sources of contagious opinion and behavior were measured with sociometric choice data. Survey respondents were asked to name their friends or the people with whom they discuss things, then asked about the opinions or behavior of the cited people. A body of research emerged in which people connected by a sociometric link were reported to have similar opinions and behaviors. To name a few of the more influential studies (see Rogers, 2003, for broad review), connected people had similar

---

[1] Sherif (1936:69–70) cites precedent experiments by Allport (1924:260–285) in which groups had what he termed a "leveling" effect, truncating the distribution of personal opinion and behavior to less extreme evaluations (which reflects a "basic human tendency to temper one's opinions and conduct by deference to the opinion and conduct of others," Allport, 1924:278). For the purposes of this book, Sherif's experiment seems to me the precedent for the body of research on contagion launched from MIT and Columbia University that provided the foundation for social capital research. See Turner (1990) on Sherif's links to sociology more broadly.

presidential preferences (Lazarsfeld, Berelson, and Gaudet, 1944; Berelson, Lazarsfeld, and McPhee, 1954), similar student opinion and activity (Festinger, Schachter, and Back, 1950), similar consumer preferences (Katz and Lazarsfeld, 1955), and similar professional practices (Coleman, Katz, and Menzel, 1957).[2]

Following the precedent of Sherif's study, the survey research focused on ambiguous stimuli, stimuli that had no obvious empirical referent, because ambiguous stimuli were likely to reveal social forces at work. Festinger, Schachter, and Back (1950:168–169) gave a working definition often cited in subsequent work:

> If a person driving a car down a street is told by his companion that the street ends in a dead end, this piece of information may be easily checked against physical "reality." He has only to drive on and soon he will find out whether or not the street really does end in this manner.... The situation with regard to social opinions and attitudes is quite different, however. There is no such "physical reality" against which to check. If one person offers the opinion to another that if the democratic candidate for president is elected economic ruin may be expected, the second person may agree or not but he cannot definitely check this opinion against "reality."... The "reality" which settles the question in the case of social attitudes and opinions is the degree to which others with whom one is in communication are believed to share these same attitudes and opinions.

Festinger (1954:118) extrapolated the empirical research into a perspective he termed social comparison theory: "To the extent that objective, non-social means are not available, people evaluate their opinions and abilities by comparison respectively with the opinions and abilities of others." Building on that intuition, Schachter (1959:126) noted that our wide variation in emotions is generated by a narrow range of physiological states occurring in a wide variety of social situations. Emotion is physiology matched to a situation. There can be ambiguity in identifying the emotion appropriate to a situation. I feel anxious. Is it excitement about the task at hand? Am I afraid? Angry? How should I interpret this feeling? The answer lies in watching people "like me" respond, which leads to Schachter's results showing that people afraid of an event are drawn to affiliate with people facing the same event (also see Schachter and Singer, 1962). Schachter (1959:129) concludes: "...the emotions or feelings, like the opinions and abilities, require social evaluation when the emotion-producing situation is ambiguous or uninterpretable in terms of past experience." Toward the end of the era, Coleman, Katz, and Menzel (1966:118–119) offered a similar description of doctors influencing one another's decision to begin prescribing a new antibiotic: "Confronted with the need to make a decision in an ambiguous situation—a situation that does not speak for itself—people turn to each other for cues as to the structure of the situation. When a new drug appears, doctors who are in close interaction with their colleagues will similarly interpret for one another the new stimulus that has presented itself, and will arrive at some shared way of looking at it."

---

[2] Agency in social networks is a contemporary excitement, but it has long been waiting in the wings. Reviewing Katz and Lazarsfeld (1955) in the *American Sociological Review*, Gold (1956:793) concludes with an uneasy feeling: "The acting person seems to have got lost in the decision-making. An outside influence—another person or the mass media—is always the most important factor. I am prompted to predict that, now that Katz and Lazarsfeld have 'rediscovered the primary group' in mass communications, the next episode of 'rediscovery' will involve personality and the self. It can only be a matter of time and serendipity before this crucial 'intervening' variable will be explored." Quite a bit of time, apparently.

Equivalence mechanism: Competition

The concept of structural equivalence emerged in the 1970s as contemporary network analysis evolved from sociometry, so it was not a consideration in the early experiments and survey research on contagion.[3]

Equivalence implicit in early research

Equivalence was nevertheless implicit in the early research. For example, people were sometimes aggregated into groups by factor analyzing sociometric choice data (e.g., MacRae, 1960; Lankford, 1974). A group defined by factor analysis is actually a set of structurally equivalent people because people are put into the same group (load high on the same factor) to the extent that they have similar relations with other people (see e.g., Burt, 1982:47–49, 73–89). Further, some people analyzed as strongly connected were also structurally equivalent because of the overlap between the connectivity and equivalence criteria. Recall the similar spatial distributions by connectivity in Figure 8.5 and structural equivalence in Figure 8.6. More generally, people within groups are structurally equivalent in a population of disconnected, cohesive groups (relation pattern is strong ties within group and no ties beyond group). At the same time that evidence of contagion within the groups is evidence supporting the connectivity criterion, it is often also evidence supporting the equivalence criterion—but the latter possibility went untested.

Turning from the field to the lab, equivalence was implicit in the early experiments. Consider the widely cited experiments by Solomon Asch (1951, 1956) showing that social reality affects evaluations even when social reality contradicts physical reality. Asch wanted to know whether the contagion evident in Sherif's study with ambiguous stimuli was strong enough to affect evaluations of unambiguous stimuli. Figure G1 is a quick overview of the experiment (using the data in Asch, 1951). The perceptual task was to match line lengths between two cards. An example pair of cards is given in Figure G1. One card contains a single vertical line. The other card contains three lines of different lengths. The task is to match the length of the single line with the same-length line on the three-line card. In Figure G1, the match is with line C. Subjects were asked to make 18 matches. The single lines varied from two to ten inches in length. Lines on the three-line card differed on average by 1.6 inches from shortest to longest (see Asch, 1951:180, for research design).

Line length in this experiment is an unambiguous stimulus. Stevens (1957:166) reports from psychophysics experiments that people perceive line length increasing linearly with the actual length of a displayed line ($v = 1$). When alone as if in a

---

[3] Connectivity and equivalence are network instances of a long-standing distinction: classifications based on similarity within categories versus similar relations with other categories. Is a bug to be classified into a category because the bug looks like other bugs in the category or because it has similar relations with categories of predators, hosts, and competitors? Should this variable be considered an indicator of concept A because it is correlated with other indicators of the concept (factor analysis, internal consistency), or because it resembles other indicators of A in its correlations with key concepts related to concept A (canonical correlation, construct validity)? With respect to network analysis, the long-standing distinction became explicit with the emergence of structural equivalence in the 1970s, first in Lorrain and White's (1971) theoretical treatment, then in White, Boorman, and Brieger's (1976) operational treatment.

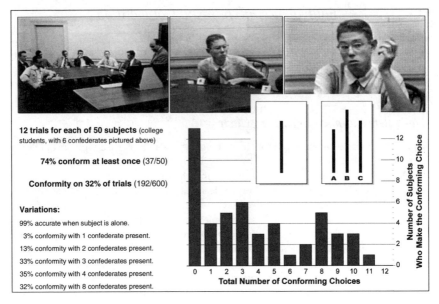

Figure G1 The Asch Experiment

psychophysics experiment, Asch's subjects were accurate in reporting line length. Asch asked a control group of students to go through 12 trials writing down their matches. In 444 matches, the students only made three errors (Asch, 1951:181).

The accurate perceptions when people are alone make all the more impressive the erroneous line lengths people report in a social setting. The left photo in Figure G1 shows seven students sitting around a table facing the experimenter, Asch. Asch sits next to a board on which the two stimulus cards are pasted. All but one of the students are confederates hired by Asch. The second from the last, in Figure G1, is the experiment subject. On the first two trials, the confederates each verbally select the correct match. The subject comfortably goes along with what everyone else is saying. On the third trial, the confederates unanimously select the wrong line; say line B in Figure G1. The subject reaction is illustrated in the middle picture: he cannot believe his eyes. Everyone has picked line B, but we know from the baseline results that the subject sees that line C is the correct match. One can imagine the subject in the third photo in Figure G1 saying to himself, "I must be blind," as he conforms to the majority in announcing that line B is the match. The experiment continues for 18 trials, of which 12 involve the majority making an erroneous match. Every so often, the majority makes a correct match to keep the subject uncertain.

The bar graph in Figure G1 tabulates the results (Asch, 1951:181). One subject conformed to the erroneous majority opinion in 11 of 12 opportunities. Thirteen subjects never conformed (0 conforming choices). In all, subjects conformed to the clearly erroneous majority in 32 percent of 600 trials, and 74 percent of 50 subjects conformed at least once. Varying the number of peers (Asch, 1951:188), shows that conformity continues to be about a third of trials whether there are eight, four, or three peers. Conformity is less likely with two other people expressing erroneous opinion, and unlikely with a single other person. As Asch (1956:12) summarized the results: "The unanimously wrong majority produced a marked and significant distortion in the reported estimates." Replications of Asch's experiment show varying levels of conformity, but the experiment continues to show people conforming to the majority (Bond and Smith, 1996).[4]

The results are simultaneously evidence of social comparison between structurally equivalent people. First, the students are socially similar; they have what Lazarsfeld and Merton (1954) termed homophily. I know nothing about the social network among the students, but look at the photo in Figure G1. The students are all male. They are all about the same age. They are the same race. They are all enrolled in courses at the same elite, New England college, familiar with the same courses taught by the same professors. They are all in the college's subject pool for psychology experiments. They likely draw female companions from the same local schools. A subject looks around the room and sees people "like me." One can imagine the photograph looking different for Sherif's experiment in the early 1930s at Columbia University, but homophily must have been similarly high.[5]

---

[4] It could seem reasonable to go beyond the Sherif–Festinger–Lazarsfeld–Katz–Coleman focus on ambiguous stimuli and argue instead that social reality can dominate physical reality—as illustrated by Asch's subjects reporting perceptions consistent with social reality but clearly inconsistent with physical reality (e.g., see Hardin and Higgins, 1996, for such an argument). There is even evidence of a biological foundation for the Asch results. Berns *et al.* (2005) report MRI evidence of activity in emotion areas of the brain when subjects contradict the group opinion (versus activity primarily in routine perception areas of the brain when subjects conform to group opinion). The authors offer the results as "the first biological evidence for the involvement of perceptual and emotional processes during social conformity."

I have two reasons for staying with the original focus on ambiguous stimuli. The first reason is my wish to run tests between the connectivity and equivalence criteria for distinguishing peers. The bent preference model links concrete stimuli (the x_i and x_j in equation 4) with ego's social frame of reference (the w_{ij}). For ambiguous stimuli, the concrete stimuli do not exist so I can compare alternative definitions of the network weights in predicting similar evaluations by pairs of people.

My second reason for staying with the original focus on ambiguous stimuli is confidence. The paragraph quoted in the text from Festinger, Schachter, and Back sets up a continuum of stimuli ranging from evaluations that are clearly grounded in empirical fact (as in "this street is a dead-end road") to evaluations that have no clear empirical referent (as in "the economy will suffer if a Democrat is elected"). I am confident that people use other people as a frame of reference for evaluations that have no clear empirical referent, they feel tension contradicting a peer group of unanimous opinion, and they might be affected by other people when making evaluations clearly grounded in empirical fact—but then again they might not. A substantial number of Asch's subjects show the effects of contagion on an evaluation clearly grounded in empirical fact, but some of those subjects did not believe their own reports. They go along with the majority while privately believing what their eyes told them. This public lies versus private truths phenomenon (Kuran, 1998) is illustrated by participant remarks such as (Asch, 1956:32): "When in Rome you do as the Romans," or "I agreed less because they were right than because I wanted to agree with them. It takes a lot of nerve to go in opposition to them." More, subjects are less likely to go along with the majority when the majority is obviously in error (Cohen, 1963:28–29), and subjects are more likely to conform if they have to recall the image of the line rather than having it displayed in front of them when they evaluate its length (Deutsch and Gerard, 1955). In short, physical reality intrudes even into the social reality of complete consensus among peers, or as Asch (1951:189) himself put it: "we find that the majority effect grows stronger as the situation diminishes in clarity."

[5] Homophily is often discussed in network analysis since relations tend to occur between similar people (e.g., same gender, same function, same business, etc.). McPherson, Smith-Lovin, and Cook (2001) provide broad review, distinguishing baseline homophily from inbreeding. The former is homophily expected by random chance. For example, Blau (1977) predicts that when friendships

A second point to note with respect to structural equivalence is that the contagion in Asch's experiment does not require influencer and influencee to talk to one another, yet there is pressure to conform.[6] The influence predicted between structurally equivalent people not talking to one another—such as the salesmen in Figures 8.5 and 8.6—was familiar in social psychology long before Asch's study in 1951, or Sherif's in 1936. In fact, such influence was the subject of Triplett's (1898) analysis, which is often deemed the first experiment in social psychology (Stube, 2005). Triplett describes men competing in bicycle races, and children competing on the speed with which they can wind a fishing reel. The racing bicyclists and competing children are structurally equivalent—standing in common relation to the rule-making authority, the goal, one another, and non-competing spectator elements in the environment. Though not talking with one another, the competitors influence one another. Consistent with the discussion of relative deprivation and motivation in Chapter 8, Triplett (1898:533) shows that people work faster when they are pitted against a competitor:[7] "the bodily presence of another

---

emerge from random encounters in a population containing few men, women will often have other women as friends and men will often have female friends. The greater tendency for women to have gender-homophilous networks need not indicate that the women are biased by gender. The homophily can be predicted from the lack of available men. Feld's (1981) social foci are another factor in baseline homophily. Relations can occur between homophilous people because opportunities for relations are concentrated between homophilous people (cf. Denrell and Le Mens, 2007, for a similar idea in which homophilous opinion arises from friends similarly sampling events). For example, the tendency for children to have friends the same age need not indicate that children have limited capacity for friendship beyond their own age; the homophily can be predicted from the fact that children form friendships in school, which is segregated into age homophilous grades. The homophily between subjects in early social psychology experiments and illustrated in Figure G1 was likely baseline induced, but its etiology matters less for my point here than the fact that everyone in the experiment was "like me." A second point to note on homophily is that Lazarsfeld and Merton (1954) distinguished two kinds: status homophily and value homophily. Status homophily refers to people having similar social status characteristics, regardless of their expressed opinions or behaviors. Different leaders can express contradictory opinions but recognize one another as similarly leaders. Value homophily refers to people who express similar opinions and behave similarly, regardless of status. In modeling preferences bent by network position, I focus on status homophily. For an emphasis on value homophily, see Festinger's (1954) social comparison theory in which ego is assumed to compare herself to people who express opinions similar to hers and display similar abilities (especially hypothesis III in the theory).

[6] I focus on the Asch experiment as an exemplar. Gartrell (2002) offers a broader discussion of the early research on communication and influence in the course of assuming that network connectivity defines the peers with respect to whom ego feels relative deprivation. His chapter is useful in directing research attention to network criteria for ego's selection of peers for social comparison. For the purposes here, however, I put aside Gartrell's assumption that the peers responsible for relative deprivation are defined by connectivity because Gartrell did not consider the structural equivalence implicit in the early research, and did not have the empirical evidence reported here supporting structural equivalence over connectivity as the criterion defining network peers.

[7] Triplett presented his results in graphs and tabulations that were sophisticated for the time, but can leave questions for contemporary scholars about the statistical significance of the oft-cited results (Stube, 2005). Triplett's competitor-induced speed improvement stands up to routine statistical scrutiny. The below two regression equations predict task time in seconds from variables in Triplett's (1898:521–522) data tables (t-tests in parentheses, adjusted for repeated observations of the same children using the CLUSTER option in STATA). The equation in the first row describes all 40 children across six trials ($R^2 = .44$). The second equation describes the 20 children Triplett identified after running the experiment as affected positively by a competitor ($R^2 = .53$). Having a competitor increased the average child's task speed by a second (3% gain on an average of 38.3 seconds) and increased speed by two and a half seconds for the average positively affected child (6% gain on an

contestant participating simultaneously in the race serves to liberate latent energy not ordinarily available." In Allport's (1924) influential textbook a generation later, he felt the need to explicitly separate evidence of social influence into two kinds, one describing influence between people not talking to one another (Triplett is cited as an example), and the other describing influence between people who talk to one another (pages 260–261): "Groups, in turn, may be classified under two heads: *co-acting* groups and *face-to-face* groups. In the former the individuals are primarily occupied with some stimulus other than one another. . . . Pupils in a classroom reading a lesson in concert from the blackboard illustrate this type of group. In the face-to-face group, which is necessarily small, the individuals react mainly or entirely to one another. A committee of three or four directors discussing a business project is a group of this sort." Allport (1924) discusses at length the evidence on co-acting groups, and bemoans the lack of research on face-to-face groups ("the face-to-face group has been neglected," page 285). The neglect was corrected in the following decades, although the subsequent studies by Sherif (1936) and Asch (1951) that are today deemed classics in the mid-century research wave that established the connectivity criterion were both instances of influence in co-acting groups. The point for this appendix is that influence between structurally equivalent people who do not talk to one another—a point of contention between connectivity and structural equivalence criteria defining "like me"—was a phenomenon familiar early in social psychology.

In the bent preference model, all social influence results from a single process of interpersonal evaluation, but different outcomes can result from the process occurring in different situations. Ego puts herself in the position of a peer to see what ego's options would look like if viewed from the position of a peer (equation 2). This image of symbolic communication is familiar from a school of sociology established in the early 1900s with the work of Cooley, Mead, and Thomas (e.g., Collins, 1994: chap. 4). The interpersonal comparison in equation (2) has ego putting herself in the roles of other people, from which a generalized other emerges to guide ego in her own opinion and behavior (Mead, 1934:154–155). Ego needs to be aware of the peer sufficient to imagine herself in the peer's position, but no behavioral communication is necessary. Peer pressure could be stronger with contact and discussion, but neither is required. I do not need to talk to my peers to feel that I am ahead of them (relative advantage) or falling behind (relative deprivation). I do not need to talk to my peers to feel that I am fortunate to have my current compensation, or exploited for the pittance I receive. Inconsistency draws attention. If I hear, or see, or become aware of someone "like me" making an evaluation that contradicts my own evaluation, I am puzzled. Perhaps my peer has information I do

---

average of 41.9 seconds). The control variables in the equations show that the children became faster on successive trials, girls were about the same speed as boys, older children were able to do the task more quickly, and the two left-handed children were disadvantaged by the equipment being set up for right-handed children.

	Constant	Competitor	Trial (1–6)	Female	Age (8–17)	Left-handed
All	66.90	−1.04	−1.17	0.55	−2.14	11.90
		(−2.77)	(−7.15)	(0.36)	(−5.06)	(5.86)
Positive	70.54	−2.67	−1.66	0.56	−2.03	9.15
		(−8.38)	(−7.22)	(0.25)	(−3.80)	(4.37)

not have, or vice versa. Perhaps the light is different from where he sits. If the contradiction between our evaluations is persistent or too great, perhaps we are not as similar as I thought. "Like me" is it's own motivation. Ego makes the interpersonal comparison in equation (2) when ego would be surprised if the other person, presented with the same stimulus, made an evaluation obviously different from ego's. Ego would feel pressure to explain the difference, moving closer to the other person's evaluation or expecting the other person to move closer to ego's evaluation.

Competition

Where the connectivity criterion uses socializing communication as the mechanism responsible for interpersonal influence, the equivalence criterion uses competition (Burt, 1992: chap. 1). Two people arc network equivalent when they engage in similar relationships, which makes them potential substitutes for one another. You and I are equivalent professors to the extent that we are expert in the same specialty, our work is popular with the same constituencies, we teach the same courses, and try to place students in the same jobs. The competition between structural equivalents can be destructive, but it need not be any more than the feelings of relative advantage and deprivation induced between similar people who use one another as a frame of reference for the social comparisons described in Chapter 8.

At the same time, the concept of equivalence in network analysis is identical to the concept of industry or niche in competitive strategy: Establishments are in the same industry to the extent that they compete to sell output to the same customer markets and purchase inputs from the same supplier markets. Industry establishments are of a kind defined by a unique pattern of supplier and customer relations (see Burt, 1983:60–63; 1992:85–89, 208–215, for details and references on equivalence definitions of industry and niche boundaries). Each organization in an industry has relations with customers and suppliers, but each knows that their customers and suppliers are in other industries. More precisely, the organizations "like me" are the ones that could replace me in my relations with customers and suppliers. Among the structural or role equivalent establishments within an industry, anything new that makes one establishment more attractive to suppliers or customers can be expected to elicit feelings of relative deprivation in the other establishments, so the new practice is adopted quickly by other industry establishments. Most studies of business fads and fashion report on the tendency for organizations to imitate one another within industries.[8]

---

[8] Here are some specific examples: Fligstein (1987:53–54) shows that the odds of a CEO having a specific functional background increase with the percentage of other large firms in the industry that drew their CEO from the functional background. Mizruchi (1989:414) shows that firms in the same industry make contributions to the same political candidates. Davis (1991) predicts the probability of a focal firm adopting a poison pill defense from (1) adoptions by other study firms in the focal firm's industry and (2) adoptions by firms connected by interlocking directorate with the focal firm. Focal firm adoptions are correlated .07 with the first predictor, .11 with the second predictor, and the two predictors are correlated .53, so it is difficult to reliably disentangle independent effects within the statistically significant aggregate effect (Davis, 1991:602). Greve (1995) studies diffusion between radio stations abandoning an easy listening format, so all of his establishments are in the same industry. Imitation is consistently more likely between market contact stations, that is stations in

The fact that industry competitors calibrate against one another is so obvious that it is easily taken for granted. It is productive for at least two reasons to recognize the equivalence concept implicit in the definition of industry boundaries.

First, analogy between equivalence in economic and social networks makes it easier to see competition in social networks. Competition is obvious and familiar within an industry. The equivalence that defines industry boundaries similarly defines the boundaries around positions in social networks, and the people in those boundaries are similarly affected by the feelings of relative advantage and deprivation known as competition.[9]

Second, competitive pressure between establishments in the same industry originates in their equivalent relations with suppliers and customers, not from the industry category used as a shorthand to reference their network equivalence. Calibrating research results in terms of industry categories instead of the underlying equivalence condition responsible for competitive pressure can generate inconsistent measures of competitive pressure, and reify legacy categories. This is not as much of a problem as it could be because the transaction patterns defining broad American industries were stable from the 1960s into the 1980s (Burt and Carlton, 1989). However, the same analysis shows that transaction patterns were not stable for information technology, where advances in electronics changed the industry. Just because the patterns of buying and selling that define aggregate industries have been stable does not mean that they will always be stable. The best preventative against erroneous definitions of industry boundaries is to look beneath the category labels to the transaction patterns that define when organizations are competitors. More generally, I expect that the observed stability in broad industry categories masks substantial change in local or specialized industries.

---

separate cities owned by the same parent company. Being owned by the same parent makes two stations structurally equivalent beyond whatever they have in common by dint of being in the same industry. Competition must be more severe between stations reporting to the same parent than it is between stations reporting to different parents. The between cities (Greve, 1995:450–451), but anyone who has witnessed the competition, one could say sibling rivalry, that occurs between business units within a company will sympathize with my interpretation of the evidence as an illustration of competition between network equivalent peers as discussed in the text. Bothner (2003) studies the diffusion of a new generation of computer chip across computer manufacturers. Like Greve, Bothner gets analytical traction from variable equivalence between firms in the same industry. Measuring equivalence with respect to the channels through which companies reach customers, Bothner (2003:1198–1199) shows, especially for smaller firms, that diffusion is more likely between companies that sell through the same sales channels.

[9] The analogy is productive in the opposite direction as well. People have long been discussed for comparing themselves to certain other people to feel good about themselves. The tendency varies between people. Some people have to surround themselves with weaker people to feel good about themselves (and we all feel better when someone gets in line behind us). Some people feel sufficiently good about themselves that they seek out stronger people, but on average, people avoid the pain of comparing themselves to others who are so much prettier, or have so much more in assets, or have so much more in career potential. Strategic selection of social peers carries over to the industry level. There is a subjective component in defining industry boundaries: Different people in an industry can see themselves facing different primary competitors depending on their personal location in the network structure of the industry (e.g., Porac *et al.*, 1995; Hodgkinson, 2005). This issue is discussed in the "Perception Defines the Network" section of Chapter 8 (Figure 8.9 is based on the network data reported in Porac *et al.*, 1995).

Corresponding developments in economics

In the year that Stouffer in the Harvard Sociology Department published the first volumes of *The American Soldier*, which became the touchstone for the concept of relative deprivation in sociology, an assistant professor in the Harvard Economics Department published *Income, Saving, and the Theory of Consumer Behavior* (Duesenberry, 1949), which become a touchstone for the relative income hypothesis in economics. Another key work was in press, appearing a year later in Harvard's *Quarterly Journal of Economics*, the independent work of a graduate student at Princeton (Leibenstein, 1950). To my outsider sociologist eyes, Duesenberry (1949) and Leibenstein (1950) were milestone developments in economics corresponding to the concepts of social pressure, social comparison, reference groups, and relative deprivation emerging at the same time in sociology and psychology.

The work in economics did not receive the welcome enjoyed by corresponding work in sociology or psychology. Duesenberry (1949) and Leibenstein (1950) stood for years a neglected outpost, scarecrow warning to young economists. The relative income hypothesis is based on an assumption that ego's consumption—how she spends her resources—is affected by the usual factors of market price and ego's income, plus factors defined by the way other people spend their resources. People want what they see other people want (or, to use Duesenberry's, 1949:29, term, what other people "demonstrate" they want). The assumed interdependence contradicted the neoclassical assumption widely used in mid-century economics that people make their evaluations independently. In particular, the absolute income hypothesis proposed by Keynes said that consumption increased as a proportion of ego's income, and the permanent income hypothesis proposed by Friedman said that consumption increased as a proportion of ego's long-run expected income. The absolute and permanent income hypotheses were consistent with the reigning neoclassical economics and prospered accordingly (Mason, 2000). For example, citations to the book in which Friedman (1957) proposed the permanent income hypothesis were high from the outset. The Web of Science shows that the book was cited in 21.3 articles per year through 1969, 32.8 per year from 1970 through 1989, and 30.4 per year after 1989. In contrast, the Web of Science shows one citation to Duesenberry (1949) in the five years after it was published, an average of 2.7 citations per year for the first decade after the book was published, then after 50 years, when most mid-century work had been forgotten, Duesenberry (1949) receives a healthy average of 18.3 citations per year. Social diffusion is more obvious in the use of Leibenstein's article. Well-known today, the article was cited only three times in its first decade, and articles citing it during the first 20 years after its publication were themselves rarely cited (from 1951 through 1971, the ten articles citing Leibenstein, 1950, were cited an average of 3.7 times over their lifetime—through 2008). Duesenberry (1949) showed the same pattern of its few early citations coming from peripheral articles that were themselves rarely cited. With the exception of a Modigliani article on the life-cycle-income alternative to the relative income hypothesis, articles citing Duesenberry (1949) in the first 20 years after the book's publication were themselves rarely cited. As Frank (1985:146) described the situation at a time when social comparison was not yet fashionable in economics, "Duesenberry's relative income hypothesis has been relegated to a historical footnote in most modern economics textbooks." And as Frank (2005) continued to bemoan the lack of attention to Duesenberry 20 years later: "This is surprising because his theory of consumer behavior clearly outperforms the alternative theories that displaced it in the 1950s—a striking reversal of the usual pattern in which theories are displaced by alternatives that better explain the evidence. His disappearance from modern economics textbooks is an intriguing cautionary tale in the sociology of knowledge.''

Implications of the relative income hypothesis are illustrated in Leibenstein's (1950) analysis of what he described as the "nonfunctional" market demand that can result from social comparison. (Sanders, 2008, provides useful didactic introduction to the relative income hypothesis.) Leibenstein's bandwagon effect refers to ego's demand for a product increasing because other people are buying it (cf. Duesenberry's, 1949, demonstration effects). Leibenstein's taboo effect refers to ego not wanting a product because too few other people are buying it. His snob and Veblen effects refer to ego not wanting a product because too many other people have it or can afford it. The neoclassical prediction is that a decrease in price triggers an increase in demand along the market demand curve. If there is a bandwagon effect, however, increased demand triggers new demand from people entering the market, people who were not interested before but are now interested because other people are buying the product. Decreasing price therefore has two effects on demand: it increases demand from people in the market, and it increases demand from new people entering the market (Leibenstein, 1950:195). Where a bandwagon effect is operating, price decrease triggers a disproportionately large increase in demand (because new buyers are attracted by the larger number of people consuming at the lower price). Where a snob effect is operating, in contrast, price decrease triggers a disproportionately small increase in demand, and a Veblen effect can trigger decreased demand, because potential buyers are repulsed by the larger number of people consuming at the lower price (Leibenstein, 1950:201–202).

Note the lack of attention to the process of social comparison. Social comparison is assumed. The analytical focus is on aggregate market behavior. If people engage in social comparison, then there are predictable implications for the association between market price and demand; changes in price can trigger disproportionately large or small changes in demand.

One implication of the analytical focus on aggregate market behavior is that the empirical evidence offered to justify attention to social comparison processes is at the market level, far from the interpersonal processes presumed responsible. For example, Duesenberry (1949) offers empirical support from income put aside as savings. The absolute and permanent income hypotheses predict savings in proportion to income, the higher ego's income, the more that can be put aside in savings. The relative income hypothesis predicts that keeping up with the Joneses consumes a larger proportion of income for low-income people, leaving less for savings, so wealthier people are predicted to put a higher proportion of their income into savings, which is the observed pattern of savings (Duesenberry, 1949: chap. 3; Frank, 1985:144–149). Similarly, Easterlin (1974) is a popular citation for evidence legitimating the need for concepts of social comparison: happiness and income are correlated within countries but not across, implying that happiness is a response to relative income, not absolute income.

A second implication of the lack of attention to interpersonal processes is an indifference to criteria that distinguish the peers to whom ego compares herself. Liebenstein's (1950) concepts of bandwagon, taboo, snob, and Veblen effects are defined with respect to all other consumers. Leibenstein (1950:190) acknowledges that ego's demand could be affected by a subgroup of other people, but decided in the interest of simplicity to assume that ego's demand is affected by everyone else ("Initially, therefore, we assume that A's demand is a function of the units demanded by all others collectively" Leibenstein, 1950:191). That simplifying assumption about social comparison continues to be useful (e.g., Rayo and Becker, 2006:236–237). Duesenberry distinguishes individual peers, but leaves the distinction intuitive. He had a connectivity criterion in mind (consistent with the Festinger research he cites in justification of social comparison). He (1949:32) begins his formal model with ego comparing herself to people with whom she associates: "... the frequency and strength of impulses to increase expenditures for one individual depend entirely on the ratio of his expenditures to the expenditures of those with whom he associates." He (1949:48) is more explicit about connectivity when presenting empirical evidence: "Any particular consumer will be more influenced by the consumption of people with whom he has social contacts than by that of people with whom he has only casual contacts." Duesenberry's (1949:32) formal expression for social comparison contains network weights and an ego to peer resource ratio: $C_i/(\Sigma_j \alpha_{ij} C_j)$, where C_i is ego i's consumption, ego i is not included in the summation across other people j, and α_{ij} is "the weight applied by the ith consumer to the expenditure of the jth." The α_{ij} weights define an aggregate peer to which ego i compares herself. The weights are left intuitive in the sense that they remain buried inside the ratio of ego to aggregate-peer consumption, and the ratio is used to analyze implications of social comparison. This is not a flaw in the analysis. There was no authoritative evidence available at the time defining network weights, and a specific definition of the weights was not essential to the economic analysis (cf. Bagwell and Bernheim, 1996:353, on Veblen effects defined with respect to a representative social contact, where representative is left to intuition). The point for this book is only that the network criteria distinguishing peers in these economic analyses are intuitive rather than concrete.

In sum, empirical research on the relative income hypothesis in economics described aggregate market implications of social comparison while corresponding work in psychology and sociology described the process by which, and circumstances in which, social comparison occurred. This is the reason for my statement in Chapter 8 that the relative income hypothesis and its component effects in economics had a great deal to say about population implications of social comparison, but little to say about the situations in which social comparison was likely so I drew little from that work for Chapter 8.

The disconnect between economics and social psychology on the topic of social comparison is an opportunity. It is yet another place for a productive micro–macro bridge between the two disciplines (for broader discussion, see Coleman, 1990: chap. 1). Social psychology is articulate about the mechanism by which interpersonal influence occurs, debating the relative merits of connected people socializing one another into a shared opinion versus structurally equivalent people competing with one another to be attractive to their shared constituency. Economic theory is articulate about macro hypotheses implied by people acting under specified constraints. Given people guided by bent preferences, what are the macro implications for demand, supply, and price? The social psychology of bent preferences narrows the variety of circumstances in which social comparison occurs, which can enhance the power of empirical research testing the macro hypotheses. For example, as discussed in Chapter 8, Frank (1985) shows that wage schedules are flatter than predicted for competitive labor markets so that people can avoid the pain of relative deprivation. However, wage schedules are predicted to be especially flat within groups of people made especially sensitive by structural equivalence to relative deprivation—as in a high-performance team.

Testing the alternative mechanisms

Evaluations with no clear grounding in physical reality have been a strategic research site because people have to rely on social reality in lieu of physical reality, so the operation of social factors can be studied in high relief. Physical stimuli drop out of the preference prediction. You are equally well off having your hair long or short, but it is fashionable to have it not too different from the way that peers have theirs. In the absence of physical stimuli (the x_i and x_j in equation 4), feelings of relative advantage and deprivation are determined only by the way the surrounding network exposes ego to peers (the w_{ij}). As more peers adopt an opinion or behavior, the opinion or behavior becomes more contagious for ego such that a correlation develops between ego's response, y_i, and the response typical of ego's peers, y_i^*:

$$y_i* = \Sigma_j \ w_{ij} \ y_j, \quad i \neq j \tag{G1}$$

where y_j measures person j's evaluation, ego i's own evaluation is excluded from the summation, and network weight w_{ij} is a fraction increasing with the extent to which ego sees j as "like me" ($\Sigma_j \ w_{ij} = 1$). Alternative definitions of "like me" can be compared for the extent to which ego and her peers make similar evaluations. The more accurate the definition of w_{ij}, the more similar y_i should be to y_i^*.

Network weights for connectivity

Where connectivity is responsible for contagion, ego is most affected by the opinion and behavior of the people with whom she has the strongest connections, so the network weights would be: $w_{ij} = f(z_{ij})$, where z_{ij} measures the strength of connection between ego and person j (ignoring ego herself; $w_{ij} = 0$, $\Sigma_j \ w_{ij} = 1$). For example, w_{ij} is often set to $1/N$ for each person that ego cites as a close discussion partner, and N is the number of people that ego cited, whereupon y_i^* in equation (G1) is the average response of ego's discussion partners. The salesmen in Figure 8.5 only discuss their work with the head of sales, so w_{ij} would equal 1.0 for each salesman i's relationship with the head of sales j and zero for each of the other two salesmen. The marketing staff discuss their work with one another and the head of marketing, so w_{ij} would equal .25 from individual contributor i to each of their four colleagues j in marketing.

Network weights for equivalence

If equivalence is responsible for contagion, ego is affected by the opinion and behavior of people who seek the same other people as ego and who are themselves sought by the same people who seek ego, so the network weights are defined by equation (6) in Chapter 8 as a function of equivalence distances from ego. Under a perceptual exponent v equal to 1.0, equation (6) defines w_{ij} as $f([dmax_i - d_{ij}] / \Sigma_k [dmax_i - d_{ik}])$, where $dmax_i$ is the maximum distance from ego i in a population, and equivalence d_{ij}. The w_{ij} are fractions that sum to one for each ego i.

For example, a salesman in the Figure 8.5 hypothetical organization will treat the other two salesmen as most "like me," followed by the people above him in the chain of command, followed by people in the other functional groups. This sentence is based on a transformation of the structural equivalence distances d_{ij} in the bottom row of Table F3 into network weights w_{ij}. For distances from salesman 19 specifically, $dmax_i$ is 3.16, and the w_{ij} under exponent v equal to one for each person j from 1 to 19 are as follows: .06, .07, .01, .10, .04, .00, .00, .01, .01, .01, .01, .01, .01, .04, .04, .04, .17, .17, and .17 (see Figure 8.8 for salesman 19 network weights under higher values of the exponent, all of which emphasize more strongly the other two salesmen as peers). Salesman 19 takes the other two salesmen as peers, followed to a lesser extent by the head of sales, followed by the division head of sales and marketing, followed by the senior leader, followed by everyone else.

The network weights defined by equivalence distances include self-weight, w_{ii}, that measures the extent to which ego is structurally unique. The self-weight will be useful at the end of this appendix, but has to be removed here to compute y_i^* in equation (G1). I remove w_{ii} by excluding i from the summation in the denominator defining w_{ij}, whereupon network weights w_{ij} sum to one across j excluding ego i. For salesman 19, for example, y_i^* in equation (G1) using the above weights is primarily the average response by the two other salesmen, persons 17 and 18.

Similarity and contradiction between the alternatives

As discussed in Chapter 8, the connectivity and equivalence criteria can yield similar definitions of "like me" at the same time that they can differ in two ways significant for peer pressure. With respect to similarity, the relative location of people in Figure 8.5, based on the connectivity criterion, is about the same as their relative location in Figure 8.6, based on the equivalence criterion. Further, the only structurally equivalent people in the organization—the individual contributors in each functional group—are with one exception strongly connected directly and indirectly. Structurally equivalent people often have direct connections with one another. When they do, equivalence and connectivity define the same peers for ego.

With respect to equivalence broadening the connectivity criterion, people can be structurally equivalent without having any direct contact to one another. The three salesmen in the hypothetical organization (persons 17, 18, 19) talk to the head of sales (person 4), but not one another. They are busy chasing sales in their respective regions. Yet the three salesmen are on top of each other in the Figure 8.6 spatial map of equivalence distances because they are equivalent in talking with the head of sales and no one else. The three salesmen are an example of the situation described in Triplett's (1898) early social psychology of influence between competitors. They are an example of the co-acting groups that Allport (1924) felt the need to distinguish from face-to-face groups in his *Social Psychology*, but we can now treat as an instance of structural equivalence.[10]

---

[10] This is a convenient place to put aside the idea that connectivity is responsible for influence between people who do not talk to one another (see footnote 13 in Chapter 8). Structurally equivalent

With respect to equivalence limiting the connectivity criterion, people who talk together need not be structurally equivalent. For example, people prominent in a network often attract satellites. The satellites are indicated by their unreciprocated claims to relations with prominent people and the lack of relations from people elsewhere in the network. The prominent and their satellites are in direct contact, but the prominent are only structurally equivalent to one another. The satellites are equivalent to one another and nonequivalent to the prominent with whom they claim connection.

Given the history of research reporting influence between connected people, a critical empirical question is whether the equivalence adjustments to connectivity are accurate in predicting where people have similar opinion and behavior. For the purposes here, I present evidence on networks and similarity in three populations analyzed in detail elsewhere, one population from business, one from politics, and a third from medicine.

Evidence of contagion in business

I begin with a moderately complex social structure. The study population is managers of corporate philanthropy in large corporations in the twin cities of Minneapolis and St. Paul in the early 1980s. The population is described in Galaskiewicz (1985, and a follow-up survey is described in Galaskiewicz, 1997). Galaskiewicz and Burt (1991) analyze the relative importance of cohesion and structural equivalence for contagion processes among the managers. Figure G2 is a summary of social structure and contagion among the managers.

A social structure of managers

Social structure is based on sociometric citations among 61 managers. Interviewed managers were presented with a list of all publicly held companies in the Twin Cities area and asked to "check off those firms where you know personally individuals involved in corporate contributions, i.e., on a first name basis, would feel comfortable calling for lunch or drinks after work, etc." Their responses define a (61,61) choice matrix. The bar graph in Figure G2 shows close connections between the managers (16% direct citations, and another 33% indirect connections through one intermediary) at the same time that there are distinct groups among the managers (34% of the manager pairs disconnected in the sense that they cannot reach one another through any chain of intermediaries among the other 59 managers).

---

people who do not talk to each other can be viewed as communicating indirectly through mutual contacts. For example, the three salesmen in Figure 8.5 are structurally equivalent and not connected directly to one another, but information could pass between them through their mutual exchanges with the head of sales. The bit of evidence that makes such an interpretation implausible is that direct connections between people are not associated with opinion or behavioral similarity once structural equivalence is held constant. In the discussion of Figure G6 below, note in the section labeled "Contact Is Insufficient" that direct contact does not increase similarity between structurally nonequivalent people, and note in the section labeled "Contact Is Superfluous" that direct contact does not increase similarity between structurally equivalent people. Given that direct connection does not increase opinion or behavior similarity, then indirect connection, a weaker channel for socializing communication, cannot be responsible for the similarity observed between structurally equivalent people who do not talk to one another.

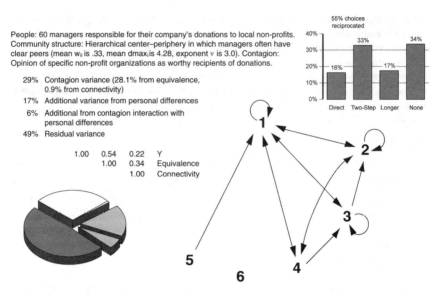

People: 60 managers responsible for their company's donations to local non-profits. Community structure: Hierarchical center–periphery in which managers often have clear peers (mean w_{ii} is .33, mean $dmax_i$ is 4.28, exponent ν is 3.0). Contagion: Opinion of specific non-profit organizations as worthy recipients of donations.

29%   Contagion variance (28.1% from equivalence, 0.9% from connectivity)

17%   Additional variance from personal differences

6%   Additional from contagion interaction with personal differences

49%   Residual variance

1.00	0.54	0.22	Y
	1.00	0.34	Equivalence
		1.00	Connectivity

Figure G2 Contagious Evaluation of Non-Profits among Managers of Corporate Giving in Early-1980s Minneapolis and St. Paul

Routine structural equivalence analysis reveals a center–periphery structure; a social hierarchy stratified across six positions.[11] Relations within and between positions are summarized in the sociogram in Figure G2. Numbers identify sets of structurally equivalent managers, and arrows indicate where the density of sociometric choices is above average. Managers at the top of the hierarchy, position 1, have strong contacts with one another and the densest contacts with other positions. All are managers in the largest firms. All but two of the firms have their headquarters in Minneapolis or its suburbs. The managers in positions 2, 3, and 4 form a hierarchy of decreasingly prominent positions below the top position. Positions are linked to geographic boundaries. Managers in positions 2 and 4 are principally affiliated with firms headquartered in Minneapolis and its suburbs. Managers in position 3 are all affiliated with firms headquartered in St. Paul and its suburbs. There are two positions at the bottom of the hierarchy. Position 5 is a satellite to the most prominent managers. Managers in position 5 have little contact with one another, but claim to have contacts with the managers at the top of the

---

[11] By routine structural equivalence analysis I mean that: (a) path distances were derived from the (61,61) matrix of sociometric choices and converted (frequency decay function, Burt, 1982:28–29) to measure the strength of the direct or indirect relation from each manager to each other manager, (b) Euclidean distances were computed to identify the extent to which each pair of managers were structurally equivalent in the sense of having identical relations with other managers, (c) the distances were cluster analyzed to identify sets of structurally equivalent managers, (d) the identified sets of structurally equivalent managers were tested for the degree to which they were structurally equivalent, and (e) network structure was summarized in a density table which is displayed here as a sociogram. For more detail, look up structural equivalence and density tables in a network analysis textbook such as Wasserman and Faust (1994: chaps. 9–10) or online in Hanneman and Riddle (2005: chaps. 12–13).

hierarchy, in position 1. Contact with other positions is minimal. All but one of these managers is affiliated with a small firm. Finally, there is an isolate position—managers in position 6 have no contact with one another and little or no contact with managers in other positions. Social isolates are structurally equivalent in having no contact with anyone. They are the recognized-by-one-another wallflowers surrounding a social activity. The social isolates in this community of managers are varied, drawn from large and small firms, some headquartered in St. Paul and some in Minneapolis.

Contagious evaluations

The evaluation being tested for contagion is manager opinion of specific non-profit organizations in the Twin Cities area. Selecting among organizations for corporate gifts is the central business of the managers. Managers are compared here for the extent to which they had similar opinions of the ten non-profit organizations given the most variable ratings. Sixty of the managers provided opinion data. Four of the criterion non-profits are cultural services organizations (Twin Cities Public Television, Minnesota Public Radio, the Minnesota Orchestral Association, and Film in the Cities). The other six are health and welfare organizations (the Fairview Community Hospitals, the Harriet Tubman Women's Shelter, the Wilder Foundation, the Opportunity Workshop, the Sabathani Community Center, and St. Mary's Rehabilitation Center).

Contagion is measured by correlating a manager's opinion (y) with the average opinion of his contacts (connectivity y* in equation G1) and the average opinion of his structural peers (equivalence y* in equation 6). Following Galaskiewicz's original analysis, the network weight for connectivity is set to 1/N when i and j cite each other (where N is the number of managers with whom i has reciprocal sociometric citations), and zero otherwise. Alternative network weights for connectivity computed from path distances, or with weaker criteria for a tie between managers, yield similar results (Galaskiewicz and Burt, 1991). When these network weights are put into equation (G1), the manager opinion predicted by connectivity, y*, is the average opinion of a manager's contacts. Structural equivalence distances are computed as they were computed to generate the spatial map in Figure 8.6, then used to define network weights as explained above using equation (6) in Chapter 8. Alternative equivalence measures yield similar or weaker evidence of contagion.[12]

Twenty-nine percent of the variance in manager opinion can be predicted from the average opinion of contacts and peers. This is the white area in the variance pie chart in Figure G2. Structural equivalence is the primary effect (28% of the variance can be attributed to structural equivalence, versus 0.9 percent for connectivity). Opinion varies

---

[12] The data were reanalyzed for contagion effects using popular variations on the raw Euclidean distance measure. Euclidean distances were computed directly from the raw binary sociometric choice data (which ignores indirect relations). This reduces the correlation between manager opinion and the average opinion of structurally equivalent peers only slightly to .48 from the .54 in Figure G2. Euclidean distances were also computed from z-score measures of relations (as in CONCOR, ignoring mean and variation differences between relation patterns). This reduces the equivalence contagion correlation from .54 to .34. These results are not offered to justify a general preference for the distance measure selected here. The results only show that the general measure used here is suited to this study population.

significantly between the managers. The managers work in different industries, different firms, play different roles within their firms, and come from different backgrounds. An additional 17 percent of the opinion variance can be predicted with variables distinguishing individual managers, and another 6 percent is gained with analysis of covariance adjustments for stronger contagion effects among certain managers. These are the two light-grey areas in the variance pie chart. That leaves 48 percent unexplained variance in manager opinion, indicated by the dark area in the variance pie chart.[13] My summary conclusion is that manager evaluations of the non-profits were strongly affected by contagion, primarily between structurally equivalent peers.

Evidence of Contagion in Politics

Consider a less complex structure. Heinz, Laumann, Nelson, and Salisbury (1993) describe the social system of elite lobbyists active in US Government policy in agriculture, energy, health, and labor during the early 1980s. Among the elite lobbyists are a few that Heinz *et al.* (1993: chap. 10) describe as notables because of their special prominence as representatives. The 63 notables are the study population here. All lobbyists analyzed here are notables, so I drop the adjective. Social structure and contagion among the lobbyists is summarized in Figure G3.[14]

A social structure of lobbyists

Social structure is based on sociometric citations. Presented with a roster of the study population, each lobbyist was asked to indicate potential sources of support: "Please place a check by the names of people you know well enough to be confident that they would take the trouble to assist you briefly (and without a fee) if you requested it." The bar graph in Figure G3 shows closer connections between the lobbyists than between the

---

[13] The partitioned variance is a heuristic. Regression coefficients computed from the correlation matrix in Figure G2 are .526 for structural equivalence and .041 for cohesion, with a .290 squared multiple correlation. The .290 squared multiple correlation defines the 29% pie slice in Figure G2, for which the independent contributions of structural equivalence (.281 = .526 × .535) and cohesion (.009 = .041 × .218) are also given in the figure. The correlations are computed across the 60 managers, each expressing an opinion of 10 nonprofit organizations, creating 600 observations. Without defining specific qualities of the managers that might affect evaluations, I can get a sense of how much differences between them matter by regressing the 600 evaluations across dummy variables that distinguish each manager from every other. When I add 59 dummy variables distinguishing the 60 managers to the contagion prediction, the squared multiple correlation increases by .169 to .459 (thus the 17% in Figure G2 attributed to personal differences). When I use the dummies to capture interactions with contagion to test for slope adjustments to the aggregate contagion effect, the squared multiple correlation increases by .055 to .514 (thus the 6% in Figure G2 attributed to contagion slope adjustments). I cannot give a specific meaning to this additional explained variance, but I know that it has something to do with differences between the managers. In short, I am not estimating network autocorrelation effects, nor testing contagion against personal differences. That work is reported elsewhere (Galaskiewicz and Burt, 1991). I get a rough estimate of the contagion correlation between manager opinion and the average opinion of contacts and peers, then measure how much personal differences matter beyond the estimated contagion.

[14] I appreciate Ed Laumann and his colleagues allowing me to make use of their data for this comparison.

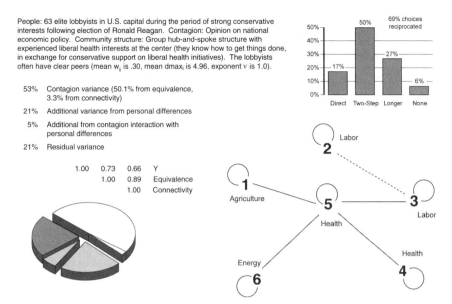

People: 63 elite lobbyists in U.S. capital during the period of strong conservative interests following election of Ronald Reagan. Contagion: Opinion on national economic policy. Community structure: Group hub-and-spoke structure with experienced liberal health interests at the center (they know how to get things done, in exchange for conservative support on liberal health initiatives). The lobbyists often have clear peers (mean w_{ij} is .30, mean $dmax_i$ is 4.96, exponent v is 1.0).

53%   Contagion variance (50.1% from equivalence, 3.3% from connectivity)

21%   Additional variance from personal differences

5%   Additional from contagion interaction with personal differences

21%   Residual variance

1.00	0.73	0.66	Y
	1.00	0.89	Equivalence
		1.00	Connectivity

Figure G3 Contagious National Economic Policy among Elite Lobbyists in Early-1980s Washington, D.C.

corporate managers in Figure G2. The density of direct connections is similar (17%, versus 16% in Figure G2), but the lobbyists are much more often friends-of-friends (50% indirect connections through one intermediary, versus 33% in Figure G2), and very few lobbyists are isolated from one another (6% of the lobbyist pairs cannot reach one another indirectly through other lobbyists, versus 34% of the manager pairs).

The frequent indirect connections through one intermediary suggests that the population has a center–periphery structure in which members are connected indirectly through shared relations with central leaders. The structure displayed in the Figure G3 sociogram is a simple star-shaped center–periphery pattern—five cliques distributed around a center position. The sociogram is from a routine structural equivalence analysis (see footnote 11 to this appendix). Numbers identify sets of structurally equivalent lobbyists, and arrows indicate where the choice density is above average. The generic pattern for a position in this structure is for people to expect support from other people in the position, and the central position. The one exception is position 2, occupied by people who do not have direct access to the central position.

The positions are linked to policy domains. All 14 of the agriculture lobbyists occupy position 1. The 15 energy lobbyists occupy position 6. Positions 2 and 3 contain all but one of the labor lobbyists, with position 2 containing the lesser players (lesser in the sense of not having direct access to the central position and in the sense of having an asymmetric acquaintance tie to position 3). Positions 4 and 5 contain all but one of the health lobbyists, with position 4 containing the lesser players (lesser in the sense of not being as widely connected to other policy domains).

The four lobbyists in position 5 operate at the center of the population. They have support contacts in all four of the distinguished policy domains. They come from the health policy domain, but their interests and contacts spill over into the other domains. All lawyers, the four lobbyists represent the interests of the Affiliated Food Producers, the American School Food Service Association, the California and Hawaii Sugar Companies, Farmland Industries, Land O'Lakes, the National Milk Producers' Federation, and the United Mine Workers. The boundary around them is nicely illustrated by considering the lobbyist most equivalent to them as a potential fifth member of the central position. That next person is another health lobbyist, the only person outside the agricultural domain who occupies position 1. However, he is more equivalent to his colleagues in position 1 than anyone in the central position 5.[15]

The four lobbyists in position 5 are not the only intermediaries that hold the other positions together. Heinz *et al.* (1993) emphasize the strength of ties between lobbyists in adjacent policy areas rather than through central people. There are 1,711 pairs of lobbyists not in position 5. The average path distance through support contacts between these 1,711 other pairs through support contacts is 1.95 if the four position 5 lobbyists are included in the network. The average path distance is almost unchanged (2.00) if the four are excluded from the network. In other words, the lobbyists are separated by a single intermediary whether or not the four central people in position 5 are available to connect them.

Contagious economic policy

The criterion variable is lobbyist opinion on national policy. Each lobbyist was asked to express on a scale from 1 to 5 his or her agreement with eight opinion items concerning government policy. The lobbyists share some beliefs. They agree that Americans should have equal access to quality medical care regardless of ability to pay. Reflecting their own positions and the interests they represent, they share a disbelief in the need to reduce income differences between occupations. I am more interested in ideas on which they disagree. The lobbyists have diverse beliefs regarding government regulation on behalf of consumers. They vary widely in their views on whether profits and power are too concentrated, and the extent to which labor unions are a benefit to the country. Still, lobbyist opinion is sufficiently correlated across items to construct a meaningful measure by averaging responses across the eight items. I have taken the average from Heinz *et al.* (1993), and following their analysis, I refer to the average as a measure of lobbyist economic ideology. The measure distinguishes lobbyists on an ideological continuum ranging from extreme conservative to welfare-state liberal.

Contagion is again measured by correlating each lobbyist's ideology (y) with the average ideology of supporters (connectivity y*), and structural peers (equivalence y*), as described above for the managers.[16] There is strong evidence of contagion.

---

[15] This sentence is based on factor-analysis measures of equivalence. The equivalence reliability for the additional person is .79 if he is put in position 1 versus .49 if he is put in position 5, so I leave him in position 1. Explained with illustrations in Burt (1982:73ff.), factor analysis can be a useful guide to deciding whether to add a person to a network position, and is isomorphic with the concept of structural equivalence, but it never caught on as standard practice.

[16] The strong evidence of contagion by connectivity and equivalence between lobbyists is robust over alternative measures of connectivity and equivalence. In keeping with Heinz *et al.* (1993),

Connectivity and equivalence combine to describe 53 percent of the variance in lobbyist opinion; the white area in the variance pie chart. Personal differences between the lobbyists matter about as much as they did for the corporate managers, but with the stronger contagion effect, all but 21 percent of the variance in lobbyist ideology is explained.[17]

Structural equivalence contributes most of the contagion effect (50% of ideology variance can be attributed to structural equivalence, versus 3.3% for connectivity), but it is difficult to partition the contagion variance in this population. This is a structure in which connectivity and structural equivalence make similar predictions. Lobbyists are organized into non-overlapping cliques. People in each clique are strongly connected with each other, and are structurally equivalent in having similarly strong relations in their clique and similarly weak relations outside their clique. The result is that a lobbyist's supporters are often structural peers, so it is difficult to distinguish evidence of structural equivalence contagion from evidence of contagion by connectivity. The correlation between y* defined by connectivity and equivalence in Figure G3 is higher than either variable's correlation with the criterion variable (.89 versus .73 and .66). Collinearity between the alternatives makes it difficult to separate a connectivity contribution from an equivalence contribution. The most reliable conclusion is that economic ideology is clearly contagious between the lobbyists, and that connectivity and structural equivalence reinforce one another as the network conditions responsible.

Evidence of contagion in medicine

My third study population has a relatively complex structure. The study population is doctors in the mid-1950s in four Illinois cities: Bloomington, Galesburg, Peoria, and Quincy. The criterion variable is the date by which each doctor begins writing prescriptions for a new antibiotic. These are the doctors in Coleman, Katz, and Menzel's (1966) classic study, *Medical Innovation*. The study was the first to combine mathematical models with extensive network data and a behavioral measure of adoption. The study is often cited for its evidence of discussion partners beginning to prescribe the new drug

---

lobbyist j is a key supporter for i if i cites j for support. I tried more extensive and more intensive measures. The more extensive measure was to include indirect connections. The proximity of j to i is the strength of the direct or indirect relationship from j to i as used to compute structural equivalence. This yields a contagion correlation for connectivity slightly stronger than reported in Figure G3, but less robust in the sense that the correlation generates a slightly weaker jackknife t-test (6.9 t-test versus 7.6 for the .66 correlation in Figure G3). The more intensive measure was to limit connections to mutually recognized relations in which lobbyists i and j cite one another (as among the managers in the previous section). Contagion through these relations is again slightly stronger than in Figure G3, but again less robust in the sense of generating a weaker jackknife t-test (5.7 t-test versus 7.6 for the correlation in Figure G3). I also reanalyzed the data with alternative equivalence weights. Euclidean distances were computed directly from the raw binary sociometric choice data, which reduced the contagion correlation for equivalence in Figure G3 only slightly from .73 to .69. Euclidean distances were computed from z-score measures of relations, which generates a contagion correlation of .71, just about identical to the .73 result in Figure G3.

[17] Detailed analysis of the diverse background data gathered in for the study led to a focus on 13 dummy variables to hold constant contagion-relevant personal differences between the lobbyists. The variables distinguish lobbyists by the policy domain in which they primarily operate (agriculture, energy, health, labor; from Laumann *et al.*, 1992), political party (Republican, Independent, Democrat), profession (lawyer, lawyer-manager, manager), and prominence (low, average, high).

at about the same time.[18] The data are ancient history in terms of contemporary medicine, but the analysis is an exemplar for academic research and practitioners (e.g., Sawai, 1994), and has continuing policy relevance (e.g., Carrin, 1987). Social structure and contagion among the doctors are summarized in Figure G4.

Four communities of doctors

Social structure is based on two kinds of sociometric citations in the survey. Doctors were asked to name advisors: "When you need information or advice about questions of therapy where do you usually turn?" They were asked for discussion partners: "And who are the three or four physicians with whom you most often find yourself discussing cases or therapy in the course of an ordinary week—last week for instance?" Their responses define a (240,240) matrix of sociometric choices where a 1 indicates that the row doctor cited the column doctor as an advisor or discussion partner. Embedded in the large network are 125 prescription sample physicians whose behavior is to be explained. There are no citations between cities, so the large matrix can be analyzed in four sections, one for each of the four study cities.

The doctors lived in a complex social structure. The complexity is apparent from the connections between individuals, and the aggregate structure of their relations. The bar graph in Figure G4 shows that the doctors were not closely connected. Only 5 percent of

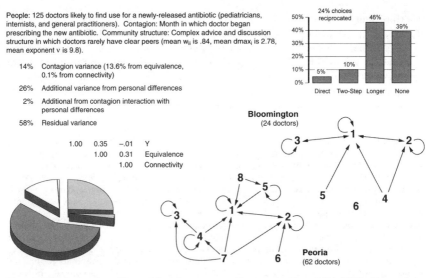

People: 125 doctors likely to find use for a newly-released antibiotic (pediatricians, internists, and general practitioners). Contagion: Month in which doctor began prescribing the new antibiotic. Community structure: Complex advice and discussion structure in which doctors rarely have clear peers (mean w_{ii} is .84, mean $dmax_i$ is 2.78, mean exponent v is 9.8).

- 14% Contagion variance (13.6% from equivalence, 0.1% from connectivity)
- 26% Additional variance from personal differences
- 2%   Additional from contagion interaction with personal differences
- 58% Residual variance

1.00	0.35	−.01	Y
	1.00	0.31	Equivalence
		1.00	Connectivity

24% choices reciprocated

Direct 5% / Two-Step 10% / Longer 46% / None 39%

Bloomington (24 doctors)

Peoria (62 doctors)

Figure G4 Contagious Drug Adoption among Doctors in Four Mid-1950s Downstate Illinois Communities

---

[18] The sentence in the text is correct, but there are multiple explanations for why it is correct. For Coleman, Katz, and Menzel (1966:114–130), doctors central in the discussion network were early adopters and socialized others, but it seems more likely that contagion was between structurally

the doctor pairs are directly connected, and another 10 percent are connected indirectly through one intermediary. The average physician is connected either directly or indirectly with the majority of other physicians in his city, however, that connection is typically through multiple intermediaries, and 39 percent of the doctor pairs have no chain of intermediaries through whom they are connected. The network image portrayed is one of communities held together by strands of asymmetric professional relations through one or more intermediaries. It is correct to view the physicians in each city as connected for the most part within a single professional community. At the same time, it would be incorrect to think of them as members of cohesive cliques.

The sociograms in Figure G4 illustrate the structural complexity of the networks. Peoria and Bloomington are presented. Each city was subjected to a routine structural equivalence analyses (see footnote 11 to this appendix). Numbers identify sets of structurally equivalent doctors, and arrows indicate where choice density is above average. Doctors are organized around central positions in each city, but the center is rarely one-dimensional. Galesburg (not presented) is the least complicated, with a strong center position, an isolated clique, and a satellite position occupied by doctors who are not cited as advisors or discussion partners but claim direct access to the most central physicians. Bloomington has a strong center position (position 1), but there are also two internally connected cliques affiliated with, but distinct from, the center (positions 2 and 3). Quincy has two center positions. The social structure of Peoria doctors is the most complicated, with two interlocked center positions (positions 1 and 2) and three internally cohesive cliques affiliated with the center (positions 3, 4, and 5).

Contagious adoptions of a new drug

The criterion variable is the date by which each physician began writing prescriptions for the new antibiotic. Local pharmacy records were searched for prescriptions written by the 125 prescription sample doctors. The result is an adoption variable ranging from 1 to 17 roughly indicating the month after tetracycline's release in which a doctor first began prescribing the new antibiotic. Sixteen doctors were nonadopters in the sense that the

---

equivalent doctors regardless of direct contact (for more detail on the original Coleman, Katz, and Menzel evidence, see Burt, 1987:1304–1306, 1313n). Either way, adoption was more determined by personal background than colleague behavior. The new drug spread without the slow-start period typical of early innovation (Burt, 1987:1304–1306), and less variance in adoption dates was predicted by colleague adoptions than by characteristics of a doctor's background and practice (respectively, 14% versus 26% in Figure G4). Marsden and Podolny (1990) report no event-history evidence of contagion when they impute missing adoption dates from a doctor's personal background (see their appendix, pp. 210–211). The cross-sectional evidence of contagion in Burt (1987) also disappears if missing adoption dates are imputed from a doctor's personal background. Strang and Tuma (1993:633–634) report event-history evidence of contagion by equivalence (multiplying or adding to personal background) and cohesion (additive only), but in both cases, doctor background strongly predicts adoption date. In fact, just holding constant monthly advertising on the new drug in three magazines to the individual doctors can fully account for the evidence of contagion (Van den Bulte and Lilien, 2001), though there is an endogeneity issue in whether drug-company advertising caused or anticipated the generic diffusion curve for the spread of the new antibiotic. The above analyses predict when a doctor began prescribing the new drug as a continuous function of peer behavior. The evidence of contagion conditional on weak equivalence to be highlighted in Figures G5 and G6 below would not be detected in the analyses.

prescription sampling turned up prescriptions that they had written, but no tetracycline prescriptions. As in the original study, I use these doctors to define a final point in tetracycline's diffusion, category 18 on the date-of-adoption variable.[19]

Contagion is again measured by correlating each doctor's adoption date (y) with the average adoption date of his advisors and discussion partners (y* defined by connectivity weights), and the average adoption date of his structural peers (y* defined by structurally equivalent peers), where the y* are weighted averages computed as described above for the managers.[20] The correlation matrix in Figure G4 shows evidence of contagion by structural equivalence, but no evidence of contagion by cohesion. The two variables combine to describe 14 percent of the variance in adoption dates (white area in the variance pie chart). Personal differences between the doctors matter. Five variables distinguishing personal differences among the doctors describe another 26 percent of the variance in adoption dates (gray areas in the variance pie chart). The doctors predisposed toward adopting the new antibiotic were professionally young, kept up to date with scientific developments in medicine, and believed that such behavior was important to being a good physician. The stronger effect of contagion by structural equivalence, and the stronger effect of personal predisposition toward adoption, are points developed at length in Burt (1987). The conclusion here is that social contagion affected doctor adoption, but contagion is entirely between structurally equivalent peers, and is a weaker cause than the doctor's own personal predisposition toward adoption.

Clear, near, and not peers

Connectivity interacts with equivalence to bring network brokers back into the picture. The interaction is illustrated in Figure G5, taken from an analysis reported elsewhere (Burt and Uchiyama, 1989). The unit of analysis is a pair of *Medical Innovation* doctors practicing in the same city. The vertical axis is the months that pass between the first doctor's adoption until the second doctor's adoption. The minimum is zero, for two doctors who adopt in the same month. The maximum is 17 months, the interval between a doctor who adopted in the first month and a second doctor who had not adopted before the last month of the study.

---

[19] Assigning the non-adopters to month 18 is conservative in that the 17-month interval between first-month adopters and doctors who had not adopted by the end of the study is probably longer than 17 months. The non-adopter might have adopted in month 18, or 19, or 20, or not at all, or might be a sampling error (only three days of prescriptions each month were audited to determine the month when a doctor began writing prescriptions for the new drug). For the purposes of this appendix, I am content to include the non-adopters as adopting a month later than the end of the study because (a) prescriptions were found for most of the doctors (87%), (b) network effects are visually apparent in Figure G5 and Figure G6, and (c) I ran an event-history model to check on my statistical inferences. In the event-history model, non-adopters enter the model only as doctors who have not yet adopted.

[20] I follow the original study in using direct sociometric choices to define sources of contagion. Cohesion weight w_{ij} is one over the number of i's cited advisors and discussion partners. I get similar results with alternative measures of cohesion and alternative measures of structural equivalence (Burt, 1987; Burt and Uchiyama, 1989).

The solid line in Figure G5 describes contagion by structural equivalence. Doctor pairs range from nonequivalent at the left in the graph, to strongly equivalent at the right. The solid line is high for nonequivalent doctors, showing that about six months passed between their adoptions. The average difference between all pairs of doctors is six months, which shows that most doctor pairs are toward the left of the graph. In other words, structural equivalence was rare. A pair of doctors selected at random in a city would have each had their own circle of advisors and discussion partners. To the extent that two doctors were equivalent, however, they were likely to begin prescribing the new antibiotic soon after one another. The bold line in Figure G5 declines almost linearly as the network weight for structural equivalence increases.

Now connectivity: The dashed line describes the time interval between adoptions by pairs of doctors in which one cited the other as an advisor or discussion partner. Across much of the horizontal axis, the dashed line adds nothing to the solid line. Non-equivalent doctors are separated by about six months whether or not they talked together. Above a certain level of structural equivalence (about .2 in Figure G5), the dashed line runs parallel to the solid line showing that equivalent doctors adopted soon after one another, whether or not they talked together. The point of the graph is the big gap between the dashed and solid lines at low levels of equivalence. A pair of doctors for whom the equivalence network weight is .1, for example, were separated in their adoptions by 5.79 months on average, but were a month and a half closer together if they discussed cases (4.19 month average interval between adoptions for dashed line at w_{ij} equal to .1). In short, connectivity contributes to contagion in combination with equivalence. At low levels of equivalence, connectivity makes a big difference.

I find the same pattern among the managers and lobbyists, distinguishing three qualitative levels of structural equivalence with respect to contagion: Not-peers are pairs of people for whom the equivalence network weight is within rounding error of zero. Not-peers have networks as different as any in their community and show no evidence of contagion even if they are connected directly.

Clear-peers are pairs of people for whom the equivalence network weight is high and contagion is likely even if the two people are not connected. Most people in the three populations have a small number of these close comparison points. I selected a threshold of network weights three or more standard deviations greater than zero. The cut-off has no theoretical foundation. It is based on comparing the three study populations to find a level of equivalence after which contagion is likely and direct contact irrelevant. Among the *Medical Innovation* doctors, the interval of the horizontal axis marked clear-peer in Figure G5 contains pairs of doctors who sought advice from the same colleagues, discussed cases with the same colleagues, and were themselves sought out by the same colleagues for advice and discussion.

Near-peers are pairs of people neither equivalent nor clearly nonequivalent. These are the people between whom contagion is as likely as connectivity is strong. Among the *Medical Innovation* doctors, the interval of the horizontal axis marked near-peer in Figure G5 contains pairs of doctors who had similar relations with some colleagues, but also had advisors and discussion partners that the other did not.

Across the populations

Connectivity is binary in Figure G5, two people are connected or not by a sociometric citation. Expanding connectivity to distinguish levels of connection reveals a Z-pattern

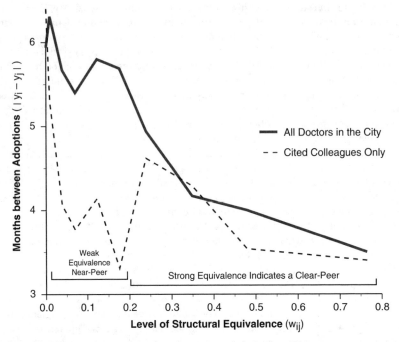

Figure G5 Detail on Network Conditions for Contagion between the *Medical Innovation* Doctors

by which contagion varies with connectivity and equivalence in all three populations. Elements of the pattern are stronger or weaker in specific populations, but the Z-pattern is apparent in each as displayed in Figure G6. The Z-pattern recurs in each graph, so I focus on the summary graph across all three populations (Figure G6A).

The horizontal axes in Figure G6 distinguish levels of connection. The strongest is two people mutually citing each other as colleagues with whom they discuss their work. The next level of connection is when one, but not both, cites the other. The next lower level is when the two people have no direct contact, but they discuss their work with colleagues who know one another such that there is *some* chain of intermediaries through whom information could travel between the two people. The lowest level of connection is when the two people discuss their work with disconnected colleagues such that there is *no* chain of intermediaries (measured) through whom information could travel between the two people.

In the population graphs, the vertical axes in Figure G6 are difference scores on whatever measure was tested for contagion. For the *Medical Innovation* doctors (Figure G6D), the differences are months between doctor adoptions as in Figure G5. In the summary graph across the three populations (Figure G6A), the vertical axis is a z-score measure of opinion or behavior within each community. The score for a pair of *Medical Innovation* doctors, for example, is the (z-score) difference between the dates when the doctors began prescribing the new drug. One doctor began prescribing the new drug in

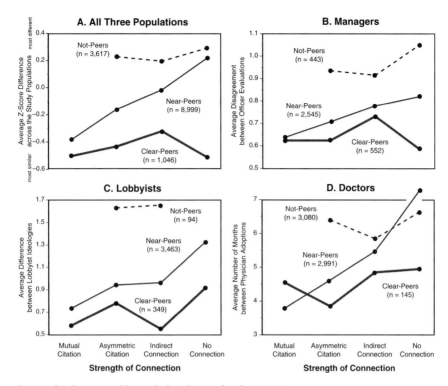

Figure G6 Summary Network Conditions for Contagion

month A and the other began in month B. The time between their adoptions ($|A-B|$), minus the average difference for other pairs of doctors in their community, divided by its standard deviation is a z-score measure of the extent to which the adoption difference between the two doctors was larger than the average in their community (high on the vertical axis), or smaller than the average (low on the vertical axis). The score for two managers is the z-score difference in their evaluations of the ten local non-profit organizations on which officer opinion differed sharply. The score for two lobbyists is the z-score difference between their respective opinions about national economic policy.

Not-peers: contact is insufficient

The dashed lines across the top of the Z-patterns in Figure G6 show no evidence of contagion between clearly nonequivalent people, regardless of connection between the people. On average, nonequivalent people are further far apart on the contagion variable than the average pair of people in a community (.29 mean z-score). Their difference remains if the nonequivalent people have a chain of indirect connections through whom they could communicate (.20 mean z-score), or one of them cites the other as a discussion partner (.23 mean z-score). There is no mean reported in Figure G6 for mutual citations on the dashed line because the mutual strength of connection did not occur between nonequivalent people.

Clear-peers: contact is superfluous

At the other extreme, the bold lines across the bottom of the Z-patterns in Figure G6 show consistent evidence of contagion between structurally equivalent people, regardless of connection between the people. The bold lines show that structurally equivalent people who talked to one another directly were similar in their opinions and adoption dates, but no more similar than structurally equivalent people who had no direct connection with one another.[21] Contact is superfluous to alignment between structurally equivalent people. Competitive pressure keeps them aligned as described above in the "Equivalence Mechanism" section. Social comparisons between equivalent people make them alert to one another such that they become similar whether or not they talk together. This point is implicit in early research conclusions about evidence recognized thirty years later to be evidence of contagion by equivalence. Merton (1949:465–466) concludes that: "One gains the impression that although a relatively few people—the top influentials—exert influence upon people on all levels of the influence-structure, there occurs a secondary tendency for people to be otherwise most influenced by their peers in that structure.... people in each influence stratum are more likely to be influenced by their peers in this structure than are people in the other strata." Katz and Lazarsfeld (1955:331) conclude that: "The flow of influence in this arena tends—as it does in every arena—to remain within the boundaries of each status level, but when it does cross status lines, there is no indication that the direction of flow is any more from high to low than it is from low to high."

Structural equivalence is the primary criterion

My conclusion is that structural equivalence is the primary criterion defining network weight w_{ij} in the bent-preferences model. In addition to the evidence supporting equivalence over connectivity, equivalence is an attractive criterion for the bent-preferences model because the role-playing mechanism in equation (2) allows interpersonal influence with or without direct contact between influencer and influencee. By shifting from behavioral communication to symbolic communication, the role-playing mechanism can account for structurally equivalent people using one another as a frame of reference even when the equivalent people have no direct contact with each other. What this does is make the empirical evidence more understandable. There is no evidence of contagion

---

[21] Average z-scores are well below zero for structurally equivalent people at each level of connection ($-.51$, $-.32$, $-.43$, and $-.50$ for the four points on the horizontal bold line at the bottom of Figure G6A). There is no statistically significant trend across the points (0.4 t-test adjusted for clustering between relations involving the same person) and the mean of .47 for the people in direct contact is not significantly higher than the mean of .38 for the people with no direct contact to one another (1.4 t-test adjusted for clustering between relations involving the same person). Clustering adjustment was applied with the CLUSTER option in STATA.

between structurally nonequivalent people, whether or not they are connected (not-peers in Figure G6). There is evidence of contagion between structurally equivalent people, again whether or not they are connected (clear-peers in Figure G6).

Brokers, near-peers, and opinion leaders

What about the near-peers, the pairs of people for whom connectivity is associated with contagion? These pairs contradict the conclusion that structural equivalence is the primary criterion defining network peers, and they are the most numerous pairings in the three study populations (8,999 of 13,662 dyads in Figure G6A, or 66 percent, are near-peers).

Near-peers are weakly equivalent pairs of people who have some friends and colleagues in common, but more that are different. Near-peers need not be aware of similarity until conversations reveal what they have in common. For example, sociologists and economists move in different academic circles, but conversations between a sociologist and economist at the same university can reveal to each the many people they know, admire, or disdain in common. Upward-sloping thin lines in Figure G6 show that contagion for near-peers depends on contact. The stronger the connection, the more likely the contagion. For pairs of weakly equivalent people who are disconnected from one another, which is the upper-right corner of the graphs in Figure G6, differences in opinion and behavior are as wide between near-peers as the differences between completely non-equivalent people. Strong connection between weakly equivalent people increases the probability that the people display similar opinions and behaviors (of course, similar opinions and behaviors could be why weakly equivalent people tolerate close contact). The rate at which contagion is more likely with stronger connections varies across the study populations (managers the lowest, doctors the highest), but all three populations show contagion more likely with stronger connection between near-peers.

Table G1 shows that the contagion associated with near-peer connectivity is through network brokers. Mutual-citation near peers are similar in opinion and behavior ($-.38$ mean z-score difference on contagion variable, thin solid line in the lower-left corner of Figure G6A). Disconnected near peers are dissimilar (.22 mean z-score difference, thin solid line in the upper-right corner of Figure G6A). The last column in Table G1 makes the link to network brokers. Contagion is concentrated in near-peers directly connected to each other, and the people most involved in those kinds of near-peer dyads are network brokers. Figure 2.4 showed the returns to brokerage as higher levels of residual performance associated with low levels of network constraint. The last column in Table G1 shows that network constraint has strong negative correlations with the two kinds of near-peer dyads in which contagion is concentrated: mutual-citation near-peers, and asymmetric-citation near-peers. Network constraint is computed as it was in the text (equation B1 in Appendix B). Involvement in kinds of dyads is the number of a person's near-peer dyads that are each of the four kinds distinguished by rows in Table G1. For example, each of the 63 managers in Minneapolis and St. Paul was involved in 62 dyads with the other managers. Some number of the dyads were mutual-citation near-peers, some number were clear-peers, and so on. I regressed the number of each kind of dyad in which a person was involved across the log network constraint on the person and the number of people available in the person's city. Prediction is across 248 people: the 60 managers in Figure G2, 63 lobbyists in Figure G3, and 125 doctors in Figure G4 from

Medical Innovation. The coefficients in the last column of Table G1 are standardized regression coefficients for log network constraint predicting the number of row dyads in which a person was involved, holding community size constant. The −.54 and −.68 coefficients in the table show that brokers (people in low-constraint networks) were involved in a disproportionately large number of direct-contact near-peer dyads—the near-peer dyads in which contagion was most likely. The .46 coefficient shows that brokers were disproportionately uninvolved in disconnected near-peer dyads—the near-peer dyads in which contagion was least likely.

Once identified, the near-peers for whom personal connection is so influential are quickly recognized. They are the opinion leaders and cosmopolitans described by Katz, Lazarsfeld, and Merton in the early public opinion surveys from Columbia University's Bureau of Applied Social Research. One of the Bureau's early projects was a study of the 1940 presidential election, later published as *The People's Choice*. As so often quoted thereafter (Lazarsfeld, Berelson, and Gaudet, 1944:151), the researchers were surprised to find almost no direct media effect on voters, instead finding "...that ideas often flow from radio and print to opinion leaders and from these to the less active sections of the population." The role of opinion leaders in innovation diffusion was elaborated in Merton's (1949) contrast between cosmopolitan versus local leaders, and studied in subsequent Bureau projects, most notably Katz and Lazarsfeld (1955) on opinion leaders in consumer purchases. The two-step flow—a process of information moving from the media to opinion leaders, and influence moving from opinion leaders to their followers—became a guiding theme for diffusion and marketing research (Katz and Lazarsfeld, 1955:309ff; Rogers, 2003:285).

Figure G6 and Table G1 show that the familiar two-step flow of communication is a compound of two very different network mechanisms; ideas enter a group through weakly equivalent, near-peers on the edge of the group, then relative deprivation and advantage trigger adoptions between strongly equivalent, clear-peers within the group. In other words, opinion leaders are more precisely opinion brokers who transmit information across the boundaries between status groups. These need not be leaders with superior authority, nor leaders in the sense of others wanting to imitate them. Defining opinion leaders by function (people whose conversations make new ideas and behaviors contagious) and structural location (people communicating with, and weakly equivalent

Table G1   Near-Peer Contagion is Concentrated in Network Brokers

Kind of Near-Peer Dyad	Number Observed	Evidence of Contagion	Mean Z-Score Difference in Opinion-Behavior	Association with Network Constraint
Mutual Citation	454	Strong	−.38	−.54
Asymmetric Citation	1,034	Weak	−.16	−.68
Indirect Contact	6,013	No	−.02	−.19
No Contact	1,498	No	.22	.46

Note: Dyad results are for the thin, solid line in Figure G6A. The final column is a standardized regression coefficient predicting the number of the row kind of dyads in which a person is involved from the natural log of network constraint on the person, and the number of people available for dyads in the person's city. Prediction is across the 248 people in the three study populations.

to, the individuals they influence) removes the vertical distinction implicit in the contrast between opinion leaders and followers. Opinion leaders are not people at the top so much as people at the edge, not leaders within groups so much as brokers between groups. They are in some ways structurally similar to the people they influence, but in one important way distinct; they have strong connections to other groups. They are what Merton (1949) described as cosmopolitans (see Rogers, 2003:293–294, for a similar conclusion, and Rogers', 2003:336 ff., discussion of change agents as linkers).

Brokers and other structurally unique people

Making the link between network brokers and the familiar role of opinion leader leaves unanswered the question of how brokers escape the competitive pressure of structurally equivalent peers. One explanation is the unique network around a broker. There is no one quite like ego in Figure 1.1. Ego is the person who connects across groups while most people focus on ties within their group. The intrepid broker and network identity hypotheses in Chapter 8 are based on the assumption that a person surrounded by a structurally unique network is less subject to the competitive pressure of relative advantage and deprivation. Specifically, the more unique the network around ego i, the higher the equivalence self-weight w_{ii} defined by equation (6), the closer to zero the equivalence weights w_{ij} for other people j, and the more the bent preferences model in equation (4) reduces to equation (1) describing people alone in a psychophysics lab (see the discussion of self-weights that precedes the network identity hypothesis in Chapter 8).

The graph in Figure G7 shows that brokers on average are more structurally unique. The vertical axis of the graph in Figure G7 is each person's self-weight w_{ii}. Higher scores indicate people who are more structurally unique within their population. The horizontal axis in the graph is network constraint, the index used in the text to distinguish brokers from people in closed networks. The horizontal axis in Figure G7 is the same as the horizontal axis in the Figure 2.1 summary graph, and the many similar graphs in the text. The regression line at the top of the graph, through the solid squares, shows that brokers were more structurally unique among the *Medical Innovation* doctors. A zero-order t-test of −6.01 shows a strong tendency for people in closed networks to be less structurally unique than brokers.

Structurally equivalent peers were more obvious among the managers (Figure G2) and lobbyists (Figure G3), so individuals are less structurally unique on average. The regression line through the circles representing the manager and lobbyist data in Figure G7 is well below the line describing the *Medical Innovation* doctors. Still, the zero-order t-test of −5.98 for the managers and lobbyists shows a strong tendency for people in closed networks to be less structurally unique than brokers.

Although brokers are more often structurally unique within their communities, differences between communities explain more of the individual differences in structural uniqueness across communities. The table in Figure G7 shows the results of predicting self-weight w_{ii} from network constraint (as in the Figure G7 graph) while holding constant some community differences. Network constraint accounts for only 1 percent of the variance in structural uniqueness across communities. In comparison, 39 percent of the variance is predicted by a dummy variable distinguishing the *Medical Innovation* doctors from the lobbyists and managers. That is the difference between the two regression lines in the Figure G7 graph. Another 31 percent of the variance is predicted from the number of people in the community. Another 23 percent of the variance is attributable to ego's maximum distance from others in the community. Maximum distance, $dmax_i$ in equation (6), is 4.96 on average for the lobbyists, slightly lower for the managers (4.28), and much lower for the doctors (2.78). Maximum distance increases with the extent to which one or more groups are clearly distinct in a community. Figure 8.8 in Chapter 8 illustrates the point. The maximum distance from a salesman in the hypothetical organization in Figure 8.5 is greater than the maximum distance from a doctor on the periphery of Quincy, one of the *Medical Innovation* cities ($dmax_i$ is respectively 3.23 versus 2.36). The Quincy network is larger. There are 51 doctors in the Quincy network versus 19 people in the hypothetical organization. However, Quincy is a more complex network of long, asymmetric connections. Only 24 percent of discussion citations between the doctors were reciprocated (versus 55% of citations between the managers and 69% of citations between the lobbyists), and 85 percent of the connections between doctors were longer than a friend of a friend (versus 49% of connections between the managers and 67% of connections between the lobbyists). The result is that every doctor is a little bit different from every other doctor. In the hypothetical organization, people are more clearly in this group and not in that group, so maximum equivalence distances are larger. The more clearly distinct a person's group, the larger the maximum distance to the person. The maximum distance to salesman 19 in Table F3 is high at 3.23, but the maximum distance to the other individual contributors is higher (3.63) because of the direct connections between individual contributors within each of the other functional groups. The senior leader has the shortest connections on average to people in the organization, so she is the least segregated in a group apart from the organization, and has the smallest maximum distance in the network

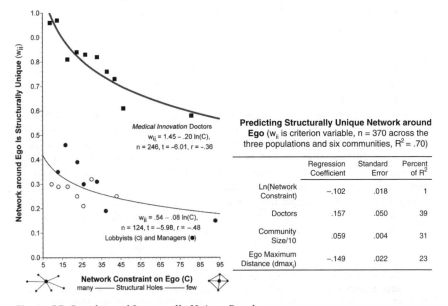

Figure G7 Correlates of Structurally Unique People

(2.52). The negative regression coefficient for dmax$_i$ in Figure G7 shows that larger maximum distance from ego means more obvious structural-equivalence peers for ego, which means that ego is less structurally unique. My summary conclusion is that structural-equivalence peers are less obvious for network brokers, especially in the more complex networks characteristic of larger communities.

Where peers are difficult to identify, peer pressure has less effect on opinion and behavior. Across the three study populations, the evidence of peer pressure is strongest among the lobbyists (53% of opinion variance in Figure G3), weaker among the managers (29% of opinion variance in Figure G2), and weakest among the doctors (14% of behavior variance in Figure G4). That is the reverse of network complexity. The lobbyists had the simplest network structure (short paths of often-reciprocated citations defining distinct groups). Group boundaries were sufficiently clear among the lobbyists that actual structural equivalence functioned as felt equivalence in defining network peers for social comparisons. A value of one for exponent v is sufficient to reveal the evidence of structural equivalence defining network peers. The doctors worked in the most complex networks (long indirect connections of rarely reciprocated citations defining a relatively unique position for each doctor). Exponent v averages a much higher 9.8 across the four physician networks. Group boundaries were difficult to identify in the complex advice and discussion networks. Exponents well above one were needed in equation (6) to distinguish physician peers (illustrated in Figure 8.8B for doctor 3 in Quincy).

Role equivalence [22]

With structural equivalence failing to define network peers for brokers, brokers are predicted by the network identity hypothesis in Chapter 8 to use more abstract images of social structure to define peers, images in which broker peers are more obvious. One such abstraction is role equivalence, illustrated in Figure 8.10. This final section explains the distances used in Figure 8.10.

Measures of structural equivalence drew criticism as quickly as they began to be used in research during the mid-1970s. Grounding equivalence in relations between individuals, and analyzing those relations to detect roles, lost much of the substantive meaning of status and role. This was the theme of two key papers released in the late 1970s; Lee Sailer's (1978) article on structural relatedness and a paper presented by Michael Mandel and Christopher Winship in the Social Networks session of the 1979 annual meetings of the American Sociological Association. Sailer's paper reflected ideas under debate at the University of California at Irvine, ideas eventually formalized in a later article on regular equivalence by White and Reitz (1983). Mandel and Winship's paper reflected debate in the mid 1970s (sketched in a 1974 manuscript by Winship) among students working with Harrison White at Harvard on generalizing structural equivalence. The Mandel and Winship paper was later published (Winship and Mandel, 1983), followed several years later by Winship's 1974 commentary (Winship, 1988).

---

[22] This section draws on Burt (1990). Further details and numerical illustrations can be found there. Wasserman and Faust (1994: chap. 12) provide a textbook review of regular and role equivalence (useful discussion is also available online in Hanneman and Riddle, 2005: chaps. 14, 15). I wrote my own software to get the results on role equivalence reported here. Options beyond structural equivalence are available in the popular UCINET and PAJEK software packages

The two extensions of structural equivalence had similarly important goals and suffered from a similar problem. Both were intended to enrich the substantive meaning of structural equivalence by defining equivalence in terms of relations between roles rather than individuals. There is little disagreement over the point that both models capture the substantive meaning of status and role better than the popular operational definitions of structural equivalence. Both models suffered from the lack of a simple operational model. Equivalence was a difficult concept and measures were obtained numerically rather than analytically.

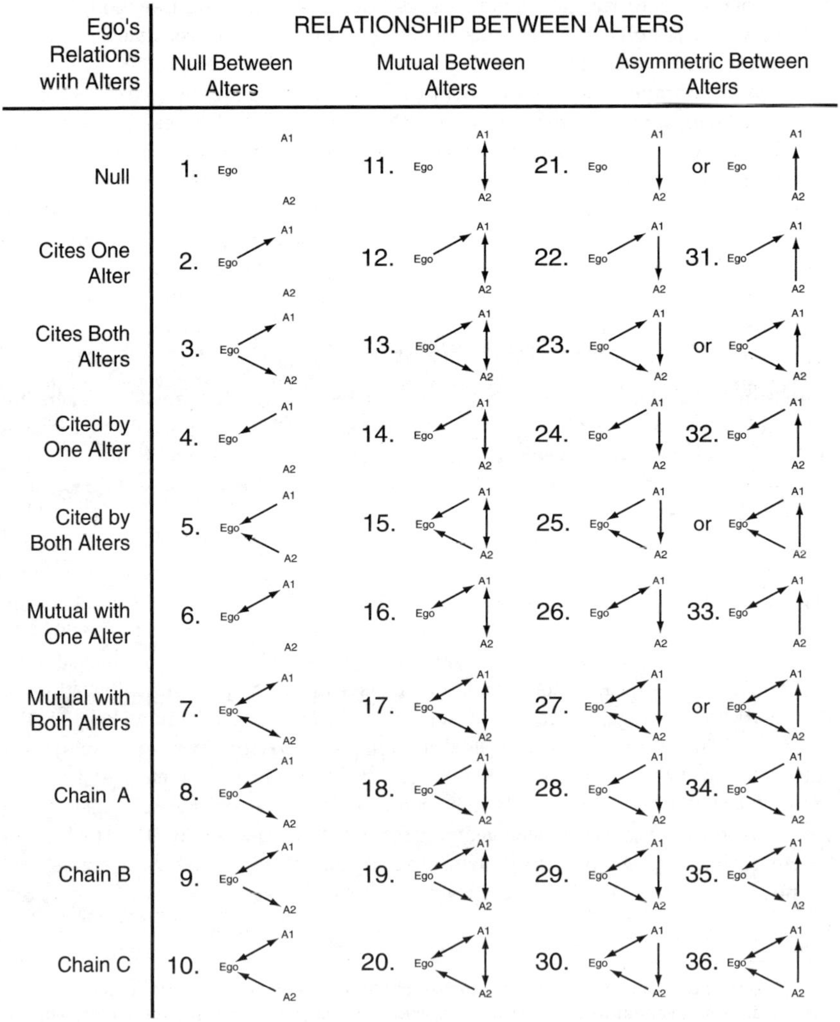

Ego's Relations with Alters	RELATIONSHIP BETWEEN ALTERS		
	Null Between Alters	Mutual Between Alters	Asymmetric Between Alters
Null	1.	11.	21. or
Cites One Alter	2.	12.	22. 31.
Cites Both Alters	3.	13.	23. or
Cited by One Alter	4.	14.	24. 32.
Cited by Both Alters	5.	15.	25. or
Mutual with One Alter	6.	16.	26. 33.
Mutual with Both Alters	7.	17.	27. or
Chain A	8.	18.	28. 34.
Chain B	9.	19.	29. 35.
Chain C	10.	20.	30. 36.

Figure G8 Interaction Triads Defining Ego's Role in a Network

A simple operational model was provided by Hummell and Sodeur (1987) in the course of their efforts to link their work on the triad census with the ongoing structural equivalence debate. Their equivalence measure is very similar (not identical) to Winship and Mandel role equivalence in direct and two step indirect connections. The Hummell and Sodeur measure is intuitively simple, involves no numerical iteration, and handles symmetric and asymmetric relations equally well. Hummell and Sodeur's solution was to express ego's role in a network as a triad census, a pattern of relative frequencies with which kinds of triads describe the role implicit in the immediate network around ego, then compute Euclidean distances between the triad patterns for people to measure the extent to which the people play the same role. By expressing an individual's role as a pattern of triads in which the individual is involved, and comparing individuals in terms of their respective triad patterns, Hummell and Sodeur generalize equivalence beyond having the same relations with the same individuals.

Figure G8 contains a table of 36 triad structures that distinguish ways in which ego is connected within the immediate network around her. Ten rows distinguish patterns of relations between ego and the two alters. For example, the first row contains triads in which ego has no connection with either alter. The seventh row contains triads in which ego sends relations to both alters and both reciprocate. The three columns in Figure G8 distinguish triads by the connection between alters. In the first column, no connection. In the second column, symmetric connection. In the third, asymmetric connection.[23]

The important point in Figure G8 is that the alters are defined by the pattern of their relations with each other and ego. They are not identified as individuals. The microstructural orientations toward others represented by the triad types are components in roles. Figure G8 is an inventory of the components, and the relative frequency with which any one person, group, or institution as ego plays each of the triad types within a network defines ego's role in the network. Two individuals then play the same role in a network to the extent that they are equivalently involved in the role components tabulated in their respective triad patterns. Each individual in a network of N individuals is involved in $(N-1)(N-2)/2$ triads distinguished in Figure G8. Let t_{jq} be the frequency with which individual j is involved in triads of type q. The triad pattern for individual j is then an array of 36 such frequencies; t_{j1}, t_{j2}, t_{j3}, ... t_{j36}.

To illustrate, consider a division leader in Figure 8.5. This is an extension of the educational hierarchy used as numerical illustration in Winship and Mandel (1983). Each individual in the 19-person organization is involved in 153 triads from Figure G8; $(N-1)(N-2)/2$ is here 18*17/2. Being a division leader is described by the following pattern of triad frequencies (88 of triad 1, 17 of triad 11, and so on):

88	0	0	0	0	38	3	0	0	0
17	0	0	0	0	7	0	0	0	0
0	0	0	0	0	0	0	0	0	0
0	0	0	0	0	0				

---

[23] Two triad types are distinguished in some rows of the third column. Distinctions occur where ego has different relations with the two alters, therefore making it significant to know which alter has which relation with ego. In the first row, for example, there is no distinction between which alter cites the other. Ego has no relation with either alter, so their relations with one another do not affect ego's relation pattern. Illustrating the other condition, there is a distinction in the second row

Putting aside the null triad (triad 1 in which ego is disconnected from two people who are disconnected from each other), triad 6 with 38 instances is the most frequent for a division leader. Figure G8 shows that triad 6 is an exclusive relationship; Sam is connected with John and both are disconnected from Tom. An example in Figure 8.5 for division leader 2 is the relationship between 1 and 2, which excludes person 3. Triad 7 with 3 instances is the least-frequent triad in the division-leader role. This is a broker role in which ego is connected with two people disconnected from one another. The three such triads in Figure 8.5 for division leader 2 are his brokerage between the two group leaders who report to him (persons 2, 4, and 5), and his brokerage between each group leader and the senior leader (the triad among persons 1, 2, 4 and the triad among persons 1, 2, 5).

Now consider the role of being a group leader. The triad profile for the head of marketing, person 5, is the following:

73	0	0	0	0	54	3	0	0	0
18	0	0	0	0	2	3	0	0	0
0	0	0	0	0	0	0	0	0	0
0	0	0	0	0	0				

Group leader 5, like the division leaders, is involved in many triads 1, 6, and 18. In contrast to the division leaders, the group leader is involved in fewer triads 16 (there are 7 instances for the division leaders, 2 for group leader 5), and more triads 17 (0 instances for the division leaders, 3 for group leader 5). Figure G8 shows that triad 16 is a chain; Sam is connected to Sue who is connected to John and Sam has no connection with John. The two instances of this for group leader 5 are the connection through his division leader to the senior leader (persons 5, 2, 1), and the connection through his division leader to the head of sales (persons 5, 2, 4). Figure G8 shows that triad 17 is a closed triad; Sam, Sue, and John are all connected. The senior leaders have no such experience. The three instances for group leader 5 are his connections with his direct reports (triad 5, 14, 15; triad 5, 14, 16; and triad 5, 15, 16).

No information is retained on which individuals are in which triads. Individuals have been abstracted out of the relations defining the role ego plays in the immediate network around her.

Role equivalence can now be measured by differences between the triads in which two people are involved. Hummell and Sodeur propose Euclidean distance. With respect to triad patterns, the distance between the role that individual j plays in a network and the role that individual i plays is given as follows:[24]

---

between two kinds of triads in the third column. Ego directs a relation to the first alter and has no contact with the second. If there is an asymmetric relation from the second alter to the first, then ego is one of two individuals directing relations to the first alter. If there is an asymmetric relation from the first alter to the second, then ego is in a chain of asymmetric relations from ego to alter one to alter two.

[24] Two practical points on using equation (G2): First, it can be useful to zero out some triad types, such as the null triad (triad 1 in Figure G8). The null triad occurs frequently, so it can greatly affect the distances defined by equation (G2). This can obscure roles because two people similarly disengaged

$$d_{ij}^{\,2} = \Sigma k\,(t_{jq} - t_{iq})^2 \qquad\qquad (G2)$$

where q varies from 1 to 36 across the kinds of triads in Figure G8. Distance d_{ij} is zero when i and j play identical roles within their immediate network. Role-equivalence distances defined by equation (G2) for the organization in Figure 8.5 are given in Table F3 in Appendix F. These are the distances used to construct the spatial map in Figure 8.10. Network weights based on role-equivalence distances replacing structural-equivalence distances in equation (6) are given in Table F5. Distance d_{ij} increases as i and j play different roles in the organization. This is illustrated by the difference above between the two division leaders and group leader 5. It is illustrated in Figure 8.10 by the slight distance between the head of sales and the other group leaders because the other group leaders participate in closed triads, which never occur for the head of sales.[25] The two division leaders supervise entirely different people, so they are not structurally equivalent. However, they are identically engaged in the immediate network around them as reflected by their identical triad patterns, so they are separated by zero role-equivalence distance in Table F3 and Figure 8.10. Role equivalence provides an unambiguous and intuitively appropriate frame of reference for the division leaders and group leaders at the same time that structural equivalence does not.

---

from many people can play very different roles within their immediate network. Second, distance based on triad counts can be large numbers in large networks. Before computing distance, it can be convenient to convert triad frequencies to percentages; 100 times a triad frequency divided by ego's total number of triads, $(N-1)(N-2)/2$. Relative distance between people is unaffected for cluster and spatial analysis since every profile is divided by the same constant.

[25] Specifically, here is the triad profile for the head of sales, group leader 4, and the closed triad (number 17 in Figure G8) occurs with zero frequency:

70	0	0	0	0	54	6	0	0	0
21	0	0	0	0	2	0	0	0	0
0	0	0	0	0	0	0	0	0	0
0	0	0	0	0	0				

The three triads with subordinates that are closed triads for the other group leaders are for the head of sales just more brokerage triads (triad 7 occurs 6 times in the above triad profile versus 3 times in the profile for group leader 5 given in the text).

REFERENCES

Abrahamson, Eric (1996). "Management fashion." *Academy of Management Review* 21: 254–285.

Allen, Thomas J. and Stephen I. Cohen (1969). "Information flow in research and development laboratories." *Administrative Science Quarterly* 14: 12–19.

Allport, Floyd Henry (1924). *Social Psychology*. New York: Houghton Mifflin.

Amabile, Teresa M., Sigal G. Barsade, Jennifer S. Mueller, and Barry M. Staw (2005). "Affect and creativity at work." *Administrative Science Quarterly* 50: 267–403.

Ancona, Deborah G. and David F. Caldwell (1992a). "Demography and design: predictors of new product team performance." *Organization Science* 3: 321–341.

—— —— (1992b). "Bridging the boundary: external activity and performance in organizational teams." *Administrative Science Quarterly* 37: 634–665.

Anderson, Marc H. (2008). "Social networks and the cognitive motivation to realize network opportunities: a study of managers' information gathering behaviors." *Journal of Organization Behavior* 29: 51–78.

Aral, Sinan and Marshall Van Alstyne (2007). "Network structure and information advantage: structural determinants of access to novel information and their performance implications." Paper presented at the annual meetings of the Academy of Management, Philadelphia.

Asch, Solomon E. (1951). "Effects of group pressure upon the modification and distortion of judgments." Pp. 177–190 in *Groups, Leadership and Men*, edited by Harold Guetzkow. Pittsburgh, PA: Carnegie Press.

—— —— (1956). "Studies of independence and conformity: a minority of one against a unanimous majority." *Psychological Monographs* 70 (Whole no. 416).

Atwater, Leanne and David Waldman (1998). "Accountability in 360 degree feedback." *HR Magazine* 43: 96.

—— —— (1998). "Accountability in 360 degree feedback." *HR Magazine* 43: 96.

Bagwell, Laurie Simon and B. Douglas Bernheim (1996). "Veblen effects in a theory of conspicuous consumption." *American Economic Review* 86: 349–373.

Baker, Wayne E. (1984). "The social structure of a national securities market." *American Journal of Sociology* 89: 775–811.

Balwin, Nancy S. and Ronald E. Rice (1997). "Information-seeking behavior of securities analysts: individual and institutional influences, information sources and channels, and outcomes." *Journal of the American Society for Information Science* 48: 674–693.

Bandura, Albert (1997). *Self-Efficacy*. New York: W. H. Freeman.

Barker, James R. (1993). "Tightening the iron cage: concertive control in self-managing teams." *Administrative Science Quarterly* 38: 408–437.

Baron, James N. and Jeffrey Pfeffer (1996). "The social psychology of organizations and inequality." *Social Psychology Quarterly* 57: 190–209.

Baron, Robert A. (2008). "The role of affect in the entrepreneurship process." *Academy of Management Review* 33: 328–340.

Barsade, Sigal G. (2002). "The ripple effect: emotional contagion and its influence on group behavior." *Administrative Science Quarterly* 47: 644–675.

Barsade, Sigal G. and Donald E. Gibson (2007). "Why does affect matter in organizations." *Academy of Management Perspectives* 21: 36–59.

Baum, Joel A. C., Tony Calabrese, and Brian S. Silverman (2000). "Don't go it alone: alliance network composition and startups' performance in Canadian biotechnology." *Strategic Management Journal* 21: 267–294.

Baum, Joel A. C. and Timothy J. Rowley (eds.) (2008). *Advances in Strategic Management, 25*. Oxford: JAI/Elsevier.

Baum, Joel A. C., Diederik W. van Liere, and Timothy J. Rowley (2008). "Between closure and holes: hybrid network positions and the performance of U.K. investment banks." Unpublished manuscript, University of Toronto Rotman School of Management.

Belliveau, Maura A., Charles A. O'Reilly, and James B. Wade (1996). "Social capital at the top: effects of social similarity and status on CEO compensation." *Academy of Management Journal* 39: 1568–1593.

Berelson, Bernard R., Paul F. Lazarsfeld, and William N. McPhee (1954). *Voting*. Chicago: University of Chicago Press.

Berns, Gregory S., Jonathan Chappelow, Caroline F. Zink, Giuseppe Pagnoni, Megan E. Martin-Skurski, and Jim Richards (2005). "Neurobiological correlates of social conformity and independence during mental rotation." *Biological Psychiatry* 58: 245–253.

Bidwell, Matthew and Isabel Fernandez-Mateo (2007). "Relationship Duration and Returns to Brokerage in the Staffing Sector." Unpublished manuscript, INSEAD, Singapore.

Blau, Peter M. (1968). "Interaction: social exchange." Pp. 452–458 in *The International Encyclopedia of the Social Sciences*, edited by David L. Sills. New York: Free Press and Macmillan.

—— (1977). *Inequality and Heterogeneity*. New York: Free Press.

Bonacich, Phillip (1972). "Factoring and weighting approaches to status scores and clique identification." *Journal of Mathematical Sociology* 2: 113–120.

—— (1987). "Power and centrality: a family of measures." *American Journal of Sociology* 92: 1170–1183.

Bond, Rod and Peter B. Smith (1996). "Culture and conformity: a meta-analysis of studies using Asch's (1952b, 1956) line judgment task." *Psychological Bulletin* 119: 111–137.

Borgatti, Stephen P. (2002). *Netdraw*. Boston, MA: Analytic Technologies.

Borgatti, Stephen P., Candace Jones, and Martin G. Everett (1998). "Network measures of social capital." *Connections* 21: 27–36.

Bothner, Matthew S. (2003). "Competition and social influence: the diffusion of the sixth-generation processor in the global computer industry." *American Journal of Sociology* 108: 1175–1210.

Bothner, Matthew S., Jeong-han Kang, and Toby E. Stuart (2007). "Competitive crowding and risk taking in a tournament: evidence from NASCAR racing." *Administrative Science Quarterly* 52: 208–247.

Bott, Elizabeth (1957). *Family and Social Network*. New York: Free Press.

Boyer, Paul and Stephen Nissenbaum (1974). *Salem Possessed*. Cambridge, MA: Harvard University Press.

Brass, Daniel J. (2009). "Connecting to brokers: strategies for acquiring social capital." pp. 260–274 in *Social Capital*, edited by Viva Bartkus and James H. Davis. Northhampton, MA: Edward Elgar.

Briscoe, Bob, Andrew Odlyzko, and Benjamin Tilly (2006). "Metcalfe's law is wrong." *IEEE Spectrum* (July): 26–31.

Brooks, E. Bruce and A. Taeko Brooks (1998). *The Original Analects*. New York: Columbia University Press.

Brown, John Seely and Paul Duguid (2000). *The Social Life of Information*. Boston, MA: Harvard Business School Press.

—— —— (2002). "Local knowledge: innovation in the networked age." *Management Learning* 33: 427–437.

Brown, Jonathan D., Natalie J. Novick, Kelley A. Lord, and Jane M. Richards (1992). "When Gulliver travels: social context, psychological closeness, and self-appraisals." *Journal of Personality and Social Psychology* 62: 717–727.

Brüderl, Josef and Andreas Diekmann (1995). "The log-logistic rate model: two generalizations with an application to demographic data." *Sociological Methods and Research* 24: 158–186.

Burt, Roger (2003). "Freemasonry and business networking during the Victorian period." *Economic History Review* 56: 657–688.

Burt, Ronald S. (1980). "Autonomy in a Social Topology." *American Journal of Sociology* 85: 892–925.

—— (1982). *Toward a Structural Theory of Action*. Academic Press: New York.

—— (1983). *Corporate Profits and Cooptation*. New York: Academic Press.

—— (1987). "Social contagion and innovation, cohesion versus structural equivalence." *American Journal of Sociology* 92: 1287–1335.

—— (1988). "The Stability of American Markets." *American Journal of Sociology* 94: 356–395.

—— (1990). "Detecting role equivalence." *Social Networks* 12: 83–97.

—— (1992). *Structural Holes*. Harvard University Press: Boston.

—— (1998a). "The gender of social capital." *Rationality and Society* 10: 5–46.

—— (1998b). "Partitioning the American Economy for Organization Research." Unpublished manuscript, University of Chicago Booth School of Business (http://faculty.chicagogsb.edu/ronald.burt/research/PAEOR.pdf).

—— (2000). "The network structure of social capital." Pp. 345–423 in *Research in Organizational Behavior*, Volume 22, edited by Robert I. Sutton and Barry M. Staw. Greenwich, CT: JAI Press.

—— (2002). "Bridge decay." *Social Networks* 24: 333–363.

—— (2004). "Structural holes and good ideas." *American Journal of Sociology* 110: 349–399.

—— (2005). *Brokerage and Closure*. Oxford: Oxford University Press.

—— (2007). "Secondhand brokerage: evidence on the importance of local structure for managers, bankers, and analysts." *Academy of Management Journal* 50: 119–148.

Burt, Ronald S. and Debbie S. Carleton (1989). "Another look at the network boundaries of American markets." *American Journal of Sociology* 95: 723–753.

Burt, Ronald S., Miguel Guilarte, Holly J. Raider, and Yuki Yasuda (2002). "Competition, Contingency, and the External Structure of Markets." Pp. 165–215 in *Advances in Strategic Management*, Volume 19, edited by Paul Ingram and Brian S. Silverman. New York: Elsevier.

Burt, Ronald S., Robin M. Hogarth, and Claude Michaud (2000). "The social capital of French and American managers." *Organization Science* 11: 123–147.

Burt, Ronald S., Joseph E. Jannotta, and J. T. Mahoney (1998). "Personality correlates of structural holes." *Social Networks* 20: 63–87.

Burt, Ronald S. and Don Ronchi (2007). "Teaching executives to see social capital: results from a field experiment." *Social Science Research* 36: 1156–1183.

Burt, Ronald S. and Tetsuji Uchiyama (1989). "The conditional significance of communication for interpersonal influence." Pp. 67–87 in *The Small World*, edited by Manfred Kochen. Norwood, NJ: Ablex.

Buskens, Vincent and Arnout van de Rijt (2008). "Dynamics of networks if everyone strives for structural holes." *American Journal of Sociology* 114: 371–407.

Buunk, Abraham P. and Frederick X. Gibbons (2006). "Social comparison orientation: a new perspective on those who do and those who don't compare with others." Pp. 15–32 in *Social Comparison and Social Psychology*, edited by Serge Guimond. Cambridge: Cambridge University Press.

—— —— (2007). "Social comparison: the end of a theory and the emergence of a field." *Organizational Behavior and Human Decision Processes* 102: 3–21.

Cairncross, Frances (1997). *The Death of Distance*. Boston, MA: Harvard University Press.

Carrin, Guy (1987). "Drug prescribing—a discussion of its variability and (ir)rationality." *Health Policy* 7: 73–94.

Carter, Richard and Steven Manaster (1990). "Initial public offerings and underwriter reputation." *Journal of Finance* 45: 1045–1067.

Casciaro, Tiziana and Mikolag Jan Piskorski (2006). "Power imbalance, mutual dependence, and constraint absorption: a closer look at resource dependence theory." *Administrative Science Quarterly* 50: 167–199.

Caves, Richard E. (1992). *American Industry*. Englewood Cliffs, NJ: Prentice-Hall.

Centola, Damon and Michael Macy (2007). "Complex contagions and the weakness of long ties." *American Journal of Sociology* 113: 702–734.

Cialdini, Robert B. "Indirect tactics of image management: beyond basking." Pp. 45–56 in *Impression Management in the Organization*, edited by Robert A. Giacalone and Paul Rosenfeld. Hillsdale, NJ: Erlbaum.

Clance, Pauline Rose and Suzanne Imes (1978). "The imposter phenomenon in high achieving women: dynamics and therapeutic intervention." *Psychotherapy Theory, Research and Practice* 15: 241–247.

Cohen, Bernard P. (1963). *Conflict and Conformity*. Cambridge, MA: MIT Press.

Coleman, James S. (1966). "Foundations for a theory of collective decisions." *American Journal of Sociology* 71: 615–627.

—— (1972). "Systems of social exchange." *Journal of Mathematical Sociology* 2: 145–163.

—— (1988). "Social capital in the creation of human capital." *American Journal of Sociology* 94: S95–S120.

—— (1990). *Foundations of Social Theory*. Cambridge, MA: Harvard University Press.

Coleman, James S., Elihu Katz, and Herbert Menzel (1957). "The diffusion of an innovation among physicians." *Sociometry* 20: 253–270.

—— —— (1966). *Medical Innovation*. New York: Bobbs-Merrill.

Collins, Norman R. and Lee E. Preston (1969). "Price–cost margins and industry structure." *Review of Economics and Statistics* 51: 271–286.

Collins, Randall (1994). *Four Sociological Traditions*. Oxford: Oxford University Press.

—— (1998). *The Sociology of Philosophies*. Cambridge, MA: Harvard University Press.

—— (2004). *Interaction Ritual Chains*. Princeton, NJ: Princeton University Press.

Cook, Karen S. and Richard M. Emerson (1978). "Power, equity and commitment in exchange networks." *American Sociological Review* 43: 712–739.

Cook, Karen S., Richard M. Emerson, Mary R. Gillmore, and Toshio Yamagishi (1983). "The distribution of power in exchange networks: theory and experimental results." *American Journal of Sociology* 89: 275–305.

Coser, Lewis A. (1974). *Greedy Institutions*. New York: Free Press.

Crane, Diana (1969). "Social structure in a group of scientists: a test of the 'invisible college' hypothesis." *American Sociological Review* 34: 335–352.

Cross, Rob and Robert J. Thomas (2008). *Driving Results Through Social Networks*. San Francisco, CA: Jossey-Bass.

Csermley, Peter (2008). "Creative elements: network-based predictions of active centres in proteins and cellular and social networks." *Trends in Biochemical Sciences* 33: 569–576.

Cyert, Richard M. and James G. March (1963). *A Behavioral Theory of the Firm.* Englewood Cliffs, NJ: Prentice-Hall.

Dacin, M. Tina (1997). "Isomorphism in context: the power and prescription of institutional norms." *Academy of Management Journal* 40: 46–81.

Davenport, Noa, Ruth D. Schwartz, and Gail Pursell Elliott (1999). *Mobbing.* Collins, IA: Civil Society Publishing.

Davis, Gerald F. (1991). "Agents without principles? The spread of the poison pill through the intercorporate network." *Administrative Science Quarterly* 36: 583–613.

Davis, Gerald F. and Henrich R. Greve (1997). "Corporate elite networks and governance changes in the 1980s." *American Journal of Sociology* 103: 1–37.

Dean, James W. and Mark Perlman (1998). "Harvey Leibenstein as a pioneer of our time." *Economic Journal* 108: 132–152.

Denrell, Jerker and Gaël Le Mens (2007). "Interdependent sampling and social influence." *Psychological Review* 114: 398–422.

Deutsch, Morton and Harold B. Gerard (1955). "A study of normative and informational social influences upon individual judgment." *Journal of Abnormal and Social Psychology* 51: 629–636.

Diekmann, Andreas and Henriette Engelhardt (1999). "The social inheritance of divorce: effects of parent's family type in postwar Germany." *American Sociological Review* 64: 783–793.

Diekmann, Andreas and Peter Mitter (1984). "A comparison of the 'sickle function' with alternative stochastic models of divorce rates." Pp. 123–153 in *Stochastic Modelling of Social Processes*, edited by Andreas Diekmann and Peter Mitter. Orlando, FL: Academic Press.

DiMaggio, Paul and Hugh Louch (1998). "Socially embedded consumer transactions: for what kinds of purchases do people most often use networks?" *American Sociological Review* 63: 619–637.

Doreian, Patrick (1981). "Estimating linear models with spatially distributed data." *Sociological Methodology* 12: 359–388.

—— (1986). "Measuring relative standing in small groups and bounded social networks." *Social Psychology Quarterly* 49: 247–259.

Douglas, Mary (1991). "Witchcraft and leprosy: two strategies of exclusion." *Man* 26: 723–736.

Dow, Malcolm M., Michael L. Burton, and Douglas R. White (1982). "Network autocorrelation: a simulation study of a foundational problem in regression and survey research." *Social Networks* 4: 169–200.

Duesenberry, James S. (1949). *Income, Saving, and the Theory of Consumer Behavior.* Cambridge, MA: Harvard University Press.

Dunbar, Robin (1996). *Grooming, Gossip, and the Evolution of Language.* Cambridge, MA: Harvard University Press.

Durkheim, Émile (1933) [1893]. *The Division of Labor in Society,* translated by George Simpson. New York: Free Press.

Eagly, Alice H. and Linda L. Carli (2007). *Through the Labyrinth.* Boston, MA: Harvard Business School Press.

Easterlin, Richard (1974). "Does economic growth improve the human lot? Some empirical evidence." Pp. 89–125 in *Nations and Households in Economic Growth,* edited by Paul A. David and Melvin W. Reder. Palo Alto, CA: Stanford University Press.

Eccles, Robert G. and Dwight B. Crane (1988). *Doing Deals.* Boston, MA: Harvard Business School Press.

Economist (1992). "The luxury-goods trade." 325 (7791): 95–98.

Eifenbein, Hillary Anger (2007). "Emotion in organizations: a review and theoretical integration." *Academy of Management Annals* 1: 315–386.

Elias, Norbert and John L. Scotson (1994) [1965]. *The Established and the Outsiders.* Thousand Oaks, CA: Sage.

Ellickson, Robert C. (1991). *Order without Law.* Cambridge, MA: Harvard University Press.

Emirbayer, Mustafa and Jeff Goodwin (1994). "Network analysis, culture, and the problem of agency." *American Journal of Sociology* 99: 1411–1154.

Epstein, Seymour (1979). "The stability of behavior: I. on predicting most of the people much of the time." *Journal of Personality and Social Psychology* 37: 1097–1126.

Erickson, Bonnie H. (1996). "Culture, class, and connections." *American Journal of Sociology* 102: 217–251.

—— (2001). "Good networks and good jobs: the value of social capital to employers and employees." Pp. 127–158 in *Social Capital,* edited by Nan Lin, Karen S. Cook, and Ronald S. Burt. New York: Aldine de Gruyter.

Erickson, Kai T. (1966). *Wayward Puritans.* New York: John Wiley.

Fang, Lily H. & Yasuda, Ayako (2005). "Analyst reputation, conflict of interest, and forecast accuracy." Working Paper No. 24-04. Rodney L. White Center for Financial Research, University of Pennsylvania.

Feld, Scott L. (1981). "The focused organization of social ties." *American Journal of Sociology* 86: 1015–1035.

—— (1997). "Structural embeddedness and stability of interpersonal relations." *Social Networks* 19: 91–95.

Fernandez-Mateo, Isabel (2007). "Who pays the price of brokerage? Transferring constraint through price setting in the staffing sector." *American Sociological Review* 72: 291–317.

Ferrier, Walter J. and Ken G. Smith (1999). "The role of competitive action in market share erosion and industry dethronement: a study of industry leaders and challengers." *Academy of Management Journal* 42: 372–388.

Festinger, Leon (1954). "A theory of social comparison processes." *Human Relations* 7: 117–140.

Festinger, Leon, Stanley Schachter, and Kurt W. Back (1950). *Social Pressures in Informal Groups.* Stanford, CA: Stanford University Press.

Fine, Gary Alan (1994). "The social construction of style: Thorstein Veblen's *The Theory of the Leisure Class* as contested text." *Sociological Quarterly* 35: 457–472.

Fine, Gary Alan (1996). "Reputational entrepreneurs and the memory of incompetence: melting supporters, partisan warriors, and images of President Harding." *American Journal of Sociology* 101: 1159–1193.

Finifter, Bernard M. (1972). "The generation of confidence: evaluating research findings by random subsample replication." *Sociological Methodology* 4: 112–175.

Fleming, Lee and David M. Waguespack (2007). "Brokerage, boundary spanning, and leadership in open innovation communities." *Organization Science* 18: 165–180.

Fleming, Lee, Alexandra Marin, Jonathan McPhie, and Lyra J. Colfer (forthcoming). "Why the Valley went first: agglomeration and emergence in regional collaboration networks." In *Market Emergence and Transformation*, edited by John Padgett and Walter W. Powell. Boston, MA: MIT Press.

Fleming, Lee, Santiago Mingo, and David Chen (2007). "Collaborative brokerage, generative creativity, and creative success." *Administrative Science Quarterly* 52: 443–475.

Fligstein, Neil (1987). "The intraorganizational power struggle: rise of finance personnel to top leadership in large corporations, 1919–1979." *American Sociological Review* 52: 44–58.

Foster, George M. (1965). "Peasant society and the image of limited good." *American Anthropologist* 67: 293–315.

—— (1972). "A second look at limited good." *Anthropological Quarterly* 45: 57–64.

Frank, Robert H. (1984). "Are workers paid their marginal products?" *American Economic Review* 74: 549–571.

—— (1985). *Choosing the Right Pond*. Oxford: Oxford University Press.

—— (2005). "The mysterious disappearance of James Duesenberry." *New York Times*, June 9.

Frankort, Hans T. W. (2008). "Technological resources, structural holes, and innovation: a longitudinal study of an interfirm R&D network." Unpublished manuscript, Maastricht University, School of Economics and Business Administration.

Fredrickson, Barbara L. (1998). "What good are positive emotions?" *Review of General Psychology* 2: 300–319.

Freeman, Linton C. (1977). "A set of measures of centrality based on betweenness." *Sociometry* 40: 35–40.

—— (1979). "Centrality in social networks: conceptual clarification." *Social Networks* 1: 215–239.

Friedkin, Noah E. (1983). "Horizons of observability and limits of informal control in organizations." *Social Forces* 62: 54–77.

Friedman, Milton (1957). *A Theory of the Consumption Function*. Princeton, NJ: Princeton University Press.

Friend, Ronald M. and Joel Gilbert (1973). "Threat and fear of negative evaluation as determinants of locus of social comparison." *Journal of Personality* 41: 328–340.

Gabbay, Shaul M. (1997). *Social Capital in the Creation of Financial Capital*. Champaign, IL: Stipes.

Galaskiewicz, Joseph (1985). *Social Organization of an Urban Grants Economy*. New York: Academic Press.

—— (1997). "An urban grants economy revisited: corporate charitable contributions in the Twin Cities, 1979–81. 1987–89." *Administrative Science Quarterly* 42: 445–471.

Galaskiewicz, Joseph and Ronald S. Burt (1991). "Interorganization contagion in corporate philanthropy." *Administrative Science Quarterly* 36: 88–105.

Gambetta, Diego (1994). "Godfather's gossip." *Archives Europeennes de Sociologie* 35: 199–223.

Gartrell, C. David (2002). "The embeddedness of social comparison." Pp. 164–184 in *Relative Deprivation*, edited by Iain Walker and Heather J. Smith. Cambridge: Cambridge University Press.

Gibbons, Frederick X. and Abraham P. Buunk (1999). "Individual differences in social comparison: development of a scale of social comparison orientation." *Journal of Personality and Social Psychology* 76: 129–142.

Gladwell, Malcolm (2000). *The Tipping Point*. New York: Little, Brown and Company.

Gluckman, Max (1963). "Gossip and scandal." *Current Anthropology* 4: 307–316.

Gold, David (1956). "*Personal Influence*, review." *American Sociological Review* 21: 792–793.

Goodman, Leo (1984). *The Analysis of Cross-Classified Data Having Ordered Categories*. Cambridge, MA: Harvard University Press.

Goolsebee, Austan and Peter J. Klenow (2002). "Evidence of learning and network externalities in the diffusion of home computers." *Journal of Law and Economics* 45: 317–343.

Granovetter, Mark S. (1973). "The strength of weak ties." *American Journal of Sociology* 78: 1360–1380.

—— (1983). "The strength of weak ties: a network theory revisited." *Sociological Theory* 1: 201–233.

—— (1985). "Economic action, social structure, and embeddedness." *American Journal of Sociology* 91: 481–510.

—— (1992). "Problems of explanation in economic sociology." Pp. 29–56 in *Networks and Organizations*, edited by Nitin Nohria and Robert G. Eccles. Boston, MA: Harvard Business School Press.

Greif, Avner (1989). "Reputation and coalitions in medieval trade: evidence on the Maghribi traders." *Journal of Economic History* 49: 857–882.

Greenberg, Jerald, Claire E. Ashton-James, and Neal M. Ashkanasy (2007). "Social comparison processes in organizations." *Organizational Behavior and Human Decision Processes* 102: 22–41.

Greenwood, John D. (2004). "What happened to the 'social' in social psychology?" *Journal for the Theory of Social Behavior* 34: 19–34.

Greve, Henrich R. (1995). "Jumping ship: the diffusion of strategy abandonment." *Administrative Science Quarterly* 40: 444–473.

Griliches, Zvi (1992). "The search for R&D spillovers." *Scandinavian Journal of Economics* 94: S29–S47.

Guimond, Serge (ed.) (2006). *Social Comparison and Social Psychology*. Cambridge: Cambridge University Press.

Grinblatt, Mark, Matti Keloharju, and Seppo Ikäheimo (2008). "Social influence and consumption: evidence from the automobile purchases of neighbors." *Review of Economics and Statistics* 90: 735–753.

Gulati, Ranjay (2007). *Managing Network Resources*. Oxford: Oxford University Press.

Gulati, Ranjay and Martin Gargiulo (1999). "Where Do Interorganizational Networks Come From?" *American Journal of Sociology* 104: 1439–1493.

Hamblin, Robert L. (1971). "Mathematical experimentation and sociological theory: a critical analysis." *Sociometry* 34: 423–452.

Hannan, Michael T. and John H. Freeman (1989). *Organizational Ecology.* Cambridge, MA: Harvard University Press.

Hanneman, Robert A. and Mark Riddle (2005). *Introduction to Social Network Methods.* Riverside, CA: University of California, Riverside. Online textbook available at http://faculty.ucr.edu/~hanneman.

Hansen, Morten T. (1999). "The search-transfer problem: the role of weak ties in sharing knowledge across organization subunits." *Administrative Science Quarterly* 44: 82–111.

—— (2002). "Knowledge networks: explaining effective knowledge sharing in multiunit companies." *Organization Science* 13: 232–248.

Hansen, Morten T., Joel M. Podolny, and Jeffrey Pfeffer (2001). "So many ties, so little time: a task contingency perspective on the value of social capital in organizations." *Research in the Sociology of Organizations* 18: 21–57.

Hardin, Curtis D. and E. Tory Higgins (1996). "Shared reality: how social verification makes the subjective objective." Pp. 28–77 in *Handbook of Motivation and Cognition*, Volume 3, edited by Richard M. Sorrentino and E. Tory Higgins. New York: Guilford.

Hargadon, Andrew and Robert I. Sutton (1997). "Technology brokering and innovation in a product development firm." *Administrative Science Quarterly* 42: 716–749.

Hayek, F. A. (1945). "The use of knowledge in society." *American Economic Review* 35: 519–530.

Hayward, Mathew L. A. and Warren Boeker (1998). "Power and conflicts of interest in professional firms: evidence from investment banking." *Administrative Science Quarterly* 43: 1–22.

Hedström, Peter (2005). *Dissecting the Social.* New York: Cambridge University Press.

Heinz, John P., Edward O. Laumann, Robert L. Nelson, and Robert H. Salisbury (1993). *The Hollow Core.* Cambridge, MA: Harvard University Press.

Heise, David R. (1972). "Employing nominal variables, induced variables, and block variables in path analysis." *Sociological Methods and Research* 1: 147–73.

Hitler, Jennifer M. (2009). "Social capital in Asia: do managers in collective cultures benefit from boundary spanning?" Paper presented at annual meetings of the Academy of Management, Chicago.

Hochschild, Arlie R. (1983). *The Managed Heart.* Berkeley, CA: University of California Press.

Hodgkinson, Gerard P. (2005). *Images of Competitive Space.* New York: Palgrave Macmillan.

House, James S. (1977). "The three faces of social psychology." *Sociometry* 40: 161–177.

—— (2008). "Social psychology, social science, and economics: twentieth century progress and problems, twenty-first century prospects." *Social Psychology Quarterly* 71: 232–256.

Hsu, David H. and Kwanghui Lim (2006). "Knowledge bridging by biotechnology start-ups." Unpublished manuscript, University of Pennsylvania Wharton School.

Hubbell, Charles H. (1965). "An input–output approach to clique identification." *Sociometry* 28: 377–399.

Hummell, Hans and Wolfgang Sodeur (1987). "Strukturbeschreibung von positionen in sozialen beziehungsnetzen," Pp. 177–202 in *Techniken der Empirischen Sozialforschung: 1, Methoden der Netzwerkanalyse*, edited by Franz U. Pappi. Munich: Oldenbourg.

Hyman, Herbert and Eleanor Singer (eds.) (1968). *Readings in Reference Group Theory.* New York: Free Press.

Ingram, Paul and Peter W. Roberts (2000). "Friendships among competitors in the Sydney hotel industry." *American Journal of Sociology* 106: 387–423.

Ingram, Paul and Lori Qingyuan Yue (2008). "Structure, affect and identity as bases of organizational competition and cooperation." *Academy of Management Annals* 2: 275–303.

Isen, Alice M., Kimberly A. Daubman, and Gary P. Nowicki (1987). "Positive affect facilitates creative problem solving." *Journal of Personality and Social Psychology* 52: 1122–1131.

Isen, Alice M., Mitzi M. S. Johnson, Elizabeth Mertz, and Gregory F. Robinson (1985). "The influence of positive affect on the unusualness of word associations." *Journal of Personality and Social Psychology* 48: 1413–1426.

Jackson, Matthew O. (2008). *Social and Economic Networks.* Princeton, NJ: Princeton University Press.

Jaffe, Adam B. (1986). "Technological opportunity and spillovers of R&D: evidence from firms' patents, profits, and market value." *American Economic Review* 76: 984–1001.

Janicik, Gregory A. and Richard P. Larrick (2005). "Social network schemas and the learning of incomplete networks." *Journal of Personality and Social Psychology* 88: 348–364.

Jennings, Helen (1937). "Structures of leadership-development and spheres of influence." *Sociometry* 1: 99–143.

Jensen, Michael (2003). "The role of network resources in market entry: commercial banks' entry into investment banking." *Administrative Science Quarterly* 48: 466–497.

—— (2008). "The use of relational discrimination to manage market entry: when do social status and structural holes work against you?" *Academy of Management Journal* 51: 723–743.

Kadushin, Charles (1995). "Friendship among the French Financial Elite." *American Sociological Review* 60: 202–221.

Kahn, Jeffrey H., Renée M. Tobin, Audra E. Massey, and Jennifer A. Anderson (2007). "Measuring emotional expression with the Linguistic Inquiry and Word Count." *American Journal of Psychology* 120: 263–286.

Kahneman, Daniel and Amos Tversky (1984). "Choices, values, and frames." *American Psychologist* 39: 341–350.

Kahneman, Daniel, Paul Slovic, and Amos Tversky (eds.) (1982). *Judgment under Uncertainty.* Cambridge: Cambridge University Press.

Kang, Eugene (2008). "Director interlocks and spillover effects of reputational penalties from financial reporting fraud." *Academy of Management Journal* 51: 537–555.

Karpoff, Jonathan M. and John R. Lott, Jr. (1993). "The reputational penalty firms bear from committing criminal fraud." *Journal of Law and Economics* 36: 757–802.

Katz, Daniel and Robert L. Kahn (1966). *The Social Psychology of Organizations.* New York: John Wiley.

Katz, Elihu and Paul F. Lazarsfeld (1955). *Personal Influence.* New York: Free Press.

Kenny, David A. and Linda Albright (1987). "Accuracy in interpersonal perception: a social relations analysis." *Psychological Bulletin* 102: 390–402.

Kets de Vries, Manfred (2005). "The dangers of feeling like a fake." *Harvard Business Review* 83: 108–116.

Kilduff, Martin and David Krackhardt (1994). "Bringing the individual back in: a structural analysis of the internal market for reputation in organizations." *Academy of Management Journal* 37: 87–108.

—— —— (2008). *Interpersonal Networks in Organizations*. Cambridge: Cambridge University Press.

Killworth, Peter D. and H. Russell Bernard (1978). "The reverse small world experiment." *Social Networks* 1: 159–192.

Kohn, Melvin L. (1969). *Class and Conformity: A Study in Values*. Homewood, IL: Dorsey.

—— (1971). "Bureaucratic man: a portrait and an interpretation." *American Sociological Review* 36: 461–474.

Kohn, Melvin L. and Carmi Schooler (1978). "The reciprocal effects of the substantive complexity of work and intellectual flexibility: a longitudinal assessment." *American Journal of Sociology* 84: 24–52.

—— —— (1983). *Work and Personality: An Inquiry into the Impact of Social Stratification*. Norwood, NJ: Ablex.

Krackhardt, David (1998). "Simmelian ties: super strong and sticky." Pp. 21–38 in *Power and Influence in Organizations*, edited by Roderick M. Kramer and Margaret A. Neale. Thousand Oaks, CA: Sage.

Krippner, Greta R. and Anthony S. Alvarez (2007). "Embeddedness and the intellectual projects of economic sociology." *Annual Review of Sociology* 33: 219–240.

Kuran, Timur (1998). *Private Truths, Public Lies: The Social Consequences of Preference Falsification*. Cambridge, MA: Harvard University Press.

Labianca, Giuseppe and Daniel J. Brass (2006). "Exploring the social ledger: negative relationships and negative asymmetry in social networks in organizations." *Academy of Management Review* 31: 596–614.

Labianca, Giuseppe, Daniel J. Brass, and Barbara Gray (1998). "Social networks and perceptions of intergroup conflict: the role of negative relationships and third parties." *Academy of Management Journal* 41: 55–67.

Lankford, Philip M. (1974). "Comparative analysis of clique identification methods." *Sociometry* 37: 287–305.

Laumann, Edward O. (1965). "Subjective social distance and urban occupational stratification." *American Journal of Sociology* 71: 26–36.

—— (1966). *Prestige and Association in an Urban Community*. New York: Bobbs-Merrill.

Laumann, Edward O., Tony Tam, John P. Heinz, with Robert L. Nelson and Robert H. Salisbury (1992). "The social organization of the Washington establishment during the first Reagan administration: a network analysis." Pp. 161–188 in *Research in Politics and Society*, Vol. 8, edited by Gwen Moore and J. A. Whitt. Greenwich, CT: JAI Press.

Lawson, Ann M. (1997). "Benchmark Input–Output Accounts for the U.S. Economy, 1992." *Survey of Current Business* 77: 36–82.

Lawson, Ann M., Kurt S. Bersani, Mahnaz Fahim-Nader, and Jiemin Guo (2002). "Benchmark Input–Output Accounts of the United States, 1997." *Survey of Current Business* 82: 19–109.

Lawson, Ann M. and Teske, D. A. (1994). "Benchmark Input–Output Accounts for the U.S. Economy, 1987." *Survey of Current Business* 74: 73–115.

Lazarsfeld, Paul F., Bernard Berelson, and Hazel Gaudet (1944). *The People's Choice*. New York: Duell, Sloan and Pearce.

Lazarsfeld, Paul F. and Robert K. Merton (1954). "Friendship as a social process: a substantive and methodological analysis." Pp. 18–66 in *Freedom and Control in Modern Society*, edited by Morroe Berger, Theodore Abel, and Charles H. Page. New York: Van Nostrand.

Leana, Carrie R. and Frits K. Pil (2006). "Social capital and organizational performance: evidence from urban public schools." *Organization Science* 17: 353–366.

Leibenstein, Harvey (1950). "Bandwagon, snob, and Veblen effects in the theory of consumers' demand." *Quarterly Journal of Economics* 64: 183–207.

Leifer, Eric M. (1988). "Interaction preludes to role setting: exploratory local action." *American Sociological Review* 53: 865–878.

Lin, Nan (2001). "Building a network theory of social capital." Pp. 3–29 in *Social Capital*, edited by Nan Lin, Karen Cook, and Ronald S. Burt. New York: Walter de Gruyter.

—— (2002). *Social Capital*. Cambridge: Cambridge University Press.

Lin, Nan and Mary Dumin (1986). "Access to occupations through social ties." *Social Networks* 8: 365–385.

Lin, Nan, Mary Dumin, and Mary Woelfel (1986). "Measuring community and network support." Pp. 153–170 in *Social Support, Life Events and Depression*, edited by Nan Lin, Alfred Dean, and Walter Ensel. New York: Academic Press.

Lin, Nan, Walter Ensel, and John Vaughn (1981). "Social resources and strength of ties: structural factors in occupational status attainment." *American Sociological Review* 46: 393–405.

Lin, Nan and Bonnie Erickson (eds.) (2008). *Social Capital*. Oxford: Oxford University Press.

Lin, Nan, Yang-chih Fu, and Ray-May Hsung (2001). "The position generator: measurement techniques for investigations of social capital." Pp. 57–81 in *Social Capital*, edited by Nan Lin, Karen S. Cook, and Ronald S. Burt. New York: Aldine de Gruyter.

Lin, Nan, Xiaolan Ye, and Walter M. Ensel (1999). "Social support and depressed mood: a structural analysis." *Journal of Health and Social Behavior* 40: 344–359.

Lorrain, Francois P. and Harrison C. White (1971). "Structural equivalence of individuals in social networks." *Journal of Mathematical Sociology* 1: 49–80.

Luce, R. Duncan (2002). "A psychophysical theory of intensity proportions, joint presentations, and matches." *Psychological Bulletin* 109: 520–532.

McPherson, Miller (1983). "An ecology of affiliation." *American Sociological Review* 48: 519–532.

MacRae, Duncan Jr. (1960). "Direct factor analysis of sociometric data." *Sociometry* 23: 360–371.

March, James G. and Herbert A. Simon (1958). *Organizations*. New York: John Wiley.

Marsden, Peter V. (1983). "Restricted access in networks and models of power." *American Journal of Sociology* 88: 686–717.

—— (1990). "Network data and measurement." *Annual Review of Sociology* 16: 435–463.

—— (2005). "Recent developments in network measurement." Pp. 8–30 in *Models and Methods in Social Network Analysis*, edited by Peter J. Carrington, John Scott, and Stanley Wasserman. Cambridge: Cambridge University Press.

Marsden, Peter V. and Joel M. Podolny (1990). "Dynamic analysis of network diffusion processes." Pp. 197–214 in *Social Networks through Time*, edited by Jeroen Weesie and Henk Flap. Utrecht, Netherlands: ISOR.

Marshall, Alfred (1920). *Principles of Economics*. London: Macmillan.

Martin, John Levi and King-To Yeung (2006). "Persistence of close personal ties over a 12-year period." *Social Networks* 28: 331–362.

Mason, Roger (2000). "The social significance of consumption: James Duesenberry's contribution to consumer theory." *Journal of Economic Issues* 34: 553–572.

Mayer-Schönberger, Viktor (2009). *Delete*. Princeton, NJ: Princeton University Press.

McClelland, David C. (1961). *The Achieving Society*. Princeton, NJ: Van Nostrand.

McGahan, Anita M., N. Argyres, and Joel A. C. Baum (2004). "Context, Technology and Strategy: Forging New Perspectives on the Industry Life Cycle." Pp. 1–21 in *Advances in Strategic Management, 21*, edited by Joel A. C. Baum and Anita M. McGahan. Oxford: JAI/Elsevier.

McPherson, Miller, Lynn Smith-Lovin, and James M. Cook (2001). "Birds of a feather: homophily in social networks." *Annual Review of Sociology* 27: 415–444.

Mead, George Herbert (1934). *Mind, Self, and Society*, edited by Charles W. Morris. Chicago: University of Chicago Press.

Mehra, Ajay, Andrea I. Dixon, Daniel J. Brass, and Bruce Robertson (2006). "The social network ties of group leaders: implications for group performance and leader reputation." *Organization Science* 17: 64–79.

Mehra, Ajay, Martin Kilduff, and Daniel J. Brass (2001). "The social networks of high and low-self monitors: Implications for workplace performance." *Administrative Science Quarterly* 46: 121–146.

Menon, Tanya and Jeffrey Pfeffer (2003). "Valuing internal vs. external knowledge: explaining the preference for outsiders." *Management Science* 49: 497–513.

Menon, Tanya, Leigh Thompson, and Hoon-Seok Choi (2006). "Tainted knowledge vs. tempting knowledge: people avoid knowledge from internal rivals and seek knowledge from external rivals." *Management Science* 52: 1129–1144.

Merry, Sally Engle (1984). "Rethinking gossip and scandal." Pp. 271–302 in *Toward a General Theory of Social Control*, Volume 1, edited by Donald Black. New York: Academic Press.

Merton, Robert K. (1968) [1949]. "Patterns of influence: local and cosmopolitan influentials." Pp. 441–474 in *Social Theory and Social Structure*, edited by Robert K. Merton. New York: Free Press.

—— (1968) [1957]. "Continuities in the theory of reference groups and social structure." Pp. 335–440 in *Social Theory and Social Structure*, edited by Robert K. Merton. New York: Free Press.

—— (1984). "Socially expected durations: a case study of concept formation in sociology." Pp. 262–283 in *Conflict and Consensus*, edited by Walter W. Powell and Richard Robbins. New York: Free Press.

Merton, Robert K. and Alice S. Rossi (1968) [1957]. "Contributions to the theory of reference group behavior." Pp. 279–334 in *Social Theory and Social Structure*, edited by Robert K. Merton. New York: Free Press.

Meyerson, Eva M. (1994). "Human capital, social capital and compensation: the relative contribution of social contacts to managers' incomes." *Acta Sociologica* 37: 383–399.

Mintz, Beth and Michael Schwartz (1981). "The structure of incorporate unity in American business." *American Sociological Review* 29: 87–103.

Mischel, Walter (1968). *Personality and Assessment.* New York: Wiley.

—— (2004). "Toward an integrative science of the person." *Annual Review of Psychology* 55: 1–22.

Mischel, Walter and Yuichi Shoda (1995). "A cognitive-affective system theory of personality: reconceptualizing situations, dispositions, dynamics, and invariance in personality structure." *Psychological Review* 102: 246–268.

Mizruchi, Mark S. (1989). "Similarity of political behavior among large American corporations." *American Journal of Sociology* 95: 401–424.

Mizruchi, Mark S., Peter Mariolis, Michael Schwartz, and Beth Mintz (1986). "Techniques for disaggregating centrality scores in social networks." *Sociological Methodology* 16: 26–48.

Mizruchi, Mark S. and Linda B. Sterns (2001). "Getting deals done: the use of social networks in bank decision making." *American Sociological Review* 66: 647–671.

Moran, Peter (2005). "Structural versus relational embeddedness: social capital and managerial performance." *Strategic Management Journal* 26: 1129–1151.

Moreno, Jacob L. (1934). *Who Will Survive?* Washington, DC: Nervous and Mental Disease Publishing.

Morris, Michael W., Joel M. Podolny, and Sheira Ariel (2000). "Missing relations: incorporating relational constructs into models of culture." Pp. 52–90 in *Innovations in International and Cross-Cultural Management,* edited by P. Christopher Earley and Harbir Singh. Thousand Oaks, CA: Sage Publications.

Munshi, Kaivan and Mark Rosenzweig (2005). "Economic development and the decline of rural and urban community-based networks." *Economics of Transition* 13: 427–443.

—— —— (2007). "Network decay in traditional economies." Pp. 183–209 in *The Missing Links,* edited by James E. Rauch. New York: Russell Sage Foundation.

Nachman, Steven R. (1986). "Discomforting laughter: 'schadenfreude' among Melanesians." *Journal of Anthropological Research* 42: 53–67.

Nanda, Ashish and Christopher A. Bartlett (1990). "Corning Incorporated: a network of alliances." *Harvard Business School Case 9-391-102.* Boston, MA: Harvard Business School Press.

Newman, Matthew L., James W. Pennebaker, Diane S. Berry, and Jane M. Richards (2003). "Lying words: predicting deception from linguistic styles." *Personality and Social Psychology Bulletin* 29: 665–675.

Obstfeld, David (2005). "Social networks, the tertius iungens orientation, and involvement in innovation." *Administrative Science Quarterly* 50: 100–130.

Oh, Hongseok and Martin Kilduff (2008). "The ripple effect of personality on social structure: self-monitoring origins of network brokerage." *Journal of Applied Psychology* 93: 1155–1164.

Oliver, Christine (1992). "The antecedents of deinstitutionalization." *Organization Studies* 13: 563–588.

Ord, Keith (1975). "Estimation methods for models of spatial interaction." *Journal of the American Statistical Association* 70: 120–126.

Orzechowicz, David (2008). "Privileged emotion managers: the case of actors." *Social Psychology Quarterly* 71: 143–156.

Owen-Smith, Jason and Woody W. Powell (2004). "Knowledge networks as channels and conduits: the effects of spillovers in the Boston biotechnology community." *Organization Science* 15: 5–21.

Padgett, John F. and Christopher K. Ansell (1993). "Robust action and the rise of the Medici, 1400–1434." *American Journal of Sociology* 98: 1259–1319.

Pennebaker, James W., Janice K. Kiecolt-Glaser, and Ronald Gleser (1988). "Disclosure of traumas and immune function: health implications for psychotherapy." *Journal of Consulting and Clinical Psychology* 56: 239–245.

Pennebaker, James W., Matthias R. Mehl, and Kate G. Niederhoffer (2003). "Psychological aspects of natural language use: our words, our selves." *Annual Review of Psychology* 54: 547–577.

Peterson, Christopher, Steven F. Maier, and Martin E. P. Seligman (1993). *Learned Helplessness*. Oxford: Oxford University Press.

Pfeffer, Jeffrey and Gerald R. Salancik (1978). *The External Control of Organizations*. New York: Harper & Row.

Phillips, Damon J. and Ezra W. Zuckerman (2001). "Middle-status conformity: theoretical restatement and empirical demonstration in two markets." *American Journal of Sociology* 107: 379–429.

Podolny, Joel M. (1993). "A status-based model of market competition." *American Journal of Sociology* 98: 829–872.

—— (2005). *Status Signals*. Princeton, NJ: Princeton University Press.

Podolny, Joel M. and James N. Baron (1997). "Relationships and resources: social networks and mobility in the workplace." *American Sociological Review* 62: 673–693.

Podolny, Joel M. and Toby E. Stuart (1995). "A role-based ecology of technological change." *American Journal of Sociology* 100: 1224–1260.

Podolny, Joel M., Toby E. Stuart, and Michael T. Hannan (1996). "Networks, knowledge, and niches: competition in the worldwide semiconductor industry, 1984–1991." *American Journal of Sociology* 102: 659–689.

Polanyi, Michael (1958). *Personal Knowledge: Towards a Post Critical Philosophy*. London: Routledge.

Pooley, Jefferson and Elihu Katz (2008). "Further notes on why American sociology abandoned mass communication research." *Journal of Communication* 58: 767–786. Porac, Joscph F. and Howard Thomas (1990). "Taxonomic mental models in competitor definition." *Academy of Management Review* 15: 224–240.

Porac, Joseph F., Howard Thomas, Fiona Wilson, Douglas Paton, and Alaina Kanfer (1995). "Rivalry and the industry model of Scottish knitwear producers." *Administrative Science Quarterly* 40: 203–227.

Porac, Joseph F., James B. Wade, and Timothy G. Pollock (1999). "Industry categories and the politics of the comparable firm in CEO compensation." *Administrative Science Quarterly* 44: 112–144.

Portmann, John (1999). *When Bad Things Happen to Other People*. London: Routledge.

Porter, Michael E. (1980). *Competitive Strategy*. New York: Free Press.

Powell, Walter W., Douglas R. White, Kenneth W. Koput, and Jason Owen-Smith (2005). "Network dynamics and field evolution: the growth of interorganizational collaboration in the life sciences." *American Journal of Sociology* 110: 1132–1205.

Pugh, S. Douglas (2001). "Service with a smile: emotional contagion in the service encounter." *Academy of Management Journal* 44: 1018–1027.

Putnam, Robert D. (1993). *Making Democracy Work*. Princeton, NJ: Princeton University Press.

—— (2000). *Bowling Alone*. New York: Simon and Schuster.

Rao, Hayagreeva, Henrich R. Greve, and Gerald F. Davis (2001). "Fool's gold: social proof in the initiation and abandonment of coverage by Wall Street analysts." *Administrative Science Quarterly* 46: 502–526.

Rayo, Luis and Gary S. Becker (2006). "Peer comparisons and consumer debt." *University of Chicago Law Review* 73: 231–248.

Reagans, Ray E. and Bill McEvily (2003). "Network structure and information transfer: the effects of cohesion and range." *Administrative Science Quarterly* 48: 240–267.

Reagans, Ray E. and Ezra W. Zuckerman (2001). "Networks, diversity, and performance: the social capital of corporate R&D units." *Organization Science* 12: 502–517.

—— (2008). "Why knowledge does not equal power: the network redundancy trade-off." *Industrial and Corporate Change* 17: 903–944.

Reagans, Ray E., Ezra W. Zuckerman, and Bill McEvily (2004). "How to make the team: social networks vs. demography as criteria for designing effective teams." *Administrative Science Quarterly* 49: 101–133.

Rodan, Simon and Charles Gallunic (2004). "More than network structure: how knowledge heterogeneity influences managerial performance and innovativeness." *Strategic Management Journal* 25: 541–562.

Rogers, Everett (2003) [1962]. *Diffusion of Innovations*. New York: Free Press.

Rosen, Emanuel (2000). *The Anatomy of Buzz*. New York: Doubleday.

Rosen, Sherwin (1997). "Austrian and neoclassical economics: any gains from trades?" *Journal of Economic Perspectives* 11: 139–152.

Rosenkopf, Lori and Atul Nerkar (2001). "Beyond local search: boundary-spanning exploration, and impact in the optical disk industry." *Strategic Management Journal* 22: 287–306.

Rosten, Leo (1989). *The Joys of Yinglish*. New York: McGraw-Hill.

Roth, Louise Marie (2007). "Women on Wall Street: despite diversity measures, Wall Street remains vulnerable to sex discrimination charges." *Academy of Management Perspectives* 21: 24–35.

Rotter Julian B. (1966). "Generalized expectancies for internal versus external control of reinforcement." Psychological Monographs 80 (Whole No. 609).

Rowley, Timothy J. and Joel A. C. Baum (2004). "Sophistication of interfirm network strategies in the Canadian investment banking industry." *Scandinavian Journal of Management* 20: 103–124.

Rowley, Timothy J., Henrich R. Greve, Hayagreeva Rao, Joel A. C. Baum, and Andrew V. Shipilov (2005). "Time to break up: social and instrumental antecedents of firm exits from exchange cliques." *Academy of Management Journal* 48: 499–520.

Ryall, Michael D. and Olav Sorenson (2007). "Brokers and competitive advantage." *Management Science* 53: 566–583.

Sailer, Lee D. (1978). "Structural equivalence: meaning and definition, computation and application." *Social Networks* 1: 73–90.

Saltzer, Jerome H., David P. Reed, and David D. Clark (1984). "End-to-end arguments in system design." *ACM Transactions in Computer Systems* 2: 277–288.

Sanders, Shane (2008). "A pedagogical model of the relative income hypothesis." Unpublished manuscript available at SSRN: http://ssrn.com/abstract=1262991.

Sawai, K. (1994). "A study on how Coleman's book on diffusion of new drugs has been cited in subsequent published articles." *Library and Information Science* 32: 105–122.

Schachter, Stanley (1959). *The Psychology of Affiliation*. Stanford, CA: Stanford University Press.

Schachter, Stanley and Jerome E. Singer (1962). "Cognitive, social, and physiological determinants of emotional state." *Psychological Review* 69: 379–399.

Schmalensee, Richard L. (1989). "Inter-Industry Studies of Structure and Performance." Pp. 951–1009 in *Handbook of Industrial Organization, Volume 1*, edited by Richard L. Schmalensee and Robert D. Willig. New York: North-Holland.

Scott, W. Richard (2004). "Reflections on a half-century of organizational sociology." *Annual Review of Sociology* 30: 1–21.

Scott, W. Richard and Gerald F. Davis (2007). *Organizations and Organizing*. Upper Saddle River, NJ: Pierson Prentice Hall.

Seibert, Scott E., Maria L. Kraimer, and Robert C. Liden (2001). "A social capital theory of career success." *Academy of Management Journal* 44: 219–237.

Seligman, Martin E. P. and Mihaly Csikszentmihalyi (2000). "Positive psychology: an introduction." *American Psychologist* 55: 5–14.

Seligman, Martin E. P., Tracy A. Steen, Nansook Park, and Christopher Peterson (2005). "Positive psychology progress: empirical validation of interventions." *American Psychologist* 60: 410–421.

Sepra, Stefanie P., Eric D. Buhrfeind, and James W. Pennebaker (1994). "Expressive writing and coping with job loss." *Academy of Management Journal* 37: 722–733.

Sewell, William H. (1989). "Some reflections on the golden age of interdisciplinary social psychology." *Social Psychology Quarterly* 52: 88–97.

Sherif, Muzafer (1935). "A study of some factors in perception." *Archives of Psychology*, No. 187.

—— (1936). *The Psychology of Social Norms*. New York: Harper & Brothers.

Shipilov, Andrew V. (2006). "Network strategies and performance of Canadian investment banks." *Academy of Management Journal* 46: 590–604.

Silverman, Brian S. and Joel A. C. Baum (2002). "Alliance-based competitive dynamics." *Academy of Management Journal* 45: 791–806.

Smith, Allen C. and Sherryl Kleinman (1989). "Managing emotions in medical school: students' contacts with the living and the dead." *Social Psychology Quarterly* 52: 56–69.

Sorenson, Olav and Pino Audia (2000). "The social structure of entrepreneurial activity: geographic concentration of footwear production in the United States, 1940–1989." *American Journal of Sociology* 106: 424–462.

Sorenson, Olav and Toby E. Stuart (2001). "Syndication networks and the spatial distribution of venture capital investments." *American Journal of Sociology* 106: 1546–1588.

Spence, Michael (2002). "Signaling in retrospect and the informational structure of markets." *American Economic Review* 92: 434–459.

Steingrimsson, Ragnar and R. Duncan Luce (2006). "Empirical evaluation of a model of global psychophysical judgments: III. a form for the psychophysical function and intensity filtering." *Journal of Mathematical Psychology* 50: 15–29.

Stevens, S. S. (1957). "On the psychophysical law." *Psychological Review* 64: 153–181.

—— (1970). "Neural events and the psychophysical law." *Science* 170: 1043–1050.

—— (1975). *Psychophysics*. New York: Wiley Interscience.

Stickel, Scott E. (1992). "Reputation and performance among security analysts." *Journal of Finance* 47: 1811–1836.

Stouffer, Samuel A. (1962). "The concept of relative deprivation." Pp. 13–38 in *Social Research to Test Ideas*, edited by Samuel A. Stouffer. New York: Free Press.

Stouffer, Samuel A., Edward A. Suchman, Leland C. DeVinney, Shirley A. Star, and Robin M. Williams Jr. (1949). *The American Soldier: Adjustment During Army Life.* Princeton, NJ: Princeton University Press.

Strang, David and Nancy Brandon Tuma (1993). "Spatial and temporal heterogeneity in diffusion." *American Journal of Sociology* 99: 614–639.

Stuart, Toby E., Ha Hoang, and Ralph C. Hybels (1999). "Interorganizational endorsements and the performance of entrepreneurial ventures." *Administrative Science Quarterly* 44: 315–349.

Stuart, Toby E. and Joel M. Podolny (1996). "Local search and the evolution of technological capabilities." *Strategic Management Journal* 17: 21–38.

Stube, Michael J. (2005). "What did Triplett really find? A contemporary analysis of the first experiment in social psychology." *American Journal of Psychology* 118: 271–286.

Suls, Jerry and Ladd Wheeler (eds.) (2000). *Handbook of Social Comparison.* Boston, MA: Kluwer Academic/Plenum.

Sutton, Robert I. (1991). "Maintaining norms about expressed emotions: the case of bill collectors." *Administrative Science Quarterly* 36: 245–268.

—— (2007). *The No Asshole Rule.* New York: Warner Business Books.

Taylor, Shelley E., Rosemary R. Lichtman, and Joanne V. Wood (1983). "It could be worse: selective evaluation as a response to victimization." *Journal of Social Issues* 39: 19–40.

Tennen, Howard, Tara Eberhadt McKee, and Glenn Affleck (2000). "Social comparison processes in health and illness." Pp. 443 in *Handbook of Social Comparison,* edited by Jerry Suls and Ladd Wheeler. Boston, MA: Kluwer Academic/Plenum.

Tortoriello, Marco and Krackhardt, David (forthcoming). "Activating cross-boundary knowledge: the role of Simmelian ties in the generation of innovations." *Academy of Management Journal,* In Press.

Triplett, Norman (1898). "The dynamogenic factors in pacemaking and competition." *American Journal of Psychology* 9: 507–533.

Tullock, Gordon (1985). "Adam Smith and the prisoner's dilemma." *Quarterly Journal of Economics* 100: 1073–1081.

Turner, Jonathan H. and Jan E. Stets (2005). *The Sociology of Emotions.* Cambridge: Cambridge University Press.

Turner, Ralph H. (1990). "Some contributions of Muzafer Sherif to Sociology." *Social Psychology Quarterly* 53: 283–291.

Uzzi, Brian (1996). "The sources and consequences of embeddedness for the economic performance of organizations: the network effect." *American Sociological Review* 61: 674–698.

—— (1999). "Embeddedness in the making of financial capital: how social relations and networks benefit firms seeking finance." *American Sociological Review* 64: 481–505.

Uzzi, Brian and J. J. Gillespie (2002). "Knowledge spillover in corporate financing networks: embeddedness and the firm's debt performance." *Strategic Management Journal* 23: 595–618.

Uzzi, Brian and Ryon Lancaster (2004). "Embeddedness and the price of legal services in the large law firm market." *American Sociological Review* 69: 319–344.

Uzzi, Brian and Jarrett Spiro (2005). "Collaboration and creativity: the small world problem." *American Journal of Sociology* 111: 447–504.

Van de Ven, Andrew H., Douglas E. Polley, Raghu Garud, and Sankaran Venkataraman (1999). *The Innovation Journey.* New York: Oxford University Press.

Van den Bulte, Christophe and Gary L. Lilien (2001). *"Medical Innovation* revisited: social contagion versus marketing effort." *American Journal of Sociology* 106: 1409–1435.

van der Gaag, Martin, Tom A. B. Snijders, and Henk Flap (2008). "Position generator measures and their relationship to other social capital measures." Pp. 27–48 in *Social Capital*, edited by Nan Lin Nan and Bonnie Erickson. Oxford: Oxford University Press.

van Liere, Diederik W. (2007). *Network Horizon and the Dynamics of Network Positions*. Unpublished doctoral dissertation, Erasmus University, Rotterdam.

van Liere, Diederik W., Otto R. Koppius, and Peter H. M. Vervest (2008). "Network Horizon: An Information-Based View on the Dynamics of Bridging Positions." Pp. 595–639 in *Advances in Strategic Management, 25*, edited by Joel A. C. Baum and Timothy J. Rowley. Oxford: JAI/Elsevier.

Veblen, Thorstein (1899). *The Theory of the Leisure Class*. New York: Macmillan.

Vehovar, Vasja, Katja Lozar Manfreda, Gasper Koren, and Valentina Hlebec (2008). "Measuring ego-centered social networks on the web: questionnaire design issues." *Social Networks* 30: 213–222.

von Hippel, Eric (1994). "Sticky information and the locus of problem solving: implications for innovation." *Management Science* 40: 429–439.

Waley, Arthur (1938). *The Analects of Confucius*. New York: George, Allen and Unwin.

Walker, Gordon, Bruce Kogut, and Weijian Shan (1997). "Social capital, structural holes and the formation of an industry network." *Organization Science* 8: 109–125.

Walker, Iain and Heather J. Smith (eds.) (2002). *Relative Deprivation*. Cambridge: Cambridge University Press.

Wasserman, Stanley and Katherine Faust (1994). *Social Network Analysis*. Cambridge: Cambridge University Press.

Watts, Duncan J. and Steven H. Strogetz (1998). "Collective dynamics of 'small-world' networks." *Nature* 393: 440–442.

Weber, Max (1930) [1905]. *The Protestant Ethic and the Spirit of Capitalism* (translated by Talcott Parsons). New York: Charles Scribner's Sons.

Weick, Karl E. (1969). *The Social Psychology of Organizing*. New York: Addison-Wesley.

Weiss, L. W. (ed.) (1989). *Concentration and Price*. Cambridge, MA: MIT Press.

White, Douglas R. and Karl P. Reitz (1983). "Graph and semigroup homomorphisms on networks of relations." *Social Networks* 5: 193–234.

White, Harrison C., Scott A. Boorman, and Ronald L. Breiger (1976). "Social structure from multiple networks, I. blockmodels of roles and positions." *American Journal of Sociology* 81: 730–780.

Wills, Thomas Ashby (1981). "Downward comparison principles in social psychology." *Psychological Bulletin* 90: 245–271.

Winship, Christopher (1988). "Thoughts about roles and relations: an old document revisited." *Social Networks* 10: 209–231.

Winship, Christopher and Michael Mandel (1983). "Roles and positions: a critique and extension of the blockmodeling approach." *Sociological Methodology* 14: 314–344.

Wong, Peter Leung-Kwong, and Paul Ellis (2002). "Social ties and partner identification in Sino-Hong Kong international joint ventures." *Journal of International Business Studies* 33: 267–289.

Woolcock, Michael J. V. (1999). "Learning from failures in microfinance: what unsuccessful cases tell us about how group-based programs work." *American Journal of Economics and Sociology* 58: 17–42.

Xiao, Zhixing and Anne S. Tsui (2007). "When brokers may not work: the cultural contingency of social capital in Chinese high-tech firms." *Administrative Science Quarterly* 52: 1–31.

Zucker, Lynne G. (1977). "The role of institutionalization in cultural persistence." *American Sociological Review* 42: 726–743.

Zuckerman, Ezra W. (1999). "The categorical imperative: securities analysts and the illegitimacy discount." *American Journal of Sociology* 104: 1398–1438.

INDEX